POPULAR CULTURE AND NATIONALISM
IN LEBANON

Based on an award-winning thesis, *Popular Culture and Nationalism in Lebanon* is a pioneering study of musical theater and popular culture and its relation to the production of identity in Lebanon in the second half of the twentieth century.

In the aftermath of the departure of the French from Lebanon and the civil violence of 1958, the Rahbani Brothers (Asi and Mansour) staged a series of folkloric musical-theatrical extravaganzas at the annual Baalbeck Festival which highlighted the talents of Asi's wife, the Lebanese diva Fairouz, arguably the most famous living Arab singer. The inclusion of these folkloric vignettes into the Festival's otherwise European-dominated cultural agenda created a powerful nation-building combination of what Partha Chatterjee calls the "appropriation of the popular" and the "classicization of tradition." This musical-theatrical movement coincided with the confluence of increasing internal and external migration in Lebanon, as well as with the rapid development of mass-media technology, of which the Baalbeck Festival can be seen as an extension. Employing theories of nationalism, modernity, globalism, and locality, the book shows that these factors combined to give the project a potent, if not always constructive, identity-forming power. Small wonder then that with the start of the civil war in 1975 would come the collapse of this project. In the ashes of these events Ziad Rahbani, the son of Fairouz and Asi, began to author, compose, and star in his own series of exceedingly popular musical plays. These works comically and parodically confronted the gap between his parents' Lebanon and the Lebanon of brutal internecine war. Ziad's plays portray a much more heteroglossic and complex Lebanon than that of his parents. He achieves this, however, without completely breaking free from the strong pull of his parents' project. In the space of intertextual connections and the interpersonal and intergenerational relationships among the figures in question, one can see how the nation comes to be debated, imagined, and represented.

This book is the first study of Fairouz and the Rahbani family in English and will appeal to students and researchers in the field of Middle East Studies, Popular Culture, and Musical Theater.

Christopher Stone is an Associate Professor of Arabic and Head of the Arabic Division at Hunter College of the City University of New York. He received his PhD in Near Eastern Studies from Princeton University.

ROUTLEDGE STUDIES IN MIDDLE EASTERN
LITERATURES
Editors
James E. Montgomery
University of Cambridge

Roger Allen
University of Pennsylvania

Philip F. Kennedy
New York University

Routledge Studies in Middle Eastern Literatures is a monograph series devoted to
aspects of the literatures of the Near and Middle East and North Africa both
modern and pre-modern. It is hoped that the provision of such a forum will lead to
a greater emphasis on the comparative study of the literatures of this area, although
studies devoted to one literary or linguistic region are warmly encouraged. It is
the editors' objective to foster the comparative and multi-disciplinary investigation
of the written and oral literary products of this area.

POPULAR CULTURE AND NATIONALISM IN LEBANON

The Fairouz and Rahbani nation

Christopher Stone

Routledge
Taylor & Francis Group

LONDON AND NEW YORK

Transferred to digital printing 2010

First published 2008
by Routledge
2 Park Square, Milton Park, Abingdon, Oxon, OX14 4RN

Simultaneously published in the USA and Canada
by Routledge
270 Madison Ave, New York, NY 10016

*Routledge is an imprint of the Taylor & Francis Group,
an informa business*

© 2008 Christopher Stone

Typeset in Times New Roman by
Newgen Imaging Systems (P) Ltd, Chennai, India

British Library Cataloguing in Publication Data
A catalogue record for this book is available from the
British Library

Library of Congress Cataloging in Publication Data
A catalog record for this book has been requested

ISBN10: 0–415–77273–7 (hbk)
ISBN10: 0–415–78166–3 (pbk)
ISBN10: 0–203–93932–8 (ebk)

ISBN13: 978–0–415–77273–0 (hbk)
ISBN13: 978–0–415–78166–4 (pbk)
ISBN13: 978–0–203–93932–1 (ebk)

TO KAVITA AND ZUNE

CONTENTS

CONTENTS

Conclusion: Beiteddine 2000 and beyond **170**

ACKNOWLEDGMENTS

I would like to thank the following people for their generous help with this project. None of them bear any responsibilities for its shortcomings:

The Stones and the Misras, Mohammed Abi Samra, Nabil Abou Mourad, Ziad Abu Absi, Suzanne Abu Ghaida, Ghazi Abuhakema, As'ad AbuKhalil, May Ahmar, Roger Allen, Georges Atty, Hussein Ayyub, Amer Barghouth, Beth Baron, Adel al-Batal, Mahmoud al-Batal, Lisa Bernasek, Harry Bone, Ryan Brown, Kristen Brustad, Joseph Bulbulia, Doha Chams, Nicole Choueiry, Robyn Creswell, Rada Dagher, Hassan Daoud, Lara Deeb, Alex Elinson, Adrienne Fricke, Camillo Gomes-Rivas, Tamara Green, Ken Habib, Zeina Halabi, Andras Hamori, Michelle Hartman, Heiko Henkel, Jeanette Herman, Samah and Kirsten Idris, Hiba and Dida Jordy, Phil Kennedy, Samir Khalaf, Akram Khater, Ilyas Khouri, Toby Lester, Adel Louka, Tina Lupton, Annes Mcann-Baker, Barbara Mann, Nisrine Mansour, Kavita Misra, James Montgomery, Natalja Mortensen, Suleiman Mourad, Suad Najjar, Newgen, Basil Qasim, Jim Quilty, Akram Rayess, Dwight Reynolds, Nabil Saab, Nada Saab, Zaynab Saleh, Lisa Salem, Samah Selim, Rima Semaan and her family, Jonathan Shannon, Heather Sharkey, Susan Spektorsky, Fawwaz Traboulsi, Samer Traboulsi, Ines Weinrich, Joe Whiting, and Kate Wilson.

I would also like to thank the respective journals for providing permission to reprint earlier and condensed versions of Chapters 1, 2 and 3. Chapters 1 and 2: "The Ba'labakk Festival and the Rahbanis: Folklore, Ancient History, Musical Theater and Nationalism in Lebanon." *Arab Studies Journal*, 11.2–12.1 (Fall 2003/Spring 2004): 10–40. Chapter 3: "Ziyad Rahbani's 'Novelization' of Lebanese Musical Theatre or The Paradox of Parody." *Middle Eastern Literatures*, 8.2 (July 2005): 151–70.

NOTE ON TRANSLITERATION

I have used a simplified system of dropping the diacritics (dots under emphatic consonants) but of keeping macrons (the lines above long vowels). A *tā' marbūta* is represented by "a." The *hamza*, except for the initial *hamza* which is not marked, is represented with a single closing quotation mark and the letter *'ayn* with a single opening quotation mark. Proper names that are used widely in French or English or that appear with any frequency in this book – aside from most sources – are spelled the way they most commonly appear in those languages. Thus, "Fayrūz" becomes "Fairouz" and "Ba'labakk" becomes "Baalbeck." When transliterating material from spoken Arabic, I have tried to a certain extent to mimic the pronunciation in my transliteration, thus in some cases the *tā' marbūta* is written as an "i," not an "a."

INTRODUCTION

The claims of this book rest on the idea that popular culture and modern forms of nationhood and national subjectivity have a profound relatedness. In Lebanon, this phenomenon manifests itself, among other forms, in the struggles to define, shape, and claim Lebanese identity in the second half of the twentieth century and beyond. It is not surprising that the most prominent artistic family in Lebanon in the second half of the twentieth century – that of the Lebanese diva Fairouz (Fayrūz, nee Nuhād al-Haddād, b. c.1933), her husband Asi Rahbani ('Āsī, 1923–86), her son Ziad Rahbani (Ziyād, b. 1956), and her brother-in-law Mansour Rahbani (Mansūr, b. 1925) – would have played a role in these struggles. No artistic family or individual in Lebanon comes close in this period to the influence of Fairouz and the Rahbanis' thousands of songs and tens of musical-theatrical works.

Fairouz and the Rahbanis came to prominence at a time of increased internal and external migration and a global explosion of mass media technologies. It was a time, in other words, when representations of the nation were particularly potent. Lebanon in the mid-1950s was just thirty some years old and had only enjoyed about a decade of independence from France. What constituted this Lebanon remained an open question. Since the country's founding, Christian groups had been accorded the bulk of power over various Muslim factions through a variety of power sharing agreements. By the mid-1950s these Christian groups were finding themselves on the short end of the demographic stick. This change did not result, however, in a substantially more equitable distribution of power sharing with the country's growing Muslim population. This increasing imbalance, in fact, played a part in the short-lived civil violence of 1958 and was a major factor in the outbreak of civil war in 1975.

It is my contention that Fairouz and the Rahbanis were and continue to be key players in the protracted struggle over the identity of this new nation. Fairouz and the Rahbani Brothers (Asi and Mansour) have always been thought of as unifying forces in Lebanon and beyond, and this seems to have been their intention. In a recent celebration of Lebanese unity in the wake of the assassination of the Lebanese politician and businessman Rafik Hariri (Rafīq al-Harīrī), and the subsequent increased pressure on Syria to withdraw its troops from Lebanon, for example, one of Fairouz's musical films – *Exile* (*Safar barlak*, 1966) – a film about the oppressive policies of the Ottomans during World War One, was shown on an outdoor screen in downtown Beirut. The message was clear: in the face of outside interference and aggression we Lebanese have to stick together. This book argues, however, that the national sentiment evoked in their powerful works did not always convey a unifying message. By showcasing in their musical and musical-theatrical performances a narrow Lebanon analogous to the Christian Mount Lebanon village, the Rahbanis in fact participated in a discourse that exacerbated sectarian tensions.

The book also covers the rise to fame of Ziad Rahbani – the son of Fairouz and Asi – from the ashes of civil-war torn Lebanon. Much of Ziad's work, particularly his theater, was aimed at uncovering the dissimulation that was the Rahbani nation. The war prompted nostalgia for prewar Lebanon. Suddenly, the 1960s were a golden age, a different Lebanon from that of 1975 onwards. Ziad's polyvocal, parodic, and acerbic musical-theatrical works of the 1970s and early 1980s worked hard to argue that these two Lebanons were one and the same. Simultaneously, these works make the case eloquently for the existence of multiple synchronic Lebanons. Ziad's works celebrate the linguistic and cultural diversity of Lebanon while at the same time disabusing his audience of the notion of a golden prewar age full of miracles. He is not, however, as we see in his recent collaborations with his mother, immune to the seduction of nostalgia for those prewar days or for the Rahbani works that embody them. This ambiguity can be seen in the events surrounding the return of Fairouz to the last of this book's main characters – Lebanon's Baalbeck (Ba'labakk) Festival – after a near quarter-century hiatus due to the 1975–90 Lebanese civil war.

Fairouz at the 1998 Baalbeck Festival

In the summer of 1998, the Lebanese diva Fairouz performed at the "International Baalbeck Festivals" (mahrajānāt Baalbeck al-dawliyya) after a twenty-four-year hiatus. The Festival was founded in 1955, after a sporadic series of cultural happenings there, as an annual summer event featuring a wide array of international and then local cultural icons. Baalbeck and its Festival very quickly came to be associated almost tautologically with Fairouz and the Rahbani Brothers. It is at this venue, starting in 1957, that they completed their rise to fame via their almost annual musical-theatrical extravaganzas in the folkloric section of the Festival called "the Lebanese Nights" (al-Layālī al-Lubnāniyya). The workings of the Festival were suspended with the start of the civil war in 1975 and would not be resumed until the summer of 1997.

Of her 1998 return to the ruins of Baalbeck after her long absence, the Lebanese journalist 'Abduh Wāzin writes:

> The return of Fairouz is not just a return to the fortress and its steps, but is a recalling of the myth that the Rahbani Brothers and Fairouz created,

and which was the only myth that withstood the destructive war. There was Fairouz in her white clothes like a statue of the pure Virgin [Mary].

(Wāzin 1998: 18)

Journalist Abū al-Asbar opines similarly: "Fairouz the art and Baalbeck the civilization are twins that have never and will never separate over time. It is as if she, beside the six columns, were the seventh column of art embodied by her white clothes" (Abū al-Asbar 1998: 24). The event was portrayed, in other words, as the most natural of homecomings.

The magnitude of the event is reflected in the fact that the Lebanese President Elias Hrawi (Ilyās al-Harāwī) bounded up onto the stage to congratulate Fairouz at the end of her performance, saying, "with her success comes Lebanon's success" (Bāshā 1998: 1). It is said that he had wanted to congratulate her prior to the concert, but that she had asked him to wait until after the show (Abī Samrā 1998: 9). This power over the president in 1998 stands in contrast to a meeting that took place between then President Camille Chamoun (Kāmīl Sham'ūn) and the Rahbani Brothers in 1957, just before their controversial debut at the same Festival. According to Mansour, President Chamoun told them that he would either shoot them or award them a medal after the show depending on its outcome (Zoghaib 1993: part five, 72). This jocular threat is emblematic of the tension that surrounded their original inclusion in a festival that had been conceived as a showcase for international acts. According to Lebanese actor and theater historian Nabīl Abū Murād, the Festival's committee members "could barely hide their anger, concern and fear about including a program of local art in this international festival" (qtd. in Abī Samrā 1998: 9). This was not just snobbery, but also because the Festival was an integral part of a larger elite nationalist project that aimed to highlight the Christian and European faces of the new nation.

Despite this shaky beginning, the Rahbani Brothers and Fairouz would quickly become institutions at the Festival, performing their musical-theatrical works there for five successive years and then, after a two-year hiatus, appearing there five more times before the outbreak of civil war in 1975. It would seem, however, that despite their success at this venue, some of the original tension persisted. This can be seen in the controversy surrounding the absence of Fairouz and the Rahbani Brothers from the first postwar version of the Festival in 1997. The general puzzlement at their nonparticipation is summed up in the following newspaper article headline: "The Creators of the Glory of Baalbeck are Absent from It" (Suwayd, H. 1997: 58). Accounts of the reasons for their absence vary. The Festival committee claims that the Rahbani Brothers asked for more money than it could pay. The committee also expressed concern that there would not have been enough time for the Rahbani Brothers to write a new play and thus that they would have been compelled to put on one of their old works (Suwayd, H. 1997: 58). Reporter Hudā Suwayd concludes that the Festival committee never actually intended to have Fairouz and Mansour Rahbani participate in the rebirth of the Festival (Suwayd, H. 1997: 58).

3

After the Festival committee held a press conference explaining their version of the events, Mansour Rahbani – his brother Asi having passed away in 1986 – held one of his own to tell his side of the story. About his meeting with the Festival committee, which was presided over by one of its original members, Mayy 'Arīda, he said,

> I met with the ladies of the committee, and after a long preamble about the Rahbani Brothers and Fairouz and their popularity and about how there can be no festival without them, I raised the topic of our participation, and they welcomed the idea and their eyes welled up with tears and everyone rejoiced, and they told me that these plays have become the memory of the nation, and how great it would be to re-live the past, even if for one night.
>
> (qtd. in "Rahbani yarudd 'alā lajnat mahrajānāt
> Baalbeck" 1997: 9)

Mansour also contested the Festival committee's claim that they were asking for too much money, pointing out that international groups received similar sums. And as to the issue of their inability to perform a new and original work, he argued that dance and music groups coming from abroad rarely perform "new works," so why should local groups be prohibited from staging repeat performances ("Rahbani yarudd 'alā lajnat mahrajānāt Baalbeck" 1997: 9)? Though Mansour would not go so far as to agree with the opinion that "Fairouz's nonparticipation in the Festival appeared to be a new episode in the conspiracy woven to keep 'our Ambassador to the stars' away [from Baalbeck]," he did attribute it to a "lack of appreciation" and an "absence of deep thought" on the part of the Festival committee (Suwayd, H. 1997: 58). He is also quoted as saying, "We created the glory of Baalbeck, and it will never again be what it once was" (qtd. in Suwayd, H. 1997: 59).

Differences between the two sides, however, seem to have been resolved by the next year. At the 1998 version of the Festival, Fairouz and company, it was agreed, would put on sections of three of the Rahbani Brothers' prewar musical plays, all of which had debuted at Baalbeck: *The Moon's Bridge* (*Jisr al-qamar*, 1962), *Granite Mountains* (*Jibāl al-Sawwān*, 1969), and *The Guardian of the Keys* (*Nāṭūrat al-mafātīh*, 1972).[1] The evening's events opened with Fairouz singing "Baalbeck: I am a candle on your steps" ("Baalbeck, anā sham'a 'alā darājiki") a song she had sung there first in 1961. The show ended with her singing two new songs, one by Mansour Rahbani, who produced the show, and one by Mansour and Asi's younger brother Elias (Ilyās),who conducted the orchestra.

Though this was not the first time that Fairouz had sung in Lebanon since the end of the war, her return to Baalbeck, as we have seen above, was a special event. One might have expected that because of its reunion atmosphere, along with the fact that the program was full of old favorites, the show could not have been anything but a great success. In actuality, though it is clear that many were star struck by the diva's return, there were a significant number of negative reviews. One critic opined that the concert, for its lackluster presentation of mostly old material, felt more like a funeral than a celebration (Abī Samrā 1999: 9). The same Wāzin article cited above that celebrates the fact of Fairouz's return to Baalbeck goes on to criticize the program itself: "The chosen scenes seemed anachronistic, especially those full of political clichés and nationalistic speeches" (Wāzin 1998: 18). Also targeted in more than one review were the new songs written for Fairouz that concluded the show. Again, a comment from Wāzin,

> As for the two surprises that the fans had every hope in, by which I mean the two new songs by Mansour and Elias, they were not worthy of the fans' expectations. Mansour's nationalistic song entitled "The Last Time I Sang For You" ["Ākhir marra ghannayt laka"] appeared to be Rahbani-esque in form, but to be empty of the fire which Mansour usually ignites in poetry and music and it had a large number of nationalistic slogans which are no longer convincing, for what nation is this "green nation" that Fairouz is going to build? [Furthermore,] is it still possible for our diva to announce, according to what Mansour has written for her, that she is going to build her nation as she likes?
>
> (Wāzin 1998: 18)

Wāzin's observations are full of pregnant assumptions and important ellipses. It seems that it took the war to draw attention to the emptiness of the Rahbanis' utopian vision for Lebanon. What the quote does not hint at is the Rahbanis' arguable participation in the heating up of tensions that would lead to the war. Nor does Wāzin's critique inform us that at least one informed observer sensed the danger in their representations of Lebanon even before the war began. I speak of Fairouz and Asi's son Ziad Rahbani.

The aspect of the concert that received the most criticism, however, was the fact that all of it – the music and the singing – was prerecorded. In a confrontational interview with Elias Rahbani after the concert, Journalist Maralīn Khalīfa confronts the show's conductor.

> After an absence of twenty-five years from the Baalbeck Festival, the Rahbani Brothers' fans and the new generation were surprised by the complete reliance on the technique of "play-back," in the plays and even in the new songs since they had been eagerly waiting to hear Fairouz's voice. Why?
>
> (Khalīfa, Maralīn 1998: 18)

Another critic wonders why Fairouz's fans abroad get to hear her voice live, whereas those at home have to settle for a thirty-five-year-old facsimile (al-Zībāwī 1998: 10).

The most noted critic of this aspect of the show, however, was Ziad Rahbani, Fairouz and Asi's son, the sometimes *enfant terrible* and sometimes collaborator with the Rahbani Brothers' musical-theatrical project. Ziad, which is how he is referred to in Lebanon, had been slated to contribute an original song to the concert and to accompany his mother on the piano. He apparently made a last minute decision not to participate, as on the first night of the performance the empty piano remained on stage, its notes audible in the concert's prerecorded sound track. The significance of Ziad's absence can be seen in the fact that it is noted in the headlines of many of the articles about the concert. For example, Khalīfa's above-cited interview is entitled: "Elias Rahbani: 'We Went to Baalbeck and Waited for Ziad, but He Did not Come' " (Khalīfa, Maralīn 1998: 18). The 'Abduh Wāzin article mentioned above ran with the following subtitle: "Ziad Rahbani Withdrew, Protesting the Deception of the Play-Back" (Wāzin 1998: 18). When asked whose idea it was to prerecord the show, Elias Rahbani quipped cryptically that it was Asi's (Khalīfa, Maralīn 1998: 18). How can this be when his brother had passed away some twelve years earlier? What he meant to say was that this technique was first and widely used by the Rahbani Brothers in the original staging of the very productions from which the scenes presented in 1998 had been culled. This raises an interesting question: if this technique was so widely used, even, according to Elias, by Ziad Rahbani in his own theatrical productions (Khalīfa, Maralīn 1998: 18), why the disappointment in 1998? I will venture an answer to this question in the book's Conclusion.

I start with this recent event because it raises a variety of issues that I will explore in my treatment of the musical-theatrical projects of the Rahbani family over the past fifty years or so. It highlights, first of all, the issue of the triangular relationship between the Rahbani Brothers and Fairouz, Baalbeck, and a particular brand of Lebanese nationalism. This recent event also provides a glimpse of the complicated relationship between Rahbani the father, mother, and uncle; and Rahbani the son. In the chapters to come I will discuss this constellation of relationships and events, primarily but not exclusively through a study of the musical plays of the Rahbani Brothers and Fairouz on the one hand, and those of their son Ziad Rahbani on the other.

The academic marginalization of theater

According to Raymond Williams, the critical treatment of the theater has been overshadowed by that of the novel (Williams 1968: 11). Until recently, musical theater was even less studied than other types of theater.[2] This problem exists in the Arab World as well, where the question of the place of theater is further complicated by the issue of language. While the use of colloquial language in literature written in European languages has not been completely unproblematic (Anderson 1991), it remains a highly contentious issue in the Arab World for a variety of political, cultural, and religious reasons.[3] The spoken dialects very quickly diverged from the language of the Qur'ān and have continued to develop over the centuries. Because the Qur'ān has remained in its original language, classical Arabic is the linguistic standard by which other texts are judged. Despite

6

the fact that these dialects are all rooted in classical Arabic, speakers of Arabic do not usually consider their spoken language to be worthy of being written down. The fact that so much theater in the Arab World is written in dialect, then, may help to explain why it has been even more shunned in academic circles than has theater in the West. Even more ignored critically than theater in the dialect is *musical* theater in the dialect, this despite the fact that up until the 1930s theater in the Arab World was almost always *musical* theater (Shāwūl 1989: 471).

So strong is the association of musical theater with the nonliterary and the low, that describing the place of the project of the Rahbani Brothers in the history of Arab theater – when they are mentioned at all – becomes problematic and tension-filled, as can be seen in 'Alī al-Rā'ī's estimation of their contribution to Arab theater:

> These operettas must be considered Lebanon's main contribution to the art of theater. But for drama proper, that is fixed texts of literary merit which are actable, Lebanon had to wait until the poet 'Isām Mahfūz produced his *avant-garde* plays such as *The China Tree* (*al-Zanzalakht*, 1968), an absurdist play attacking political tyranny.
>
> (al-Rā'ī 1992: 392)

With some exceptions, musical theater has suffered the same critical fate in writing in Arabic.[4] In light of this, it cannot be surprising that academic writing on the Rahbani Brothers and Ziad is rare. Take, for example, Khālida Sa'īd's monumental work on Lebanese theater between 1960 and 1975 which was sponsored by the Baalbeck Festival committee. Although this work covers the very decade and a half when the Rahbani Brothers and Fairouz dominated the theatrical scene in Lebanon, in her 700-page work the Rahbani Brothers and Fairouz are mentioned, in passing, just 20 times. Sa'īd says that she considers the folkloric acts of the Rahbani Brothers and Fairouz at Baalbeck to have been "a first step" toward the development of indigenous theater in Lebanon, but that since it has its own "special components and origins," it demands a separate study (Sa'īd, Kh. 1998b: 44–5).[5]

Sources

This is not to say that there are no written sources on the Rahbani Brothers. In their 1966 musical play *The Days of Fakhr al-Din* (*Ayyām Fakhr al-Dīn*), the prince Fakhr al-Din appoints 'Atr al-Layl, the character played by Fairouz, to be the singer laureate of the play's Lebanon. It is her job to unite the country through song. Fakhr al-Din informs her that it is *he* who history will remember, and that *her* role will remain hidden. No one, he tells her, will write about or remember her (Rahbani, A. and M. 1966: 7). It is likely that the Rahbani Brothers meant for this line to be taken ironically. As one of their biographers has written: "In the whole history of the Arab press, never has anything been written about as much or as well as has the rich experiment presented by the Rahbanis" (Aliksān, J. 1987: 11).

This is in part because the press has a much simpler relationship to celebrity and popular culture than does academe. As a result, there are innumerable articles on this family in both the culture and gossip sections of regional – but particularly Lebanese – newspapers and journals. There are also several book-length studies on the Rahbani Brothers and Fairouz, some of which also contain sections on Ziad.[6] It is on these mainly journalistic sources that I have relied heavily for my secondary sources.

In terms of primary sources, I benefited greatly from the fact that performances of all of the musical plays of both the Rahbani Brothers and Ziad Rahbani are available on compact disc. Furthermore, one of the Rahbani Brothers' original musical plays was converted into a feature film that is available on videocassette and DVD. Even though none of Ziad's plays that I am focusing on in this book were converted into feature films or released on film in their stage versions, all of his plays are available on compact disc.[7] Both the Rahbani Brothers and Ziad, as will be seen, produced non-theatrical musical works from which I will draw as well. Six of the Rahbani Brothers musical plays were recently published in book form, and others exist as part of Festival programs, preperformance promotional newspaper articles, or in manuscript form. In contrast, all of Ziad's plays on which I focus have been published in book form. I also consider the Baalbeck Festival's annual festival programs to be primary sources. This includes the coffee table book on the Baalbeck Festival that I will call the Festival's "official history." I have also drawn on a number of tourist guides and travelers' accounts of Baalbeck specifically and Lebanon generally. This book also benefits from the availability of hours of television programming on both generations of the Rahbani family. The fact that nothing about this family that appears on Lebanese television goes unrecorded and uncirculated says much about its place in the Lebanese and regional popular imaginations. Another valuable combination of primary and secondary source material for this book is the various web sites devoted to the family.[8]

Methodology

This is not a work of Ethnomusicology.[9] It is perhaps best defined as a mode of literary analysis. I have discussed above the problematic relationship between musical theater and the literary branches of the academy in and out of the Arab World. In the Western academy, the study of popular culture has been gaining rapid acceptance. These studies are often carried out from departments of Anthropology or Cultural Studies. They have or have come to have, in other words, a disciplinary home. In terms of the study of the Arab World, even so-called high literature has had difficulty penetrating discipline-based departments, it being usually placed within Area Studies programs or regional language and literature departments. It is still not clear where the study of the popular culture of the Arab World will fall discipline-wise.[10] Edward Said has written on the methodological and genealogical problems of Middle Eastern studies as an academic field (Said 1979: 284–328). Said's and other's critiques of the field have led to a great deal of methodological introspection.[11] At the same time there has been a proliferation of calls recently for more cross-disciplinary work in academia (e.g. Moran 2002). In my mind, there is no reason why Area Studies departments cannot use this lack of "discipline" as a point of strength as both Armbrust (2000b) and Bayat (2001) have argued. While one needs to exercise vigilance in order to avoid the traps of essentialism and exceptionalism,[12] Area Studies offers an ideal place for the confluence of a number of disciplines: Anthropology, Comparative Literature, History, Political Science, and so on. I also believe that it is important for studies of literature and popular culture in the region to keep at least "one foot" in area studies. On the dangers of Middle Eastern Studies without literature, Edward Said wrote

> One of the striking aspects of the new American social-science attention
> to the Orient is its singular avoidance of literature. You can read through
> reams of expert writing on the modern Near East and never encounter a
> single reference to literature. What seems to matter far more to the
> regional experts are "facts," of which a literary text is perhaps a disturber.
> The net effect of this remarkable omission in modern American awareness
> of the Arab or Islamic Orient is to keep the region and its people
> conceptually emasculated, reduced to "attitudes," "trends," statistics: in
> short, dehumanized.
>
> (Said 1979: 291)

It is with this in mind that I call this work a literary study in the context of area studies.

Chapter outline

Chapter 1 establishes the confluence of the evolution of the ancient site of Baalbeck into a Lebanese national symbol and the founding of an annual festival there beginning in 1955. Based on work done by Ussama Makdisi, I first show how Baalbeck was for centuries a site for Orientalist historiography that showed no interest in the local surroundings and population. I then demonstrate how it came to be seen as a space with some connection to its local context by the end of the nineteenth century. Its evolution into an actual symbol for the nation, I argue, would take longer. It was not complete, in fact, until more than thirty-five years after the establishment of modern Lebanon in 1920. Baalbeck did not become a symbol for Lebanon, in other words, until the founding of the Annual Arts Festival at the site in 1955 and the subsequent inclusion of Lebanese folkloric acts dominated by the Rahbani Brothers and Fairouz into the festival beginning in 1957.

Before discussing in some detail the founding of the Festival in the late 1950s, I trace the genealogy connecting that site to cultural acts and the ideologies it came to represent, from the time of the creation of Le Grand Liban as a French Protectorate in 1920. This Grand Liban was cobbled together by annexing to the predominantly Christian Mt Lebanon, former Ottoman provinces and states North, East, and South of the mountain, including the cities of Tripoli, Sidon, and the country's new capital, Beirut. Although this new nation had a roughly fifty-fifty Christian/Muslim composition at its founding in 1920 – one that would quickly and significantly change in favor of the Muslims – the French ruled mostly with the help, and in favor, of the Maronite Christians of Mt Lebanon. By the time the French left in 1946 then, the political structure of the country had been set in favor of this ever-shrinking portion of the Lebanese population. One of the goals of the Baalbeck Festival, I argue, was to protect this political advantage by representing Lebanon as the Christian village Lebanon of Mt Lebanon. It is in this regard that the inclusion of the folkloric vignettes of the Rahbani musical-theatrical productions into an otherwise European dominated cultural agenda created a powerful nation-building combination of what Partha Chatterjee calls the "appropriation of the popular" and the "classicization of tradition" (Chatterjee 1993: 72–4). While I study the texts of the plays themselves in Chapter 2, in Chapter 1, I focus on the official rhetoric surrounding the Festival and its founding.

Chapter 2 is dedicated to a study of some of the Rahbani Brothers' early musical-theatrical plays, almost all of which featured Fairouz in the starring role. I suggest that the Lebanon depicted in many of these works is not the diverse Lebanon espoused by President Fouad Chehab (Fu'ād Shihāb) who came to power after the civil violence of 1958, but rather one modeled on the much-narrower Lebanon of the Christian mountain village envisioned by the founders of the Baalbeck Festival and their political sponsors as discussed in Chapter 1. While I look at a number of plays, my focus in this chapter is on *The Holiday of Glory (Mawsim al-'izz*, 1960), *The Moon's Bridge (Jisr al-qamar*, 1962), *The Night and the Lantern (al-Layl wa-al-qindīl*, 1963), *The Ring Seller (Bayyā' al-khawātim*, 1964), and *The Days of Fakhr al-Din*. In addition to engaging Partha Chatterjee's work on nineteenth-century Indian nationalism and Arjun Appadurai's writing on transnational processes and the production of modern subjectivities, I also draw in this chapter on theories of the formation of national communities developed by Benedict Anderson (Anderson 1991 and 1994) and others. All of these theorists are indebted to the work of Michel Foucault, whose critical project can be said to have revolved around the discursive creation of modern subjectivities.[13] In the chapters to come I will speak often about the "subject forming" power of the musical and musical-theatrical works of the Rahbani family. The formation of modern identities is very much linked to narratives we both receive and create about ourselves and others. One of the main premises of this book is that because of a confluence of circumstances mentioned briefly here and to be elaborated on in the chapters to come, the musical and musical-theatrical works of the Rahbani family were a very powerful source of subject-forming narratives for the Lebanese in particular and speakers of Arabic in general. In other words, because this project coincided with the confluence of increasing migration both out of Lebanon and to its urban centers, as well as with the rapid development of mass media technology, it had potent subject-forming power across Lebanon's diverse population. I argue that this project played a central, powerful, and sometimes problematic role in providing citizens of this nascent state with their new "Lebanese" identity. In order to stress the importance of the development of mass media in this equation, I begin Chapter 2 discussing the pre-Baalbeck radio careers of the Rahbani Brothers and Fairouz in the 1950s.

Adding to the subject-forming power of their musical-theatrical works at Baalbeck and elsewhere is the fact that the Rahbani Brothers' musical-theatrical project is a model of modern representation – as theorized by Timothy Mitchell 1999 – whereby the very gap between the representation and the represented can make the former seem paradoxically more real than the "original." I show that at times this gap is present as a self-conscious device in the theater of the Rahbani Brothers. In other instances, I argue that it is the necessary result of the act of exhibition in general, no matter how centrally accurate is the goal. I will argue that this phenomenon may help partially to explain the increasing extravagance and decreasing folkloricness of these works. I end the chapter by suggesting that this move away from "folklore," again in combination with the phenomena of mass media and migration, may help to reveal how the Rahbanis and Fairouz could come to stand for a variety of different nationalisms and localisms all at once: an impressive accomplishment, I conclude, but not without potentially dangerous consequences.

Chapter 3 traces the rise of the artistic project of the son Ziad Rahbani from the ashes of both the nation itself and the musical-theatrical work of his parents. The Rahbani Brothers and Fairouz responded to the Arab military defeat of 1967 with a burst of artistic activity that may have played a role in the decline of Asi's health and thus the de facto breakup of this artistic trinity. I will show that despite a continued move away from the village toward a kind of urban "social realism" in their post-1967 works, the Rahbani Brothers never broke free from the pre-1967 ideologies outlined in Chapter 2. While I survey a number of their post-1967 plays I look most closely at their epic *Petra* (*Batrā*, 1977). At first it seemed as if the young Ziad and other family members might have been able to salvage the family project. Buttressing this sense was Ziad's very Rahbani-esque first play: *An Evening's Celebration* (*Sahriyya*, 1973). Just a year later, however, Ziad would announce a new parodic positioning vis-à-vis his parents' project in his *Happiness Hotel* (*Nazl al-surūr*, 1974). While this work marks a clear ideological and artistic break from that of his parents' project, it is also an expression of an ambivalence that Ziad's musical theater and music would never rid itself of. *Hotel* and future plays like *What Do We Need to do Tomorrow* (*Bi-al-nisba li-bukrā shū*, 1977), *A Long American Film* (*Fīlm Amīrkī tawīl*, 1979), and *A Failure* (*Shī fāshil*, 1983) evidence, among other things, a paradox of parody that, by very definition, straddles a line between homage and mockery. In the remainder of the chapter I will show how Ziad struggled with this thin line, all the while creating a theatrical Lebanon much more polyvocal – at times veritably cacophonous – than that of his

11

parents. I rely on Bakhtin's work on dialogism and heteroglossia in the novel to tease out the links between many of the above concerns; and to show the connection between parody and ambivalence on the one hand, and between parody and heteroglossia on the other.

Chapter 4 is dedicated to a discussion of the role of Fairouz in both Rahbani projects. If Fairouz's voice is largely absent from this family's narrative in the first three chapters, it is the goal of this chapter to explain this paradoxical silence that extends well beyond this particular text. After looking at some of the literature on the role of women in national projects both in and outside of the region, as well as considering the precarious social position of performers – particularly female and particularly in the region – I conclude not only that Fairouz's striking silence, but also her well-known motionlessness on stage, result from the fact that women, in many different cultural contexts, are often burdened with largely metaphoric roles in the nation-building process. Women tend to be the maternal producers of citizens, and not full citizens themselves in this process. At the same time they must be stripped of their sexuality or, at the very least, have their sexuality be placed in the service of the nation. Fairouz found herself doubly trapped because her representations of the nation were being executed, very literally, in the socially problematic space of the stage. This leads to another paradox as some of her musical-theatrical characters had very active nation-building roles in the contexts of the plays themselves, because these were enacted on stage, Fairouz seemed to have to work extra hard in her "private life" to prove her appropriateness as a symbol for the nation. Offstage, in other words, she had to exaggerate her maternalness, her angelicness, and her silence.

With the start of the civil war came the breakdown of the Rahbani Brothers' project. This decline was not disconnected from personal ruptures in the trinity including Asi's stroke in 1973 and the separation of Fairouz and Asi later in that decade. These events coincide with the beginning of a musical collaboration between Fairouz and her son Ziad; works such as *How Are You?* (*Kīfak inta*, 1991) and *To Asi* (*Ilā Asi*, 1995). One result of this mother-son project was to free Fairouz from her dehumanized and desexualized pedestal/prison, and to free her from allegory. The final chapter will end, however, by asking if Fairouz did not find herself in yet another type of "prison," as Ziad gained more and more artistic control over the project.

It is tempting to read the irony and paradox-filled saga of this family as a metaphor for the turbulent history of modern Lebanon. I hope that the chapters to come convince the reader that the relationship between art and society is more complex than that, that Lebanon and this musical project do not just *stand* for each other, but also *inform* each other. Furthermore, as we see the lives of this family and the history of the country bleed into each other in the pages to come, I hope that this book establishes not just the dialectical relationship between art and life, but also the need to question the phrasing that too as a strict binary.

1

BAALBECK AND THE RAHBANIS

Folklore, ancient history, and nationalism

At a certain point in their careers Fairouz and the Rahbani Brothers had become virtually synonymous with Baalbeck's ancient ruins and annual festival. This fact is reflected in some of Fairouz's nicknames, such as "the star of Baalbeck" (najmat Baalbeck) and "the seventh pillar" (al-'amūd al-sābi') (Wāzin 1996: 20). In this chapter I begin tracing the formation of the tautological relationship between Baalbeck the site, Baalbeck the Festival, Lebanon, and Fairouz and the Rahbani Brothers. Different combinations of these elements are often linked in a variety of sources. In the program to the 1998 Baalbeck Festival, the Lebanese literary critic Khālida Sa'īd writes on the occasion of the return of Fairouz to Baalbeck after an absence of almost a quarter of a century:

> Fairouz is a unique phenomenon who...became the symbol of Baalbeck. It is one of those rare times when an artist is transformed into a symbol for the nation.... In the darkest days she did not give up her belief that art is the most lasting face of Lebanon, nor did she lose faith in the ability of art to save the world. Thus she became a symbol of Lebanon and a sign of a desired utopian Lebanon. With this inspiration and symbolic voice she returns to the ruins of Baalbeck. We greet her return like the renewal of the promise and we hope for the resurrection of the utopian dream from its ashes.
>
> (Sa'īd, Kh. 1998a: 125)

One concern of this chapter and Chapter 2 is to address what it means to say that this place, this Festival, and this family came to equal Lebanon.

It is at the very moment that the Rahbanis and the Baalbeck Festival are being linked, in fact, that the site *itself* reaches a period of peak potency as a symbol for the nation. *Which* nation it symbolized was a contested issue, a fact that the story of the Rahbanis' difficult entrance into the Festival will demonstrate. I will show that the eventual metaphoric and metonymic relationship between the Rahbanis, the ruins, the Festival, and Lebanon itself was not the given that it can appear to be from the vantage-point of today.

13

Baalbeck: whose site is it anyway?

Before Baalbeck could become a productive site in Lebanon's post–independence nation-building process, the connection between the ruins and present-day Lebanon had to be established. This process was paradoxically facilitated by eighteenth- and nineteenth-century European identity searching in the region (Makdisi, U. 1998: 138). Partha Chatterjee's study of nationalism in nineteenth-century India reminds us that this phenomenon was in no way peculiar to Lebanon. If the English could lay cultural claim to ancient Greece, nineteenth-century Indian nationalists argued, could not India do the same for its Vedic age, a civilization the greatness of which had already been established by European Orientalists? This is an example of what Chatterjee terms the "classicization of tradition" (Chatterjee 1993: 73).[1]

The process of the classicization of traditions has been documented, with some variation, for other European colonies. Before taking up the case of Lebanon, I will refer to a few other examples. Chatterjee's work traces how nineteenth-century European historiography of India marveled at its classical and glorious past and bemoaned its present state of decay and decline. This decline was blamed on centuries of despotic Islamic rule, a conclusion that, among other things, served as a convenient justification for colonialism (Chatterjee 1993: 102). In parts of the world with Islamic majorities, the wholesale disparaging of Islam was more problematic. The requisite period of decline, in other words, had to be formulated differently. The process, however, was often virtually identical. Timothy Mitchell, in his treatment of the transplanted Levantine Christian Jūrjī Zaydān's prolific historiographic writing on Islamic History, documents this phenomenon in late nineteenth- and early twentieth-century Egypt. Through his scholarly works, historical novels, school textbooks, and his highly influential magazine *al-Hilāl*, Zaydān, as read by Mitchell, helps propagate the idea of a truncated Islamic golden age being followed by centuries of decline culminating in "our present backwardness" (Mitchell 1988: 169). As in India, such historiography is arguably influenced by Orientalist "groundwork." Mitchell argues, for example, that Zaydān was influenced by works such as Gustave Le Bon's *La civilisation des Arabes* (Mitchell 1988: 170). This mode of writing about Egyptian and Islamic history – with some variation as to when the decline actually began – remains prevalent today (Piterberg 1997). Mitchell's examination of Zaydān's works also gives us insight into another aspect of the classicization of tradition process: namely, how the colonial discourse of great classical cultural flow followed by centuries of ebb was eventually co-opted by local national elites (Mitchell 1988: 169–71). Thus the same historical construct that paved the way for colonization could, ironically, do the same for independence: "You were once great and need our help to become so again," becomes tweaked to read, "We were once great without you and can become so again."

Egypt has an additional period that is a candidate for a former-greatness/current-decline narrative: the Pharaonic age. Some of the most influential intellectuals of early twentieth-century Egypt such as Muhāmmad Husayn Haykal, Salāma Mūsā, and Tawfīq al-Hakīm fell under the spell of the achievements of European Egyptology. The nascent Pharaonic movement was catalyzed in particular by the near confluence of the Egyptian Revolution of 1919 and the 1922 discovery of the fantastically intact tomb of the Pharaoh Tutankhamun.[2] For the remainder of that decade, traces of this strain of Egyptian nationalism can be found in all types of writing and artistic expression (Gershoni and Jankowski 1986). Haykal, the author of *Zaynab* (*woman's name*, 1913), arguably one of the first Arab novels,[3] would eventually outline the importance of Egypt's Pharaonic past in his literary manifesto *The Literary Revolution* (*Thawrat al-adab*, 1933) in which he states that Pharaonic History, the Nile, and its valleys

> are capable of being the source of inspiration for a national literature that
> would depict Egypt's past and present powerfully and truthfully and
> impress the spirit of her children as well as foreigners.... Thus they
> would know the authentic Egypt, not the Egypt that propaganda has
> defaced out of political, and other motivations.
>
> (qtd. in Selim 2004: 82–3)

As an example of a literary text making the link between the Pharaohs and the contemporary Egyptian peasant, Samah Selim offers the case of the French archeologist in al-Hakīm's novel *The Return of the Spirit* (*'Awdat al-rūh*, 1937) who compares the happily toiling Egyptian peasant to his uncomplaining and industrious Pharaonic ancestor: "We are simply unable to comprehend those feelings that united this people into a single unit, capable of carrying huge blocks of stone on their shoulders for twenty years and smiling all the while..." (qtd. in Selim 2004: 118–19). With these huge blocks of stone we move closer to Lebanon's Baalbeck, for while Islam is not without its monuments of architecture, its classicization is mainly textual. And while texts certainly play an important role in Egyptology, it is the large stones of the pyramids referred to by al-Hakīm's French archeologist, as well as other spectacular nontextual artifacts, that provide the most striking evidence for a link between the residents of ancient and modern Egypt.

The same narrative of European interest and then nationalist appropriation can be told for the impressive pillars of Baalbeck, a thesis developed by Ussama Makdisi in his article on the "rediscovery" of this ancient site (Makdisi, U. 1998). A work that links European interest in classical pasts in both Egypt and Lebanon is Volney's 1787 *Voyage en Égypte et en Syrie*. This work, which is said to have had a substantial influence on Napoleon's 1798 Egyptian expedition (Said 1979: 81), is based on his 1783 tour of those areas. It focuses on Giza's pyramids and Baalbeck's ruins as symbols, not of former glory, but rather of the despotism of their rulers throughout history, a characteristic he is quick to link to present-day Ottoman decline (Makdisi, U. 1998). But Makdisi's account of European interest in Baalbeck starts even earlier, with European travelers such as Richard Pococke and Robert Wood, whose visits to the area were characterized by a search for a

European past. Like Volney, their accounts of sites such as Baalbeck and Palmyra share a disregard for their contemporary settings, as well as for their Islamic pasts. The main difference between Pococke and Wood on the one hand and Volney on the other is that the latter saw the history of Baalbeck as being potentially related to *present-day* European civilizing missions. In Egypt, Volney saw no hope of enlightened self-rule and thus recommended straight colonization. However, in the people of the mountains of Lebanon – somewhat removed from direct Ottoman tyranny and significantly non-Muslim – he saw a kindred race whose nascent republican spirit could, under French tutelage, prosper. His theory was, in a word, that despotism flourishes in plains and coastal regions (Makdisi, U. 1998).

Almost a century later France would heed Volney's advice and use the sectarian violence of 1860 as a pretext for sending its army to Lebanon to protect the very mountain-inhabiting Maronites who had inspired such hope in him. By this time, Baalbeck had become a regular stop on European grand tours of the East. In the context of this development, and under the protection of French troops, the philologist Ernest Renan visited Baalbeck. Eschewing the site's Roman and Hellenistic aspects (i.e. Europe's past) Renan, as he outlined in his 1864–74 *Mission de Phénecie*, focused instead on its Phoenician heritage. While he did not make an explicit connection between the present-day Maronites and the ancient Phoenicians, he provided the key that would allow future Maronite nationalists to open that door (Makdisi, U. 1998: 150).

Next in Makdisi's article is a section on the joint German-Ottoman excavations of the site at the very end of the nineteenth century, which Makdisi reads as an Ottoman attempt to debunk the European discourse about its backwardness among other things ("Look, we too, like Europe, take an interest in our Empire's pre-Islamic sites"). In fact, the Ottomans not only ignored the Arab aspects of the site, they actually effaced at least one of them by filling in the moat of the Arab fort, thus "restoring the ancient relationship between the sanctuary and the surrounding land" (Ragette 1980: 81). Finally, Makdisi arrives at the first "local" account of Baalbeck's history that connects the ancient and present sites: Mīkhā'īl Allūf's *History of Baalbeck*. Not only is Allūf a local writing in Arabic, his narrative is also the first to recount a history of the ruins right up to the present day. In addition, he is also the first to write extensively and not wholly disparagingly about the local population and environs. Allūf picks up on Renan's Phoenician focus and claims, in a similar fashion, that Baalbeck is of Phoenician origin. Whereas Renan based his conclusions on the belief that the massive three-stone base of the Jupiter Temple – the so-called trilithon – was the work of the Phoenicians (Makdisi, U. 1998: 149), Allūf focuses on etymology:

> What was the origin of Baalbeck? This town was of Phoenician origin, in spite of the fact that the German excavations have discovered no traces of Phoenician origin. Its name Baal-bek plainly indicates that here Baal was first worshipped, and the renown in which Baalbeck was already held, induced the Romans to build the marvelous temples we

admire to-day, out of the materials, employed by the Phoenician, to build the primitive temples of which no traces remain.

(Allūf 1914: 40)[4]

Makdisi is right to note that Allūf is a proto-nationalist. In other words, the direct connection between Baalbeck and a coherent Lebanese nationalism would have to wait (Makdisi, U. 1998: 155). It is clear from the 1914 English edition of Allūf's work on the site, for example, that he does not even consider the ruins to lie in a place called Lebanon: "It [the district of Baalbeck] is bounded by the *caza* [district] of Bekaa [Biqā'] on the South; on the East by Anti-Lebanon; on the North by the *caza* of Homs; and on the west by the Lebanon" (Allūf 1914: 2). The 1922 English edition, calls Baalbeck "one of the best-known towns in Syria" and then on the same page says that it forms part of "the Great Lebanon" (Allūf 1922: 1). This shift in nomenclature is due, of course, to the creation of "Greater Lebanon" – "Lebanon" as we know it today geographically – in 1920. The 1926 Arabic edition changes the word Syria to "Lebanese Syria" (Allūf 1926: 7), showing that there is some ambiguity as to whether or not "the Great Lebanon" is considered to be part of Syria or an entity of its own.

The Baalbeck Festival: "Finally/forever anchored in Lebanese life"

In the 1962 Egyptian film *Letter from an Unknown Woman* (*Risāla min imra'a majhūla*, dir. Salāh Abū Sayf) the character played by Farid El Atrache (Farīd al-Atrash) travels from Cairo to Lebanon. The film's sole Lebanese scene has him singing in front of Baalbeck's six famous pillars. A mere five years prior to that in *The Glory* (*al-Majd*, 1957, dir. Sayyid Badīr), another Egyptian film in which the lead actor plays a role with parallels to his personal life, the character played by Farīd Shawqī goes to Lebanon to work on a script that he has been having trouble writing at home in Cairo. In this film, Lebanon is represented by its mountain resorts, cabaret acts, and Pigeon Rocks.

It is possible to speculate that in 1957 Baalbeck would not have been used to represent Lebanon because the Baalbeck Festival was in its nascent phase. By 1962, however, the Festival had not only become established in its own right, but had transformed the ruins of Baalbeck themselves into a symbol for modern Lebanon. This might explain why we do not see Farid El Atrache roaming the ruins touristically, but rather singing there. The Festival's accompanying literature makes it clear that this is not just a matter of this ancient space being transformed into a venue for art, but rather of reclaiming its original role. As the Festival committee's president Aimée Kettaneh (Aymīh Kitāna) writes in the official program for the 1960 Festival season:

The International Baalbeck Festival is forever/finally anchored in Lebanese and Near Eastern life. Years of effort and promise and initiatives

17

are harvested today in a rich program spread out over five weeks on this plentiful Bekaa plain to restore to it its cultural glow which was promised it two thousand years ago by the builders and great priests.

(qtd. in Munassā 1994: 16)

Mīkhā'īl Allūf had laid the groundwork for Baalbeck's ancient past to be linked to its present. The founders of the Baalbeck Festival seem to have built the bridge that would "finally/forever" connect that glorious past to Lebanon's present.

By 1962, Baalbeck and its Festival were appearing in more than just Egyptian films. A 1962 travel guide to Lebanon is full of images of the site. As Baalbeck has long been a central element of Lebanon's tourism industry, it is not surprising that an official travel guide to the country would allot considerable space to these ruins. What is perhaps somewhat remarkable is that so many of the book's pictures of the ruins were taken in the context of the Festival. The very first page of the book, for example, is equally divided between four pictures: Pigeon Rocks, a mountain ski scene, bikini-clad women on the beach, and a picture of Baalbeck with its Festival in progress (*Tourist and Hotel Guide* 1962: 1). The remainder of the book is peppered with photos of the Festival. The book echoes Ms Kettaneh's discourse about art constituting the connection between Baalbeck's past and present:

> The authorities in contemporary Lebanon, in organizing this annual festival, in which dramatic Art, Music, Ballet Dancing and Folklore Representations revive ancient rites, have sought mainly to *re-associate* [italics mine] the present with those fervent eras during which all of the Arts were used as a means to better serve divinity.
>
> (*Tourist and Hotel Guide* 1962: 10)

The travel guide states directly what Ms Kettaneh did not go so far as to say: namely, that this "re-association" was something "sought," not just something found. What the travel guide shares with her statement, however, is the notion that there *is* an association between the present and a certain idea of the past, and that one of the Festival's roles is to remind the Lebanese and foreign visitors of it.

It is not just the *official* guides to Lebanon and Baalbeck proper that reiterate the idea of Baalbeck and its Festival representing the link between ancient and modern Lebanon. Most of the guides and travel narratives that I looked at – both on the ruins specifically and on Lebanon generally – replicate this discourse (e.g. Biani 1972, Harding 1963, Ragette 1980, and al-Sir'alī 1966). Gerald Harding's guide to the ruins, published soon after the release of *Letter From an Unknown Woman*, further demonstrates how quickly such a discourse became "anchored":

> The presentation each year of the Baalbeck Festival is a bold and imaginative stroke on the part of the Lebanese people. The steps of the two temples make fabulous settings for Opera, Ballet, Plays, Orchestras, and Folk

Dancers and singers, and some of the sense of glory, almost of worship, of these magnificent buildings is thereby revived, but with effects and lighting never dreamed of by the ancients. Yet these ancients were always ready for new ideas and experiments, and one cannot but feel that they would have given whole-hearted approval to the innovations, and would have clapped and cheered as enthusiastically as any modern audience at some of the magnificent spectacles displayed in this two thousand year old setting.

(Harding 1963: 69)

If these books do not make the connection between ancient and modern Lebanon, they at least almost invariably mention the Festival when writing about Baalbeck (e.g. Izzard 1959 and Kuntz 2000). In contrast, texts written between the publication of Allūf's *History* and the founding of the Festival continue either the trend explicated by Makdisi of not making the connection between Baalbeck the ancient and Baalbeck the present (e.g. Inchbold 1906) or, if focused on modern Lebanon, of downplaying the importance of Baalbeck in Lebanese history (e.g. *Republic of Lebanon at the New York World's Fair* 1939).

In translating Kettaneh's statement about the Festival being "finally/forever anchored in Lebanese life," I rendered the word *nihā'iyyan* as both "finally" and "forever" because of its semantic flexibility. If we choose to read her meaning ambiguously, we can see not only it as a mixture of hope for the future ("forever"), but also feel pride and relief in the completion of a difficult task ("finally"). Both readings, however, raise important questions that I will examine below. The former provides a glimpse of the possibility that this employment of Baalbeck as part of a nationalist vision of Lebanon offers. Before taking up the nature of this vision for Lebanon that was literally staged at Baalbeck, it will be necessary to consider the implications of the latter reading of *nihā'iyyan* which looks back to a process completed. In other words, while I have shown that by the early 1960s Baalbeck and its Festival had become potent symbols for Lebanon, it is now important to go back and at least partially fill in the space between Allūf and the "anchoring" of the Baalbeck Festival. This will make it easier to understand more fully how this connection was "finally" made.

In 1955, on the occasion of what would be the first of nineteen consecutive times that the Baalbeck Festival was held (excepting the violence-marked summer of 1958) Camille Chamoun, Lebanon's second post-independence president, wrote:

The historical role of Lebanon has been since time immemorial, is now, and will continue to be primarily the development of culture and civilization. In organizing this International Festival in the magnificent temples of Baalbeck at which great classic works of music and drama of rare beauty and power have been presented, Lebanon has been conscious of and faithful to its heritage.

(qtd. in Tueni 1994: xxii)

In 1960 the Baalbeck Festival committee chairperson Aimée Kettaneh made the connection between ancient and contemporary Baalbeck via art. In 1955 Chamoun had already declared this fact to be a keystone in Lebanon's civilizational mission. This is not just art for art's sake; this is art for a purpose. It is not surprising, then, that both agree that such a venture should be the responsibility of the "authorities." In fact, as we will see below, Chamoun's rhetoric cannot be dismissed as merely a *pro forma* official endorsement of this venture, for both he and his wife took great personal interest in the Festival, as would future leaders of Lebanon. What remains to be explained, however, is how the annual event came to be seen in such weighty terms.

In 1893, three years after Allūf published his work on Baalbeck, which not only confirmed Renan's conclusions about its Phoenician roots but also implicitly connected that past to Allūf's present, Yusuf al-Dibs, the Maronite archbishop of Beirut, published his *The Book of Syria's History* (*Kitāb tārīkh Sūriyya*). While he too does not yet draw a direct connection between the ancient Phoenicians and the present-day occupants of the land he does, more broadly than Allūf, portray the Phoenicians in a way that would be echoed by Maronite Lebanese nationalists in the near future. He focuses, in other words, on their non-Semitic origins, their seafaring skills, their business acumen, their craftsmanship, etc. (Kaufman 2001: 179). A half century earlier another Maronite patriarch, Nicolas Murad, had written perhaps the first text by a Maronite calling for a separate political unit in and around Mt Lebanon (Kaufman 2001: 179). Eventually these two discourses would converge.

There are parallels between specific strands of Lebanese and Egyptian nationalisms. Asher Kaufman argues, in fact, that Pharaonic nationalism had a direct impact on Lebanese thinkers, most specifically on Lebanese intellectuals who had been drawn to Egypt and particularly Alexandria at the turn of the twentieth century for a myriad of reasons.[5] Though the Pharaonic nationalist movement was not yet fully developed, its ideas were mature enough in the first decade of the twentieth century to influence a group of Lebanese there that called itself the "Alliance libanaise." This coalition would not only take the lead in the call for the creation of a French-assisted Greater Lebanese state at the end of the Great War, it would also produce pre–Lebanese independence Phoenician nationalists such as Yusuf al-Sawda (Yūsuf al-Sawdā), Hektor Klat (Haktūr Khalāt), and Michel Chiha (Mīshāl Shīhā). While I will discuss the latter two figures below, here I will say about al-Sawda that his *For the Cause of Lebanon* (*Fī sabīl Lubnān*, 1919) was one of the first books to link directly the Phoenician past and the Lebanese present (Kaufman 2001: 181). In it he writes:

As a nation is proud of its roots and draws its good virtues from its good progeny, so is Lebanon proud to remember and remind us that it is the cradle of civilization in the world. It was born at the slopes of its mountain and ripened on its shores, and from there, the Phoenicians carried it to the four-corners of the earth. Just as Europe has to be committed to Italy and Greece it also has to be committed to a land that is the teacher of Rome and the mother of Greece.

(qtd. in Kaufman 2001: 181)

At the Versailles treaty conference that concluded the Great War, Europe seemed to show just such a commitment to the "cradle of civilization" by creating *Grand Liban* out of the former area of self rule in Mt Lebanon and other ex-Ottoman provinces to its North, East, and South, including Baalbeck and the Bekaa plain where it lay. A mere two years later in 1922, the first theatrical performance was staged at the ruins of Baalbeck in what the "official history" of the Festival records as the beginning of the revival of the cultural duties befitting the inheritors of this cradle (Munassā 1994: 6).[6]

The beginnings of the Baalbeck Festival and the beginnings of the nation

On a summer night in 1922 a group of French military officers and their friends and family (including the first French High commissioner for Syria and Lebanon, General Henri Gouraud) that had been touring the Chouf (al-Shūf) region of the recently formed Grand Liban, found themselves at nightfall at Baalbeck. As the Festival's official history tells it, they were inspired by their surroundings to recite French poetry (Munassā 1994: 6). They were so encouraged by this evening that they decided to stage a play there based on a classical "Lebanese" myth. A French journalist wrote the work and it was performed – in French – by a mixed group of French and Lebanese elite (the group included the wife of the future president Charles Dabbas (Shārl Dabbās)) before approximately four hundred spectators at Baalbeck in the autumn of that same year (Abū Murād 1990: 44). Lighting was provided by the anti-aircraft lights of the French Airforce (Munassā 1994: 6).

It is telling that the official narrative of the establishment of the Baalbeck Festival would virtually coincide with the post–World War One transfer of the stewardship of Lebanon to France. It would also coincide with the annexation of Baalbeck, among other areas, to Mt Lebanon to create The Grand Liban in 1920. The very fact of French military officers roaming the Lebanese countryside and reciting poems at ancient ruins and then subsequently using advanced military technology to stage their play in conjunction with the Christian elite not only speaks volumes about the initially cozy and intimate relationship between the French mandate officials and some Maronites, but also hints at the complexity of the role that Baalbeck and its Festival would come to play in the subsequent nation-building process. This event also illustrates that the reclaiming of history as a stage of postcolonial nation building is no simple affair. For a time, a particular site may have both local and European "claimants." The Arabic section of the official history of the Festival (it is omitted in the French) describes just such a state before narrating the events of 1922:

> Baalbeck was not only a source of inspiration for the Orientalist poets and artists who came with the diplomatic missions in the eighteenth and nineteenth centuries. As soon as the foot of [any] visitor had tread on its steps, the gift of creativity would pour over him and he would be inspired by its history enough to satisfy his nostalgia for its past. Before the Festival appeared in 1956 came those who blew life into it and returned to it some of what was buried under the rubble of time.
>
> (Munassā 1994: 6)

The next chapter in the official history of the Festival comes after twenty years of cultural inactivity at Baalbeck. In light of the fact that much had changed in Lebanon, the region, and the world in those years, it would be expected for the next installment to have a distinctly more "Lebanese" character. The year 1944 is the next significant date in the official version of the founding of the Baalbeck Festival. While the French were still physically in Lebanon at that time, their days were numbered.[7] This was no time, in other words, for the French and Maronite elite to be doing collaborative amateur classical theater at Baalbeck.

Or was it? Though the organization that sponsored the play that was staged there that summer was called "L'association nationale pour le maintien et le développement de la culture *libanaise* [italics mine]," and though the play was staged "sous le haut patronage" of the president of the republic Bishara Khoury (Bishāra al-Khūrī) (Tueni 1994: 36–7), the leader of the Constitutional Bloc which was calling for the end of the French presence in the country, the scene at Baalbeck in the fall of 1944 would have been virtually indistinguishable from that of 1922. A classical play (*Les Perses d'apres la tragedie d'Eschyle*) – acted in costumes designed in France and performed to music composed there as well – was staged. Even the lighting, provided by the ostensibly still-French-assisted Air Force, was the same. There were, of course, differences. This time, all of the actors were Lebanese. The fact that Mrs Charles Dabbas once again played the lead female role, however, is indicative of the elite nature of that participation. The festivities were opened with the singing of a Greek poem and the play itself was framed by the performance of two "classical" dances.

The apparent paradox of a joint French-Lebanese production in a time of increasing tension between the two sides is at least partially explained, however, when one discovers that behind "L'association nationale pour le maintien et le développement de la culture libanaise" were the likes of Michel Chiha, Said Akl (Sa'īd 'Aql), and Fouad Boustani (Fu'ād Bustānī).[8] While I will have more to say about Akl in Chapter 2, a brief look at Chiha's thought and influence here will help us to understand this particular version of "la culture libanaise" that would inform the vision of the founders of the Baalbeck Festival some sixteen years later.

Chiha was part of the Alexandria-based "Alliance libanaise." There he got to know al-Sawda, one of the early Phoenician nationalists, as we saw above from

22

his *For the Cause of Lebanon*. Chiha's adherence to Phoenicianism can be deduced from the fact that he translated al-Sawda's work into French (Traboulsi 1999: 21). The Arabic of al-Sawda and the French of Chiha, however, are significant, for they represent their one major difference. While both saw the contemporary Lebanese as the rightful heirs to the Phoenicians; while both had a geographically deterministic view of Lebanese nationalism; while both envisioned a Greater Lebanon including the Chouf, the Bekaa Valley, and Beirut, al-Sawda did not share Chiha's view that their nationalist goals had to be achieved under the aegis of a French mandate (Traboulsi 1999: 21). This fissure with al-Sawda is seen clearly in the slogan of the political party al-"Taraqqī" (advancement) that Chiha helped to form the year following the declaration of Greater Lebanon: "For the sake of Lebanon, with France" (Traboulsi 1999: 22). At this time Chiha also became a member of a group called the "New Phoenicians," which was centered on Charles Corm's (Shārl Qurm) *La revue phénicienne*. Both the newspaper and the party were, as the names would indicate, Francophone and phile, the latter promulgating the idea that the modern Lebanese had inherited the role of free-trading businessmen from their Phoenician ancestors. Both also supported the concomitant theory that the true Lebanese were not Arabs (Amīn 1997: 73 and Traboulsi 1999: 23). Chiha, who had close ties to many Mandate officials, would enjoy a short parliamentary career that coincided with the enactment of the Lebanese constitution in 1926. However, he would soon give up a direct role in politics to focus on his family's banking interests. In spite of this he would continue, until and even after his death in 1954, to exert considerable influence on the thought of the Lebanese political elite, the extent of which would be difficult to exaggerate. Such influence would be practiced through his news-paper *Le jour* (Beirut 1935–46), his copious writing in that and other sources and through his closeness to his brother-in-law and sometimes President Bishara Khoury (Traboulsi 1999: 12–13). This influence is perhaps best summarized by the words of Lebanon's fourth president, Charles Helou (Shārl al-Halū):

> He used to fill the country with his powerful personality, to the point that in the course of a century, it was our solace [to think] that he personified the country. And it is our solace that we can compare this Lebanese [citizen] – in terms of his thought and character – to the great figures of this world and this age .... Even those who did not know him personally or thought that they did not know him were indebted to him more than they knew.

(qtd. in Traboulsi 1999: 13)

Traboulsi (Tarābulsī) argues that his influence can continue to be seen in post–civil war Lebanon, even on those in the Lebanese national movement who were the most virulent opponents of his philosophy (Traboulsi 1999: 13). If this is the case, then it can hardly be surprising that one finds elements of his thought in the cultural events held by his philosophical, social, and political bedfellows at Baalbeck in 1955, just one year after his death.[9]

In such an atmosphere of persistent Francophilia and Phoenicianism among certain sectors of the Lebanese elite, it is not surprising that the 1955 rebirth of the idea of staging plays at Baalbeck would occur not in Beirut but in Paris, despite the final departure of the French from Lebanon in 1946. It is also not surprising that the four plays that would be staged later that summer at Baalbeck would be of French provenance and be staged with aid from a French theater company. At some point during the following year, the official narrative goes, at an official function at the presidential palace, President Chamoun proposed that what had until then been highly sporadic cultural events at Baalbeck be turned into an organized annual event. This suggestion would lead to the formation of a committee – composed mostly of wealthy Maronite women who would come to be called "les dames du festival" (Tueni 1994: xxviii) – to undertake the organization of the event. They were given six months to put together a program that would ultimately consist of French and English theater, as well as a German symphony orchestra.

Theater historian Khālida Sa'īd rightly praises these women for their spirit of volunteerism (Sa'īd, Kh. 1998b: 50). She is also careful to point out the committee's relative independence from the government. The very possibility of such fiscal independence is, of course, also indicative of the financial means and connections of their families and the businesses they owned. It is also a reflection of the liberal principle of favoring a relatively weak public sector as seen in the thought of Chiha and others. Despite the committee's financial dependence on the private sector, however, there is no denying both a keen government interest in the project and a resonance between the visions of the two sectors, both at its establishment and, as I will demonstrate in Chapter 2, under subsequent regimes. So much so that Sa'īd's assessment that "It is possible to say that the activity of the committee translated to a great extent the current ideological discourse of the Lebanese government before the [civil] war [of 1975]" (Sa'īd, Kh. 1998b: 50), reads like an understatement. Even the official history's depiction of the Festival's importance to Chamoun almost seems not to go far enough when it says that Baalbeck had become for him like "a sacred duty parallel in its importance to the affairs of the nation..." (Munassā 1994: 8). That nation's very existence was about to be challenged by the civil violence of 1958. That event and the tension leading up to it convinced some among the national Maronite elite that they would have to engage in more than nominal power sharing with the country's other confessional groups. On the level of the Baalbeck Festival, this realization was reflected in the inclusion of local folkloric acts starting in 1957. There seemed to be an understanding that a wholesale dependence on European classical theater, dance, and music in such an environment was not expedient.

Folklore at Baalbeck: the appropriation of the popular, part one

By the early 1960s the Baalbeck Festival and Baalbeck itself had become potent symbols of Lebanon. In light of the violence of 1958, perhaps the symbol had become more stable than the nation itself. The fact that Baalbeck would serve as the single representative image of Lebanon in the 1962 Egyptian film *Letter from an Unknown Woman* demonstrates that the site's representational powers were working beyond Lebanon's borders as well. This might not have been possible if the local folkloric acts pioneered by the Rahbani Brothers and Fairouz had not been made an integral part of the Festival. Once again, I offer details of that film's sole Lebanon scene as evidence. While I mentioned above that Farid El Atrache sings in front of the pillars of Baalbeck, I did not specify that at least part of the song he is performing is a folksong of the *mawwāl* variety.[10] He is also accompanied by a troupe of elaborately costumed "folk" dancers, who move in a highly choreographed way that is reminiscent of and perhaps inspired by the dance troupe that performed with the Rahbani Brothers at Baalbeck. While the ancient site had already successfully and incrementally been linked to modern Lebanon by the writings of Allūf, Sawda, and others, and by the activities of nationalist thinkers such as Chiha and Akl, the addition of "folklore" to the program at the Baalbeck Festival would serve to strengthen those ties.[11] Now the connection would not only be the *fact* of performance, but the *content* of it as well.

The establishment of the Baalbeck Festival allowed its founders to claim a connection to the classical past represented by that site. A way to further connect the past and the present of a place is through what Chatterjee calls "the appropriation of the popular" (Chatterjee 1993: 72). As we saw in Tawfīq al-Hakīm's *The Return of the Spirit*, for example, Egypt's Pharaonic past and present are connected via the cheerily working Egyptian peasant. Chatterjee would say that this is an example of the popular becoming "...the repository of natural truth, naturally self-sustaining and therefore timeless.... The popular is...the timeless truth of the national culture, uncontaminated by colonial reason" (Chatterjee 1993: 73). The Baalbeck Festival is a perfect example of how the classicization of tradition and the appropriation of the popular often and powerfully go hand in hand. The official history of the Festival certainly demonstrates an awareness of the potency of this combination:

> In our folklore we perceive what is coming from that glorious age...
> most [of it] drawn from ancient forms sung by our ancestors as they
> danced to its rhythms thousands of years ago in worship of the gods,
> especially Bacchus who was mentioned by Euripides. The circles that
> male and female dancers form at national occasions and rural holidays
> have preserved their deep heritage that did not disappear in the dusk of
> forgetfulness, for it continued to narrate our culture and our customs in
> this land despite hundreds of years of foreign guardianship.
> (Munassā 1994: 12)

It is thus that Bacchic rites and the folkloric *dabka* become siblings reunited after thousands of years of foreign intervention.[12] Those attending the Festival were meant, then, to see the link between the ruins, the high-brow European acts, and the colorful local folklore. Their Lebanon boasted not only of a glorious past, but

25

also of a past that was very much connected, through its folklore, to its present.[13] It is this decision of the Festival committee to include folklore into the annual program that brings the Rahbani Brothers and Fairouz, as I will elaborate on below, into the Baalbeck picture.

While the "appropriation of the popular" may be a common feature of post-colonial nation building, it does not always occur at the same juncture in the process of achieving independence. In Bengal, for example, Chatterjee describes this phenomenon as happening well before political independence was achieved. He describes the situation there by employing Gramsci's idea of the incremental revolution. In other words, before the national elite were able to take political control of their country, they took cultural control, carving out a domestic cultural space that was off-limits and superior to the culture of their English colonizers. Both the classicization of tradition and the appropriation of the popular were carried out, in other words, well before independence (Chatterjee 1993). While the former was begun in Lebanon in the nineteenth century, the latter seems to have been delayed until after independence, perhaps because a condition for it in Lebanon would be rural-to-urban migration, a trend that would begin significantly and not coincidentally during the mandate period. Once in power France, as part of its divide-and-rule strategy in Lebanon, began to cultivate ties with Maronite families that had thus far remained for the most part in the mountains. This caused a flow of more well-to-do Maronites to Beirut. More significant in terms of numbers were the waves of migration of less well-off mostly Christian families affected by economic changes on Mt Lebanon. Despite the fact that many of these moves were made under great duress, apparently some of the national elite celebrated such migration as exemplifying the Phoenician spirit of travel and adventure (Traboulsi 1999: 24). Even on the mountain itself, many former farmers, especially among the Maronites, left their work as they entered modern schools and then took posts in administrative positions in the population centers there (Abī Samrā 1999: 7). All of this movement and change surely heightened the sense that the true nature of Lebanon lay in the folk of the villages or farms – or in one's own childhood or past – left behind. A result of all of this movement was the production of a nostalgia which Asi Rahbani called "the nostalgia of the mountain for itself" (qtd. in Abī Samrā 1999: 6). Though I will discuss migration at greater length below and in the following chapters, here I will suggest that migration and its concurrent nostalgia were key factors in the appearance of a movement to preserve and record folk culture in Lebanon.

One example of this movement is the work of the Arabic Professor Anis Frayha (Anīs Furayha) at the American University in Beirut. At the time that local folkloric performance was about to enter the Baalbeck Festival, Frayha published several books in a conscious attempt to record a mountain culture which, as can be clearly seen from one of the following titles, he saw as being in danger of extinction (Abī Samrā 1999: 7): *Listen Rida* (*Isma' yā Ridā*, 1956) and *The Lebanese Village: A Civilization on its Way to Disappearing* (*al-Qarya al-Lubnāniyya: hadāra fī tarīq al-zawāl*, 1957). The first text is a collection of village stories presented as being told to his son. The second is a catalogue of aspects of village folk life that he feared were in danger of dying out. One of the predominant features of these two works is their clear nostalgia: they rely heavily on memories of life in the Greek Orthodox and Druze village of Ra's Matn, which the author had left years before (Frayha 1957: 8). Chatterjee observes that a distinctive feature of the appropriation of the popular is the presentation of the folk in childlike terms (Chatterjee 1993: 72). This tendency is replicated in Frayha in what seems to be a clear projection of his childhood memories onto his object of study. This is seen in his very definition of folklore: it is the lullabies sung to a child by his mother, the games children play in the village square, the stories of spirits and ghouls told to children sitting around the fire in the winter, or when a child becomes ill and the grandmother blames it on the evil eye, and so on (Frayha 1957: 16–19). *Listen Ridā*, for its part, is dedicated to all children. They are the ones, after all, who can appreciate village life, who love its simplicity, even if they have not actually seen it for themselves (Frayha 1956: jīm, dāl, and hā').

Folklore is the realm not just of the child but the childlike, a category that for Frayha includes the segment that he credits with creating most of it: women (Frayha 1957: 19). It is also the realm of the poor, the middle class having nothing but disdain for it (Frayha 1957: 16–20). Folklore, of course, may be created and preserved in these segments, but it is certainly not safe in them. Children, women, and the poor – in other words, what is "unthinking, ignorant, superstitious, scheming, quarrelsome, and also potentially dangerous and uncontrollable" (Chatterjee 1993: 73) – are not where we place our trust. It must, rather, be mediated by "enlightened leadership" in order "to shine forth in its natural strength and beauty" (Chatterjee 1993: 73). For Frayha, this is the role of the "upper classes," who, with their "mature mindsets," can appreciate folklore and realize its value. It is they, through their societies and organizations, who strive to record and preserve it (Frayha 1957: 21).

Recording and preserving, of course, are not neutral acts. Whether it is deciding what to include in a semi-scholarly work on folklore or how to perform it for an audience, choices have to be made, and they are not devoid of ideology. In the preface to his book on the Lebanese village, Frayha is quite clear about *his* choices: he will not include the folklore of coastal cities, for example, because they were "never part of old Lebanon, Lebanon the mountain and the village," nor will he treat the folklore of the Muslims, because their folklore differs from that of the "inhabitants of old Lebanon" (Frayha 1957: 10). Because folklore is a mirror of any society, he avers, one must study it if one is really to understand a particular society. In Lebanon, this means studying the country's "original" inhabitants, the people of its [presumably non-Muslim mountain] villages (Frayha 1957: 12). This act of selection is part of the larger process of drawing boundaries – cultural, cartographic, and otherwise – between one's nation and the next, between oneself and the Other.[14] On the subject of choice, it is interesting to note that Frayha also decides not to include folk music and dance in his study. This not because they are not worthy of study or reflective of an original Lebanon, but rather because he does not see them as being in danger of extinction due to the efforts that were being made on several fronts, not only to collect and preserve them, but also to "put them on a higher artistic level" (Frayha 1957: 9). This is presumably a reference, at least in part, to the pre–Baalbeck Festival efforts of the Rahbani Brothers and Fairouz that will be examined in Chapter 2.

In the work of Frayha one can see signs of awareness that

> Claims to the past lay the ground for present and future claims. Having a past, a history, a "folklore" of one's own, and institutions to bolster these claims is fundamental to the politics of culture: those who are concerned with demonstrating the possession of a national folklore, particularly as legitimated by a national museum and troupe, cite this attribute as a mark of being civilized.
>
> (Kirshenblatt-Gimblett 1991: 423)

Let us return to "les dames du festival" to see how such an awareness reached them, to see how the Festival became a leading player in the creation of a "national folklore" in Lebanon.[15]

By most accounts, the Festival committee was not quick to realize the potential power of staging appropriations of the Lebanese popular at Baalbeck. The decision to include folklore into the program was imposed on the Festival committee by Lebanon's First Lady, Zalfa Chamoun. It was she, according to the official narrative of the Baalbeck Festival, who would lead the campaign not just for the inclusion of Lebanese folklore at the Baalbeck Festival, but also for a systematic study of it. These efforts would result in "folklore coming into its own on the dirt of Baalbeck and then spreading throughout Lebanon and the rest of the world" (Munassā 1994: 13). The context in which the official narrative describes this idea occurring to Mrs Chamoun is instructive in that it demonstrates that what was happening in Lebanon was part of a larger local, regional, and international movement.

Khālida Saʿīd talks about the years between 1956 and 1958 as ones of great cultural and artistic foment in Lebanon, with each new cultural phenomenon or movement affecting the others. In the visual arts the Artists Group was formed in 1957, as was the Spring Exhibition at the UNESCO Palace. In that same year the modernist poetry journal *Poetry Magazine* (*Majallat al-shiʿr*) was founded. The field of music during this period was active as well, through the efforts of The Musical Group and the National Conservatory. This activity is part of the atmosphere in which the Baalbeck Festival was founded, which in turn opened the door for the further development of music – particularly popular music – and theater (Saʿīd, Kh. 1998b: 15).

It was in this context that in 1956 the Lebanese National Committee for UNESCO, the United Nation's main cultural organ, brought the Soviet folk dance specialist Igor Moiseyev to Lebanon to perform with his folkloric troupe. The president's wife was apparently so taken with the performance that she commissioned Mr Moiseyev to visit the Lebanese countryside and to prepare a report on the state of folk culture there. He reported back that there was a distancing from traditional clothes, song, and rhythm. The report goes on to reveal the tension that exists between the preservation of folklore and its development: "Dance, that most expressive and emotive form of expression coming to us today across thousands of years is the most endangered folk art of all" (qtd. in Munassā 1994: 12). To save it, he suggests, it must not just be preserved, but developed:

> the popular and natural roots which gives birth to dance ought to be directed by a choreographic system which must have strict standards... without, however, effacing all of the magical steps, rhythms or ethnic characteristics. Its goal should be to develop [the dance] into a folklore that covers all of Lebanon and its popular customs relating to peace, war, marriage and death.
>
> (qtd. in Munassā 1994: 12)

To "develop" such dance, the report goes on to suggest, members of the proposed professional national folkloric troupe must have close ties to the countryside. They must, in other words, have all of the natural dance moves "stored within them" (qtd. in Munassā 1994: 12). All that is left for the dance teachers "are the technical aspects that are based on strict anatomical rules and which push the dancer toward the development of harmony and movement" (qtd. in Munassā 1994: 12). Training for two leading dancers, it was suggested, should take place in the USSR.

The president's wife and the members of the Baalbeck Festival's new Folklore committee apparently saw no contradiction in the suggestion of sending dancers to the USSR to perfect their own "genuine" Lebanese dances. And thus Marwān and Wadī'a Jarrār were sent to Russia with the following results: "What this couple learned at Moiseyev's school was the yeast which would eventually lead to the formation of popular dance groups and which opened up closed wells" (Munassā 1994: 13). This returns us to the need to take folklore out of the hands of the poor, the women, and the children, and to place it into the capable hands of the elite; for the popular is not simply to be appropriated, but rather "appropriated in a sanitized form, carefully erased of all marks of vulgarity, coarseness, localism and sectarian identity" (Chatterjee 1993: 73). But dance alone does not make up a folkloric festival. It is at this juncture that the Rahbani Brothers and Fairouz, along with the dance troupe formed by the Jarrārs, would enter the Baalbeck Festival by way of the new folkloric portion of the Festival that would come to be called "The Lebanese Nights." The details of events leading up to the Rahbanis' debut at the Festival are worth pausing over, demonstrating as they do that at the Festival's inception there was tension surrounding what the content and goals of this ambitious cultural event should be.

The Baalbeck Festival: "A mirror with two faces"

The relationship between the Rahbanis and the Baalbeck Festival committee was fraught from the very beginning. In the official narrative of the Baalbeck Festival, however, this tension is presented as excited anticipation. It is not that the committee was not sold from the very beginning on the inclusion of folklore in the Festival or that the Rahbanis – chosen at the highest levels – were not the clear choice for the inauguration of the folkloric Lebanese Nights, but just that no one knew, right up until the opening night, exactly what to expect (Munassā 1994: 14).

Other sources on the Rahbani Brothers and the Festival present accounts that contradict the official narrative of the decision to include them in the program (Abī Samrā 1993: 63 and 1998: 9; Abū Murād 1990: 59; Aliksān, J. 1987: 109; and Suwayd, H. 1997: 58). None of them differ with the official version as virulently as does Mansour Rahbani himself in an interview conducted in 1993–4 in the news weekly al-Wasat by the poet Henri Zoghaib (Hanrī Zughayb). Mansour claims that not only was the participation of the Rahbani Brothers and Fairouz agreed upon reluctantly by the "ladies of the committee," but that many of them were loath to sully the event with local acts in the first place. He relates:

> We were called in the spring of 1957 to meet with the Baalbeck Festival committee. At that time the Festival was limited to foreign acts presented by international theater, opera and ballet groups. That year Mrs. Zalfa Chamoun had decided to insert "The Lebanese Nights" into the Festival. The meeting with the ladies of the committee was in the office of the Minister of the Interior Habib Abou Chahla [Habīb Abū Shahlā]. They did not have a clear idea as to what they wanted to present there [at the Festival], and even were not enthusiastic about the idea of The Lebanese Nights, feeling that it would be less prestigious than the foreign nights' international groups. But they had deferred to the First Lady's idea and had attended the meeting.[16] They began by cautioning us against the length of Arab songs and "tatrīb"[17] which "our audience has an aversion to after becoming accustomed to the foreign works at Baalbeck." We assured them that we were against long songs, and that they would have to wait to see our proposal for The Lebanese Nights before judging it ahead of time with those snobbish and arrogant bourgeois looks. They asked us: "Who is going to sing at your concert?" We told them: "Fairouz." They yelled disapprovingly: "No, never. She will sing on and on and wail and start tearing the handkerchief in her hand."[18] We understood that they did not know Fairouz, nor what Fairouz sings. Then they imposed on us a crew that they had previously hired.... We politely refused this arrangement and told them that these matters were our concern. We asked for a bit of time to outline the broad scheme of a scenario and then to meet again. They agreed begrudgingly, and the meeting ended with that arrogant look which sees itself as being in the right and all that is against it as being wrong.
>
> (qtd. in Zoghaib 1993: part five, 72)

This tension was not, as some of the accounts make it seem, simply a matter of personal difference, but rather it was an issue of potential conflicting visions not so much as to the role of this Festival in Lebanese life, but as to the version of Lebanon that would be presented there.

Making the stakes particularly high was the fact that the insertion of local folkloric performances into the Festival's program would result, as we saw above, in powerfully combining the classicization of tradition and the appropriation of the popular. The presence of the popular, literally in the space of the classicized ruins, would represent a muscular claim to that past. An example of a similar combination of the classicization of tradition and the appropriation of the popular in a different context can be seen in the unveiling of Mohammad Mukhtar's (Muhammad Mukhtār) sculpture "The Revival of Egypt" ("Nahdat Misr") in Cairo at the height of Egypt's Pharaonic movement in 1928. The sculpture depicts a sturdy peasant woman next to, and with her arm around, a kneeling and muscular sphinx-like figure. The work of art not only confirms that the link between Egypt's past and its present is its peasant, but also points to the future, since the woman is depicted as removing her headscarf. The massive sculpture was prominently displayed and unanimously well received (Gershoni and Jankowski 1986: 186–8).

The popular and the ancient together also represent a potent mix of mimesis and metaphor. Museum and ethnographic displays are, according to Kirshenblatt-Gimblett, either mimetic, metonymic, or some combination of the two. A metonymic display, whether it be an ethnographic object or a ruin, is a piece of a putative whole, the promise of something more: showing a fragment "in all its partiality enhances the aura of its 'realness'" (Kirshenblatt-Gimblett 1991: 388–9). The exhibition of humans – whether the plaster-of-paris models of dioramic museum displays or the performance of folk dance at a festival is an example of a combination of mimesis and metonymy. The message is that if the viewer could cross the temporal or geographic boundaries that make such displays necessary, this slice of life represents what the viewer would see. What both types of displays share, no matter how accurate the presentation of a ruin or how precise a series of ethnic dance steps, is both a pretense to neutrality and a necessary lack of it (Kirshenblatt-Gimblett 1991). It is in this lack, perhaps, that the source of tension between the Rahbanis and the Festival committee can be located, for the producers of these displays and performances are not just presenting the part that the viewer *sees*, but also the whole that the display or performance *evokes*. The whole in the case of the Lebanese Nights at the Baalbeck Festival is nothing less than the nation itself. But which nation? While it seems to have quickly come to pass that Baalbeck and its Festival represented Lebanon – both metonymically and mimetically – the question of *which* Lebanon it represented was the main cause of this tension.

As it turned out, the committee members need not have worried. The Festival very quickly became, as the official narrative has Chamoun expressing his vision of it, like a "... mirror with two faces: one on World culture and the other on Lebanese heritage and the legacy of its ancestor" (qtd. in Munassā 1994: 8). His and his wife's involvement in the founding of the Festival is evidence of a realization that more was at stake than revenue from tourism. This combination of local and international acts centered on the majestic and evocative ruins of Baalbeck allowed for the propagation of an image that the Maronite national elite was keen to project: a Westward looking nation that had reclaimed its original Phoenician role as a cultivator of culture and civilization. The Festival's role in the first half of this equation was easy enough to manage. With the sufficient funds and knowledge of the world arts scene, neither of which the Festival committee members lacked (Sa'īd, Kh. 1998b), high-brow international acts could be brought from abroad. These acts included The New York Philharmonic Orchestra (1959), the Royal Ballet (1961 and 1964), the Opera de Paris (1962), the Bolshoi Ballet (1971), and Miles Davis (1971). The establishment of the connection between modern-day Lebanon and the Phoenician inventors of art, however, was potentially more difficult to pull off, especially in light of the fact that the groups and personnel needed to stage Lebanese folklore – the key to this link – did not as yet exist. What I will show in Chapter 2 is that the First Couple and the Festival committee could not have made a better choice than the Rahbani Brothers and Fairouz. From its inception, the Rahbani-dominated Lebanese Nights was a resounding success. Leaving nothing to chance, however, the Festival committee published an elaborate program to accompany each year's event. It is these texts that I turn my attention to before focusing in Chapter 2 not just on the success of the Rahbanis' participation in the Festival, but also on the consequences of that success. As the following on the Festival program will begin to make clear, the powerful presentation of a specific vision of Lebanon at the Baalbeck Festival implied the dangerous exclusion of other national imaginings.

The Festival program: "A Festival in and of itself"

A 1994 review of the official history that I have been citing is entitled "The Baalbeck Festivals in a book" ("Mahrajānāt Baalbeck fī kitāb", 1994). Even if not intentional, this title can be read as an astute comment on the elaborate textual side of the Festival. This aspect of the Festival is represented not just by the 1994 book in question, but by the similarly elaborate annual Festival programs. Why should a festival that is based on live performances need more than a simple program? Kirshenblatt-Gimblett points out that since festivals are less openly textual and didactic than, say, museums, any formal "discoursing" has to take place in the program booklet (Kirshenblatt-Gimblett 1991: 417). Logic would suggest, then, that the size of the program would be some indicator of the Festival's didactic aspirations. The program for the 1962 Festival, which will be the focus of this section, is almost two hundred and fifty pages long. These literally weighty texts served to establish the continuity and conceptual monumentality of the event, adding the literal and metaphorical weight of the printed page to the grandeur of the setting and the ambition of the performances. The importance of these annual programs can be gleaned from the writing on them in the official history:

> The International Baalbeck Festivals would begin with the book-program, which was, in its form and design, a festival in and of itself. We

look upon this book of memory and recollection today as if it were an
amulet that preserved the myth of the cultural Baalbeck from extinction
(Munassā 1994: 10)

In this section I investigate the significance of these "amulets."

The 1962 Festival program is sandwiched between a number of full-page
advertisements: 24 at the beginning of the book and 10 at the end. The presence of
these ads reminds us of the commercial aspect of both the Festival and the site.
As mentioned briefly above, tourism had been an important sector of the local
economy well before modern Lebanon itself was created. Baalbeck, soon after its
"rediscovery," became a key site for tourists and travelers, with admission being
charged as early as the beginning of the twentieth century (Makdisi, U. 1998). The
importance of the ruins as a source of income for the local private sector economy
can be seen in the inclusion of several advertisements at the beginning of the 1926
Arabic Edition of Allūf's *History of Baalbeck*.

Folk festivals are intrinsically related to tourism:

Tourists who have difficulty deciphering and penetrating the quotidian
of their destination find in festivals the perfect entrée. Public and
spectacular, festivals have the practical advantage of offering in a
concentrated form and at a designated time and place what the tourist
would otherwise search out in the diffuseness of everyday life, with no
guarantee of ever finding it.
(Kirshenblatt-Gimblett 1991: 418)

Sa'īd reminds us that one of the very *raison d'êtres* of the Baalbeck Festival was
tourism (Sa'īd, Kh. 1998b: 53). Entrance to the Festival itself has never been cheap
and admission was charged as early as 1944 (Munassā 1994: 8).[19] In 2005, tickets
ranged in price from 20 to 120 US dollars (not including transportation), no small
sum in a country where the annual per capita income is approximately 6,000 US
dollars.[20] This raises the issue of audience. Who, in other words, could afford to
attend these shows? Though there is no hard data on the subject, it is clear that from
the very beginning this was an important issue for some of those involved with the
Festival who wanted to balance its otherwise elitist image, especially those
committee members attached to the folklore or Arab theater committees (Sa'īd, Kh.
1998b: 54).[21] With the additional audience brought in by the folkloric shows came
additional revenue. Khālida Sa'īd reports, for example, that it was the revenue from
The Lebanese Nights which financed the nonfolkloric Lebanese theatrical productions at Baalbeck (Sa'īd, Kh. 1998b: 59). This may help to explain the warming of
the Festival committee's attitude to the place of folklore at the Festival.

In any case, by 1962, advertising in the Festival brochure was fairly copious.
The majority of the ads are for international companies (e.g. banks, airlines, and
oil companies) and are written in either French or English. Several of them were
obviously prepared either specifically for Lebanon or for the Festival, including

notes of congratulations or references to the grandeur and ancient history of Baalbeck. A French-language advertisement for Marlboro cigarettes, with the slogan "un moment de detente," seems particularly customized to its context. The ad's picture features a woman of unclear origin smoking. She is dressed in Western clothes and is seated next to an ornately finished door in what looks like the courtyard of an old Lebanese palace such as Beiteddine (Bayt al-Dīn).[22] In the middle of the courtyard spouts a refreshing looking fountain. In the background is what appears to be a "typical" Lebanese village: a terraced mountain studded with trees and traditional Lebanese homes. This targeting of an apparently urban audience with a village scene is consistent with the message both of the Festival itself and its annual program.[23]

The tri-lingualism of the advertisements, with French being the predominant language, reflects the linguistic makeup of the rest of the book. The program can be read from left to right or from right to left, the left-hand side written entirely in French and the right-hand side consisting of Arabic peppered with French and English. Even though one of the motivations for including folklore in the program was to attract a broader and less elite audience, French remains the dominant language of the program. Of the approximately 185 pages of the program which contain text, 140 of them are in French or, in a few instances, English. This leaves 43 pages of text in Arabic and 2 pages, both advertisements, containing a mixture of French and Arabic. The program contains information on each portion of that summer's Festival, which included in 1962 – in addition to The Lebanese Nights – a French theater company, two French classical music ensembles, a French sound and light show, and a French opera company. The portions of the program that cover the French acts are all in French. Nowhere in the program are even their names and dates included in Arabic. The section of the program on The Lebanese Nights, on the other hand, is presented consecutively in Arabic, French, and English, the assumption being perhaps that no non-French speakers would attend the foreign acts, but that non-Arabic speakers might attend "The Lebanese Nights." Of the program's 250 pages, only 37 are devoted to information about that summer's acts. Aside from the 34 pages of advertisements already mentioned, what role do the remaining 190 pages play?[24]

Each year's program, according to the Festival's official history, was devoted to a different topic, such as Lebanese architecture, theater, visual arts, and traditional garb, as proof "of the heritage, culture, art and civilization of Lebanon" (Munassā 1994: 10). In 1962, the theme was "Lebanese art." Much of the program's art is accompanied by poems and prose texts, many of them in French including some written by figures discussed above such as Michel Chiha and Hektor Klat. Taken as a whole, these texts and images can be seen as echoing the philosophy of these writers, that the heart of Lebanon is its Christian mountain people who are the true descendants of the Phoenicians and who thus represent their direct link to France. Briefly, the argument goes as follows: while it is true that the Phoenicians were primarily ocean-crossing merchants who lived on the coast of Lebanon, with the succession of invasions that followed the fall of their empire, they took refuge in Mt Lebanon (Kaufman 2001: 174). And as Asher Kaufman points out elsewhere, in the writing of Phoenician nationalists such as Corm and Akl, the Phoenicians are presented as proto Christians (Kaufman 2000: 326–7). Thus, the "folk" being represented on the stage of The Lebanese Nights at Baalbeck are the direct descendants of these culture and language inventing seafaring Phoenicians.

Small wonder that Baalbeck itself, having become the clearest symbol of that link, would be featured in a large number of the programs' texts and images. The first poem in the 1962 program is by Klat who, according to Kaufman, was "...one of the most prolific Francophile Phoenician poets" (Kaufman 2001: 183). If his poetic contribution to the Baalbeck Festival program is any indication, he was also a great believer in Baalbeck being an important link between Lebanon's present and its glorious past. His poem opens describing Baalbeck as a:

> Lyre à six cordes d'or
> Sur nos fastes dressée
> Qu'exalte leur accord
> Notre gloirie passée!
> (*VIIème festival international de Baalbeck* 1962: 5)

In the third verse he makes the connection between the present and "our glorious past" explicit:

> D'ambre et d'ombre adornée,
> Par quel subtil lien
> Tu joins le jour ancien
> A la neuve journée!
> (*VIIème festival international de Baalbeck* 1962: 5)

Baalbeck, Phoenician in origin and witness to a succession of civilizations, is the perfect symbol for the propagation of the image of Lebanon as the cradle of civilization. The Festival and its program are responsible both for reminding us of and reclaiming these temporal and geographic ties. The 1962 Baalbeck Festival program is full of other such texts.

In a piece by Emmanuel Robles entitled "Baalbeck Avant Le Festival," the link between Baalbeck's past and present is confirmed, and another of Chiha's favorite themes – the Lebanese miracle – is alluded to

> Cette nuit de juillet, à Baalbeck; j'écoutais donc les voix lointaines des ouvriers et des techniciens, je regardais ces clartés ordonnées dans la douceur des ombres et je savais qu'on préparait un rite très ancien qui n'a jamais cessé de rassembler des foules au long des siècles. Dans quelques jours, en effet, les prestiges de la musique, du théâtre et de la danse vont créer le miracle.
> (*VIIème festival international de Baalbeck* 1962: 23–4)

The same message is repeated in an Arabic text by Kāmil Murūwa, though he emphasizes more explicitly Lebanon's Baalbeck-based civilizational mission:

> If the earthquakes and the normal course of life have turned the edifices of Baalbeck into rubble, then its heritage has refused extinction. In these edifices a culture that was like preventive armor against the turmoil of time has become rooted.... In this spirit we look today to what is around us in this place. The Festival breathes into it the breath of new life. It ties the present to the past, and these pillars return to being live minarets, once again sending out their call into the world: the call of art and beauty and magic, the call of the eternal civilization.
>
> *(VIIème festival international de Baalbeck* 1962: 165)

Other Arabic texts similarly emphasize, without necessarily mentioning Baalbeck by name, the connection between past greatness and present potential. Though Lebanon has lived through many civilizations in its 3,000-year history, "It has not," Fu'ād Haddād tells us, "changed since its Phoenician days," since that is when its identity became clear (*VIIème festival international de Baalbeck* 1962: 108–11).

The majority of the Arabic texts, however, focus on the virtues of Lebanese village life. Like the Marlboro advertisement mentioned above and the Festival as a whole, the target audience of these texts is not the villager but rather the neo-urbanite pining for the simple life of the countryside. The message of "My Village, My Soul ("Qaryatī wa-nafsī") by Khalil Takieddine (Khalīl Taqī al-Dīn) is that leaving the village means losing one's soul. "Once upon a time," he writes, "I had a quiet village, lost between the olive and evergreen trees, resting on the shoulder of an ageless boulder on one of Lebanon's hills, happily opening its windows to the sun, its chest to the breeze, its heart to life" (*VIIème festival international de Baalbeck* 1962: 107). He goes on to say that he, like the rest of his compatriots, left the village one day without looking back, and that was the day that he lost his soul. Another text about the village which addresses the city dweller is by the preserver of village customs about whom we read above: Anis Frayha. His "Holiday in the Village" (" 'Id fī al-day'a") claims that the dances and songs that are performed after the church bell, "the music of Lebanon," is rung and the holiday of St George is underway are more authentic than the dances and songs that are seen in the city (*VIIème festival international de Baalbeck* 1962: 160–1). Elsewhere he makes clear that these mountain Christian holidays have Phoenician roots and that those celebrating holidays such as that of St Sargis (Mār Sarqīs) – whose church is said to stand on top of an old Phoenician temple – often get carried away and slip back into pagan and Phoenician-style celebration (Frayha 1957: 265–6). The message of these texts is that the true Lebanese are the Lebanese Christian villagers. Like the ruins themselves, they are the link between Lebanon's storied past and its potentially glorious future.

The program's images serve to punctuate this message. On the first page of the Arabic side, for example, there is a nude drawing by the painter and sculptor Joseph Hayek (Yūsuf Hayāk) (*VIIème festival international de Baalbeck* 1962: n.p.). Elsewhere in the program, a text on him informs us that "Lebanese yearning for the strong-hold of art, on the other shore of our sea [i.e. Europe], began at the beginning of the [nineteenth] century and continues to today" (*VIIème festival international de Baalbeck* 1962: 113). Among such pioneers was Hayek, who spent years between Rome and France drawing, it seems, mostly nudes. At one point he realized the emptiness of living so far from home, so not only did he return to Lebanon, but to his father's village, where he found great inspiration in the village girl (*VIIème festival international de Baalbeck* 1962: 112–13) and a patron in the prominent Phoenicianist Charles Corm (Kaufman 2004: 142). At one point the reader is presented with a pregnant combination of the nudes that were his prior focus, and the rural landscapes that he took to painting upon his return to Lebanon. The image in question is made up of a sketch of a nude reclining against what appears to be a boulder. A solitary cedar tree, a traditional symbol of Lebanon, stands in the distance. Even when such themes are not combined in the program, the frequent juxtaposition of abstract painting and bucolic rural scenes speak the same message as the written texts: the borders between Lebanon and the West are fuzzy, if they exist at all. Just as the true Lebanese Phoenician is comfortable in both Paris and the smallest Lebanese village "lost between the mountains" (*VIIème festival international de Baalbeck* 1962: 113), just as the Baalbeck Festival is as much a place for local folklore as it is for French theater, so can the true Lebanese artist create a hybrid of the modern and the traditional.

The messages of all of these texts and images overlap but rarely contradict one another. The Lebanon presented here is the Christian legate of an ancient Phoenician civilization that revels in its position as somewhere betwixt and between Europe and Asia. Lebanon is a cradle of art and civilization. Through its Festival at Baalbeck, with its ancient local and high-brow international acts, it has reclaimed its role as propagator of this civilization, a civilization that has been kept pure and alive in its mountain people despite centuries of invasions and occupations, a civilization that has, in fact, fared better than the crumbling ruins themselves.

I will mention one last aspect of the 1962 program that will take us back to where we started at the beginning of this chapter, that is, to the Europeans who did the "groundwork" for this reclamation project. The 1962 program contains within it eleven pages from the French translation of the eighteenth-century account of Baalbeck by the English traveler Richard Pococke who, as we saw above, had little interest in the Islamic past or present context of the site (Makdisi, U. 1998). This is a trait shared, as should be apparent from the above, by the mid–twentieth-century Lebanese Christian elite involved in staging the Festival. Islam had no place in this textual and performance-based enactment of the nation.

37

This despite the fact that with the creation of Greater Lebanon in 1920, Muslims would make up approximately 50 percent of the country's population.

Chatterjee's study of nineteenth-century Indian nationalism is again useful for some perspective. In the context that he speaks of, the Hindu national elite worked assiduously at crafting a national narrative that did not include that country's sizeable Muslim presence. Chatterjee shows that this was a not a religious but a political move:

> The idea that Indian nationalism is synonymous with Hindu nationalism is not the vestige of some pre-modern religious conception. It is an entirely modern, rationalist, and historicist idea. Like other modern ideologies, it allows for a central role of the state in the modernization of society and strongly defends the state's unity and sovereignty.
>
> (Chatterjee 1993: 110)

If we agree that the elite involved with the Baalbeck Festival were similarly creating a Lebanese narrative that did not involve at least half of the country's population, then the texts and subtexts of the Festival brochure and the Festival itself should not be taken lightly. They are particularly important if I am right that by 1962 – the year that Farid El Atrache sang his folksong under the site's six famous pillars in *Letter from an Unknown Woman* – the Baalbeck Festival, its particular Lebanon, and the Rahbanis had become synonymous with one another.

In Chapter 2, I will look specifically at the musical-theatrical participation of the Rahbanis at Baalbeck. Despite the Festival committee's initial reservations about placing the presentation of folklore in their hands, it turned out that their works were the perfect vehicles to catalyze the subject forming power of the classicization of tradition and the appropriation of the popular. I will show that this was partly a matter of content and partly a matter of timing. Their participation in the Festival was accompanied by new and improved recording and transmission technologies. In other words, those both in Lebanon and abroad who could not attend the Festivals could follow their works on the radio, records, and tapes. This would be necessitated by financial hardship or migration, both of which were significant and related phenomena in Lebanon at this time. The intersection of migration with mass media and their related influence on "the work of the imagination" is, according to Arjun Appadurai, the pivotal point around which modern subjectivity is constituted (Appadurai 1996: 6).

What I will argue in Chapter 2, in other words, is that the folkloric musical theatrical works staged by the Rahbanis at Baalbeck was not just a project that reflected a certain vision of Lebanese locality, but one that actively participated in producing it. Appadurai has theorized that the production of locality in such circumstances is dangerously fraught because such locality formation requires the enhancement of the significance of borders, both real and imaginary, and both internal and external. The case of the Rahbanis at Baalbeck will eloquently and tragically prove him right. I began this chapter with a quote by Khālida Sa'īd about Fairouz's return to the Baalbeck Festival in its post–civil war reincarnation. In this quote Sa'īd hopes that Fairouz will help to resurrect a national dream from the ashes of a long civil war. What she does not say is that, at least in some way, the participation of the Rahbani Brothers and Fairouz in The Lebanese Nights at the Baalbeck Festival played some part in the creation of just such unstable subjectivities, which, in turn, played a role in the sparking of Lebanon's tragic fifteen-year civil conflict.

2

THE MUSICAL THEATER OF
THE RAHBANI BROTHERS

Representation and the formation of subjectivities

The "stunning" reception of the Rahbanis and
Fairouz at Baalbeck in 1957

By all accounts, the debut of the Rahbani Brothers and Fairouz at the Baalbeck Festival in 1957 was a rousing success. This is how Mansour Rahbani, reminiscing to the poet Henri Zoghaib some thirty-five years later, remembers their first performance there, a series of folkloric musical and dance scenes called *Days of Harvest* (*Ayyām al-hasād*):

> Opening night came and none of the ladies of the committee knew what was going to be in the show. At the beginning of the first scene the director Sabri Sharif [Sabrī al-Sharīf] put Fairouz on the base of one of the columns and shined the light on her from the bottom of the pillar and from different angles. This made it seem to the audience that she was flying in the air while singing "Lebanon, How Beautiful and Green." The first scene was stunning in terms of the audience's reception, the applause igniting in a wave that was a mixture of excitement, tears and bliss. The whole event was put on before a very responsive crowd. We did the show for just two nights, as had been previously decided (each night approximately 5000 spectators came to see what Lebanon would present between the foreign acts).... The press praised us, and we were happy to see that they understood what we were trying to do... and they focused on the necessity of repeating these "Lebanese Nights" at Baalbeck.
>
> (qtd. in Zoghaib 1993: part five, 72–3)

And repeat them they would. The Rahbanis staged the folkloric "Lebanese Nights" section of the Festival for five years in a row, and then, after a two-year hiatus, appeared there five more times over nine years. It should be recalled that President Chamoun had felt so invested in the outcome of the introduction of local acts into the Festival that he had jokingly warned the Rahbanis about the dire consequences of failure. The official history of the Festival reassures the reader on this note, informing him or her that the Rahbanis and Fairouz received congratulations from the President and his wife after the opening performance. Fairouz actually received the medal that was jokingly promised to the Rahbanis should their show succeed. In that very year the First Lady presented the singer with "The Cavalier Medal," apparently the highest honor ever given to an artist (Boulus 1981: 33). Moreover, the event – a series of folkloric dance and musical numbers from a village wedding celebration – was described in the press as "a miracle" (Munassā 1994: 14). Unreported in the official history is the chilly initial reception of the Rahbanis by the Festival committee. It is perhaps the committee's change in attitude toward the family that speaks most eloquently to that opening night's success. Of their first meeting after the performance, Mansour Rahbani says: "We were called once again to meet the Baalbeck Festival committee, and its ladies received us with a different tone and attitude. They came to the meeting to hear what we had to say, not to impose their project on us" (Zoghaib 1993: part five, 73).

The success of these folkloric musical shows was also cited by those wondering how to draw bigger crowds to theatrical events both at Baalbeck and elsewhere. In 1964 the Rahbani Brothers participated in a colloquium on theater held by the leftist journal *al-Tarīq* which, among other issues, posed the question of attendance generally and asked specifically why the Rahbani Brothers' productions were so much more successful than other types of theater in terms of attracting audiences. Some of the theories suggested were their heavy dependence upon music, the use of colloquial Arabic, and the presence of Fairouz (Shahhāda 1964). To these suggestions I would like to add the combination of the appropriation of the popular and the classicization of tradition, as well as the mix of metaphor and metonymy, that these events signified. Chapter 1 – through an examination of how Baalbeck and the festivals that came to be held there became potent symbols of the nation – focused on the first binary. In this chapter, which follows the arc of the early musical-theatrical career of the Rahbani Brothers and Fairouz, I will have more to say about the second, about how their "successes" *and* their "failures" were very much connected to the way their works *represented* Lebanon. This will allow the completion of the quadrilateral tautology that I suggested at the beginning of Chapter 1: Baalbeck equals the Baalbeck Festival equals the Rahbanis equals Lebanon.

While Chapter 1 demonstrated how Baalbeck and the Baalbeck Festival came to stand for each other and how they had begun to stand for Lebanon as well, in this chapter I will show how this equation becomes complete with the Rahbani Brothers' series of folkloric shows beginning with *Days of Harvest* in 1957. The ambition of this chapter, however, is not only to complete this equation but also to show how the signifying power of the Rahbani Brothers and Fairouz eventually breaks free, both literally and metaphorically, from Baalbeck, and eclipses both site and Festival in terms of representational productivity. While the Rahbani Brothers' project was in need of the Baalbeck Festival to establish its representational authority, once developed, it became to a great extent independent of that site and Festival. In other words, once connected to the potent signifying powers of the site and the Festival, the Rahbani Brothers began to take their increasingly extravagant and decreasingly folkloric acts and music elsewhere: Beirut, the Cedars Festival, the International Damascus Festival, Egypt, Tunisia, Algeria, Europe, North and South America, and even the celluloid space of the cinema. Once no longer tethered to the Festival, this chapter asks, did their works break free from its ideological project?

These questions and issues cannot be examined in isolation from the context of the civil violence that rocked Lebanon in 1958, a year after the Baalbeck debut of the Rahbani Brothers and Fairouz.[1] That burst of civil violence with its myriad of global, regional, and local causes, called into question the utopian idea of Lebanon as a land of liberal peace and harmony. Politically, it resulted in the ascension to power of General Fouad Chehab, a reformer bent on reconciling internal differences and inequalities in the country through state building and resource distribution. Like his predecessor and despite their differences, Chehab was not only the honorary Chairman of the Baalbeck Festival committee (Sa'īd, Kh. 1998b: 50), but also took a keen interest in the Baalbeck Festival in general and perhaps The Lebanese Nights in particular. This chapter explores the theater of the Rahbani Brothers in the context of this war and the regime change in which it resulted. Though there is abundant evidence to suggest that the Rahbani Brothers identified with this project much more than they did with that of Chamoun, I will argue that in many ways their work – at Baalbeck and elsewhere – can be seen as an extension of the ideological project begun at the ruins *before* the violence of 1958. There is no debating, however, the fact that their plays changed in both form and content over time. This chapter asks how much their works' development can be attributed to the violence of 1958 and the changes it effected. Some of the development, I hope to show, had nothing to do with the political or cultural environment in which they were working, but rather was a necessary result of the very act of the repeated transferring of folklore from the Christian mountain village to the stage, radio waves, record, and screen.

Before looking at the effects of the changes wrought by the 1958 violence on the project of the Rahbani Brothers and Fairouz, however, this chapter will explore their pre-Baalbeck careers, showing how they arrived there after a start in the new and powerful medium of radio. While there is no denying the importance of that Festival to their careers, I hope to show that this triad of artists had already achieved a substantial measure of success and fame before a seemingly "flying" Fairouz burst into song at Baalbeck in the summer of 1957. This is not an attempt at comprehensive artistic biography. Rather, I wish to suggest that the seeds of both their project's representational power and some of its contradictions can be found in their early careers in this powerful medium. It was in the decade or so before their debut at the Baalbeck Festival that Asi, Mansour, and Fairouz began to work in radio. It was, in fact, at the studio of Lebanese Radio that the trinity of these artists was formed both by the artistic success of their collaborations and by the marriage of Asi and Fairouz. The Rahbanis' early careers in radio and their success both locally and abroad provide a glimpse of the power of the combination of mass media and migration in the formation of subjectivities.

Radio and the pre-1957 Rahbani Brothers: Rumba, refrigerators, and the Lebanese song

We have seen the difference in reception given to the Rahbani Brothers by the Baalbeck Festival committee before and after their first appearance at that event. One point of tension at that first meeting was the decision to include Fairouz in the program, worried as they were that she would sing long *tarab*-style songs like Oum Kalthoum. That Fairouz's debut in the inaugural version of The Lebanese Nights changed her status in their minds is evident in the official program for the second edition of The Lebanese Nights in 1959. That program contains a full-page photograph of Fairouz in peasant headscarf with the following caption: "Lebanon's leading folklore singer" ("Mahrajān al-fann al-sha'bī" 1959: n.p.). It stands to reason that her primary songwriters – her husband Asi and brother-in-law Mansour Rahbani – were seen as Lebanon's leading folkloric songwriters. In fact, their names would eventually come to be associated with the development of a distinct genre called "fūlklūr" (Racy 2002: n.p.).[2] This seemingly automatic link to folklore, however, was not a given at the start of their careers, when much of what they wrote was of the Latin dance music variety that was so popular in Europe and the US at this time.

A 1953 article on the Rahbani Brothers by the music critic Nizār Murūwa – son of the well-known Marxist thinker and journal editor Husayn Murūwa – begins by congratulating them on their musical achievements and by observing the large measure of fame and praise that this had won them. Then comes a rebuke. Murūwa notes that most of their work is of the light dance variety, which merely entertains the listener without lifting him up. "Is it not a shame," he continues,

> for the Rahbani Brothers to waste their efforts in the translation of dance songs, which everyone can hear on dance music programs?[3] Is it not more worthwhile for them to exert efforts **to create popular and national art** [bold in the original], to awaken noble emotions and to participate in the artistic and literary message which today is joining headlong the all-out war against colonialism and the forces of evil?
>
> (Murūwa 1998: 106)

It should be clear from this rebuke that much of the Rahbani Brothers' early work was a far cry from the folkloric vignettes they would initially present at Baalbeck's Lebanese Nights.

Murūwa's statement, with its reference to "dance music programs," also hints at the growing regional importance of radio – a medium that would be central to the advancement of the career of the Rahbani Brothers (Abī Samrā 1999) – not just for the propagation of music, but for ideas as well. I will pause at some length on the early intersection of the Rahbanis and radio because this medium and other forms of mass media – of which the Baalbeck Festival can be seen as an extension – were central to the relationship of their careers to subject formation both in and outside of Lebanon. For earlier nationalisms Anderson has demonstrated the importance of the coincidence of capitalism and print-media in fostering imagined national communities. He describes both newspapers and novels as presenting separate events synchronically and thus demanding that the reader imagine the connection between them. At the same time, the reader would imagine other readers simultaneously going through the same process in the same language. Thus were national communities first imagined in colonial America and Europe (Anderson 1991).

In a later work, Anderson discusses the irony of later nation-state formation (Anderson 1994). Though early nations could not have been imagined without print capitalism, the technological manifestations of late capitalism would threaten the very form of community it had, in a sense, created. Advances in transportation and communication meant increasingly wide-scale migration on the one hand, and the development of radio, television, and recording technologies on the other. No newspaper, he argues, could compete with radio services like the BBC and the Voice of America in terms of its potential audience.

In such circumstances, producing "localities" becomes a struggle between a variety of state and other factions (Appadurai 1996: 189). The stakes of this struggle are high, according to Appadurai, because it is the intersection of mass media and migration and their related influence on "the work of the imagination" that is the pivotal point around which modern subjectivity is constituted (Appadurai 1996: 4). He contends that in recent times the real and the imagined have become dialectically formed entities; each is in turn, and simultaneously, the fodder for the other. While Appadurai sees this as a phenomenon being no more than two decades old, I believe that its basic components can be found in the Lebanon of the 1950s and 1960s. In an environment of developing mass media and increased internal and external migration, the work of the Rahbanis before, after, and including their Baalbeck period figures prominently in this very subject formation.

In the case of Lebanon and the Rahbani Brothers prior to Baalbeck, the confluence of local, regional, and international radio on the one hand and nationalist independence movements on the other placed them in a precarious position between participation in several official local and regional subjectivity-forming projects. On the level of Lebanon, for example, Tāhā al-Walī claims that Lebanese mountain tastes and mores did not spread to Beirut until the likes of Fairouz and others began to broadcast their "mountain songs" on the radio. "Bit by bit," he writes, "the infection spread" (al-Walī 1992: 19). The Rahbani Brothers adeptly and simultaneously participated in a variety of such projects. At the end of this chapter and the beginning of the next I will show that this very "success" contributed, in a sense, to the project's ultimate collapse.

Earlier on, of course, these technologies had helped to spark an artistic boom in the region. It is in the context of the intersection of these historical and technological circumstances that there was a combination of an "explosion of [musical] energies and talents" in the Arab World and also a proliferation of "national anthems and national, popular and folkloric songs" (Aliksān, J. 1987: 20–1). There were also unprecedented commercial opportunities as well as tension between the various levels of nationalism represented by the different local and regional radio stations and the regimes that controlled them. As will be seen below, one can observe aspects of all of these phenomena in the early career trajectory of the Rahbani Brothers and Fairouz.

As with most other forms of mass communication, the Arab World and Lebanon did not lag far behind Europe and North America in terms of the introduction of the radio.[4] The first radio station in the Arab World was opened in Egypt in 1934 (Boyd 1977: 4). Lebanon and Syria got their first station in 1937 (al-Zughbī 1969). The first words transmitted – "ici Liban" – are indicative of the French – cultural and literal – control of the station, which would be called Radio of the East (Rādiyyū al-sharq) until the Lebanese gained control of it with the departure of the French in 1946, at which time they renamed it Radio Lebanon (Mahattat al-idhā'a al-Lubnāniyya) (al-Zughbī 1969).[5] By 1951 there was 1 radio for every 28 inhabitants of the country ("The Radio Audience of Lebanon" 1951: 84), though it should be noted that radios were often shared in public places (Boyd 1977: 4).

It is at Radio Lebanon that the Rahbani Brothers got their start in the mid-1940s. It was not until Asi joined the station full-time in 1949 (Mansour would come on board full time in 1953, both of them having been employed as policemen up until their full-time radio employment) that the name "the Rahbani Brothers" – which is how they would thereafter sign all of their work – would begin to gain recognition (Bāshā 1995: 143–4). Their work at Radio Lebanon brought them to the attention of the powers that be at a British commercial radio station which was broadcasting under the aegis of the British Foreign Ministry from offices in Cairo and a transmitter in Cyprus: Near East Radio (Idhā'at al-sharq al-adnā) (Zoghaib 1993: part four, 74). It was in the early 1950s at Near East Radio that the Rahbani Brothers would begin to collaborate with other rising stars of the Lebanese music and musical-theatrical scene, artists like Tawfiq al-Basha (Tawfīq al-Bāshā), Zaki Nasif (Zakī Nāsīf), Sabri Sharif, and Tawfiq Sukkar (Tawfīq al-Sukkar) (Abū Murād 1990: 42).[6] It is also on Near East Radio that Fairouz would first sing a song of their arrangement (Aliksān, J. 1987: 174). Likewise, it was on the airwaves of this station that Ahmad 'Assa, the director of Radio Damascus (Idhā'at Dimashq), first heard them (Aliksān, J. 1987: 88–9), marking the beginning of a long relationship with the Syrian public that will be further commented on below.

If radio in Lebanon was not put to anticolonial use due to French control of the station (Abū Murād 2000) as well as the complicated relationship between the Lebanese nationalist elite and their French "protectors" before 1946, it was certainly used by the Lebanese and Syrian governments and national elites after the withdrawal of France – as were the Baalbeck and subsequently the Damascus Festivals – for nation-building and nationalistic ends. The early career of Fairouz certainly bears this observation out, as we are told that much of what she sang in the Radio Lebanon choir and as part of the Fulayfil Brothers military-style band consisted of nationalistic anthems (Racy 2002). The Rahbani Brothers themselves would soon enough and in their own way take up the nationalistic challenge laid out for them by Murūwa above: this not simply by writing overtly nationalistic songs but rather, as they themselves and others have described it, by the very *creation* of the "Lebanese Song" (Abū Murād 1990: 34 and 40; Nāsir 1986: part one, 34; Salām 1986: 62–3; al-Sāyigh 1986: 60; Wāzin 1996: 20; Zoghaib 1993: part four, 72). While they were not without predecessors in their efforts,[7] many narratives on their career give them the lion's share of the credit for this development. We are told that at this time the dominant musical style was "Egyptian" (Aliksān, J. 1987: 65–6; al-'Awīt 1987: 20; Barakāt 1996: 29; and Murūwa 1998: 118), meaning mostly long melancholy love tunes, sung, by Egyptians and others, in the Egyptian dialect. The 1951 survey of Lebanese radio listeners confirms the domination of the Egyptian songs at this time, with the majority of singers mentioned by name being either Egyptian by birth or by style, and with all of the four most frequently mentioned performers being in that classification ("The Radio Audience of Lebanon" 1951: 151–2).[8] It is interesting but perhaps not surprising that the Rahbani Brothers do not appear in this 1951 survey. Part of the reason may be that they had yet to begin collaborating with Fairouz and were writing either for a chorus or relying on their sister Salwā – who is said not to have had such a distinctive voice (Aliksān, J. 1987: 37) – to sing their pieces. Their absence from the list of favorites at the time also gives credence to the claim that their attempts to forge a distinct Lebanese style met with some resistance. Here, for example, are the comments of Mansour Rahbani on these developments:

> We brought to our songs a new kind of orchestration, invoking melodies that spring from this land. Into them we introduced new poetic content. At that time songs contained many perfumed and sappy words ([e.g.] violet, jasmine, rebuke, reunion), were always about deprivation and [were full of] delicate and fragile expressions. The shortest song was twenty minutes long. We came along with the three minute song with changed words (and even changed pronunciation: for example, we would pronounce "night" with a *fatha* on the *lām* and a *sukūn* on the *yā'*, whereas the widespread Egyptian way was with a *kasra* under the *lām* [i.e. "layl" as opposed to "līl"]) and [used] terms like wild, boulder, thorn, etc.[9] Many would refuse to sing with us, even in the chorus, because our words were "rough and mountainous," and the musicians would avoid playing our songs due to the musical phrases' divergence from what they knew.[10]
>
> (qtd. in Zoghaib 1993: part four, 70)

These "innovations," as we will see below, are related to their culling and development of folkloric material that would appear on the stage at Baalbeck beginning in 1957.

As the Rahbanis were developing their distinct Lebanese song with its Mt Lebanon-specific imagery and vocabulary, they were also in the process of gaining a Syrian audience through their work with Radio Damascus. From the early 1950s, in fact, the Rahbani Brothers and Fairouz dominated the airwaves of Radio Damascus (Abī Samrā 1999: 9 and Aliksān, J. 1987: 90), appeared onstage at the Damascus Festival more times than they did at Baalbeck (Abū Murād 1997: 42) and wrote at least one series for Syrian television (Yamīn 1985: 11). They obviously did not achieve such popularity there by singing Mt–Lebanon-specific songs alone. In fact, their appearances at the Damascus Festival were always opened with a new song written for the occasion praising Syria and the Syrians (Aliksān, J. 1987: 251). This would become a custom at most of their non–Lebanon Arab-World appearances.

The Rahbani Brothers and Fairouz's distinct association with the Palestinian cause also began to develop at this time, due at least in part to the intersection of radio with the displacement of thousands of Palestinians after the 1948 war with Israel and with the post–World War Two acceleration of regional nationalistic movements. Soon after Asi Rahbani and Fairouz's wedding in 1955, they received an invitation to Cairo from the official Egyptian radio station The Voice of the Arabs (Sawt al-'Arab) and were granted a six-month contract to write "songs, anthems and programs," especially for the Palestinian cause (Zoghaib 1993: part four, 72). They were brought Palestinian folk songs from the Gaza Strip on which to base their compositions (Zoghaib 1993: part four, 72). Complaining that they found them too depressing and full of despair to emulate (Murūwa 1998: 43–4), they instead came up with a hopeful fifteen-minute work for Fairouz and a chorus which they entitled "Rāji'ūn" ("We are Returning") which, when it was finally released as *Rāji'ūn* along with other songs for Palestine back in Beirut in 1957, was very popular and enjoyed extensive radio air-play (Wāzin 1992: 21).

Small wonder that such a project would come out of Egypt at this time. By the mid-1950s, the anticolonial and pan-Arab bent of Gamal Abdel Nasser's (Jamāl 'Abd al-Nāsir) young revolution had already crystallized. It is also no surprise that Radio Cairo's Voice of the Arabs service sponsored this *We are Returning* project. I have cited Anderson on the power of the BBC and the Voice of America. Competing with these in the Arab World was Egypt's Radio Cairo.[11] The Rahbanis' association both with this station and with Radio Damascus are good examples of both the opportunities and the dilemmas presented by the different levels of allegiance and nationalism in which they were operating at this time: Lebanese, Syrian, Palestinian, Arab. In an essay about *We are Returning* written some thirty years later, Nizār Murūwa calls it a mature work at a time when it was not clear what direction *Lebanese* music would take (Murūwa 1998: 181). This comment is indicative of some of these tensions. It is, in other words, a Lebanese song written in Egypt at the behest of the Egyptian government for the Palestinian cause. Just one year later the Suez Canal crisis would bring many such tensions to the surface.

In July of 1956 the Nasser government nationalized the Suez Canal thus provoking a military response from France, England, and Israel. Back in Lebanon, the Near East Radio station would be forced to close when its clear support of England's participation in the aggression against Egypt became intolerable to the local artists and staff working there (Aliksān, J. 1987: 45). Even if the Rahbani Brothers were, as they claim, the catalysts behind the closing of the station in 1956 (Zoghaib 1993: part four, 72), from the early 1950s up until that point, they and many others seemingly had no qualms about working there despite their knowledge, as Mansour admits, that the station existed primarily for British propagandistic purposes (Zoghaib 1993: part four, 71).[12] This is no doubt partially because of the artistic possibilities afforded by association with a large number of high-quality musicians and artists as seen above. On the other hand, the reason behind such a collection of talent is no doubt the fact that the Near East Radio station compensated its artists generously (Zoghaib 1993: part four, 72).

While the tension that the confluence of radio and postcolonial nationalism brought with it is reflected in the *content* of their work for Radio Damascus and Voice of the Arabs, their association with Near East Radio demonstrates such tension in terms of *form*. Despite their work outside of Lebanon, it needs to be remembered that the Rahbani Brothers were much concerned with the formulation of the distinctly "Lebanese Song." I have pointed out that one of the ways that the Rahbani Brothers claimed to have moved the Lebanese song away from the Egyptian model was to shorten it. It is possible that this change in duration had as much to do with commercial considerations as it did with nationalistic ones. While limitations of early recording technology had dictated a truncation of songs the world over, by the 1950s long-playing records and the development of recording tape had made such limitations obsolete (Racy 1977: 156–60 and 170; Weber 2002: n.p.). The advent of radio, because of the possibility of transmitting live music, also obviated such restrictions (Racy 1977: 170). At the same time, *commercial* radio encouraged short songs not for technological but rather for financial reasons. Simply put, shorter songs are more appropriate for advertising.[13] Near East Radio was unique in the Arab World at this time in that it was – despite its affiliation with the British government – a commercial station (Zoghaib 1993: part four, 71). The shorter songs of the Rahbani Brothers would allow the station to air its advertisements with greater frequency than would the long "Egyptian-style" song, not to mention the fact that working for such a station afforded the Rahbani Brothers the opportunity to write some of the very advertisements that punctuated their songs.

The Rahbani Brothers wrote the music and lyrics to a number of advertisements for Near East Radio (Munassā 1991: 7). Of their work in this field Mansour says,

> The period at Near East Radio was very fruitful. It was the first radio station [in the region] to insert commercial advertisements and Asi and I ... wrote the words and music to the first advertisement, which was for "Karūslī" refrigerators. It went: "Karūslī Karūslī, refrigerator Karūslī, standing in the house you really move me." The owner of the company

48

admitted that he sold about five hundred units thanks to that advertisement which was on the tip of everyone's tongue.

(Zoghaib 1993: part four, 74)

Simultaneously, then, the Rahbani Brothers were participating in a variety and combination of state-sponsored nationalist, artistic, and commercial projects on the local, regional, and international levels. I bring up these apparent contradictions and tensions not to negate their claims of having contributed to the pioneering of a new musical idiom, nor to argue for the impossibility of simultaneously participating in a variety of subject-forming projects, nor to criticize the intersection of commerce and art, but rather to demonstrate the tension that accompanied the musical opportunities presented by the juncture of radio and independence. These tensions – and opportunities – would not dissipate as they moved into the musical-theatrical phase of their careers. In fact, the move from the airwaves to the stage at Baalbeck would only serve to increase the subject-forming power of their works.

From Sayyid Darwish to the Rahbani Brothers: musical theater and commitment

By the end of this pre-Baalbeck period the Rahbani Brothers were doing much more musically than merely translating "Western dance music," the practice for which they had been rebuked by the music critic Husayn Murūwa in 1953. They were, in fact, producing more than just music, having started to compose short musical theatrical sketches for the radio stations mentioned above, an outgrowth of the amateur musical-theatrical numbers that they had previously staged in their hometown of Antilyas (Antilyās) (Sa'īd, Kh. 1998b: 38). Most such work was done at Near East Radio in collaboration with Sabri Sharif (Abū Murād 1990: 57) who would go on to direct many of their musical-theatrical productions at the Baalbeck Festival. They began presenting these "sketches" or "radio operettas," which would ultimately be as long as a half-hour (Aliksān, J. 1987: 70), in collaboration with him as early as 1949 (Abū Murād 1997: 47). Is this the kind of thing Murūwa had in mind when he called them to join the battle against imperialism? The answer, as will be seen, is directly related to the question of the Rahbani Brothers' musical-theatrical antecedents, as well as the cultural ideologies of the period in question.

Though the Rahbani Brothers would claim that their form of musical theater was without precedent in the Arab World (T. 1987: 44 and Abū Murād 1990: 69), it is clear from the very beginning that even their early radio sketches had direct predecessors, such as the short musical-theatrical numbers put on by Tawfiq al-Basha and an American dancer named Mrs Cook, also directed by Sabri Sharif at Near East Radio ("Mu'assasat Rahbani" 2000), as well as the radio skits of Philemon Wehbe (Fīlmūn Wahba) (Murūwa 1998: 123). All of these short radio pieces, as well as the large-scale productions to come, must be seen in light of the general history of musical theater in the Arab World (Shāwūl 1989: 471).[14] This history begins in Lebanon with the birth of modern Arab theater in the musical-theatrical works of Mārūn al-Naqqāsh in the middle of the nineteenth century,[15] and continues in the form of a cultural back-and-forth between Egypt and the Levant right up through the modest beginnings of the Rahbani Brothers' musical-theatrical performances in their town of Antilyas and their initial sketches on Near East Radio.

It has traditionally been thought that when the mantle of regional theatrical leadership was passed to Egypt in the early twentieth century that Lebanese theater went into a Rip-Van-Winkle-esque slumber until the late 1950s and early 1960s. al-Rā'ī, for example, writes: "Although Syria and Lebanon helped the Egyptian theatre to flourish, giving it whole companies as well as some dramatic fare, at home, however, theatre lights were all put out" (al-Rā'ī 1992: 391). Recent scholarship has done much to debunk this historiography. Two recent studies which attempt to treat the period between the founding of Lebanese theater and its mid–twentieth-century incarnation as one of some continuity are Abū Murād 1997 and Kurayyim 2000. In the introduction to his work, the latter asks poignantly:

> But what about the period between 1847 and 1960? Is it reasonable that there would be no theatrical activity for a period of more than one hundred years and then for there to spring up a modern renaissance replete with all of the necessary elements: writers, actors, directors and an audience?
>
> (Kurayyim 2000: 19)

The answer, obviously, is no, and Abū Murād confirms that by the late 1940s there was indeed still some musical theater in Lebanon despite the war and the stiff competition already being offered by the cinema (Abū Murād 1997). This is not to deny the fact that Egypt clearly became the center of musical and nonmusical Arab-World theatrical activity in the first few decades of the twentieth century, just as it would subsequently become the leader of Arab-World cinema. It should be pointed out, however, that many working in both arenas had Levantine backgrounds.[16]

Those writing about the musical and musical-theatrical parentage of the Rahbanis almost inevitably mention the Egyptian actor, singer, composer, and musical theater playwright Sayyid Darwish (Sayyid Darwīsh). In addition to his own short-lived theater company, Darwish composed the music for some thirty musical productions for luminaries of early twentieth-century Egypt-based musical theater such as George Abyad (Jūrj Abyad), Naguib El-Rihani (Najīb al-Rīhānī), Mounira El-Mahdiyya (Munīra al-Mahdiyya), and Ali al-Kassar ('Alī al-Kassār).[17] If the Rahbani Brothers did not themselves express their indebtedness to him in plain speech, they certainly did so artistically. Two of his songs that Fairouz has sung are "It [the sun] Has Risen: How Beautiful its Light is" ("Tala'at yā mā ahlā nūrahā") and "Visit Me" ("Zūrūnī"), the latter being a regular part of her concert repertoire over the years. In 1966, during their first visit to Cairo since their 1955 trip, there was talk, ultimately unrealized, of cooperation between the Rahbani Brothers and Egyptian artists in staging various scenes from some of Sayyid Darwish's plays. Also during that trip, Fairouz was given honorary membership into the Sayyid Darwish Society for her role in spreading his works.

When the work of the Rahbani Brothers is compared to that of Darwish, one point of musical-theatrical common ground often mentioned is their respective introduction of "Western" orchestral instruments incapable of playing the traditional Arab quarter tone – such as the piano – as well as the use of "harmony."[18] Both projects are also credited with creating more of a balance between music and song in a musical tradition in which the human voice, and thus the singer, has overshadowed instrumentation, and thus the composer. More than these musical elements, however, it is the perceived nationalist and popular nature of their respective projects that is, if not always directly compared, at least similarly described. Both projects have been categorized as nationalistic, not only for their direct patriotic discourses, but also for their accurate assimilation of the voices and musical styles of the "common people."

Sayyid Darwish is said not just to have influenced the Rahbani Brothers, but also the Lebanese music critic Murūwa with whom we began this section. It is apparently the example of Darwish that he had in mind when he suggested musical theater as the ideal genre for the further development of Arab music. This suggestion comes in response to an article written by the Syrian music critic Samīm al-Sharīf calling for the formation of symphony orchestras in the Arab World. For Murūwa, this suggestion is impractical, ignoring as it does the elevated status of the human voice in Arab music (Murūwa 1998: 96–101). Murūwa's article was written in 1957, and published just a few months after the Rahbani Brothers presented their *Days of Harvest* at the Baalbeck Festival. Some ten years later he would write that the musical theater of the Rahbani Brothers had, by depicting the present through the use of the popular and folkloric, effectively reached the people. The success of their virtually annual productions at the Baalbeck Festival was also proof for him of the importance of the involvement of government in this kind of cultural production (Murūwa 1998: 121–36), a view that would be shared in post–1958 civil violence Lebanon by the Rahbani Brothers and President Fouad Chehab. Even back in 1957, however, in an article written just before their Baalbeck debut, Murūwa seemed to forecast this success. In response to a journalistic debate as to whether or not the Rahbani Brothers employed "Western" techniques in their music, Murūwa writes that Arab music is not at the stage where such questions are important. What is important at this point, he offers, is to monitor the musical-theatrical developments of the Rahbani Brothers to see if they will be able to develop further the genre of musical theater as they come out from behind the curtain of radio. "The phenomenon of the Rahbanis," he continues,

> is of great significance for the development of Arab art, and it has many
> siblings in Lebanon and Egypt. Thus it is part of a comprehensive

movement to free Arab music from the weight of its miserable past; it is all of Arab civilization that is in the process of awakening. The future is ahead of the Rahbanis. Their vision, culture, talents and extensive efforts and experiments lead us to have great hope in them.

(Murūwa 1998: 115)

This is a far cry from the rebuking tone of his 1953 article: gone is the talk of light Western dance music and of frivolous entertainment. It would seem that wittingly or not the Rahbani Brothers, about to be firmly established with Fairouz as their voice and the Baalbeck Festival's stage as their primary venue, were in the process of responding to Murūwa's 1953 call to cultural arms.

Before moving on to the next stage of the Rahbani Brothers and Fairouz's career, however, I would like to contextualize "this comprehensive movement" mentioned above. Murūwa's call to cultural arms, the Rahbani Brothers' search for the "Lebanese song," and their composition of Palestinian resistance music at the behest of the Nasser regime's Voice of the Arabs radio station can all be seen as falling under the umbrella of a movement that was most often described by the term "commitment." In 1953, the same year that Nizār Murūwa called upon the Rahbani Brothers to take up literary arms, the first issue of the literary journal *al-Ādāb*, edited and published by Suhayl Idrīs, appeared in Beirut calling for a "committed" (*multazim*) literature. In fact, Nizār Murūwa's father Husayn was a leading proponent of commitment literature in the Arab World and wrote the introduction to one of the most important books to be published in support of the movement: Mahmūd Amīn al-ʿĀlim and Abd al-ʿAzīm Anīs's *On Egyptian Culture* (*Fī al-thaqāfa al-Misriyya*, 1955). Though the term itself may have been borrowed from Sartre's 1949 essay "What is Literature?" (Badawi, M.M. 1992b: 21) the seeds of the movement in the Arab World have been traced to the poetry and prose of the nineteenth-century cultural renaissance (*nahda*). The movement was reinvigorated by the independence and nation-building struggles of this period. Whereas Lebanese theater of the first half of the twentieth century is marked by an absence of political plays (Abū Murād 2000: 142), Egyptian theater, with that country's more direct struggles with its colonizing power, was clearly more engaged. By 1900, for example, the British started to ban certain plays from being staged in Egypt for fear that they would arouse nationalist sentiment. One of the leading figures in the artistic and literary struggle against colonialism in Egypt is seen to be Sayyid Darwish, most famously perhaps for the anthems he wrote on the occasion of the 1919 revolution. One such song is seen by some to have helped in creating an alliance between Christian, Muslim, and Jewish Egyptians during the revolution. Part of it goes: "If you really want to serve Egypt, mother of the world, and see it progress, do not say 'Christian' or 'Muslim' or 'Jew.' Oh Shaykh, learn that those who are united by their nations are never separated by religion." His work in musical theater is also portrayed as having been highly patriotic, if not committed. The play *The Ten Good Ones* (*al-ʿAshara al-tayyiba*, 1920), a metaphorical work about the tyranny of Mamluke rule in Egypt, has been given as an example of such a work (Murūwa 1998: 71–5). It was written by Muhammad Taymūr and set to music by Darwish.

The rise of the Commitment movement in the Arab World also coincided with the creation of the state of Israel and the consequent displacement of thousands of Palestinians. Commitment to the Palestinian cause would thus become one of the central concerns of this cultural trend. The Rahbani Brothers' *We are Returning*, written during their 1955 stay in Cairo, is seen as proof of their concern for that cause as well as of their "commitment" in general. Based on this work, the critic Mīshāl Abū Jawda called them "the fathers of the freedom fighters" (*abā' al-'amal al-fidā'ī*) (qtd. in Abū Murād 1990: 44). When Palestine Radio first began operating out of Cairo this song was apparently used as each day's opening and closing anthem. On their songs for Palestine in general, the Palestinian poet Mahmoud Darwish (Mahmūd Darwīsh) said that they did more for the Palestinian freedom song that anyone else (qtd. in Traboulsi 1998: 203).[19]

Returning also speaks to another characteristic of the postcolonial phase of the commitment movement: the prominent role played by governments in it. The regime of Abdel Nasser is the paradigm of this phenomenon in the Arab World. It was not just the revolutionary governments, however, that appreciated the potential political power of culture, as we have seen how even relatively conservative governments like that of Chamoun could not resist the temptation to support art for political ends. Such a project would come to seem even more urgent, and thus would be carried out with even more transparency, under Fouad Chehab in the wake of the 1958 civil violence in Lebanon. This overlapping of Chamoun and Abdel Nasser – otherwise adversaries – demonstrates that like many such terms and movements the meaning and goals of "commitment" were never fixed. What, exactly, the question remains, were such Lebanese projects committed to and what role would the Baalbeck Festival and the Rahbani Brothers musical theater play in them?

The Rahbani Brothers, Chamoun, Chehab, and Chiha: the cultural politics of nationalism

I begin this section not with the Rahbanis' first appearance at Baalbeck but with their debut performance in Beirut in December of 1962. The occasion was the marking of Lebanon's Independence Day. That year's event was more festive than most because it was also a celebration of the failure of a coup attempt against President Fouad Chehab by the Syrian Social Nationalist Party. As part of a program called "The Day of Allegiance" ("Yawm al-wafā'"), Fairouz and the Rahbani Brothers put on the short musical play called *The Army's Return* (*'Awdat al-'askar*) which, perhaps more than any other musical-theatrical works of theirs, is blatantly nationalistic and praising of the Lebanese army, a body which Fouad Chehab had headed before becoming president after the violence of 1958. As Mansour himself says about the performance: "It was a heart-felt Lebanese cry for the Lebanese army and the defense of the country" (qtd. in Zoghaib 1993: part five, 75).

Is their participation in this event representative of their association with what would come to be known as "Chehabism?"

The presidency of Chehab and thus Chehabism came about as part of the compromise ending the violence of 1958. Perhaps inspired by having seen the regions which had been annexed to Beirut and Mt Lebanon in 1920 revert to local leadership during the period of violence in 1958, Chehab was determined to head a more inclusive government and to create some semblance of a centralized state, the novelty of which can be seen from the following exclamation by Said Akl in his 1964 hagiographic book on Chehab: "We now have a state!" (Akl 1964: 44). One result of this combination of inclusiveness and etatism was significantly increased government spending, particularly in previously neglected regions (Harris 1997: 146) such as the south of the country and the Bekaa region, the capital of which is Baalbeck. In another break from the liberal economic philosophy of Chiha as embodied in the presidency of Chamoun, and an important product of Chehabism, was the creation of a central bank (Harris 1997: 147). Proof that his policies were having their intended effect up until 1964 – when by law he had to step down from office – can be seen in Harris' assessment that throughout at least the early years of his tenure almost all of the Islamic leadership in Lebanon was supportive of him, his main opposition coming from estranged fellow Maronites such as Chamoun and, until it was broken up after the failed coup attempt, the Syrian Socialist Nationalist Party (Harris 1997: 148).

How, if at all, is the association of the Rahbani Brothers with this regime reflected in the nature of their "Lebanese Nights" performances at Baalbeck. Such an examination might help us to pinpoint differences in the regimes themselves. Along with Chehab's centralization policies came increased government interest in culture. One example of the differences between the two regimes in this regard can be seen in the realm of radio. While both presidents understood the importance of government control of this medium,[20] radio in Lebanon prior to 1958 had had a kind of ad hoc quality to it (Abū Murād 1990: 33–4). As part of Chehab's goal of administrative reform and centralization, Radio Lebanon became much better organized: "Especially after 1959, the government found itself having to strengthen its radio programs to face the negative propaganda and to be able to guide its citizens in terms of what was good for Lebanon and its flourishing. This was the government's primary goal, leading it to consult with foreign broadcasting experts" (al-Hasan 1965: 100). And though the cornerstone for a modern radio facility was laid by Chamoun in 1958, the project gained momentum and was completed under Chehab in 1962.

This is not to say that the Chamoun regime was too hands-off to realize the importance of government intervention in culture for nationalistic ends. Its direct role in the founding of the Baalbeck Festival and then the Chehab regime's enthusiastic support of the continuation of that decision would seem to buttress this claim of shared national goals. However, were the two regimes' visions of the role of the Festival the same? For Chamoun, the Baalbeck Festival was important as an emblem of both the "two faces" of Lebanese civilization and the belief that

Lebanon was the "cradle of civilization." It should be recalled that the inclusion of folklore in the Festival was important to both of these claims. While conveying the message that Lebanon was part of the world cultural and civilizational community, the Festival's idea of folklore – as presented by the Rahbani Brothers in 1957 – was that "Lebanese" folklore meant the lore of the Christian folk of Mt Lebanon. While it may have been true that on opening night in 1957 no one knew what the Rahbanis were going to present, it is also true that they were by then a known quantity: the mix of commercial savvy, translated Western dance music, mountain-infused songs and folkloric sketches that was their musical and musical-theatrical resume made them the ideal musical-theatrical ambassadors to the Christian national elite's vision of the nation.

While it would be difficult to prove categorically that Chehab's view of the role of the Festival was wholly divergent from Chamoun's, his official statements in the Festival brochures make it clear enough that their concerns were not one. The most obvious differences in their governments seem to stem from the fact of the 1958 violence. Such divergences are reflected in Chehab's Festival brochure statements. Gone are the boasts of Lebanon's historic civilizing mission, of the peaceful coexistence of different groups in the country, and so on that had characterized Chamoun's proclamations. Gone too are official statements about the glory of Lebanon's past. In fact, his statement in the 1960 brochure contains a mixture of embarrassment over the events of 1958 and of hope for the future: "Allow me to express the ambition of this country, which contains ample hidden creative treasures and capabilities, for a tomorrow in which Lebanon is not a preoccupation of the whole world, but to a glorious tomorrow" in which Lebanon is seen by the world for its civilizing role in (Tueni 1994: xxiii). Similarly modest is the note in the 1962 program, which focuses on the importance of self-confidence and national unity, both of which would have been given prior to 1958:

> Les qualités et les ressources inépuisables qui destinent le Liban à vivre, libre et souverain, et à réaliser une mission; l'aptitude de ses fils à s'affirmer dans leurs richesses morales et humaines demeureraient vaines ou presque stériles sans ces deux piliers de base: la Foi en Soi et en l'Unité de la Nation.
>
> (qtd. in *VIIème festival international de Baalbeck* 1962: 1)

While both statements reflect much more modest national goals than existed in such proclamations made before 1958, they only hint at Chehab's ambition for the Lebanese state. The main goal of increased government centralization was, of course, national unity. Chehab envisioned creating a nation not just for the Christians of Mount Lebanon, but a Lebanon that equally included all of the regions and religions that came with the 1920 creation of Greater Lebanon (el Khazen 2000: 242). Is it possible to see this goal reflected in cultural production at this time?

The Moon's Bridge and the miracle of national unity:
the Rahbani Brothers and Said Akl

Several writers have drawn a connection between the content of the Rahbani Brothers' musical plays and the main ideological points of Chehabism. Without offering concrete examples, Ahmad Amīn suggests that reflected in their early musical-theatrical works is Chehab's goal of limiting the role of sectarianism and of promoting democracy in Lebanon (Amīn 1997: 72–3). Fawwaz Traboulsi is much more specific in making similar connections. He reads *The Moon's Bridge*, the 1962 musical play staged by the Rahbani Brothers at the Baalbeck Festival, as a virtual narrative summation of Chehabism (Traboulsi 1996: 57–60). It is not surprising then, that he would also see the play as a response to the 1958 civil violence.[21] *Bridge*, in other words, is primarily a work about reconciliation, a theme that we saw stressed in Chehab's statement in that year's Festival brochure above. The Rahbani Brothers' first few productions at Baalbeck had consisted of largely unconnected vignettes of village customs, as can be gleaned from the title of the larger show that their 1957 *Days of Harvest* was a part of: *Traditions and Customs* (*Taqālīd wa-ʿādāt*). By the time of *Bridge*, the productions had become more plot-driven. In other words, the same folkloric scenes that were staged in the first few years were now linked by a story line. And instead of one act, these "stories" were told in two: one to present the "problem" and the other to solve it. In *Bridge*, the problem is a conflict between two villages. The solution comes when the "girl" played by Fairouz, who has been magically held captive at the bridge by the enmity between the two villages, reveals – just as the two hamlets are about to square off in battle – that there is a treasure beneath the bridge. She tells them that instead of doing battle with the tools that they brought they should use them to dig for the treasure instead

> Look around...
> The treasure will present itself to you...
> The sound of the hoe is sweeter
> Than the ring of the sword...
> And peace is the treasure of treasures.
>   (Rahbani, A. and M. 2003c: 70–1)

The play ends, as do most of the Rahbani musical-theatrical productions, with everyone coming together for a celebratory line dance and song as a marker of peaceful resolution.

Traboulsi suggests intriguingly that the whole plot of the play is built on three slogans that came out of the violence of 1958. One of them is: "Returning the water to its course." He connects this motto to the play literally, since the source of the conflict between the two villages is the distribution of water. The play ends with the command "Let the water run," which he reads as a narrative expression of Chehab's plan to divert water from the Litani River to the poor and mostly

Shiite south. More metaphorically, he also sees it as an echo of Chehab's famous 1961 independence day speech that called for those who have benefited from Lebanon's flourishing to be concerned with "the different Lebanese" (*al-Lubnānī al-mukhtalif*) (Traboulsi 2006: 59), that is the poor.

The slogan to return the water to its course is also a call for reconciliation and unity, which Traboulsi reads as one of the signifieds of the play's central symbol: the bridge (Traboulsi 2006: 57–60). This message of reconciliation is expressed before the play even begins in the following lines, taken from the end of the play where they are spoken by Fairouz's character, that introduce the section of the 1962 Festival brochure that covers the play.

> Between every village and the world there is a moon's bridge
> And as long as it contains a heart feeling for another heart
> No matter what danger it is exposed to
> The moon's bridge will not be destroyed.
> ("al-Layālī al-Lubnāniyya" 1962: 182 and
> Rahbani, A. and M. 2003c: 72)

The poet Said Akl wrote the introduction to the play and thus chose these lines from the play to be representative of it. Though they and this theme of the play clearly represent post-1958 Chehabist thinking, the connection between Akl and the Rahbanis more generally, I would like to argue, contains within it evidence of the lingering influence of Chiha's thought in their work and in this play specifically.

The mentor-protégé relationship between Akl and the Rahbani Brothers has been well documented. Akl had links to Baalbeck and Chiha through his involvement in the organization called "L'association nationale pour le maintien et le développement de la culture Libanaise" which was responsible for staging a distinctly non-Lebanese play at Baalbeck in 1944 ("Mahrajānāt Baalbeck fī kitāb" 1994: 3). The year 1944 is also the year that Akl published his *Cadmus* (*Qadmūs*), a play based on the Greek myth of Cadmus in which he focuses on the fact that this mythical son of the king of Phoenicia gave Europe its alphabet and that his sister Europa gave the continent its name. At this point in his career, Akl was still writing in classical Arabic. He would eventually not only switch to the Lebanese dialect – which he would convince the Rahbani Brothers to use exclusively in their works in (Abī Samrā 1992b) – but would also experiment with writing that dialect in the Latin script. This was not in emulation of Europe, but rather in line with the general message of the early Baalbeck Festivals. It was, namely, an act of reclaiming from Europe what Lebanon had already pioneered (al-Khāzin 1970).

With Akl responsible for the introduction to *Bridge*, it should come as no surprise that Traboulsi also finds elements of the play that have to be seen as extensions of the Chiha ideology which infused Lebanon's pre-1958 governments. The other two slogans that came out of the 1958 violence and upon which

Traboulsi reads *Bridge* as being based are "What has passed has passed" (*mā madā qad madā*) and "No victor and no vanquished" (*lā ghālib wa-lā maghlūb*). For Traboulsi, these slogans are reflected in the play by the simplistic way that the conflict is solved, that is, without its roots ever being examined. The consequences of such a policy in real-life Lebanon would, he posits, be devastating, implying perhaps that the tragic fifteen-year Lebanese civil war could have been avoided by an examination of the underlying causes of the 1958 violence.

Also, the simplistic way in which the tension in the play's story is resolved can be seen as reflecting one of the central tenets of Chiha's philosophy: the Lebanese miracle. Traboulsi calls *Bridge* "the Lebanese miracle play *par excellence*" (Traboulsi 2006: 48). This can be seen from the very start of the play – with the girl's miraculous appearance on the bridge – right up to the end with her magical reappearance and discovery of the "treasure." Traboulsi rightly points out that this would be the beginning of a string of miracle-inducing roles for Fairouz. And while the trope of the miracle cannot be said to figure prominently in the rhetoric of Chehab himself, his regime is *described* in terms of the miracle repeatedly by Said Akl in a way not dissimilar to the miracles performed by the girl on the bridge in *Bridge*. It is, for example, a "miracle" that he was able to achieve as much as he did in such a short time, a "miracle" that he brought about national unity and a "miracle" that he was able to perform this "miracle" alone (Akl 1964: 30–1, 51, and 63). While it would eventually become painfully clear that no miracles had actually occurred during the reign of Chehab, the theatrical project of the Rahbanis would continue – largely through the characters portrayed by Fairouz – to echo Akl's insistence that they had. The theater of the Rahbani Brothers, in other words, would continue to reflect the main goals of Chehabism all the while echoing the ideology of Chehab's predecessor and nemesis Chamoun. Like Akl, the Rahbanis seemed to be straddling both eras without too much of a stretch.

The Holiday of Glory and *The Night and the Lantern*: inclusivity through exclusivity, or the "Other" in the early theater of the Rahbani Brothers

Said Akl wrote the introduction to another early Rahbani Brothers musical play: *The Holiday of Glory* (1960). Both this play and their 1963 *The Night and the Lantern* can be read as evidence of active participation in the post–1958 nation- and state-building project of Fouad Chehab's government. Again, it is the intersection of certain aspects of these works with those of Said Akl that demonstrates that these works retain some pre-1958 Chamounist ideals. Both of these works are very centrally about unification. In both cases, this desired-for-state is achieved via the exclusion of an "Other."

For Akl, *Holiday* represents nothing less than Lebanon itself (al-Akl 1960: 4). Perhaps he was thinking of the work's end, when an old man gives the female protagonist of the play, now a newly wed bride, some advice, in a now famous speech. After telling her to leave her childhood and her family behind, to stick with her husband through sickness and health, through wealth and poverty, he advises her to raise her children with love and to "Tell them that after God, they should worship Lebanon" (Rahbani, A. and M. 1960: 55–6). Underlining the importance of these lines is the fact that it is one of just two songs from the play to have its lyrics included in that year's Festival program ("Mawsim al-'izz: awparīt sha'biyya" 1960). The play ends just after these words of advice with the full cast singing:

Lebanon the strong	Lebanon the rich
Happiness and harvest	In the skies of Lebanon
The moon rose	The moon stayed up late
The moon loved	In the skies of Lebanon....
Lebanon the strong	
Lebanon the rich	
Lebanon the sweet	
Lebanon.	

("Mawsim al-'izz: awparīt sha'biyya" 1960: 56)

This union, which will result in Lebanon-worshipping offspring, could not have come about, however, without the intervention of an "Other."

The Lebanon at the end of *Holiday* is presented not just as being strong, rich, and sweet, but, as in *Bridge*, as being unified. Once again we are presented with the story of two villages being united by peace and love. The "bridge" between the two hamlets in this play is marriage. The work opens with a holiday that consists of various types of competition between the two towns: dance, feats of strength, and poetry, all of which, in addition to the marital and unification celebrations which end the play, provide ample opportunity for the display of Lebanese folklore. It is at the opening-scene holiday that Najlā and Shāhīn, two youths from neighboring and competing villages, fall in love. In the meantime Murahhij al-Qalā'ī, a hunter from the area belonging to neither village, has fallen in love with Najlā. Naljā, the female protagonist, is not played by Fairouz, as this is one of the few Rahbani Brothers' productions at Baalbeck that did not feature Fairouz, due to pregnancy. The female protagonist of this work was played by Sabah (Sabāh, nee Jānīt Fīghālī). One day Shāhīn surprises Najlā with a declaration of his love. She responds:

Murahhij you're wrong
Our heart is not your heart
Our road is not your road.
("Mawsim al-'izz: awparīt
sha'biyya" 1960: 23)

59

The synopsis of the play in the 1960 Festival program elaborates a bit on who exactly Murahhij is

> Murahhij al-Qalā'ī watches everyone. He is a hunter known to the people of this region. He has passed a thousand times in front of their doors, but he has never entered, just as no one has ever invited him to enter, and he has remained a stranger to their hearts.
>
> ("Mawsim al-'izz: awparīt sha'biyya" 1960: 88)

The program also tells us that after failing to move Najlā by his declaration of love, "he embraced his rifle and went off 'by himself' " (" 'alā ghurbat nafsihi") ("Mawsim al-'izz: awparīt sha'biyya" 1960: 88), literally to "his own alienation" or "stranger-ness."

Murahhij, quite simply, plays the role of "the Other," without whom unity cannot be achieved. The marriage ceremony includes the lifting of a heavy object – al-qayma – by a member of the groom's family, a custom still practiced according to Anis Frayha in his 1957 work on the Lebanese mountain village (Frayha 1957: 172–3). In fact, though the Rahbani Brothers have said that the story of Holiday was related to them by their grandmother (Munassā 1994: 17), there is a strikingly similar story in Frayha's The Lebanese Village. In it, Frayha tells of a wedding between two villages that almost did not happen when the bride's family surprised the groom's side by asking them to lift a qayma. No one could do it and the wedding was about to be called off when at the last moment the groom's party found a driver, whom they claimed was with them, who could lift the heavy object (Frayha 1957: 173). In the Rahbani play, two members of Najlā's village – Sab' and Makhūl, comic characters that appear repeatedly in these works played by Philemon Wehbe and Mansour Rahbani respectively – are opposed to Najlā's marrying outside the village and plot to bring to the wedding a qayma that no one could possibly lift. And this is in fact what happens on the first attempt, with the result that the groom's family asks for a night's respite before having their strong man attempt to lift the object again. The next day the designated strong man from the groom's party fails once again to lift the object. Just when it looks like there will be no wedding, Murahhij asks to represent the groom's party and saves the day by lifting the qayma, after which he disappears – presumably to "ghurbat nafsihi" again – just as the two villages burst into celebration. Everyone, except the now absent Murahhij, sings:

> Love love your love
> Welcome in your visit
> Our village has become your village
> Love love love love.
> ("Mawsim al-'izz: awparīt
> sha'biyya" 1960: 55)

The message could not be clearer: love – even the love of a stranger – unifies.

60

In his work on the interplay between globalization and locality, Appadurai notes the need for otherness in the production of what he calls "neighborhoods." Such communities are only formed in historical context, in contrast, that is, "to something else." About this something else he writes:

> In the practical consciousness of many human communities, this something else is often conceptualized ecologically as forest or wasteland, ocean or desert, swamp or river. Such ecological signs often mark boundaries that simultaneously signal the beginnings of nonhuman forces and categories or recognizably human but barbarian or demonic forces.
>
> (Appadurai 1996: 182–3)

This is certainly a common characteristic of the "something else" in the musical theater of the Rahbani Brothers, and can be observed in the character of Murahhij. He not only occupies that wild space between villages, but is also appellatively represented *as* that wild space. After performing his heroic act we are told that Murahhij "disappears into the wasteland" ("Mawsim al-'izz: awparīt sha'biyya" 1960: 50). The word given for this for this space is "qalā'ī," none other than Murahhij's surname.

A character occupying similarly wild space is Hawlū of the 1963 musical-theatrical production *The Night and the Lantern*. The play, staged at the Casino du Liban, a venue well known for its French-style cabaret acts, is about a village lamp-maker Mantūra (played by Fairouz) who is assembling a gigantic lantern to illuminate the extra-village wild space where Hawlū lives and profits from the darkness. When Hawlū gets wind of the project he does all he can to sabotage it. In the meantime, he has become enchanted by the singing of Mantūra, and when she is implicated as an accomplice in the theft of the village's money which she had been safeguarding, Hawlū not only returns it, but he and his sidekick proceed to set up the huge lantern in a high rocky spot that no one else could reach, thus jeopardizing their own livelihood. As with *Holiday*, the play ends with the liminal figure disappearing into the wilderness while the reunited village celebrates in song and dance. In addition to being another case of "Other"-dependent unity in the Rahbani musical-theatrical oeuvre, this play confirms another observation of Appadurai about community. Not only is unity based on the presence of wilderness, but also on some act carried out on that space or on those who reside in it:

> All locality building has a moment of colonization, a moment both historical and chronotypic, when there is a formal recognition that the production of a neighborhood requires deliberate, risky, even violent action in respect to the soil, forests, animals and other human beings.
>
> (Appadurai 1996: 183)

Community in *Night* is achieved when the dark space that is perceived to be jeopardizing it is daringly illuminated and thus neutralized, regardless of the impact on those of that habitat.

The idea of "the Other" as a unifying force is another shared characteristic of the literary works of Said Akl and the Rahbani Brothers at this time, for writings of the former – such as the play *Qadmūs* – demonstrate a belief that the essence of Lebanon cannot be revealed without the presence of an Other, whether this Other is outside of Lebanon or representative of internal "other Lebanons" (al-'Īd 1978: 169).[22] The need of the Other for national unity is not, of course, peculiar to Lebanon. Chatterjee, for example, posits that the cultural independence movement that preceded the political one in India was predicated on differences between the Indian "self" and the British "Other" (Chatterjee 1993). As Thongchai reminds us in his study of Thai nationalism and geography, however, the distinction between self and Other is not always clear (Thongchai 1994). Where, in other words, does one draw the various borders? From the story of the nineteenth-century Calcuttan actress Binodini, Chatterjee concludes that – as we see in *Holiday* and *Night* – some of the most important boundaries have to be drawn "internally" (Chatterjee 1993: 154–5). Despite unusual success on the stage, Binodini failed to establish a satisfactory life outside of theater notwithstanding a relationship with a man from one of the most respected families of the city. Chatterjee surmises that this is because in nation building, the Other comes from *within* as well as from without, and that

> the story of nationalist emancipation is necessarily a story of betrayal. Because it could confer freedom only by imposing at the same time a whole new set of controls, it could define a cultural identity for the nation only by excluding many from its fold; and it could grant the dignity of citizenship to some only because the others always needed to be represented and could not be allowed to speak for themselves. Binodini reminds us once more that the relations between the people and the nation, the nation and the state, relations which nationalism claims to have resolved once and for all, are relations which continue to be contested and are therefore open to negotiations all over again.
>
> (Chatterjee 1993: 154)

The lessons that Chatterjee draws from Indian nationalism are relevant to mid–twentieth-century Lebanon as well. *Holiday* and *Lantern* remind us not only that unity is predicated on the presence of difference, whether it be perceived as internal or external, but that the Rahbani Brothers bought into the idea of the importance of exclusion.

Holiday also demonstrates a different but not wholly unrelated kind of exclusivity. That play, staged at the 1960 Baalbeck Festival, marks the beginning of a kind of folkloric monopoly for the Rahbani Brothers at the Festival. Until this point I have been presenting the story of the Rahbani Brothers' participation at the Baalbeck Festival as if they alone had been chosen to present Lebanese folklore at that site. In actuality, however, the first two incarnations of the Nights were group projects (Bāshā 1995: 148). Mansour himself remembers that the first-half of the 1959 version of The Lebanese Nights at the Festival was put on by Muhammad Muhsin, Zaki Nasif, and Tawfiq al-Basha (Zoghaib 1993: part five, 72). What he does not mention is that Fairouz sang both in the first- and second-half of the show ("Mahrajān al-fann al-shaʿbī al-Lubnānī" 1959: n.p.), meaning that the Rahbani Brothers' monopoly of her, and in turn the folkloric portion of the Festival, was not yet complete. In fact, though Fairouz is given a full-page photograph in that year's brochure, Mansour warrants just a quarter-page image like the other photographed participants. Asi, often considered the more important of the two partners artistically (e.g. "Ilā Asi," 1995), is not photographed in the brochure at all ("Mahrajān al-fann al-shaʿbī al-Lubnānī" 1959).

I would like to suggest that at least a partial answer to the question of how the Rahbani Brothers would subsequently come to dominate the Lebanese Nights can be found in a comparison of the content of the folkloric scenes which were staged before their takeover was accomplished.[23] As we learn from the 1959 Festival brochure, while for the non–Rahbani Brothers half of the evening contained village weddings and celebrations, it also included a four-part "Bedouin-tent evening scene." In light of Baalbeck's location and the fact that it was historically an important destination for commercial caravans (Nasr Allāh, H. 1984), the inclusion of such vignettes into the Festival is hardly surprising. What is surprising is the fact that 1959 would not only mark the last time that the Rahbani Brothers would share the veritable spotlight at Baalbeck, but that it would also be the last time that such non-mountain village folklore would be presented at the Lebanese Nights portion of Baalbeck Festival in its pre–civil war manifestation. The introduction by Said Akl to the 1960 play Holiday with which we began this section considers the works of the Rahbani Brothers to be musical-theatrical representations of Lebanon. If we look at Akl's words closely, we see that it is a very specific Lebanon to which he is referring:

> The very Lebanese land.... You find all of it in their works in a single dance scene, in the waving of a scarf or in a radiant verse of poetry. Simplicity in their work is a building, and time in it has colors, and the colors are from here, from this mountain [italics mine].
>
> (Akl 1960: 4)

Below I will be concerned to explore in more detail just which Lebanon it was that they were representing through their folkloric works. In addition to constructing an image of this Lebanon based on a continued reading of the works themselves, I will be equally interested in looking at the consequences of this kind of representation. One of the things that I mean by this, that is, the connection between their eventual move away both from folklore and the Baalbeck Festival itself – I take up presently.

"I am the word, you are the song," or the appropriation of the popular, part two: from folkloric to operatic, from the Baalbeck Festival to Beirut

Built into the story line of the Rahbani Brothers' 1966 musical play *The Days of Fakhr al-Din* is their conception of the ideal role of folklore in the nation-building project. 'Atr al-Layl, played by Fairouz, catches the attention of a returning-from-exile Fakhr al-Din by singing a few songs for him. When asked where she learned these songs, she says that they "just appeared before me," (Rahbani, A. and M. 1966: 4) as if they had spontaneously bubbled up from some authorless collective memory. The prince is so impressed with her that he commissions her to roam the country to unite its people through song. When she does not understand what he means he clarifies things for her: "I am the sword, you are the song" (Rahbani, A. and M. 1966: 6). Later in the play an old storekeeper says that he wants to teach her an ancient song. What is it, she asks? I don't remember, he tells her, but I do remember the opening line, which I will teach you, and then your role is to go around and collect the rest. How am I going to collect it? He tells her:

> Listen. In the square of every village there is a shop, and in each shop there is an old man.... You have to ask each one to teach you one of the song's words, and thus you'll learn it from the tongues of the old-timers.
> (Rahbani, A. and M. 1966: 15–16)

Folklore in this play, then, is presented as a spontaneous and authorless material to be gathered from those who remember it, and then employed in the service of the nation. Whereas in the play itself, Fakhr al-Din tells 'Atr al-Layl that by her song she will make the people love their country (Rahbani, A. and M. 1966: 7), the summary of the play in that year's Festival program makes it seem as if her song will literally create Lebanon: "Fakhr al-Din requests that 'Atr al-Layl sings Lebanon" ("al-Fann al-sha'bī al-Lubnānī" 1966: 109). Fakhr al-Din himself tells a confused 'Atr al-Layl: "It [i.e. Lebanon] will become the song" (Rahbani, A. and M. 1966: 7).

This is precisely what the Rahbani Brothers seem to do early in their musical-theatrical career at Baalbeck. It has been said of their musical theater that the stage is turned into an anthropological and folkloric museum of Lebanese village life (Abī Samrā 1999: 7). Mansour has said that in their early works in general they were careful to be true to the folklore of Lebanon of which, he adds, they made a careful study (Aliksān, J. 1987: 59). This seems to be particularly true of *Holiday*, which Mansour Rahbani called their richest work in terms of folklore (Yamīn 1985: 11). Abū Murād implicitly seconds this opinion. His section on folklore in *The Rahbani Brothers: Life and Theater* (*al-Akhawān Rahbani: hayāt wa-masrah*, 1990) is dominated by examples from the work in question (Abū Murād 1990: 97–104). Further proof of the folkloric nature of the work can be seen in the fact that its story line is said to have been told to the Rahbani Brothers by their illiterate grandmother (Munassā 1994: 17), an oft-mentioned source of their folkloric information, for it is the poor, uneducated, and childlike who are the most important sources of folkloric material. The text of the play offers further proof of its folklore-heavy nature. Compared to the other plays, *Holiday*'s text contains the largest number of songs which have the words "old poem" written next to them, the largest number of songs that are, in other words, "authorless," one of the conventional requirements for a song or a story to be considered folklore (Murūwa 1998: 127).

Fakhr al-Din exemplifies the importance of the exhibition of folklore in the early theater of the Rahbani Brothers. In another way, the play illustrates that perhaps an inevitable result of embarking on such a project of collection and dissemination is to change it. "Lebanon's *dabka*" (Dabkat Lubnān), the title of one of the songs that 'Atr al-Layl initially sings for Fakhr al-Din, demonstrates this fact perfectly. The *dabka* is the generic name for a kind of line dance that comes in many variant forms in the Levant and, under different names, in Turkey and Eastern Europe. Before the Rahbani Brothers came along, however, there was no such thing as "Lebanon's Dabka." Rather, each region would practice several different variations of this dance, depending on the occasion (Traboulsi 1996: 45). This does not mean that one region or town could and would not learn another's dances, but simply that the idea of one standard Lebanese Dabka was unknown. But this is exactly what the Rahbani Brothers, in collaboration with the Russian-trained Jarrārs and other foreign-trained dancers and choreographers, would eventually create after representing different Lebanese versions of the dance in their first few works (Abū Murād 1990: 100–1). The results of this standardization can be seen in the complaints in the English press about the dances performed as part of the Rahbani Brothers' inaugural appearance in that country in 1962. The dances were, some averred, highly reminiscent of the Balkan dances that they had witnessed before (Traboulsi 1996: 45). While the Dabka that the Rahbani Brothers participated in developing was based on its north-Lebanese mountain versions, the result was something new. By trying to make the Dabka more "Lebanese," the Rahbani Brothers had, in fact, made it less so.

For a similar phenomenon in Egypt consider the example of Farida Fahmi. In 1957 Farida Fahmi, daughter of the well-known Egyptian engineering professor Hasan Fahmi, traveled to the USSR with her dance partner Mahmoud Reda (Mahmūd Ridā) to perform in a folklore festival there. This event inspired them to form a dance troupe that would perform in Egypt for the first time in 1959. The government adopted their troupe – "The Reda Troupe" – in 1961. Franken describes their mix of authentic and devised material in a way highly reminiscent of descriptions of the Rahbani Brothers and the dance troupes that worked with them:

> The movement was not taken directly from any existing folk dance, but the invented movements appropriately presented an image familiar from everyone's childhood. Mahmoud Reda in fact created a novel performance genre in Egypt; he invented theatrical dance that drew on the participatory

folk dances of the streets and homes of the Egyptian people, and gave it a new polish and respectability that drew also on Western, audience-oriented dance forms. These sorts of details, including actual dance "steps," familiar social scenes, and images from Egyptian life, resonated with audiences of all social backgrounds. Peasants identified with the dancers performing "their" stick dances, urban audiences recognized characters from their childhoods, and all audiences regardless of education, income, social class, or regional origin, could see aspects of their lives, their culture and *the concept of Egyptian life itself* [italics mine] celebrated, even honored on the stage.

(Franken 1998: 275)

This standardization of the Dabka is similar to what the Rahbani Brothers did to all kinds of folkloric material (Traboulsi 2000: 3). That is, what started out as "collecting and choosing" ("Fairouz tazhar" 1967: 12) turned very quickly into authoring, polishing, and developing. This can be detected in the earliest stages of their careers (Abū Murād 1990: 98; Aliksān, J. 1987: 59–61; and Yamīn 1985: 11), including such seemingly purely folkloric works as *Holiday*. According to Jān Aliksān:

In the hands of the Rahbanis folklore became something else, for they went beyond Lebanese folklore and created a more developed folklore than what was already present... they washed it, they developed it, they grew it, and made it purely Rahbani-esque. They took the givens of folklore from its primary sources: its tones, its rhythms, and resuscitated it. Or we can say that they realized the deep folkloric conscience, that they grasped the popular, group and historical conscience and sent it into a new space, a space open to all creative possibilities. Folklore with the Rahbanis and with Asi specifically did not remain a fixed and parroting material, but became a live being, that grew, developed, branched out, and rose. Baalbeck in 1957 was the illuminated space where the presentation of folklore went beyond the *dabka* and the rhythms of the *mījānā* and the *'atāba*... to a new folklore, or a new social consciousness, not stuck to the available popular material. It was a personal folklore that was generalized to become a live part of the inherited folklore.

(Aliksān, J. 1987: 50–1)

Mahmūd Nāsir goes even farther when he writes:

As far as the popular folkloric or dance songs go, people thought that these existed in their heritage when in fact they were not as they were [now] being presented. The Rahbanis re-wrote, arranged and produced them until they were no longer what they had been at all. The only thing that remained of them were their name.

(Nāsir 1986: part four, 46)

66

"Folklore," thanks in part to the Rahbani Brothers, came to mean the song and dance that was performed at festivals (Racy 2001: 339). In addition, a key element of the appropriation of the popular is that its cleaning and preservation are best left, as Frayha put it, in the hands of "the upper class." The Rahbanis' attitude towards the *dabka* echoes this sentiment. While they were clearly impressed with the spontaneity of these dances among "the peasants," they were also keenly aware of the need for polish. On the subject of training Asi once said, "Ballet is not simply a matter of steps… and the problem with the peasant is that he does not know how to practice" (qtd. in Sh. 1966: 15).

While Aliksān and Nāsir present such developments as an integral part of the genius of the Rahbani Brothers, it is also possible that "going beyond" folklore is an inevitability of staging such material for an audience, of removing it from its original context. Seen in this light, the eventual move away from folklore in the Rahbani Brothers' musical theater becomes easier to understand. It may also help to explain the eventual breakup of the tautological chain with which we began. While both the Rahbani Brothers and the Baalbeck Festival would continue to equal a certain Lebanon, the Festival would at least partially lose its automatic association with the Rahbani Brothers. This occurred at least in part, I will argue, because their works became less and less appropriate for The Lebanese Nights portion of the Festival. Not that they became less "Lebanese," but rather less folkloric. With their signifying power established through their earlier presentation of folkloric acts at the symbolically charged site of Baalbeck, however, they could then go on representing a certain Lebanon at a variety of venues.

As early as 1961 the quickly established symbiotic relationship between the Rahbani Brothers and the Baalbeck Festival would begin to show signs of stress. Though the Rahbani Brothers would appear many more times at the Baalbeck Festival, they would begin to take their progressively more extravagant and at the same time less folkloric acts elsewhere. Just one year after the great success of the 1960 *Holiday*, the Rahbani Brothers found that the Baalbeck Festival committee had reservations about their musical play *The Woman from Baalbeck* – which revolves around the interaction between a girl (played by Fairouz) from the town of Baalbeck and its gods – because it was more mythological than folkloric (Zoghaib 1993: part five, 74). The next year, however, they were back to their folkloric ways with *The Moon's Bridge*. The following year, they put on the similarly folkloric *The Night and the Lantern* in Beirut at the Casino Liban. The year after that they would skip the Baalbeck Festival as well, having been asked by the Foreign Ministry to stage something at that year's Cedars Festival which was to coincide with a convention of Lebanese living abroad ("Fairouz bi-alhān Najīb Hankash" 1964: 6). It was here that they put on the highly folkloric *The Ring Seller*, about which I will have more to say later. For now I will mention that the play was quite successful in terms of attendance (Zoghaib 1993: part five, 75) and has been called "the crown" of this early period in their musical-theatrical careers (Shāwūl 1988: 258). It has been estimated that over 72,000 spectators attended the play during its three-night run (Abī Samrā 1992a: 10).

Just as the Rahbani Brothers were reaching their folkloric peak, there were signs that the trend, which they helped to popularize, was reversing itself. In an article on the very same page of the al-Nahār newspaper issue announcing their plans to stage The Ring Seller at the Cedars Festival, there is an adjacent piece about their replacements at the Baalbeck Festival that summer. The article says that those involved in the project (including Sabah, Wadi Al-Safi (Wadī' al-Sāfī), Tawfiq al-Basha, and Zaki Nasif) preferred that the word "folklore" not be used in association with their production. They said that they "do not want their work to be thus labeled.... Because [']folklore['] here has begun to lose its meaning. Its use has spread until it has become commercialized. It has become difficult to distinguish between a folkloric and a nonfolkloric work" ("Baalbeck bi-khayr" 1964: 6). Whether or not they are referring directly to the profusion of folkloric works by the Rahbani Brothers up to that point is unclear. What is certain is that as early as 1964 this genre that the Rahbani Brothers are partially credited with having created had become so diffuse as to result in a certain amount of backlash. Later that year an article was published in the same paper promising to clear up the controversy over what is and what is not "the new bogeyman:" folklore ("Hādhā huwa al-fūlklūr" 1964: 15).

After this "crowning" folkloric moment of 1964 that was The Ring Seller, the Rahbani Brothers' plays, whether at Baalbeck or elsewhere, would become less folkloric. A 1973 article previewing the first of two musical-theatrical works they would put on at the Piccadilly theater in Beirut that year notes that the following kinds of songs would be performed: long, folkloric, rhythmic, dancing, modern, group songs, and Andalusian Muwashshahāt.[24] By the early1970s, then, folklore was just one part of a diverse repertoire, and the events of their plays had begun to move from village to urban or nonspecific setting. In fact, with Hāla and the King (Hāla wa-al-malik) in 1967, the musical theater of the Rahbanis had shifted, for the most part, to the city. By 1967 it had also grown more extravagant. A 1966 newspaper article informs us that Fakhr al-Dīn – called a "huge musical theatrical extravaganza that would occupy all of the Jupiter theater, i.e. all 30,000 of its square feet" – would involve more than 200 performers including a 30-piece orchestra and 30 dancers, and that the costumes alone would cost 50,000 Lebanese pounds ("10 Layālin fī Baalbeck" 1966: 8–10).[25] Compare this to Holiday – their most "folkloric work" – which included just four musical instruments (Munassā 1994: 17). It is perhaps ironic that Fakhr al-Dīn, the very work that so eloquently expresses their folkloric ideals would be their least folkloric work to date. Toward the end of that play Fairouz sings the song that she was supposed to learn from the various old shopkeepers. That song – "My Father Left with that Army" (Bayyī rāh ma' hāy al-'askar) – is not, of course, a song without provenance, but rather one that was written, from beginning to end, by the Rahbani Brothers. This is not to say that folklore did not remain a popular genre. While the Rahbanis were moving away from folklore by this time, the rest of the country was not necessarily following suit. In the middle of the summer of 1972, one newspaper complained that the summer was only half over and already fifty local folkloric festivals had been staged, many of them putting on renditions of the Rahbanis' musical plays (Abī Samrā 1992a: 10).

As the works of the Rahbani Brothers were maturing in a theatrical and performative sense (Murūwa 1998: 151–66 and Shāwūl 1988: 258), just as they were becoming more polished and more grand, they were also getting away from the folklore that constituted their and the Festival committee's original goals for The Lebanese Nights. Not only was this no coincidence, it may have been virtually inevitable. Kirshenblatt-Gimblett, here describing the results of the staging of folklore in general, sounds uncannily as if she is talking specifically about the transformation of the Rahbani Brothers' performances outlined above:

> Forms that are perfectly satisfying in their indigenous settings – chants, drumming, a cappella ballads, repetitive dance steps – challenge audiences who are exposed to them on stages where they are used to seeing opera and ballet. Professional folkloric companies adapt such forms to European production values. To hold the interest of new audiences, folkloric troupes design a varied and eclectic program of short selections. They also depend on musical accompaniment (such as piano or orchestra), European harmony, concertized arrangements and vocal styles on the model of European opera, and movement styles on the order of ballet to reduce the strangeness and potential boredom of a cappella song, unison music, and repetitive (and not apparently virtuosic) dance for unfamiliar audiences.
>
> (Kirshenblatt-Gimblett 1991: 420–1)

She goes on to say more about dance specifically, also almost as if she were describing the dance segments of the Rahbani Brothers musical plays:

> A tightly coordinated ensemble of trained professionals, often more or less the same age and physical type, wear stylized, often uniform, costumes, while executing highly choreographed routines with great precision. A frontal orientation accommodates the proscenium stage to which are added theatrical effects (sound, lighting, sets). There is a tendency toward the virtuosic, athletic, and spectacular.
>
> (Kirshenblatt-Gimblett 1991: 420–1)

As if to corroborate just such a description, Abī Samrā remarks on the high number of physical-education specialists participating in the dance numbers of the Rahbani Brothers musicals (Abī Samrā 1999: 8). Sherifa Zuhur's observations about the effect of public performance on Middle Eastern dance forms also meshes with the above: "Kicking and leg extensions are not common, except in contemporary staged forms of (Lebanese, Syrian, Palestinian, Jordanian) *dabka* thanks in part to the influence of Eastern European choreographers" (Zuhur 2001b: 8).

This transformation leaves the official history of the Festival in a quandary as to how to fit these latter, less folkloric works, under the folkloric rubric of "The Lebanese Nights." The result is a fine example of semantic acrobatics

> In reality, the word "folklore" does not always hit the mark, for many times, and in the works of the Rahbani Brothers specifically, the plays, songs and tunes would spill over the container of the folklore genre to become more comprehensive, while at the same time remaining attached to the people and the concept of popular art.
>
> (Munassā 1994: 14)

What we have seen above is that as soon as one attempts to perform this ever-elusive ideal called folklore, one moves instantly to the realm of the folkloric, and then ultimately to what resembles ballet and opera. One moves almost immediately from gathering and choosing, to authoring, cleaning, and developing. What we have seen, in a sense, is the built-in impossibility of presenting folklore. One can speculate that it is perhaps this move away from even the folkloric that ultimately made the Rahbani Brothers and the Lebanese Nights of the Baalbeck Festival a less than perfect fit. At the same time, this move away from folklore and the folkloric that began with their earlier works did not diminish the power of their representations of a very specific Lebanon. In fact, it may have strengthened it.

Representation and *The Ring Seller*: "The Word Became a Man" or "The Lie" versus "The Story"

Benedict Anderson has suggested that identity is a function of duality. Above I examined one of identity's basic equations: for "a" to exist there has to be a "b." There is another identity formulation that is an equally powerful component of the Rahbani Brothers' musical theater. It states that "a" comes into existence only when it meets "equals a," when it encounters, in other words, a *representation* of itself (Anderson 1998: 130). This formula can be read as a refutation of Wale Soyinka's proclamation that "the tiger has no need of tigritude" (Anderson 1998: 130). Do the Lebanese need "Lebanese-ness"? Whether yes or no, this is precisely what the musical theater of the Rahbani Brothers offers. And the self-conscious way in which it is presented is reminiscent of Timothy Mitchell's characterization of "representation." For him, representation does not simply mean the manufacture of images, but rather that

> In sphere after sphere of social life, the world is rendered up in terms of the dualism of image and reality. This corresponds, in turn, to a series of other simplifications, each of which stages the complexities and antagonisms of social experience in terms of a simple binarism: life and its meaning, things and their exchange value, activity and structure, execution and plan, content and form, object- and subject-world. In each case an

immediacy of the really real is promised by what appears in contrast to be the mere abstractions of structure, subjectivity, text, plan or idea.

(Mitchell 1999: 22)

Mitchell demonstrated in detail the centrality of this type of representation in the nineteenth-century colonization of Egypt in his *Colonising Egypt* (Mitchell 1988). Can the works of the Rahbani Brothers be treated as forms of representation in this sense? Do they, in other words, create a duality between them and what they claim to be representing? Do they suggest a Lebanese-ness to their viewers by acting not like a regular mirror but like one of those fun-house reflections that distorts one's image but at the same time, through the difference between the image the viewer sees in the mirror and the image he has of him or herself, confirms the viewer's identity?

Just as much as the musical-theatrical project of the Rahbani Brothers is about "a" meeting "b," it is perhaps even more centrally about "a" meeting "equal a," about the creation of a Lebanese identity by year after year and summer after summer reminding some and informing others of what it means to be "Lebanese." These works also – quite self-consciously at times – emphasize the gap between what they are portraying and what is real, a prerequisite for modern representation as characterized by Mitchell. The poet and essayist Unsī al-Ḥājj wrote, as early as 1965, for example:

> Of course life is not as tender or fine or sweet as it is in the songs and tunes of the Rahbanis. This contradiction does not at all weaken these songs, rather it is what gives them their unique scope, the scope of imagining and dreaming... which allows us... to compare it to what is in us and what we dream we will become.
>
> (al-Ḥājj, U. 1987: vol. one, 101)

This is not done solely by their move toward spectacle. Sometimes it is stated quite directly in the individual works themselves. The 1964 musical production *The Ring Seller* opens with a "voice" (Fairouz's) informing the audience that they are "going to tell the story of a village. Neither is the story true, nor does the village exist. But at night a bored person scribbled on paper and the story came to life and built the village" (Rahbani, A. and M. 2003a: 17). Such admission of the constructed nature of a representation is a key element of the paradoxical power of the phenomenon for Mitchell. Representations always have built-in signification of the fact that they are not "real."

At the same time, they promise to be standing in for something that *is* real, something that is separated from the performance of it only by time and space. This is what Mitchell calls the "double claim" of representation (Mitchell 1999: 23). In this sense, the Rahbani Brothers' performances of mountain/village life can be seen as saying: "just a few miles from here exists the original of the copy of the village we are presenting you." *The Ring Seller* not only exhibits this paradox, it also displays an awareness of its power. The play is about the peace of a mountain village being disrupted by the threat of a dangerous outsider named Rājih. It begins with the village headman returning from a hair-raising encounter with Rājih on the outskirts of the village. "What did he say to you?" the headman is asked. He responds that the villain said to him: "I have killed seven and you are going to be the eighth." After telling of his daring escape, a few of the listeners are a bit skeptical as to why no one save the headman has ever actually seen this Rājih. He then calls for his niece Rīmā (played by Fairouz) to confirm his heroics for any doubters. When the two of them are left alone she asks him how much longer she is going to have to vouch for him and why he does not just do battle with Rājih? He responds:

> "Don't be simple-minded, there is no Rājih. Your uncle is the one who
>   invented him."
> "You mean he's not around?"
> "Nor does he exist."
> "Uncle, why did you invent him? You've worried everybody and you've
>   worried me."
> "The villagers want a story. I created a story so that they'd say that I
>   protect them from an unknown threat."
> "So you lied to them?"
> "That, Rīmā, is not a lie. It's on the verge of lying. It's a story. A lie is
>   difficult, but a story is poetic ...."
>   (Rahbani, A. and M. 2003a: 26–7)

This tension is resolved when Rājih – to the great surprise and initial consternation of the village headman – turns out not only to "exist" but also to be "around." Rīmā later says to him:

> "Rājih has come."
> "But I'm the author of Rājih."
> "Believe me uncle, he's here and he's asking after you. Plus, he showed
>   me his identification card."
> "Did you read his name?"
> "His name is Rājih" ....
>   (Rahbani, A. and M. 2003a: 64)

The headman goes on to say: "I must be dreaming. How else could one throw out a word, thus planting a lie, and have the lie grow until the word turns into a man?" (Rahbani, A. and M. 2003a: 64). The message can be read as being: even when one admits and is aware that one is representing something that has no "real" counterpart, the very act of narrating creates the possibility of that counterpart. If Rājih turns out to be "real" though different from his narrative self, then the very imaginary village that we begin with must also have a counterpart. In the final analysis too, the real Rājih is not as different from the narrative Rājih as he first appears. Both, in fact, are outsiders that have an ultimately unifying effect on the village.

In addition to introducing the Lebanese viewers to their Lebanese-ness ("a" equals "equals a") and simultaneously recognizing the powers of representation, this play is another instance of the necessity of the Other in identity formation ("a" equals "not b"). As in *Holiday*, the Other is first the obstructer of unity and then its agent: Murahhij's love for Najlā was a potential obstacle to the wedding that would join two villages. In the end, that love proved to be unity's ultimate catalyst. In *The Ring Seller*, the "engagement holiday" was almost shelved because the local ring shop had been closed out of fear of the narrative Rājih. When the "real" Rājih appears, it turns out that he is not only a simple merchant, but a merchant of the very objects needed to allow the unifying marriages take place: wedding bands. At the end of the play he gives the rings away as a gesture to ensure the success of a larger unification project: himself and this village through the marriage of his son and Rīmā. The play ends with the usual resolution-signifying song and dance.

In both plays, this Other who induces unity is produced by narrative. In the case of *The Ring Seller*, the Other is produced by narrative twice: once by the Rahbani Brothers and once by the village headman. This demonstrates an awareness that the power of representation lies not just in its ability to reflect, but also to create. Appadurai's observations on the role of ethnography in the production of the local may be relevant here. Traditional village ethnography not only records the production of the local, but actively participates in its production as well. For Appadurai, this is not an issue of further proving ethnography to be the hand-maiden of colonialism, but rather it is

> a point about knowledge and representation…. The ethnographic
> project is in a peculiar way isomorphic with the very knowledge it seeks
> to discover and document, as both the ethnographic project and the
> social projects it seeks to describe have the production of locality as their
> governing telos.
>
> (Appadurai 1996: 181)

Appadurai's comment is apposite here not just because both ethnography and theater share narrative and representational properties, but because the early musical theater of the Rahbani Brothers can itself be seen as a kind of ethnographic project (Abī Samrā 1999: 7).

As the perception of the modern world was being divided into these representational binaries, other changes were occurring to make such representations particularly potent at this time in Lebanon and elsewhere. Here I refer to the powerful combination of mass media and migration mentioned above. *The Ring Seller* was performed at Lebanon's Cedars Festival, one of the Rahbani Brothers' first non-Baalbeck performances since debuting there in 1957. Their presence at this event was to coincide with a convention of Lebanese living abroad. "Coincide" yes, coincidence, no: the Rahbanis' appearance there was requested by the Ministry of Foreign Affairs ("Fairouz bi-alhān Najīb Hankash" 1964: 6). In an age of increased migration, it seems that the ministry realized that the presence of so many members of the Lebanese Diaspora in Lebanon at the same time was an event to be planned for with care. The Diasporic audience would come to be central to the fame of Fairouz and the Rahbani Brothers. For example, after her 1986 concert at the Royal Albert Hall in London, the Lebanese Ambassador to Great Britain said, "The main idea behind Fairouz's concert in London is to strengthen the relations between the Lebanese living at home and those living abroad" (Mahfūz, H. 1986: 43). The goal of these events, in other words, is to remind the Lebanese migrant – internal and external – of his Lebanese-ness. Migration is not a new phenomenon to Lebanon. However, the confluence of specific political and economic events along with technological developments starting in the first half of the century made migration simultaneously easier and in many cases unavoidable. While emigration to the Americas from Mt Lebanon had risen steadily from the time of the civil violence of 1860, it spiked dramatically with the turmoil of World War One and the end of the relatively prosperous period of self-rule. And with the establishment of Beirut as Greater Lebanon's capital at the end of the war, there was also mass migration to that swelling city, both from the mountain and from the other newly annexed provinces (Hourani and Shehadi 1992). These displaced peoples were particularly hungry for locality-reaffirming narratives.

Just which locality the Rahbanis and Fairouz were reaffirming, however, remains to be clarified. What remains to be examined in further detail, in other words, is *which* "Lebanese-ness" or which locality is represented – and thus produced – in the early musical plays of the Rahbani Brothers. Such an examination will then allow us to ask what, by default, is necessarily excluded or, as Chatterjee might say, "betrayed" in these representations. The Rahbani Brothers have been portrayed as being unusually inclusive in their musical theatrical portrayal of a Lebanon that has been referred to as "the Rahbani Brothers' Lebanon" (Abī Samrā 1993: 63): when there are so many different conceptions as to what the Lebanese nation is – "a religious group, a neighborhood, a school of thought, a family, a privilege" – the Rahbani Brothers

> correctly chose to represent the nation as belonging to the human who loves freedom and who loves the land as an area incompatible with tyranny and who is immediately made sick by the introduction of the stranger.
>
> (Nasr Allāh, R. 1986: 64)

Who is this "human" and who is this "stranger?" As part of the general interest in folklore at this time, Anis Frayha wrote his *The Lebanese Village*, a work that claimed to be preserving "Lebanese" folklore that was in danger of extinction.

What we discovered, in fact, was that through elision, this "Lebanese" came to mean a village, Christian and mountain Lebanon. And what this section's conclusions add is the realization that, that text was not only depicting its particular Lebanon, but participating in its production as well. That work was written, of course, before the faith-shattering violence of 1958, before the implementation of the Chehabist program of inclusion. Surely the theater of the Rahbani Brothers would have more in common with the latter than with Frayha. In fact, an investigation of the "Lebanon" in "the Rahbani Brothers' Lebanon" shows not just that it is closer to Frayha than Chehab, but that the pre- and post-1958 designation itself is perhaps yet another false binary.

"The Rahbanis' Lebanon"

In the few early musical-theatrical works that we have looked at so far, with the exception of *The Woman From Baalbeck*, the setting is very clearly the northern Lebanese mountain village: no South, no Bekaa, no coast, no Beirut. Occasionally the locale is mentioned explicitly, such as in *The Moon's Bridge*, the subtitle of which is "A Village in the North of Lebanon"[26] But even when not mentioned outright, as in *The Ring Seller*, any doubt as to the location of events is soon removed. In the very first scene of that play, for example, the townspeople greet the village headman and say that they have been waiting to hear what happened to him in "the forest." He replies:

> I was going up and up, up above the rock quarry and I cut across...the
> forest, behind the hill I was going, on the border, which is all dried-up
> tree stumps, and frowning black rocks and then ran into Rājih.
> (Rahbani, A. and M. 2003a: 21)

This is nothing less than the very "rough and mountainous" vocabulary mentioned by Mansour Rahbani above in the context of their development of the Lebanese song (Zoghaib 1993: part four, 70). And just as in the formation of that song, Lebanon in the early musical theater of the Rahbani Brothers remains equated with the rural mountain.

It remains equated with the rural mountain *village*, that is. It is instructive to see what happens, though, when an actual village is needed to represent a fictional Rahbani village. Such an investigation will provide the opportunity to briefly discuss the Rahbanis' short-lived foray into the medium of film. The year after its presentation at the Cedars Festival, *The Ring Seller* was adapted into a motion picture by the Egyptian director Youssef Chahine (Yūsuf Shāhīn), the first of three musical films that the Rahbani Brothers would make starring Fairouz. The setting for the films, like the vast majority of the early plays, is the mountain village. The village of the film-version of *The Ring Seller* is shot on a sound stage and is, not surprisingly, beautiful and quaint. Apparently the director ordered that "a model village be built with matching and evenly spaced houses..." (Nāsir 1986: part six, 49).

Their next film, however, was to be shot on location. *Exile* is a film about the Ottoman practice of conscripting its subjects into military and labor service on Mount Lebanon. Mansour tells the story of how the French director whom they hired to make the film spent two months in the Lebanese mountains unable to find what was requested of him: a typical Lebanese village with red-tiled, stone-walled and old arch-replete houses from the World War One era. While Mansour says that the French director had to be fired because he was not looking hard enough, even his replacement, the Egyptian director Henri Barakat (Hanrī Barakāt), had only marginally better luck. In the end, they used several different rural locations to make up the film's village "'Ayn al-jawz" (Zoghaib 1993: part six, 74). About this Mansour says:

> For the village of "'Ayn al-jawz" in the film we used, disregarding the map, two different places for filming: [the villages] Bayt al-Shabāb in the Matn [region] and Dūmā in the al-Batrūn [region]. It was rare that people were able to determine that it was two villages.
>
> (Zoghaib 1993: part six, 74)

One of the lessons of this anecdote is its proof of the paradox of modern representation: not only is the accurate representation of the folkloric model village impossible, as we saw above, but the village upon which such representation is based does not exist in the first place. When questioned by an interviewer about the gap between the reality of the Lebanese village as portrayed in their work and the real Lebanese village, Mansour replied: "Not every reality can be one hundred percent real" (Munassā 1991: 7).

One could argue that it is not that the Rahbani Brothers' village did not exist, but rather that it *no longer* existed. This "no longer" is indicative of another of modernity's symptoms: nostalgia. The importance of nostalgia to the musical-theatrical project of the Rahbani Brothers has certainly been oft noted (Abī Samrā 1978, 1998, and 1999; Abū Murād 1990 and 2000; Aliksān, J. 1987; Bāshā 1995; Baydūn, 'Abbās 1994; Manganaro 1999a; Murūwa 1998; Nasr Allāh, R. 1986; Seligman 1997; Traboulsi 1998 and 2006; Wāzin 2000a; and Zoghaib 1993). The question remains though: nostalgia for what? It has been suggested that the village-centered-ness of their project was influenced by the summers Asi and Fairouz spent in the village of Bakfiyya (Bāshā 1995: 158). More common is the reading that the virtual rural utopias these early works present have as their source the childhood of Asi and Mansour Rahbani in both the village of Antilyas – now a suburb of Beirut – which a reference work on Lebanese geography characterizes as a mix of mountain and coast (Mufarrij 1969: vol. one, 19), and the more mountainous hamlet of Dhur Shweir (Dūr al-Shuwayr) where they would spend their summers at their father's café (Abū Murād 1990 and 2000; Aliksān, J. 1987; and Zoghaib 1993). Their father has been repeatedly credited with introducing them to music and with providing the example for all of the "qabadāy" characters and principles in their works such as the protagonist of the film *Exile* (Zoghaib 1993: part one, 78) and the Shaykh of Shaykhs character in *Bridge* (Zoghaib 1993: part one, 70). The word *qabadāy* has connotations running from "strong-arm and bully" to "hero" and "revolutionary." Both in the works of the Rahbani Brothers and in portrayals of their father – who apparently took up residence in Antilyas because he was wanted by the Ottoman authorities – its use tends toward the latter meanings. When Mansour tells the story of quitting and encouraging other artists to quit their work for Near East Radio in 1956, he says, "We became our father's son and convinced the other musicians..." (Zoghaib 1993: part four, 73).

While these perceptions no doubt contain some truth, the nostalgia in their works seems actually to be hearkening back to an era that ended just before either one was born, that is pre–Greater-Lebanon Lebanon: the period between 1860 and the end of the Great War known as "al-Mutasarrifiyya" when Mt Lebanon enjoyed, thanks to the intervention of France on behalf of its Maronite Christian majority, a large degree of self-rule. This is the conjecture of Muhammad Abī Samrā who writes that

> This was a period seen as one of social and economic renaissance for the mountain inhabitants, what with silk trade and manufacture, and with their developed mountainous urban centers that traded with the coastal centers like Saida and Beirut, which was growing from a village into a proper city, based on its trade with the mountain
>
> (Abī Samrā 1999: 7)

In another article he calls nostalgia for this period the Rahbani Brothers' richest source (Abī Samrā 1998: 9). Adam Gopnik wrote in an article on Jazz in New York City that "It is art that puts a time in place" (Gopnik 2001: 30), that is, that connects an era to a specific setting. The musical-theatrical project of the Rahbani Brothers demonstrates that art can also put a place in a time: their work is not just clearly about the Lebanese mountain village; it is about that place at a specific time.

Their musical plays, however, do not only evoke nostalgia. They are also full of it. This is true even of their pre-Baalbeck works. Nostalgia figures prominently, for example, in their work for the Palestinian resistance *We are Returning* (Nasr Allāh, R. 1986; Traboulsi 1998 and 2006), which Murūwa calls a work of constructive nostalgia (Murūwa 1998: 185). In the title track, the breeze coming from Palestine and those singing about it arouse tears, nostalgia, and longing. The second-half of the song, though, is a call to those "whose houses are occupied by strangers and who are refugees in tents" to put these feelings to good use: "We will not sleep while the roads of righteousness are dark." We will struggle and "We shall return" (Rahbani, A. and M. 1992b: track one).

Nostalgia permeates their musical theater as well. Its presence in *The Night and the Lantern* demonstrates that it is often associated with childhood and youth.

After hiding the besieged villain Hawlū in her tent, Mantūra suddenly realizes who he is and sings:

> I remember, I remember. When we were young we would play on the arches of that balcony in the winter. I remember a long long time ago when we were neighbors and you would visit us and we'd play together and hope.... I remember that the road [of life] separated us from the old way....

> (Rahbani, A. and M. 2003d: 32–3)

This nostalgia causes her to feel pity for him, something the old village guard Nasrī warns her against. Nasrī himself, however, is not immune to nostalgia. In a scene which appears in the play's script but not its recording, he says to his heart: "Do you remember... when we were young and we used to love and hurt and get jealous.... What harm can it do to sit and remember. Memories of youth are like provisions for a trip" (Rahbani, A. and M. 2003d: 45–6). This connection between nostalgia and childhood in these works is perhaps one reason why it is often assumed that the plays are expressions of longing for the time and place of the Rahbanis' own childhood. While this is no doubt partially true, the emphasis on childhood does not have to be taken literally, but rather can be seen as standing for the longing for simpler premodern times which, Marshall Berman and others tells us, is the constant companion of modernity (Berman 1982). From the point of view of 1960s Beirut, with its bulging and diverse population, the pre–World War One Mutasarrifiyya days of Mt Lebanon must have seemed very enticing indeed.

Such urban-for-village nostalgia is literally acted out in the Rahbani Brothers' first "urban" play *Hala and the King* (*Hāla wa-al-malik*), which was staged at the Cedars Festival just before the Arab-Israeli war of 1967. The play is about a girl (played by Fairouz) who comes to the city from a mountain village with her father to sell masks for the city's Halloween-like holiday. The city is clearly portrayed as a place of corruption: the father immediately repairs to a bar for a long night of drinking and Hala is left to navigate the hypocrisy of the city on her own. Throughout her travails all that she can think about is home. Even the prospect of marriage to the king and thus instant riches does not deter her from her goal of returning home. In fact, as soon as she arrives in the city she is homesick for her village. "Don't you know why I'm sad," she says to her father. "This is the first time that I've been in the square of a city and as soon as I got here I missed the talk of my mother, my siblings, my village and the shade of the trees" (Rahbani, A. and M. 1967: 19). She describes her village, "Daraj al-lawz" – The very name, meaning "the terraces of the almonds," is evocatively bucolic – and her longing for it as follows:

> way up in the mountains, high up, [there are] just four or five houses and some trees, where my siblings are busy gathering wood for the winter.

Our house is run-down, my bed is old, but I won't sleep until I put my
head on my pillow there.

(Rahbani, A. and M. 1967: 40)

To the first- or second-generation city dweller, this must have proved to be a very
powerful image indeed.

The film *Exile* can be seen as a requiem for this perceived golden age, as it
covers the period between the end of a half century of self-rule on Mt Lebanon
and the eventual breakup of the Ottoman Empire. Because of the instability
during the war and the Ottoman Empire's unilateral call for the end of self-rule
on the mountain, it was also the beginning of a period of mass migration from
the mountain both abroad and to coastal urban centers such as Beirut, and thus the
beginning of the nostalgia that would be harvested by the Rahbani Brothers.
The mountain lost approximately a third of its population with the end of this
"halcyon" period (Abī Samrā 1999: 7).

It is interesting to look at depictions of the mountain village before the end
of the Mutasarrifiyya period as compared to the ideal way in which it is depicted
in the works of the Rahbani Brothers, Frayha, and others. In his *History of
Baalbeck*, the first edition of which was published at the end of the nineteenth
century, Allūf takes his reader on a tour up the mountain to the west of the ruins
of Baalbeck. Though the nature and particularly the views back to Baalbeck
impress him, some of the villages are described quite disparagingly:

> Having traversed the forests of oaks and juniper trees which cover this
> part of the Lebanon and walked $1\frac{1}{2}$ hour [sic], the poor wretched
> Maronite village of Mouchaytieh is reached and in another hour the
> miserable village of Ainata with its mean little houses.

(Allūf 1914: 12)

This is not to say that every pre-1914 depiction of the Lebanese mountain village
is devoid of romanticism or that every post-1914 depiction is replete with longing. Edward Said, for example, in remembering childhood summers spent in the
very village where Asi and Mansour Rahbani's father had a summer café – Dhur
Shweir – deploys language not dissimilar to Allūf, calling it a "dreary Lebanese
mountain village..." (Said 1999: 28). It does seem, however, that the place had
worked its nostalgic magic on his father for he goes on to say that he "...seemed
more attached to [it] than any other place on earth" (Said 1999: 28). Samira
Aghacy also informs us that many Lebanese women writers of the second half of
the twentieth century associate the village with restrictiveness and the city with
progress and freedom (Aghacy 2001). In general, however, nostalgia for the
mountain would prevail. This migration did not only provide a source for this
nostalgia, but also an automatic audience for the representation of it. This is
perhaps what Khālida Sa'īd meant when she said the folkloric works of the
Rahbani Brothers found their audience ready and waiting (Sa'īd, Kh. 1998b: 55).

79

The audience of these early Rahbani Brothers' work, then, is not the mountain dweller but he or she who was nostalgic for the mountain, that is, the first- or second-generation urbanite (Abī Samrā 1978).

Anderson talks in his *Imagined Communities* about the importance of wartime or postwar nostalgia for pre-violence times. During the large-scale slaughter of the Seminole Indians in Florida, James Fenimore Cooper published *The Pathfinder* in which a white man and an Indian – Natty Bumppo and Chingachgook – fraternally fight against the French. Similarly, after the US civil war, Twain's Huckleberry Finn harkens back to an antebellum brotherhood between blacks and whites as embodied in the friendship between Huck and Jim (Anderson 1991: 202–3). Manganaro notes that the early works of the Rahbani Brothers are similarly free of racial or sectarian tension or underrepresentation (Manganaro 1999a: 4). This is only because the world of these early works is a world depicted as being *devoid* of sects and the underrepresentable. These works, in other words, focus nostalgically not just on the rural and mountain locale of the period of self-rule, but on its predominant Christianity as well (al-Shamālī 1978: 10): the Lebanon of the Rahbani Brothers is not only a mountain and village Lebanon, it is also a Christian Lebanon. This Christian characteristic is not limited to their early work, as Munā Būlus argues in her book on the plays *The Night and the Lantern* (1963) and *Granite Mountains* (1969). She finds many traces of the Old and New Testament God in both of these plays (Būlus 2001).

In his recollections of working with the Egyptian directors Youssef Chahine and Hanri Barakat, Mansour Rahbani mentions that he and his brother Asi did Chahine "a big service" by helping him "reclaim" his Lebanese identity card, based on the fact that he had roots in the town of Zahle (Zahla) going back to his great grandfather. Barakat was similarly assisted in "reclaiming" his Lebanese citizenship based on ancestral roots in Shatura (Shatūra) and in the Bekaa (Zoghaib 1993: part six, 72 and 74). These two incidents can be seen as part of a wider trend of non-Lebanese Christians being able to "reclaim" Lebanese citizenship whereas Muslims of similar background had no such luck. A good example is the approximately 100,000 or so Palestinian refugees who found themselves in Lebanon after the 1948 war. Whereas most of the Christians among them – approximately 40,000 – were able to enjoy Lebanese citizenship eventually, the majority of the remaining 60,000 Muslim refugees had difficulty even getting work permits (Petran 1987: 48). For Anderson, passports have become less a sign of national identity than the right to participate in a labor market (Anderson 1994: 323). While this observation is borne-out in the case of the distribution of Lebanese citizenship, the fact that it was granted much more readily to Christians than to Muslims demonstrates that citizenship is still about more than just economics. This is the atmosphere in which the Rahbanis were producing their musical-theatrical works. On the one hand, there was the official Chehabist rhetoric of inclusion. On the other hand, there was a realization that the Muslim/ Christian population parity that existed at the time of the signing of the National Pact was quickly eroding in favor of the former. No wonder that the narrative portrayals of Lebanon might evoke a time when such tension was perceived as being nonexistent. How does this nostalgia for a Lebanese time and place without the inconvenience of sectarian minorities manifest itself in the theater of the Rahbani Brothers?

As mentioned above, the world of the early Rahbani Brothers' musicals is not just a mountain village world, it is a *Christian* mountain village world. Or so it seems to be perceived by those writing about them. On first glance it might seem as if the world of their works is neither Christian nor Muslim. Is not the absence of church bells, for example, counterbalanced by the absence of the Muslim call to prayer? Abū Murād seems to present the religiosity of their work in such a manner until he begins to talk about the role of light. Light in their works is often a metaphor for the light of God, a common feature, he tells us, in both the "old religions" and in the "new." As an example of the old and the new, the reader is given a few lines from the Old and New Testaments respectively. Suddenly we are in the realm of specific religions. From the mention of the New Testament, Abū Murād moves on to Jesus himself who, we are told, taught the Jews a new kind divine mercy (Abū Murād 1990: 229). Similarly, the book *Prayer in the Songs of Fairouz* (*al-Salāt fī aghānī Fairouz*, 1974), a work introduced by Said Akl, attempts to remain nonspecific in its categorization of religious elements in songs sung by Fairouz. At the beginning of the work, however, the author gives himself away by saying, "We have limited the work to the study of Fairouz's songs from one aspect, i.e. the extraction of the liturgical, ritualistic and spiritual aspects which cry out in them" ('Ubayd 1974: 12). In case the reader is not familiar with the word "liturgical," a footnote is provided: "This word has developed in Christianity and has become a synonym for 'ritual' ... " ('Ubayd 1974: 12, note). And while he does mention Islam at least once, specific Christian references are far more numerous. For example, when analyzing the poem "Give Me the Flute" ("A'tinī al-nāy") by Kahlil Gibran (Jubrān Khalīl Jubrān)[27] he says that when Fairouz sings "Song is the best prayer" she is echoing a Maronite liturgical principle ('Ubayd 1974: 141). In addition, it has been pointed out that some of the musical-theatrical characters that Fairouz has played are Virgin-Mary–type figures, such as "the girl" in *The Moon's Bridge*. Traboulsi, when talking about the presence of magic and myth in the play, says:

> It is interesting that all of these magical-mythical means do not succeed in solving the conflict or in discovering the treasure. This is brought about by a miraculous religious (Christian) act by the girl of *The Moon's Bridge* who is the theatrical equivalent of Sayyida Harīsā.[28] To play that role Fairouz even wore a Mary-esque costume, that is to say that which tradition claims to be the clothes of the Virgin Mary: blue the color of exaltedness and white the color of pureness.[29]
>
> (Traboulsi "Fann al-Rahābina": 75)

While there is perhaps nothing specifically Christian about the character in the play, it is hard for viewers not to see her as a Virgin Mary–type figure.

I will further discuss Fairouz's connection to the Virgin Mary in Chapter 4. I would like here, though, to comment on how it is not just the theatrical works of the Rahbani Brothers and Fairouz that are discussed in specifically Christian terms, but their lives as well. Until now I have referred to the duo of Asi and Mansour Rahbani without comment as the "Rahbani Brothers," which is exactly how they not only signed all of their work from the beginning of their radio careers onward, but also how Mansour Rahbani continues to sign his work despite the death of Asi in 1986. They are often talked about as if they were one. There are many anecdotes about them which stress the unity of the pair. One such story has the Egyptian poet Ahmed Rami (Ahmad Rāmī) in Lebanon meeting the Rahbani Brothers. Just before the meeting, Asi had to excuse himself. The person introducing him to Mansour said, "He [Mansour] remains the Rahbani Brothers" (Salām 1986: 62). Salām goes on to say, "They were one spirit in two bodies" (Salām 1986: 62). Just as common is the phenomenon of the three figures being talked about in a language reminiscent of the Christian trinity. An example is a 1995 episode of the "Future Television" talk show *The Open Night* (*al-Layl al-maftūh*) – commemorating the death of Asi nine years earlier ("Ilā Asi" 1995). The actor Aylī Shuwayrī (who played, among other roles, the drunken father in *Hala and the King*) says, for example: "When I look at Mansour Rahbani, I see Asi Rahbani, when I hear Fairouz, I remember the humming of Asi Rahbani" ("Ilā Asi" 1995). Elsewhere, the poet Henri Zoghaib wrote that "Fairouz's voice crowns the Rahbani trinity: Asi Rahbani/Mansour Rahbani/Fairouz" (Zoghaib 1998: 127).[30]

It is also well known that since early in her career Fairouz has chanted at a variety of churches throughout Lebanon every Good Friday. While she started in the 1950s doing this from churches in Asi and Mansour's hometown of Antilyas, she appeared eventually in a variety of Maronite and Greek Orthodox churches in Beirut as well (Wāzin 1999: n.p.). Though articles on these "performances" (which are broadcast on the radio and which were released on records in 1962 and 1964–5) often describe them as reaching across religious lines (Sa'īd, Kh. 1992: 12 and Wāzin 1999: n.p.) or having a Sufic quality about them (Wāzin 1999: n.p.), there can be no questioning their essential Christian nature. The following is typical of these chants' lyrics, which are taken from the Eastern Christian liturgical tradition and arranged by the Rahbani Brothers: "Miriam, daughter of David, went toward the pole lamenting her son who has been crucified by the hands of the soldiers" (*Good Friday* 1990: track four).

With such Christian mountain undertones being perceived in their lives and works, it should come as no surprise that their artistic output did not resonate with every one in Lebanon. One informant of Islamic background whose family has lived in Beirut for many generations and has no known ties to Mt Lebanon told me that prior to attending the university, songs from the Rahbani Brothers plays meant very little to him, both the village mountain vocabulary and the Christian inferences being mostly lost on him. It should be noted that exposure to the work of Fairouz and the Rahbani Brothers was in no way limited to the few days a year when they would present their work at Baalbeck or elsewhere, nor was it limited to those who could afford and had the inclination to see them live. Their annual musical plays and other concerts acted as the introduction of material "that would resonate for the rest of the year and, as time has proven, for many years to come" (Asmar 1999: 14) on the radio and on records. This same informant said that he only started listening to Fairouz with some regularity when he began attending the Lebanese University where, he told me, her songs would be played over and over again on the juke box in the cafeteria. The writer Muhammad Abī Samrā, a Muslim originally from the south of Lebanon, was won over to the voice of Fairouz earlier, for example, at the onset of puberty. He eloquently describes the alienation that resulted from the gap between the world created by the Rahbani Brothers and Fairouz and the urban world in which he lived (Abī Samrā 1978: 213–15). Similarly, in an article about Fairouz, the writer Tāhā al-Walī, who identifies himself as a Muslim born in the city of Tripoli (Tarābulus) and raised in Beirut, writes the following:

> Whenever I heard the radio broadcasting a Lebanese song, I would turn it off immediately. That was because I felt that that kind of song represented regional propaganda for Lebanese mountain life, for they repeatedly talk about the mountain and its beauty..... Fairouz's voice is beautiful but it was used for regional purposes, for Fairouz and Sabah and others were used to spread Lebanese mountain tastes among the people and to convince them of it when originally these tastes had not existed, for in her voice there is an ecclesiastical echo.
>
> (al-Walī 1992: 18)

This is not to say that these plays and songs were not extremely popular "across the religions" in the Levant of the 1950s and 1960s (Sa'īd, Kh. 1992: 12), but that for many to identify with this project meant *learning* to identify with it. This anecdotal evidence is evocative of the observation made by Muhammad Abī Samrā that in order to fit into modern Lebanon, non-Christian and non-Mountain Lebanese had to adapt to the needs and principles of this mountain ideology (Abī Samrā 1978: 216). The novelist Hasson Daoud (Hasan Dāwūd) described to me that after his family moved to Beirut from the south of Lebanon in the 1960s, he and his brother would try to imitate the dialect of the Rahbani works while on the school bus so as not to be made fun of by their peers. Earlier I showed that this gap between what was depicted in the Rahbani Brothers' plays and the reality of the recipient participated in forming that recipient's identity. This effect does not occur, however, without a certain amount of instability, which, I conclude below, was not without potentially serious consequences.

One might argue that because the Rahbanis and Fairouz *are* in fact Christians of mountain-village heritage that such aspects of their work should not be overdetermined. The fact of the matter is, however, that they repeatedly claimed to be a symbol of national unity, or had that claim made for him or her. In multiple interviews, for example, Fairouz has claimed not only to be a symbol of Lebanon (Aliksān, J. 1987: 161; Mahfūz, H. 1986: 40), but actually to *be* Lebanon (Traboulsi 2006: 32). In *Holiday* Shāhīn, before his marriage to Najlā, orders a builder to construct a house for him and his wife. He says, "Oh builder of builders, build for us a room and a house with nice windows before winter comes. Take a rock and put a rock and build, oh builder of builders, build until we build Lebanon" (Rahbani, A. and M. 1960: 27). Offstage, winter would be a long brutal war. Not brutal enough, according to Mansour, to destroy this house of Lebanon which they repeatedly constructed or had constructed in their names:

> The world of the Rahbanis is not easily destroyed, but rather what collapsed in Lebanon was the nation of political ideals, the nation of cronyism and bribes. As for the Rahbani nation, it is based on goodness and love and beauty, so it cannot collapse, and it is possible to achieve it. When honorable types come to power the Rahbani Brothers' nation will be realized....
>
> (qtd. in "Mansour Rahbani ba'da khurūjihi min al-mustashfā" 1995: 18)

In another interview in the same year he responds similarly to a question about the viability of the Rahbani nation: "Our [the Rahbani] nation is achievable. It has not yet been realized but it will be" (al-Dāhir 1995: 1).[31]

There are innumerable statements equating the works of the Rahbani Brothers and Fairouz with Lebanon, or crediting them for creating the nation in their works. The 1995 television program in commemoration of the death of Asi mentioned above was an occasion for many such statements. In a way it was a re-enactment of many of the programs, shows, and articles that appeared when Asi Rahbani died in 1986. The occasion was the release of a tribute record called *To Asi* by Ziad Rahbani and his mother Fairouz. While I will discuss this record in greater detail in Chapter 4, I will say here that its release prompted a fresh wave of programs and articles in commemoration of Asi Rahbani, such as the show in question. One of the guests, the poet Samīr al-Sāyigh, states the equation very simply: "Lebanon and the Rahbani Brothers are adjectives meaning the same thing" ("Ilā Asi" 1995). Just after this, Abū Murād quips not only that their works helped "to root the nation," but also that "in certain times geniuses appear who create their countries in their own images, such as Sophocles and Shakespeare. The Rahbani Brothers are just such geniuses" ("Ilā Asi" 1995). In the same program in an interview taped separately, the actor Aylī Shuwayrī makes a similar statement using the word "prophet" instead of "genius" ("Ilā Asi" 1995). Elsewhere al-Sāyigh has surmised that all of the themes of the Rahbani brother theater can be boiled down to one: the Lebanese nation (al-Sāyigh 1986: 60). In addition, 'Abbās Baydūn has written:

> the work of the Rahbanis was, in one way or another, a magical unification of different directions and tenors and sensitivities, and the Rahbani

foundation, in play after play, suggested for Lebanon one dream, a comprehensive myth, a shared language....

(Baydūn 1994: 52)

Such discourse on this project is not limited to Lebanon. The Egyptian novelist Yūsuf al-Qaʿīd, for example, has written that the Rahbani Brothers "have effectively participated in the creation of the image of Lebanon" (al-Qaʿīd 1992: 20). In other words, there is no shortage of claims made by or about the works of the Rahbani Brothers and Fairouz that equates their musical and musical-theatrical works to the project of the creation of Lebanon.

More important than such *claims*, however, are the Rahbanis' *representations* of Lebanon. What I hope to have demonstrated above is that the very representations of Lebanon in the works themselves are never the neutral reflection of reality that they claim to be. This is their paradox: the very act of creating such a display precludes the very neutrality that such displays claim. For Kirshenblatt-Gimblett, such folkloric displays are the most mimetic examples of what she calls "in-situ installations." No matter how good a copy, they

> are not neutral. They are not a slice of life lifted from the everyday world and inserted into the museum gallery, though this is the rhetoric of the mimetic mode. On the contrary, those who construct the display also constitute the subject, even when they seem to do nothing more than relocate an entire house and its content, brick by brick, board by board, chair by chair. Just as the ethnographic object is the creation of the ethnographer, so too, are the putative cultural wholes of which they are part....
> "Wholes" are not given but constituted, and often they are hotly contested.
> (Kirshenblatt-Gimblett 1991: 389)

It is not, then, just the verisimilitude of the representation that is called into question, but the very existence of the reality that it claims to be standing for. The very remembered folkloric Christian, village, mountain Lebanon that the Rahbani Brothers, Akl, Chamoun and Chehab were basing their Lebanons on were as much a fiction as the Lebanon presented on the stage of Baalbeck. These gaps between both the representation and the represented would not be without consequences. This is not only because they were officially sanctioned and sponsored, but because they would come to prominence at a time of the intersection of the rapid development of mass media and migration. Never before were such representations so widely available to an audience more and more uprooted, more and more in search of identity confirming narratives.

The Days of Fakhr al-Din: exception to the rule?

What about a play like *The Days of Fakhr al-Din*, one might ask? Is it not a musical play about the seventeenth-century Druze prince portrayed as a national hero that attempted to throw off the shackles of Ottoman rule and unite all regions of Lebanon into a single political unity? Is it not a play about a non-Christian hero, the settings of which are confined neither to village nor mountain? In juxtaposition to the metaphorical building of a mountain house standing-in for the building of Lebanon of *Holiday*, the epic and historic scope of this play allows things to be stated more directly. Upon returning from exile, the prince Fakhr al-Din says:

> I've been absent for five years, but never was this dear nation absent from my mind.... The day of returning is the day of promises and speeches. We have to build Lebanon.... How are we going to build it? With everything: wheat, agriculture, threshing floors, oil presses, looms, hands raised as far as the eye can see. We'll build palaces, we'll build bridges, we'll build fortress towers, small and large houses.
>
> (Rahbani, A. and M. 1966: 2)

Later in the play just such projects – carried out significantly not just in the mountain but all over Lebanon – arouse the suspicion and ire of Istanbul. A letter from the Sublime Porte reads like a reaction to a Chehabist five-year plan:

> We have learned that you have built four bridges on four rivers, that you have built forts and strongholds, that you have widened the ports in Tripoli and Saida and Beirut, made Beirut your capital, expanded your commerce and created consulates....
>
> (Rahbani, A. and M. 1966: 26–7)

Does not the play begin, in fact, with Fakhr al-Din returning from exile and being greeted and presented with gifts by delegations from all over modern-day Lebanon: the Chouf, the South, the Bekaa, the North, Beirut, and the mountain? Thus presented, *Fakhr al-Din* seems to reflect a wholly different discursive Lebanon than the ones presented above.

A closer look at the play, however, reveals this impression to be an illusion. While all regions of Lebanon are accounted for at Fakhr al-Din's homecoming ceremony, for example, the representative from the mountain (played by Fairouz) is the only delegate given a voice. While the others present their gifts silently, the mountain delegate is introduced by a blast of trumpets. She then sings songs of homage as she presents her gifts. Fakhr al-Din is so taken by her singing that he conscripts her for national service, saying to her: "I am the sword, you are the song" (Rahbani, A. and M. 1966: 6). When she does not quite understand what he means, he elaborates:

> With my sword I will free these regions and achieve Lebanon, and you with song will keep its name flowering wherever it is spoken. Take your song to the streets, to peoples' houses. Keep singing about it. Make

others sing and when everyone is singing they will love it and want it and it will become the song....

(Rahbani, A. and M. 1966: 7)

Not only does the representative from the mountain get to speak to and sing for Fakhr al-Din, she will also get to sing for all of Lebanon, which she promises to do, saying – in song – that she will devote her life, her voice and her death to Lebanon (Rahbani, A. and M. 1966: 7). In the live recording of the play, this line is greeted with tremendous applause (Rahbani, A. and M. 1991: disc one, track two, 6:10).

The mountain is also presented as being responsible for the defense of the country. We first get a hint of this with the gifts presented to Fakhr al-Din. While most other regions give agricultural products and such, the mountain delegate gives a sword and scabbard. When he asks 'Atr al-Layl what brings her to this ceremony, she says that her father is 'Abbās, a soldier from Antilyas (just mention of the hometown of the Rahbani Brothers is greeted with applause (Rahbani, A. and M. 1991: disc one: track one, 18:45)). Not only does Fakhr al-Din say that he knows her father the soldier, but also that he loves him. Later in the play, the Sublime Porte sends a force four times the size of Fakhr al-Din's army to Lebanon. When asked what the battle plan is, he lists a role for each region. He then tells them that in battle they should keep the music going at all times to keep their morale high. At this moment Fairouz's character sings "Oh resident of the highlands, look out from the above," a song calling on residents of the mountain to protect the country: "From our thresholds we call on you to protect our houses" (Rahbani, A. and M. 1991: disc one: track one, 18:18).[32] Lebanon is to be unified and protected – musically and militarily – by mountain dwellers. Lebanese nationalism in this play seems to become conflated with mountain nationalism.

At the same time, the play is full of Chehabist reminders of the importance of a strong central government. We see this when two brothers from the Taym valley come to Fakhr al-Din seeking arbitration in a dispute over rule of the land. Fakhr al-Din first says that he cannot believe that brothers would be having such a dispute, and then says that he is not going to rule by "right" but rather, in true Rahbani Brothers fashion, by "friendship and love" (Rahbani, A. and M. 1966: 16). The valley, he determines, will be divided in half and the two brothers will consult each other in the ruling of their districts. You cannot have a central government, of course, without taxation. When two Ottoman spies try to encourage protests against Fakhr al-Din's taxation policy, they are foiled by the wise Shaykh Khātir who convinces people of the need for taxation by saying,

Tell me people, what do you think? You want a state that builds and participates in industry, that encourages business, improves agriculture, helps science and art. You want a state that watches out for your interests and interferes anytime two sides fight each other, and at the same time you want to be excused from paying on tax day?

(Rahbani, A. and M. 1966: 15)

He further convinces them of the virtues of taxation by telling them that it is better for the state to get its money locally than to beg abroad. At the end of this speech the very character the Ottoman spies had influenced and who had been calling for protests is the one yelling at everyone to get back to work.

This play is perhaps the clearest example that the Rahbani Brothers' project can be seen as an ideological bridge between the pre-1958 regime of Chamoun and the post-violence rule of Chehab and his successor Helou. The Lebanon being depicted in this work is a combination of etatism and mountain-centered nationalism. This is reflected even in the play's traditional dances. "Lebanon's Dabka" is not just an attempt to create a *dabka* that represents all of Lebanon. It is representative of what the Rahbani Brothers did with the *dabka* in general by producing a synthetic dance *based* on mountain *dabka* elements (Traboulsi 1996: 45) that comes to represent the *dabka* in all of Lebanon (Abū Murād 1990: 100–1). Nostalgia for the mountain was not, of course, peculiar to post-1958 Lebanon. Traboulsi, in fact, claims that it was one of the main tenets of Chiha's New Phoenicians (Traboulsi 2000: 3).[33] Abī Samrā goes farther, surmising that the mountain rhetoric of Akl and his ilk was more than innocent nostalgia, that modern Lebanon of the National Pact was *formed* on the economic and ideological needs of the mountain. The needs of the ideological center, he goes on to say, were then imposed on the margins. And instead of seeing Chehabism as a break from this philosophy, he depicts it as a serious project to implement it on a national scale. And while he sees this philosophy as the well from which the Rahbani musical-theatrical project drank (Abī Samrā 1978: 216), it is also likely that the tenets of Chehabism did not escape the influence of the compelling and repeated message of these musical-theatrical works. Thus stated, the shift from Chamoun to Chehab seems less abrupt. The violence of 1958, in other words, begins to look less like a rupture and more like a gap bridgeable by Rahbani Brothers' musical-theatrical works such as *The Days of Fakhr al-Din*.

Finally, the historical Fakhr al-Din has been adopted by certain Maronite nationalists as one of their own. Some focus on the refuge he took with Maronites after the killing of his father and his dependence on them for his army and administration. Others go so far as to claim that he converted to Christianity on his deathbed and had been thinking about doing so for some time before his death (Baydūn, Ahmad 1979: 23). Christian or not, the Fakhr al-Din of the Rahbanis is a perfect historical predecessor for Lebanon's Christian nationalism of the twentieth century. Also, there is some indication that members of the Druze community were not pleased with the depiction of Fakhr al-Din in this work. According to Unsī al-Hājj, they put pressure on the government to cease broadcasting the work on the official radio station Radio Beirut. While they did not succeed in this, they were able to have the Rahbani Brothers remove one comical scene from the play that they found objectionable (al-Hājj, U. 1987: vol. one, 275–6).

The Rahbani Brothers and Fairouz, almost as quickly as they became established at the Baalbeck Festival, began to take the national signifying power of that place elsewhere. This did not, however, mean an ideological break from the regime that first sponsored them there, but rather a continuation of its vision of a liberal Christian West-leaning Lebanon with mountain village roots. At the same time, of course, one must be careful not to overstate the direct relation between culture and politics. In an article on the relationship between Oum Kalthoum and Gamal Abdel Nasser, Virginia Danielson cautions that "to cast Oum Kalthoum as 'Nasser's weapon' is to simplify in the extreme" (Danielson 1998: 114). The same can be said for the relationship of the Rahbanis to the regimes of Chamoun and Chehab. My commentary on ideological similarities is not a suggestion of conspiracy or collusion. In his work on the powerful confluence of mass media and migration, Appadurai differentiates between five "scapes" in an attempt to examine the various microprocesses in which communities come to be imagined in the era of mass mediation and migration: ethnoscapes, mediascapes, technoscapes, financescapes, and ideoscapes (Appadurai 1996: 33). Mediascapes are the print and electronic media that provide narratives against which we juxtapose our own lives with the consequence that

> the lines between the realistic and the fictional landscapes...are blurred, so that the farther away these audiences are from the direct experiences of metropolitan life, the more likely they are to construct imagined worlds that are chimeral, aesthetic, even fantastic objects, particularly if assessed by the criteria of some other perspective, some other imagined world.
> (Appadurai 1996: 35)

The Rahbanis' project is a combination of mediascapes thus described and ideoscapes, which are also based on "concatenations of images, but are often directly political and frequently have to do with the ideologies of states..." (Appadurai 1996: 36). Danielson seems to want to relieve popular culture of some of its political agency when she writes that

> critically, the "performances" of listeners...appropriate sound and image to their own purposes, constructing and projecting their own attitudes. By moving sound and image through time and space, listeners use performance to situate themselves socially and politically and thus enact political and social identities of their own. The process of remembering in this way draws the singer, the song, and the sound into the political world, where neither singer nor song may be expressly political.
> (Danielson 1998: 119)

This may be true of pure "mediascapes," if such a thing exists. The case of the Rahbani project is an example of the intersection – with unstable and ever-changing borders – of media and ideoscapes, which is not necessarily free of some degree of intentionality.

It was my goal here also to show quite specifically how the early musical-theatrical works of the Rahbani Brothers represented this Christian mountain village Lebanon. This representation is not without several paradoxes. As soon as the Rahbanis began to stage this mountain folklore they, inevitably, began to misrepresent it. The very performance of this folklore created a gap between their representations and its "original," a gap that seemed to increase with each iteration of it. This gap, in turn, would facilitate several things. While on the one hand it would only further establish the putative reality of the "original" that their work was self-consciously portraying, it would also allow the representations to break free from their signified in a way that parallels the Rahbani Brothers breaking away from Baalbeck. It is in this way that the Rahbanis' folkloric representations could further come to stand for different nationalities – sometimes simultaneously – within and without Lebanon.

This latter paradox was facilitated by the rapid development of mass media at this time. Earlier I cited Anderson on the paradox of the role of capitalism-driven technology in the formation of nationalisms. Late capitalism's mass media facilitates the imaginings necessary for nationalism but, as it develops, makes it difficult for nationalism to be contained within the borders of the modern nation-state. The Rahbani Brothers' project is certainly an instance of this phenomenon, the seeds of which I have shown was already evident in their work well before their first appearance at Baalbeck. At Baalbeck they would enact the Lebanese mountain village, to Syria they would sing of the Umayyad Empire and the famous Damascene gardens, to Egypt of its long civilizational history and the Nile, to Iraq of its poets, to Palestine of the sacred waters of the Jordan river, and to Jordan they would sing of the hills of Amman.[34]

If there is one thread that binds all of these works it is nostalgia. The tears shed at these concerts and shows were almost always in response to the evocation of former glory or of simpler times. Recollection always involves a certain amount of uncertainty. Nostalgic recollection is perhaps the fuzziest of all, and has been described thus in the work of the Rahbani Brothers (Abī Samrā 1978: 215 and Manganaro: 1999a: 5). It is this very fuzziness that allowed the Rahbani Brothers not just to cater to various nationalisms but also to speak to them at times *simultaneously*. Traboulsi mentions a song like "Return Me to My Country" ("Riddnī ilā bilādī" 1979) as an instance of Fairouz singing for Palestine and Lebanon at the same time (Traboulsi 1998: 204). Another writer has astutely pointed out that the song "We Shall Return One Day" ("sa-Narji'u yawman" 1972), originally meant as a Palestinian anthem, was equally effective as a cry out to the Lebanese Diaspora ("Song of Lebanon" 1986: 82). One's longing for one's occupied land, in other words, could sound much like one's longing for a return to one's ancestral mountain village. It is thus that Jān Aliksān could state without any irony that Lebanese nationalism for the Rahbani Brothers was "in continual contact with the Arab environment" (Aliksān, J. 1987: 181).

More than simply mirroring the Lebanese and regional realities – however distortedly – I hope to have shown that the intersection of this extremely talented and ambitious artistic team with mass media and migration participated in the very formation of subjectivities on a variety of local and regional levels. Such subject formation is characterized by what Appadurai terms a "new order of instability" (Appadurai 1996: 4). This arises because of the simultaneous flow of images and people across more fluid and problematic boundaries. The combination is sometimes catastrophic. As Appadurai says:

> The effects of large-scale interactions between and within nation-states, often stimulated by news of events in even more distant locations, serve to cascade through the complexities of regional, local, and neighborhood politics until they energize local issues and implode into various forms of violence, including the most brutal ones. What were previously *cool* ethnic identities ... thus turn *hot* ... [italics in the original].
>
> (Appadurai 1996: 164)

The causes of the Lebanese civil war are multiple and complex. I would like to suggest, however, that the instability created by migration and competing mass-media-facilitated localities, including the project of the Rahbani Brothers, played some role in the sparking of that conflict. This is not to claim in any way that their well-intentioned and artistic folkloric depictions of ever-celebrating mountain villagers at Baalbeck *caused* the civil war that began in 1975. It is to say, rather, that the project participated in the production – or at least the "heating up" – of ethnicities that under other circumstances might have remained "cool."

By this time the tautological chain mentioned earlier – Baalbeck equals the Baalbeck Festival equals the musical theater of the Rahbani Brothers and Fairouz equals Lebanon – has been broken in half. While Baalbeck still equaled its Festival (at least up until the start of the war in 1975) and while the musical theater of the Rahbani Brothers still equaled Lebanon, the Rahbani Brothers had broken from Baalbeck the Festival and the site. In a time of trauma for the nation as a whole and for the Mansour-Asi-Fairouz trinity personally, their own lives' narratives would come to replace Baalbeck in the tautological chain. The crisis-filled lives of the Rahbani Brothers and Fairouz – to be outlined in Chapter 3 – would come to equal the declining musical theater of the Rahbani Brothers and Fairouz just as it would equal Lebanon in the time of civil war. While the developments discussed in this chapter proved the tenuous nature of our original tautology, a closer look at the second will come in the following chapters. In Chapter 3 it will be examined in light of the musical and theatrical rise of Ziad Rahbani. Just when the personal lives and the very nation that the Rahbani Brothers and Fairouz's works were representing were falling into disrepair, along came an artistic project that seemed to feed off of all of these failures. Just as the success of the Rahbani Brothers would originally feed off of the powerful signification of the ruins of Baalbeck, Ziad's project can be seen as drawing its strength from the ruins not just of the Rahbani project, but of Lebanon itself. What makes the story of his project's rise even more compelling is that its author is the eldest son of Fairouz and Asi Rahbani. The intersection of the early theatrical and musical project of Ziad Rahbani with that of his parents in the time of civil war is the focus of Chapter 3.

At a press conference on the occasion of the opening of his sardonic 1993 play *Regarding Honor and the Stubborn People* (*bi-Khusūs al-karāma wa-al-sha'b al-'anīd*), Ziad confronts his uncle Mansour who is in the audience. Holding his hands out wide he says, "My uncle, you made something very big of Lebanon, bigger than Lebanon itself" ("Mu'tamar sahafī li-Ziad Rahbani" 1993). I have been arguing the opposite: that the Lebanon they and others created was not just *smaller* than Lebanon itself, but tragically so. As I will show in Chapter 3, one of the goals of Ziad's project was to represent a bigger, more inclusive Lebanon.

3

ZIAD RAHBANI'S THEATRICAL "NOVELIZATION" OF THE RAHBANIS' LEBANON

The decline of the trinity: the post-1967 Rahbani Brothers

This chapter is about the intersection of two musical-theatrical projects at a time of great strife in a young nation. Ziad Rahbani, son of Fairouz and Asi Rahbani, and nephew of Mansour Rahbani, began contributing to his parents' musical and theatrical works in a significant way after Asi suffered from a severe stroke in 1972. While at first it appeared as if Ziad might be the key to repairing the damaged trinity, his work quickly revealed a contrary side that would become even more apparent after the start of the civil war in 1975. This chapter proposes that Ziad's musical-theatrical works must be read both as a response to his parents' theatrical oeuvre and to sociopolitical events in Lebanon and the region, two phenomena that, I have argued, are not unrelated. By looking at his project through this double lens, I hope to show that its significance exceeds the bounds of the stage on which it was executed.

All of Ziad's plays can be categorized as musical theater in that they contain songs that are woven into the plays' plots to varying degrees. Unlike the musical theater of his parents, however, his plays contain no sung dialogue. His theatrical works include *An Evening's Celebration* (1973), *Happiness Hotel* (1974), *What Do We Need to Do Tomorrow* (1977), *A Long American Film* (1979), and *Failure* (1983). After a decade-long theatrical hiatus, Ziad went on to stage two other plays in quick succession. In 1993 he put on his *Regarding Honor and the Stubborn People*. Owing to some confusion about the relationship between the two acts of that play, in 1994 Ziad staged another play meant to serve as the narrative connector between those acts. This work was called *If Not for the Possibility of Hope* (*Law lā fushat al-amal*). Also unlike his parents' project, Ziad never took his plays on tour: all of them have been staged solely in West Beirut for a variety of reasons to be discussed below.

Using Bakhtin's work on parody and heteroglossia, I will show that whereas the Rahbani Brothers' musical-theatrical project represented the fantasy of a monolingual and monocultural Lebanon, Ziad's theatrical works not only revel in the linguistic diversity that was the reality of modern Lebanon, but also dialogically attack his parents' project through parody. This latter strategy, I will demonstrate, was not without certain dangers, as the success of parody hinges on the thinness of the line between it and homage, a line which, as we will see in Chapter 4 and Conclusion, Ziad would constantly cross. Before a detailed examination of Ziad's theater, including its constant dialogism with his parents' project in the context of the erosion of political stability in Lebanon, I will first trace at some length both the artistic and literal decline of the Asi-Mansour-Fairouz trinity. If the rise of this project to prominence was in part catalyzed by the short-lived Lebanese civil war of 1958, one place to look for roots of its decline, I argue, is in another war: the Arab-Israeli war of 1967.

This line of argument contains within it a paradox, as in general – and the Rahbani Brothers were no exception – the devastating military and political defeat of 1967 brought about something of a cultural renaissance throughout the Arab World. If the 1967 Arab-Israeli war had the short-term effect of curtailing artistic activity all over the region, it was not long before writers of all genres and artists of all mediums began to express their individual and collective mix of grief, resolve, and disappointment over the devastating loss for the Arabs (which came to be known as *al-naksa* (the setback)). As the Syrian novelist Hannā Mīna, collaborating with Najāh al-'Attār, has written: resistance literature

> exploded after the *naksa* of June 1967, especially by the pens of the Palestinian writers, but also generally by Arab writers. Its voice rose and rose until it drowned out all other literary voices, for the output was prolific, filling the pages of books, periodicals and magazines....
>
> (Mīna, H. and al-'Attār, N. 1976: 221)

Mīna and al-'Attār conclude that next to poetry, the most important genre in terms of its reaction to the events of 1967 came from theater (Mīna, H. and al-'Attār, N. 1976: 223). While Mīna does not mention any playwrights by name, perhaps the most oft mentioned writer in this regard is Sa'd Allāh Wannūs of Syria, particularly his two plays *Soirée for the Fifth of June* (*Haflat samar min ajli al-khāmīs min Hazayrān*, 1968) and *The Adventures of the Mamluke Jabir's Head* (*Mughāmarāt ra's al-Mamlūk Jābir*, 1970) (Allen 1998: 350–4). Lebanese playwrights were as quick as anyone to respond to the *naksa* (Abū Murād 1990: 166). Works such as 'Isām Mahfūz's *The China Tree* (*al-Zanzalakht*, 1968), his *The Dictator* (*al-Dīktātūr*, 1969), Raymūn Jabbāra's *The Blows of Desdemona* (*Latamat Dazdamūna*, 1970), Jalāl Khūrī's *Juha in the Front-Line Villages* (*Juhā fī al-qurā al-amāmiyya*, 1971), and Fāris Yawākīm's *Yikes, What a Country* (*Akh yā bilādnā*, 1971) (performed by the famous comic actor "Shūshū" (Hasan 'Alā al-Dīn)) can be seen in varying degrees as responses to the loss.[1] As with, for example, the Great War and Europe, this event had an impact on the language, content, and structure of Arab World literature and art to an extent that would be difficult to exaggerate.[2]

It should not be surprising that the work of the Rahbani Brothers, with their early commitment to the Palestinian cause and their association with various nationalisms in the Arab World, would be similarly affected by these events. In fact, their first *musical* response to the events of 1967 came in the summer of that very year. At a special show to mark the *naksa* at that year's Cedars Festival, Fairouz sang "The Flower of Cities" ("Zahrat al-madā'in"), a song celebrating Jerusalem. For this song she was awarded the key to that city the following year (Abī Samrā 1992a: 10). After 1967, not only did their works become more urban and, in a certain sense "realistic" (Abū Murād 1990: 145), but the years after 1967 also witnessed a sharp rise in their productivity. In 1972 Asi Rahbani would suffer a massive stroke. It came after – and can perhaps be at least partly attributed to – an extended period of intensive artistic activity beginning in 1969 with their initial theatrical response to the 1967 catastrophe: *Granite Mountains* (Traboulsi 1998). Between the staging of *Mountains* at Baalbeck and Asi's stroke, they would produce and stage the following musical-theatrical works in rapid succession: *The Person* (*al-Shakhs*, 1969, The Piccadilly Palace Theater in Beirut (hereafter "Piccadilly") and the Damascus International Festival (hereafter "Damascus")), *Live Live* (*Ya 'īsh ya 'īsh*, 1969, Piccadilly), *Wake Up* (*Sahh al-nawm*, 1971, Piccadilly), *The Guardian of the Keys* (*Nāturat al-mafātīh*, 1972, Baalbeck and Damascus), *Paper People* (*Nās min waraq*, 1972, Piccadilly and Damascus), and *Love Poem* (*Qasīdat hubb*, 1973, Baalbeck). They also toured Brazil and Argentina in 1970 and the US in 1971.

Many of these works, including *Mountains* – their initial theatrical response to the *naksa* – are more overtly political than their pre-1967 plays. *Mountains* is about popular resistance to a tyrannical occupier. *Guardian* is also about the struggle against an oppressive ruler, this one local as opposed to *Mountain*'s foreign invader. *Live* contains such direct commentary on the excesses of Lebanon's internal security apparatus "The Second Bureau" that Abū Murād expresses some surprise that it was allowed to be staged (Abū Murād 1990: 157). That play also exposes the general hypocrisy of government officials by portraying weapons smugglers as being more honorable than those employees who practice official smuggling. The plays of this period are also characterized by more urban settings, a trend harbingered by *Hala and the King* on the eve of the 1967 war. *Wake Up* and *Person*, for example, are clearly urban in setting, as are *Loulou* (*Lūlū*, 1974, Piccadilly and Damascus). This move to the city, observes Abū Murād, is accompanied by a relative shift toward "social realism" (Abū Murād 1990: 150). Abū Murād points out that he means "social realism" in a relative sense. The theater of the Rahbani Brothers, he says, never lets go of a certain degree of poeticism and symbolism. It does, however, more or less completely leave the village and begin to face the problems encountered by those living in the city. These later works can also be characterized by the fact that they deal, not with conflict between individuals, a characteristic of the pre-1967 works, but with the struggle between people and those in power: in *Person*, a poor roaming tomato seller has her cart confiscated when she does not heed official orders to clear out of the town center, which has been reserved for an appearance by the local leader; the people in *Wake Up* suffer from a narcoleptic king who does not stay awake long enough to stamp people's requests and petitions; and a woman wrongly serves a fifteen-year sentence for murder in *Loulou*.

This move toward urban "social realism" also results, according to Abū Murād, in a general retreat from the folkloric (Abū Murād 1990: 150). A good example of this distancing can be seen in the Rahbani Brothers and Fairouz's final pre–civil war appearance at the Baalbeck Festival in 1973 with the play *Love Poem*. The section of the official program of the 1973 Baalbeck Festival dedicated to "The Lebanese Nights" stresses themes and words such as "new" ("new word," "new dances," "a new mold"), "different," "modern" and "surprise" ("Qasīdat hubb" 1973: 151). To that end, the "folkloric" song is just one of several different types to be performed along with "long, rhythmic, dance, modern, group and Andalusian strophic songs" ("Qasīdat hubb" 1973: 151). In another way, however *Love Poem* is a throwback to the very early Rahbani Brothers/Fairouz appearances at Baalbeck in that the songs and dance numbers are only loosely tied by narrative elements. It is significant in that it reminds us that, in spite of the shocking events of 1967 and the subsequent social and political unrest in Lebanon leading up to the civil war, the theater of the Rahbani Brothers, despite some changes including an increased productivity, clung stubbornly to some of its original variety-show musical-extravaganza elements. 'Abduh Wāzin, for example, finds elements of their earlier works in the 1970 play *Wake Up*, a work of social realism on the surface (Wāzin 2000a).

These later works retained other elements from their early theater as well. Despite many of the Rahbanis' post-1967 works' urban-social-political sheen, more than a few of them share with their predecessors the central presence of an angelic, virginal female savior. Like Fairouz's 'Atr al-Layl of *Fakhr al-Din*, her Ghurba of *Mountains* is a peripatetic singing savior who seems to descend from the heavens. But Ghurba, in contradistinction to 'Atr al-Layl, carries the *entire* burden of saving her people. In *Mountains* there is no Fakhr al-Din–type character to do military battle while she wages her musical campaign. And whereas it is Fakhr al-Din who gives himself up for the sake of his country in that work, in *Mountains* it is Ghurba who must die in order to liberate her people. While this is the only Rahbani play in which the character played by Fairouz sacrifices her own life, in other works of this period her characters are solo-acting saviors as well. In *Person* it is the poor tomato seller played by Fairouz who, via her mellifluous voice, gains access to "the person" and informs him that his underlings are oppressing the people. Similarly, while the Fairouz character in *Live* does not save the day, she does manage to enlighten her country's overthrown ruler as to the corruption of his government, ensuring that when he is reinstated he will rule differently. In *Wake Up*, the Fairouz character steals the all-important government seal from around the slumbering king's neck, and stamps all of the pending petitions so that the country can get back to work after years of stagnation. In *Guardian*, Fairouz's character is trusted with everyone's house keys when they flee their tyrannical leader. Not only does she refuse to relinquish the keys to him so that he can take possession of the empty houses, but also she convinces him that a kingdom without people is no kingdom at all. The play ends with him promising to reform his ways and with everyone returning to their homes. In *Mais al-Rim* (*Mays al-Rīm*, name of village, 1975 Piccadilly and Damascus), Fairouz's character single-handedly, if reluctantly, resolves a town's major feud. In a nice reversal of the first "urban" Rahbani play *Hala and the King* in which Hala moves reluctantly, from village to city, Zayyūn of *Mais al-Rim* is begrudgingly on her way from her home in the city to a wedding in her ancestral village. As 'Āmil discusses, all of these works constitute examples of individual, not popular heroics. In all of them, there is no need for popular struggle as the role of the people is reduced to waiting for a savior to appear – literally and figuratively – from the sky ('Āmil 1969). An exception to the above is *Loulou*, adapted from the play *The Visit of the Old Lady* (*Der Besuch der alten Dame*, 1956) by the Swiss writer Friedrich Dürrenmatt (Shāwūl 1988: 259). Most of the play's narrative space is taken up with Loulou seeking revenge for fifteen years of wrongful imprisonment. Abū Murād argues that viewers were made uncomfortable by this new type of character for Fairouz, which may explain why in their next play *Mais al-Rim* (their last before the start of the civil war and their penultimate theatrical effort starring Fairouz), the character played by Fairouz returns to the village.

Many of these post-1967 plays also share with their predecessors examined in Conclusion a simplistic and beatific presentation of the conflict between good and evil. In the case of these later plays, however, since the tension is more often than not between an oppressive ruler and his oppressed subjects, these rulers are, we often discover by play's end, not so bad after all. The authority figure in *Person*, for example, has no idea about the corruption and oppression of his government. The same is true for the overthrown leader of *Live*. In *Guardian*, the king who has killed many of his own subjects is forgiven at play's end because he sheds tears. Ziad Rahbani and others have read something "religious" in the absence of "an eye for an eye, a tooth for a tooth" type justice in such plays (Bāshā 1995: 140 and 1987b: 43). Unsī al-Hājj has observed that the Rahbani project has not just been consistently about the triumph of good over evil, but rather about the triumph of good over evil with the additional element of forgive-ness (al-Hājj, U. 1987: vol. three, 1008). There is nothing inherently wrong, of course, in promoting one's vision of the importance of forgiveness in one's art, but it should be pointed out that there is a difference between the Fairouz character forgiving a scruffy bandit such as Hawlū in *Night* and her forgiving the oppressive king in *Guardian*. This sympathetic presentation of rulers could obviously be read as the theatrical exoneration of the leaders of Lebanon and the other countries in which the Rahbani Brothers performed. The Rahbani Brothers claimed to have learned from the poet Said Akl never to praise rulers but rather whole peoples (Abī Samrā 1992b: 14 and 1993: 63). While plays like *Guardian*, *Person*, and *Live* cannot be categorized as violating this principle, if they do castigate their fictitious rulers, they do so very gently.

The 1973 play *The Station* is typical of the persistence of the post-1967 Rahbani Brothers theater in relying on divine and semi-divine intervention over direct action, and of evil miraculously turning into good. The play tells the story of Warda (Fairouz) who proclaims that what appears to everyone else to be a potato field is actually a train station. Because of her unflagging faith in her vision, people begin buying tickets from an opportunist who has appeared to take advantage of this delusion. The play ends with the sound of a train approaching the "station." Not only does the arrival of the train turn the thief into a legitimate businessman (throughout the play Warda had refused to call him a thief as he called himself and insisted on calling him a "ticket seller"), it also rewards the faith and patience of the people. As Asi himself penned in the epigram preceding the play's script: "Waiting created the station and the desire to travel brought the train" (in Rahbani, A. and M. 2003e: 13). Traboulsi, an otherwise keen observer of the Lebanese cultural scene, misreads this play when he says that it announces the "end of the Lebanese miracle" ("Mā huwa 'al-shay' al-fāshil'," n.d.: n.p.) when in fact the inexplicable transformation of the potato field resembles very much the discourse surrounding the miracle of Lebanon outlined by him in another context (Traboulsi 1999: 227–33). The Rahbani Brothers won the "Said Akl Prize" for *The Station* (Traboulsi 1997: 45). It is fitting that this miracle-affirming play would win the literary award named after and inspired by one of Lebanon's biggest believers in miracles.[3] The point that I am trying to make is that despite the *naksa* of 1967 and the increasing domestic tensions within Lebanon as reflected, for example, in the student demonstrations and labor strikes of that period, the Rahbanis' version of the Lebanese miracle remained alive and well.

On the level of the personal, however, this was not the case, for soon after the script for this play was written, Asi suffered a stroke. He joined Fairouz, who was suffering from exhaustion, in the hospital. This event would be the initial external sign of distress in the Asi-Mansour-Fairouz trinity. Though Asi would partially recover and though Mansour would continue to sign his musical-theatrical works – even after the separation of Asi and Fairouz in 1977 and even after the death of Asi in 1986 – "The Rahbani Brothers," *Station* can be considered the final Rahbani Brothers' work. For a time, however, it looked like the trinity would be re-formed with the substitution of Fairouz and Asi's artistically precocious son Ziad for his ailing father. In fact, though *Station*'s script was written before Asi's medical demise, the music for the play had not been completely composed when opening day at the Piccadilly was approaching. Mansour asked for help from various family members as a show of support and appreciation for Asi. Ziad offered a piece of music he had previously composed, and to it Mansour wrote the song "People Asked Me" ("Sa'alūnī al-nās") (Zoghaib 1993: part eight, 69).

Another indication of the likelihood that Ziad would step in for Asi was the authorship of his own Rahbani-esque musical play that year: *An Evening's Celebration*. In a number of interviews Ziad has talked disparagingly about this work (Bāshā and Dāwūd 1983; "Hiwār al-'umr" 1997 and Murūwa 1998). Others too have written about the similarity between it and some of the Rahbanis' early works (e.g. al-Hājj, U. 1987: vol. 3, 972–3). The work was originally conceived, in fact, as a tribute to the Rahbani Brothers and Fairouz. Every year at the cultural club of Baqnāyā – a village near the Rahbani's hometown of Antilyas – young club members would stage one of the Rahbani Brothers' musical plays. In the summer of 1973 those in charge of the club asked Ziad, then just 17-years-old, to direct that year's production with the caveat that he compose his own music and songs for it. The result was *Celebration*, which Ziad himself describes not so much as a play but as a series of songs connected by a simple story (Bāshā and Dāwūd 1983: 10 and Shāmil 1981: 32). The simple plot goes as follows: the local village café, owned by the best singer in town, advertises a talent competition to look for a new singer to help him carry the entertainment burden of the establishment. All of the competitors are appallingly but comically bad, except for one young man. The owner of the café quickly realizes that were this man to perform, he would eclipse his own preeminence and so has him rudely evicted. The café owner's daughter, who has fallen in love with the young man, eventually convinces her father to welcome the young singer back to the café to perform. Similar to many Rahbani Brothers' productions, the plot's conflict is solved by love, and the play ends in a celebratory song. Ziad relates that one of the performances of his play was attended by one of the producers of his parents' work, Khālid al-'Itānī, who recommended moving it to Beirut. Its debut was postponed for two months due to the 1973 Israeli-Egyptian war, but it eventually moved to the capital and played to progressively larger crowds (Bāshā and Dāwūd 1983: 10). In addition to writing the script and the music for this play, Ziad also had a small comic role in it as the town drunkard. This character, along with the ineffectual beat policeman – *al-shāwīsh* – are common characters in the Rahbani Brothers' plays. Acting in bit parts had been, in fact, Ziad's entrée into the theatrical world of the Rahbanis. In terms of his continuing participation in the Rahbani project musically, after helping out with *Station* and *Loulou* (Shāmil 1981: 32), Ziad was asked to write the musical introduction to the Rahbani Brothers' 1975 *Mais al-Rim* (Murūwa 1998: 307). Prior to this, however, Ziad would stage his second musical-theatrical production: *Happiness Hotel*. This play was the first artistic indication that the replacement of Asi by Ziad was not going to happen as some had hoped and imagined.

Happiness Hotel: prognostication or proclamation?

At first view, the 1974 *Hotel* might not seem so different from *Celebration* or from the Rahbani Brothers' later urban works. Like *Celebration*, it was written (music and script), directed, and acted in by Ziad. It also contains a high song to dialogue ratio. Like his first play, some of its main characters are musicians who seem ready to burst into a song at the slightest provocation. Finally, most of the singing in both plays is done by Joseph Saqr (Jūzīf Saqr), a singer and actor whom viewers of Ziad's early plays would have recognized from his roles in some of the Rahbani Brothers' works. Just two years before, in fact, Saqr played one of the main roles in *Guardian*. And in the same year as *Hotel*, he would also appear in the

Rahbanis' *Loulou*. A year later he would have another substantial role in the Rahbanis' *Mais al-Rim*. He also had a small role in the 1970 *Live Live*. And though *Hotel*'s plot is a seemingly radical departure from the singing competition of *Celebration*, its strikes and revolution would not have been out of place in some of the post-1967 Rahbani musicals such as *Wake Up* and *Mountains*.

Hotel tells the story of a day in the life of an urban budget hotel. The play opens with two musicians – Barakāt and Qaysar – practicing their nightclub numbers only to be informed by a telephone call that the cabaret is closed due to the current strikes and demonstrations.[4] Their disappointment about missing another day's pay is tempered by an announcement from the widowed wife of the original hotel owner that there will be an engagement party for her daughter Sawsan that night, and that she would like them to perform at it. In the following scenes we meet the play's other characters: the hotel clerk, Tīnū; a long-winded leftist intellectual, Ra'ūf, who is ever prepared to extemporaneously pontificate; Sa'd and Adīb, two older and long-time guests; Karnīk, an Armenian-Lebanese photojournalist; a wandering haberdasher named 'Abd al-Karīm; an unemployed inveterate gambler named Zakariyyā who has been evicted by his wife after their most recent argument; and Tahayyāt, a belly dancer. Ziad plays the part of Zakariyyā, a much larger role than that of the drunkard in *Celebration*. For example, Zakariyyā's comic and confused entrance into the hotel occupies approximately 10 of the play's 83 pages (Rahbani, Z. 1994c: 19–29) and 15 of the recorded version's 137 minutes (Rahbani, Z. 1993b: disc one: 19:02–35:45). The comical first act, with only a hint of the social and political tensions in the background, ends with a string of raucous songs sung by Joseph Saqr that would very quickly become extremely popular in Lebanon, songs like: "Hotel of Happiness" ("Nazl al-surūr"), "I Sent You" ("Ba'at lak"), and "Everything's Alright" ("Māshī al-hāl") (Bāshā and Dāwūd 1983: 10).

In the play's second act we enter the realm of the political, albeit comically, when two recently fired factory workers – 'Abbās and Fahd – storm the hotel proclaiming the start of a revolution. The occupants of the hotel have the rest of the night to decide if they will join the movement or be killed. For the recalcitrant, these executions would take place in a specific order, depending on each person's relative use or harm to society. The two musicians are placed at the top of the list because they are "the opiate of society" (Rahbani, Z. 1994c: 38). In fact, these two are so dangerous to the revolution that, unlike the rest of the guests, they are not given all night to decide their fates. Either they compose a revolutionary anthem in a few hours or be killed. Their colleague, the dancer, is next on the list: "There is no time for dance," says one of the revolutionaries (Rahbani, Z. 1994c: 40). Then comes the intellectual, because, says 'Abbās, "all you do is talk, and I don't like talk" (Rahbani, Z. 1994c: 40). Once this list is complete and the hotel wired to blow up should anyone try to escape, the two revolutionaries rest for a few hours while the hotel guests stay up pondering on their fates.

At 3:30 in the morning, the specified deadline for completing the revolutionary anthem, 'Abbās and Fahd descend to hear what has been written. When

100

the musicians cannot even remember their own national anthem, the situation looks bleak. It is at this moment that the hotel clerk, Tīnū, asks to speak to 'Abbās in private. He convinces 'Abbās that the hotel owner's daughter, Sawsan, has fallen in love with him. Have you not always dreamed of marrying a rich girl? he asks him. If you marry her, he continues, you will have some stability in your life and a place from which to base your revolution:

> Marry, establish a home and settle down... and later if one night while you are sitting in front of the television and you begin thinking about your people... get up... and then start planning your revolution.... At that time the revolution will be more mature... and maybe it will last longer than a day, and at least you'll have a place to convene your revolutionary council.
>
> (Rahbani, Z. 1994c: 73)

After further cajoling, 'Abbās finally agrees. Sawsan is then persuaded that she merely needs to go along with this "marriage" for several days, after which time she can return to her fiancée. The next scene begins with the wedding between 'Abbās and Sawsan, which is accompanied by another lively song: "Even the Metal Felt Badly for Him, but You Did Not" ("Hann al-hadīd 'alā hālu, wa-inta mā hannayt"). Up to this point, I would argue, the content and form of this work would not have contradicted the expectation that Ziad would replace Asi in the Rahbani Brothers-Fairouz trinity. After the wedding song, however, Ra'ūf the revolutionary intellectual gives a speech which, by its end, places a large question mark over the position of Ziad vis-à-vis his parents' project.

While *Celebration* and to this point *Hotel* are reminiscent of the Rahbani Brothers' theatrical oeuvre, it is at *Hotel*'s wedding that we sense a real shift. This coincides with an oblique reference to the Rahbani Brothers' 1960 play *Holiday of Glory*. That play ends, as I discussed in Chapter 2, with a famous piece of advice from a wise old man to a newly wed bride: "Raise your children happily and with love and, after God, have them worship Lebanon" (Rahbani, A. and M. 1960: 55). The wedding of *Hotel* also ends with a piece of advice, and though it too involves children, it, and its deliverer are quite different: "Produce a revolutionary multitude of children. Produce a proud generation that does not yield to anyone. Secure the bloody future for your children and give them free rein. Your children are not for you, they are life's children" (Rahbani, Z. 1994c: 75). Offspring that were once squarely the province of the parents are now the children "of life." Children that were once to be worshipping God and Lebanon are now supposed to rising up against them. A few scenes later, the play ends with Sawsan escaping from 'Abbās and fleeing back to the hotel in search of her fiancée. A wrathful 'Abbās follows in hot pursuit. All escape the hotel except for a sleeping Zakariyyā and the dancer Tahayyāt. Zakariyyā wakes up to find that Tahayyāt has been seduced and 'Abbās and that the revolution has, once again, been cancelled. He is disappointed by this turn of events and asks 'Abbās's accomplice Fahd to give him a machine gun to pass on to his children: "Do you know what my children would do if they got hold of a machine gun? You don't know my children" (Rahbani, Z. 1994c: 83). In the meantime Fahd has exited without Zakariyyā noticing him. The play ends with the sound of an explosion and Zakariyyā calling out for Fahd, who has apparently blown himself up.

Hotel has been read as a prognostication of the 1975 civil war (Amīn 1997). Ziad himself has rejected this view (Murūwa 1998: 321), mentioning that it was actually based on a real incident, the taking of hostages inside the Beirut office of the Bank of America (Sa'īd, Kh. 1998b: 656–7).[5] In my view it is more manifesto than prophecy. And while on one level it may be a manifesto for a certain kind of revolution (Amīn 1997), one that should come in the future (al-Mukhkh 1983) and be better prepared for than were the efforts of 'Abbās and Fahd ('Abd Allāh 1977), it is also a statement on the relationship of the author to his parents' artistic project. This aspect of it can be most clearly seen in the scene following the wedding.

Between the wedding of 'Abbās and Sawsan and the end of the play as described above, life in the hotel is back to normal; it is back, in other words, to where it started: with the musicians Barakāt and Qaysar lounging around the hotel chatting. The scene just after the wedding opens with Barakāt telling anyone who will listen how "this government" came to "the plain" and told them that they could no longer grow marijuana. He goes on to say that they depended on this crop and that when they tried to negotiate with the authorities, they got nowhere. "In the end," he tells his audience at the hotel, "We grew corn." "Come harvest," he continues, "by the time we got to the end of the first row we were dizzy." When asked why, he explains: "If you sniff an ear you'll be stoned for three days, what are you talking about. This is a people who love corn, and a land that gives nothing but corn" (Rahbani, Z. 1994c: 77). As if to erase any doubt that what he means to say is that they ignored the government prohibition and continued to plant marijuana, he says, "Take Zakariyyā, for instance. He ate an ear last night and he's still sleeping. Just try to wake him up." Then Qaysar says, "This corn has become part of our heritage" (Rahbani, Z. 1994c: 75). Ziad, through Qaysar, is making a direct correlation between the effects of marijuana and the effects of "heritage." The word in Arabic – *turāth* – can mean many different things. What kind of "heritage" is Ziad referring to here? Let us follow Qaysar and Barakāt's conversation

Barakāt: "God bless our heritage, our heritage is vast, man. What are you talking about: the water spring, the singing bird, the chirping sparrow."
Qaysar: "And don't forget the vines of lily."
Barakāt: " 'God bless the vines of lily'... and 'But Oh! Abū al-Zuluf'[6]...and 'from the window of the shack...' "
Qaysar: "Yes, yes!"
Barakāt: " '...he sent you'."
Qaysar: "Our own music is full of herds of goats, of broken water jugs.... 'Oh spring'..."

Barakāt: " 'Oh spring'... What does he say to her? 'Meet me at the spring...'
and he's thinking that it will be quiet at the spring... quite a romankit
(*rūmānkītī*) [sic] scene at the spring. With all of the people meeting at
the spring... it's become like a public gathering at the spring."

Qaysar: "What a heritage! Wow!"

Barakāt: "They'll be exploring Mars and we'll still be trying to figure out who
wrote the Dal'ūna[7]... the Dal'ūna... Dal'ūna... We've really developed
the Dal'ūna... I heard someone play the Dal'ūna on the saxophone."

(Rahbani, Z. 1994c: 77–8)

While Ziad is not commenting solely on his parents' oeuvre here, their music and
theater is replete with this kind of language and content.

I have done a survey of 353 songs produced by the Rahbani Brothers for their
plays, concerts and records.[8] A glance at some of the results confirms that their
theater and song contain many instances of the very mind-numbing "heritage"
mentioned above, heritage that resulted in Qaysar and Barakāt being put at the top
of the list of those expendable or dangerous to the revolution. While there are only
two instances of "singing" birds and none of "chirping" sparrows in the Rahbani
songs that I surveyed, there is an abundance of reference to birds and flight.
Words with the root for "flight" and "bird" in them (tā', yā', rā') appear in ninety-
one different songs. In addition to those references, sparrows are mentioned
specifically in 29 songs, nightingales in 17 and doves in 7. And while "vines of
lily" is not so common, "lily" itself is mentioned in nineteen songs. The phrase
"vines of the lily" does occur, however, in at least one song sung by Fairouz:
"Return Me to My Country" ("Ruddnī ilā bilādī"). The last line of the song goes:
"I am vines of Lily. Break me over the soil of my country" (Rahbani, A. and M.
1992a: track eight). Said Akl wrote the lyrics to this song. The generic word for
"flower" (*zahra*), however, is much more frequent: it is mentioned in 84 songs.
The word for "rose" appears in no less than 70 songs. "Springs" are mentioned
in 24 songs, a few of them including actual assignations. The meeting of lovers
at springs is mentioned in the following songs: "Open the Water" ("Dīrū
al-mayy"), "Oh Moon, You and I" ("Yā qamar anā wa-īyyāk"), and "The Sparrow
Flew in Circles" ("Dār al-dūrī 'alā al-dāyir"). One song mentions the expected
quiet of the spring made fun of above: the song "The Sparrow Flies Around"
("Yadūr al-dūrī"). Springs also play a central role in the Rahbani plays. Water is
sometimes a source of tension in these works. In *The Moon's Bridge*, as I have
shown above, water is the source of conflict between the two villages. In *The Ring
Seller*, the spring is the setting for a playful water fight (Rahbani, A. and M.
2003a: 41–2). More often than not the spring is a place of so many assignations
that Barakāt is wise to wonder how lovers could actually expect any privacy there.
As Abū Murād says

As for other village subjects like the oil press and the flour mill, they
appear in many places, but the spring is a basic focal point: the spring in

the village is the meeting place of lovers, the destination of the thirsty, the resting place of hunters and the goal of picnickers, and these are many in the world of the Rahbanis. How many girls carry their pitchers to fill them at the spring and how many lovers meet their beloveds near the spring? The water spring is actually one of the basic symbols of the village so how could the theater of the Rahbanis not be filled with this symbol?

(Abū Murād 1990: 83)

A good example is the Rahbanis' *Holiday of Glory*. One scene opens with all of the girls of the village fetching water at dawn. No sooner do all of the other girls leave Najlā there by herself than Shāhīn arrives at the spring where they flirt innocently and begin to fall in love (Rahbani, A. and M. 1960: 18–19).

That the numbing effects of Rahbani-esque "folklore" in *Hotel* is commented on in the context of the failure of the government to prevent the growing of marijuana is significant when it is remembered that the Rahbani Brothers' project can be seen to have participated theatrically in the state-building goals of Chehabism. The mountain Christian village vision of Lebanon that infuses the theater of the Rahbani Brothers – as well as the songs discussed above – has to be seen in light of the attempts following the domestic violence of 1958 to turn Greater Lebanon into a cohesive nation and state. The fact that in *Hotel* "that government" is still unable to extend its reach effectively into the margins of the country is significant. When Barakāt talks about the government going up to the plain (*al-sahl*), he is referring to the area around Baalbeck, famous not just for its annual cultural festival but for its growing of marijuana (Yabroudi 1999: 282–3). So, despite their own theatrical efforts along with the Chehabist political projects, Baalbeck – the very epicenter of their Lebanon-uniting theater – remained at least partially outside the reach of "this government." In the Lebanon of *Hotel*, in fact, it is not just the margins that elude state control and unification, but the very seat of government, for though it is not mentioned specifically, it is clear that we are to understand the events of the play to be taking place in Beirut, a Beirut of wide-spread strikes (Rahbani, Z. 1994c: 8) and demonstrations (Rahbani, Z. 1994c: 11). It is also a city of intermittent water service (Rahbani, Z. 1994c: 12). In the play, the only regular source of water is that used by the police against the demonstrators. A nephew of the Armenian photographer, in fact, takes a bar of soap with him to demonstrations, as it is his only guarantee of a regular bath (Rahbani, Z. 1994c: 12). It is also a city of factory workers' daughters washing car windows at busy intersections for a few pennies (Rahbani, Z. 1994c: 34); and, most centrally, of a city on the verge of revolution.

The end of the play, announcing as it does a coup from within the theatrical version of the Rahbani's Lebanon, then, makes one rethink the play in its entirety. While it remains a comedy, its color quickly approaches the dark end of that genre's spectrum. And with the suicide of Fahd in the last seconds, it becomes positively black. Also toward the end of the play is a very dark twisting of the thought of Kahlil Gibran. It is pointed out to Ra'ūf that the "Your children are not your children" section of his wedding speech is a borrowing from Gibran. This sentence is adapted from the section of the bestselling *The Prophet* on children, which ends with Gibran comparing children to arrows being shot by God. God's bow is the parents. At the end of *Hotel*, however, it is the children themselves who are on the verge of getting hold of the weapon (updated to a machine gun) and of shooting it without the assistance of God. What they will shoot remains to be seen.

Hotel, as much as it is a declaration of war on their Lebanon, is also an expression of that ambivalence. Yes, Ziad does very significantly twist his parents' wedding advice and mock their facile use of folklore, and yes he does take children out of Gibran's parental bow. Let us not forget, however, the context of *Hotel's* wedding advice. In *Holiday*, it was a wise elder who advises the young bride. In *Hotel*, in contrast, it is a windbag of an armchair revolutionary whom Tahayyāt the dancer upbraids for being "all talk" who gives the advice. After scolding the other men as a group for their inability to act in the face of danger, she comes down particularly hard on Ra'ūf, telling him that the revolutionaries should have shot him straightaway, adding

> You pretend to be a big revolutionary, may God destroy your house, but no revolution or anything else has ever come out of you. Your whole life has been a waste... (yelling). You've written millions of pages, and what has changed in the world? Nothing.
>
> (Rahbani, Z. 1994c: 58–9)

Ra'ūf's empty pontification, in fact, is connected to a kind of music denigrated by Ziad at least as much as the "folk music" of his parents: namely, the type of music which induces the state of musical ecstasy called *tarab*. At the end of the wedding speech in which Gibran is invoked, the lute player Barakāt cries out "Ahh Mr Ra'ūf Ahh," similar to the response he has in the first line of the play when Qaysar strums a few bars on the lute and performs the typical introduction to the Egyptian "Layālī"[9] song: "Oh night. Oh, night. O night." To Barakāt's response ("Allāh, Allāh, Allāh, Allāh") the stage directions add: "He shouts as the *tarab* takes him away" (Rahbani, Z. 1994c: 7). Barakāt's similar reaction to the wedding speech, then, is meant to help us pass negative judgment on Ra'ūf and what he says. At least equally important is the fact that this wedding, again in juxtaposition to the wedding of *Holiday*, is a ruse.

Also exemplifying the ambivalence of Ziad's relationship to his parents' project is the form of the very "your children are not your children" sentence itself. As it turns out, Ziad is not actually quoting Gibran here, but rather quoting *his parents* quoting Gibran. *The Prophet* was first published in 1923. In its "original" English, the line in question reads: "Your children are not your children. They are the sons and daughters of Life's longing for itself" (Gibran 1923: 15). There are indications not only that *The Prophet* was a book that took many years to write, but also that at least an initial draft may have been written in Arabic during

Gibran's childhood (Waterfield: 254–5). In any case, Gibran's biographer and Lebanese-migrant colleague in New York Mikhail Naima (Mīkhā'īl Nu'ayma) subsequently translated the English version of the work into Arabic. He renders the line: "Inna awlādakum laysū bi-awlādikum. Innahum abnā'u ashwāqi al-hayāti wa-banātuhā" (Your children are not your children. They are the sons and daughters of the longings of life) (Naima 1974: 27). In 1972, the Rahbani Brothers staged the musical-theatrical work *Paper People*. Just before intermission, there is a song which is a synopsis of *The Prophet* and in which we find the line exactly as it comes in *Hotel*, which was performed a mere two years after the staging of the *Paper People*. It is rendered in both works as follows: "Awlādukum laysū lakum, awlādukum abnā'u al-hayāt" (Your children are not yours. Your children are the sons of life) (Rahbani, A. and M. 1975: 8 and Rahbani, Z. 1994c: 75). In Ra'ūf's wedding speech, then, Ziad is double-quoting his parents. While on the one hand he reformulates their vision of the role of children in *their* Lebanon, as expressed in *Holiday*, he is also directly quoting their reformulation of Gibran in a later play, *Paper People*.

There is another bit of selective translation of Gibran in the Rahbani's *Paper People*. The section of *The Prophet* on children is approximately sixteen-lines long in the Arabic version. The Rahbanis chose three of these lines for their song, two of which I have already discussed above. The other line that they include is the one that is rendered by Naima as something like: "You can erect homes for your children's bodies, but not for their souls" (*wa-tastatī 'ūn an tuqīmū al-masākina li-abdānihim wa-lā li-arwāhihim*) (Naima 1974: 27). The Rahbanis' add this directly to their first sentence to make their citation read: "Your children are not for you; they are the sons of life, and life does not live in the family's house" (Rahbani, A. and M. 1975: 8). Whereas Gibran does not seem to be suggesting that children not physically live with their parents, the Rahbanis' version can be read this way. It is perhaps then no coincidence that around this time Ziad literally did move out of the family house (Baydūn, 'Abbās 1996: part two, 53), an act that demonstrates that his artistic break from them was not without some form of personal rupture as well. And like the ambivalence of his artistic relationship with them, this physical break from the family home was not absolute. In describing his departure, Ziad says that he used "to come and go like Christopher," (Baydūn, 'Abbās 1996: part two, 51), referring to the US Secretary of State Warren Christopher's shuttle diplomacy in the region during the first Bill Clinton presidency.

By figuratively quoting the famous advice scene of *Holiday* and by having Zakariyyā suggest, at the end of a play which can be read as portraying the very antithesis of the Rahbanis' Lebanon, that the true path to revolution is to put the weapons in the hands of his children, Ziad is announcing a radical break from the artistic project on which he was raised, a project which, for a short time, it looked like he might help salvage after the decline of one of its pillars. By quoting his parents quoting Gibran, however, and by having the sentence uttered by arguably the play's least reliable speaker, Ziad also seems to be signaling an ambivalence that would be almost as consistent as the rebelling. Ziad may not be predicting the end of Lebanon in this play, as has been argued. If he is predicting the end of anything, it is the Lebanon of the Rahbanis and Fairouz. Or rather, he is announcing what would take less keen observers another year – in other words, the start of the civil war – to figure out: that the Lebanon of the Rahbani Brothers and Fairouz *never* existed.

Petra: civil war and the theater of the Rahbani Brothers

The Lebanese civil war erupted in the spring of 1975. Much has been written about its complex causes. When the fighting stopped after an Arab-league sponsored summit meeting in October of 1976, most thought that was the end of it, especially if history was to be trusted as a guide. Robert Fisk writes of the surprise of people each time the fighting reignited: "For we had been fooled, even the Lebanese themselves. We believe in the idea of national catastrophe, of national renewal, of political renaissance. We thought that an identity existed beyond the civil conflict" (Fisk 1992: 52). It did not take long for Lebanese artists to respond to the violence, and, as in the case of the *naksa* of 1967, theater responded as quickly as any other art form. No one, perhaps, was as impacted by the war as much as the Rahbani Brothers (Kāmil, S. 1983b: 68).

Their theatrical response to the war was the 1977 historical epic *Petra* that premiered, fittingly, in Jordan. In Chapter 2, I discussed the paradox of how the Rahbanis' theater and musical theater could be both so Mt-Lebanon–specific and at the same time speak to so many different nationalisms. This happened, I explained, partly because their works necessarily became less time and place specific over the years. In a related phenomenon, at the start of the civil war, some of the Rahbani Brothers' songs – such as "I love you Lebanon" ("Ba-hibbak yā Lubnān") – and plays – such as *The Woman from Baalbeck* (*al-Ba'labakkiyya*, 1961), *The Days of Fakhr al-Din*, and *Granite Mountains* – quickly came to be used as anthems by multiple sides in the conflict (Bītār 1978; Nasr Allāh, R. 1986; and Traboulsi 1998). *Petra* has been characterized as a response to this misuse of their work (Abī Samrā 1978). It was an effort, in other words, at clarity.

The play, loosely based on historical events, tells of the tiny city-state of Petra standing up to and ultimately defeating Roman aggression. While the king of Petra is off fighting these campaigns, the queen (Fairouz) is at home attempting to keep things in order on the domestic front in the face of plots and conspiracies. At one point Roman spies kidnap her daughter (named Petra after the city). The queen is informed that in order to save her daughter she must convince her husband to give up the resistance. She refuses even to inform him of the kidnappings. The war against Roman tyranny is won, but the daughter is sacrificed along the way. If this play is a reversal from the later Rahbani musical-theatrical works discussed above in respect to symbolic clarity, it can also be read as a shift in the meaning of the same symbols used in the earlier less ambiguous works. In many of the earlier plays, tension exists between two villages, or between a village and a real or imagined local "stranger" or "Other" who, in the end, was more a force of unity than of disunity. In this play, the cause of tension, even more so than in *Fakhr al-Din*, is a wholly "external" Other. Additionally, "The Other" in this work – in contrast to "Others" like Murahhij and Hawlū – is portrayed as being wholly merciless and evil. As the king tells his people before heading off for battle: "Rome is coming to make you submit, coming for plunder, to take your women as prisoners and to enslave your children" (Rahbani, A. and M. 1977: 12). And while this external Other's challenge will ultimately result in unity through resistance on the home front, it comes at great cost. The ending of *Petra* is similar to that of *Granite Mountains*, the Rahbanis' response to the *naksa*. In that play the price of freedom is the life of the ethereal character Ghurba, who is played by Fairouz. There are, however, a few important differences. That play was the story of conflict between two villages, not two separate states or even "civilizations." Also, that play ends with the brutal Fātik repenting and learning the evil of his ways. In other words, Ghurba's sacrifice in that play makes him give up his imperial designs. In this play, the queen decides to sacrifice her daughter to ensure a victory that has already been won. This play, then, is extremely clear that the causes of the civil war were wholly external to Lebanon. This necessitates a reversal of the some of the inward-looking criticism that was characteristic of other post-1967 Rahbani works. *Live Live*, for example, contains criticism of Lebanon's internal security apparatus "the Second Bureau." Conversely, in *Petra*, when a foreigner observes that each of Petra's citizens is, in a sense, an informant, a native replies: "Isn't that better than to have what happened to other [countries] happen to us?" (Rahbani, A. and M. 1977: 48). In *Petra*, it is not the "us-versus-them" dichotomy that is new, but rather the clear delineation of the two sides. Any fuzziness of us-Other boundaries from the earlier works has evaporated.

How can we be sure that the beleaguered Petra of this play is supposed to represent Lebanon of the civil war? The work was, after all, written for Jordan and based, however loosely, on historical fact. Actually, the Petra of their play bears an uncanny resemblance to the mountain Christian village national space depicted in their early Baalbeck Festival works. It is, for one, a space whose internal cohesion is based on love, justice, and freedom, three pillars of their theatrical oeuvre (Abū Murād 1990: 140). These three cornerstones are laid out at the very beginning of the play. Before the king departs to battle Rome, he refers to Petra as "one of the first shouts of freedoms" (Rahbani, A. and M. 1977: 12). And after turning over the affairs of Petra to his wife before departing for battle, his ministers advise her: "When you have been made ruler, rule with love. When you have been made judge, judge justly" (Rahbani, A. and M. 1977: 14). It is also perhaps the clearest theatrical expression of the intersection of their and Michel Chiha's visions for Lebanon. The Rahbani theatrical project and the Chehabist nation- and state-building project in which it participated were not free from the influences of Chiha's pre-1958 vision of Lebanon. This despite the fact that the Chehab project was in certain ways a break from the previous regime's interpretation of Chiha's vision in that it called for a certain kind of inclusiveness, equality and state building that is missing from Chihaism ("al-Shīhāwī").

Central to the vision of Chiha was the idea that Lebanon could be the Switzerland of the Middle East (Traboulsi 1999: 297–316). This desire had less to do with the two countries' similar topographical features than with their role as neutral countries that could serve as safe-havens. Chiha's concern, however, was not so much that Lebanon be a safe haven for people, but for capital. Financial secrecy laws were legislated to that end just after his death in 1956 (Traboulsi 1999: 305). Connected to this vision was the idea of Lebanon as a multi-continental crossroad of capital and goods (Traboulsi 1999: 13). The Rahbani Brothers' Petra embodies these roles. To one merchant who cannot understand why Petra would agree to safe-keep the treasures of those peoples threatened by Rome, the queen says, "All of its life the vaults of Petra have been a place for caravans and good people to safe-keep their goods. They pay friendship and get security in return" (Rahbani, A. and M. 1977: 36). This last sentence could easily be mistaken for one of Chiha's, who believed that security – specifically for foreign capital – had to be the top priority in a country without natural resources (Traboulsi 1999: 86–7). In the Rahbanis' Petra, this security pays off in a series of friendship treaties signed with neighbors after the defeat of Rome. The program for the play seems to have its Chihaism built into its very structure. In case the materialistic free-trade message of the play itself is not clear enough from the copious descriptions of the goods being stored in the vaults of the city, the full-page advertisements for dishwashers, car, trucks, five-star hotels and even an automatic *kibba* maker occupy almost literally every other page of the program, including the section that contains the play's script (Rahbani, A. and M. 1977).

This preoccupation with security is, according to Traboulsi, the "little sister" of preoccupation with conspiracy theories, which are always looking for security related causes – external ones in particular – for economic fluxes (Traboulsi 1999: 87). Thus it is natural that the Petra of the Rahbani Brothers, the very survival of which depends on its security, would be in need of clearly *external* foes. If the threat to security were internal, in other words, who would store their valuables there? It is no surprise then that the Rahbanis' Petra is so free from internal division that its vaults have no real guards to speak of. Or as one of its citizens puts it: "every citizen of Petra is a security agent" (Rahbani, A. and M. 1977: 52).

It is natural that a land without internal divisions would also be a land of "no slaves and classes" (Rahbani, A. and M. 1977: 10), as one minister describes the city-state. This represents yet another intersection between the Lebanon of this play and the Lebanon of Chiha. Chiha used a kind of circular logic to explain his belief in this idea: if there is poverty in Lebanon, it is among the peasants of the territories annexed to Lebanon proper in 1920. The original inhabitants of the mountains, he argued, were not poor. There are no poor in Lebanon, in other words, simply because there are no Lebanese poor. Put another way: if you are poor you are not Lebanese (Traboulsi 1999: 142). There are also no exploited in Lebanon, according to Chiha, because there is no industry, because the Lebanese themselves invest their money abroad. And at home the Lebanese are free and generous with their elsewhere-earned (and elsewhere exploiting?) capital (Traboulsi 1999: 145–9).

The Petra of this play is not, as the Rahbani Brothers claimed "every small city or country in the world that strives after freedom" (Harb 1978a: n.p.), but rather a combination of their nirvanic Lebanon of love, justice and freedom and the liberal service economy of Chiha's Lebanon. In *Petra*, in fact, the two collapse into one, for the internal logic of Chiha's vision for Lebanon can produce nothing but love, happiness and freedom. Any doubt as to the identity of Petra is settled when the queen welcomes her victorious husband home at the end of the play: "Oh king of the dazzling sword.... Oh king of victory and knights. I have compared you to a field of olives. I have compared you to Ajloun ['Ajlūn] and to the white snow on Mt Hermon, Oh cedar from Lebanon" (Rahbani, A. and M. 1977: 108). While the king is *like* the famous fortress of the Jordanian city Ajloun and *like* the snow of Syria's Mt Hermon, he *is* the cedar of Lebanon.

After runs in Amman and Damascus, *Petra* moved to Beirut. It overlapped with the staging of Ziad's third play, the 1978 *What Do We Need to do Tomorrow*. By this time, Ziad's physical separation from his family had become more final than the back and forth described above. In the first stage of the war, the battle lines inside Beirut were drawn between the eastern and western part of the city. The east of the city became even more predominantly Maronite Christian and the West more Muslim. The West also became a stronghold for Yasser Arafat's (Yāsir 'Arafāt) Palestinian Liberation Organization as well as a magnet for both leftist Christians and Muslims (Petran 1987). During the first few years of the war Ziad, out of his family home but still living in East Beirut, began to receive death threats. He went to his parent's house thinking that no one would attack such a symbolic place. His parents encouraged him to flee to Syria with them. The day they wanted to depart was the same day they released the nationalist song "I Love you Lebanon" ("B'ahibbak yā Lubnān," 1976) ("Hadīth ma'a Ziad Rahbani" 1993: 26). Ziad tells this story in a 1993 interview, the point of which seems to be to emphasize the widening chasm between himself and his family. He goes on to say, "I curse the day they made that song" ("Hadīth ma'a Ziad Rahbani" 1993: 26). In the song, Fairouz sings: "I want to stay with you" (Rahbani, A. and M. 1988: track one). Leaving your beloved on the day that you announce your love for him was too much for Ziad to bear. In 1993 Ziad would use the lyrics from this song in the title of his play *Regarding Honor and the Stubborn People* (*Bi-khusūs al-karāma wa-al-sha'b al-'anīd*). The title is an echo of the line from that song which reads: "Lebanon the honorable and its stubborn people" (*Lubnān al-karāma wa-al-sha'b al-'anīd*).[10] The gap between Ziad and his parents was about to grow even wider. Instead of going with them to Syria he moved to West Beirut. This is where his next play *Tomorrow*, as well as all of his subsequent plays, would be staged. This is also where he has lived since that day.

What Do We Need to Do Tomorrow and *A Long American Film*: the paradox of parody

Ziad's next play, the 1977 *What Do We Need to Do Tomorrow*, was highly successful. The play ran daily to full houses for at least six months (Shukr Allāh 1978) and apparently broke box-office records for Lebanese theater (Kāmil, S. 1986). *Tomorrow*'s songs became "... some of the most popular songs in Lebanon for the next ten years" (Manganaro 1999a: 5). The plot of *Tomorrow* is quite simple; it is, in fact, the stuff of gossip columns (Amīn 1997: 78). Zakariyyā and his wife Thurāyā, characters carried over from *Hotel*, have recently moved to Beirut from Mt Lebanon to improve their financial situation. Things do not go according to plan. At one point, an exasperated Zakariyyā says to his wife: "I brought you down [from the mountain] to work to increase our income, not our expenses. Maybe you did not understand me, maybe there was a misunderstanding" (Rahbani, Z. 1994a: 27).[11] They both work behind the bar of a café frequented by Westerners, vacationing Gulf Arabs, young Westernized Lebanese, and pretentious local intellectuals. Because of their poor finances, Thurāyā is forced to sleep with some of the foreign customers, who do not know that she and Zakariyyā are married. The shame that they both feel from this, on top of their desperate financial situation, leads to increased tension between them as the play proceeds. The action ends with Zakariyyā stabbing one of the bar's (and his wife's) customers.

One might well ask if this play had anything at all to do with the civil war? Compared to the epic scale of *Petra*, say, it seems almost frivolous. Despite appearances, however, it does not constitute neglect of the topic but rather can be seen as attempting to explain its underlying causes (Amīn 1997: 79). And, as I argued about *Hotel*, *Tomorrow* too was not just a reaction to the situation in Lebanon, but also a commentary on the Rahbani Brothers' response to it (Bītār 1978: n.p.). In short, while *Petra* was a celebration of Chihaism (al-Shamālī 1978: 10), *Tomorrow* is an indictment not only of Chihaism itself (Amīn 1997: 80), but also of the Rahbanis' employment of that ideology. No wonder that *Tomorrow* would be characterized as something of an "anti-*Petra*" (al-Shamālī 1978: 10).

In Ziad's *Hotel*, Arabic is the predominant language. Those who cannot speak it properly, such as the Lebanese Armenian who confuses his personal pronouns and the Italian who for most of the play is blissfully ignorant of the gravity of the situation, never become fully rounded characters, are never fully "humanized." In *Tomorrow* we find the opposite. Instead of a fleabag hotel, the setting for this play is an upscale bar and restaurant that caters to Beirut's international residents and tourists. In this play, those who do *not* speak a language other than Arabic are the ones who are handicapped. After the musical introduction, the curtain opens on the bar with an American song playing on the stereo. Later in the play, the bar's manager tells his staff to turn the music on: "Put on some music.... Keep the music on... (to himself) what a great thing music is (he exits while singing: 'et si tu n'existais pas')" (Rahbani, Z. 1994a: 48–9). Throughout the play the music, like the song at the beginning of the play and the song just cited, are predominantly Western.[12] In addition to the Western music at the beginning of the play, one also hears a mélange of Western languages as the customers seated around the bar chat: English, French, Italian, and Spanish. Arabic is the fifth language that the play's viewer hears. And one of the first things that we do hear in Arabic is Thurāyā translating orders for her monolingual husband Zakariyyā. Zakariyyā and others' poor linguistic skills are a source of humor in the play, such as when he tries to communicate with the customers without the help of his wife. At the end of the first scene, for example, the owner's girlfriend orders a "Dimple" (a brand of Scotch whiskey) from him. When it is slow in arriving, she asks Zakariyyā in English "Where is my Dimple?". He responds nonsensically in English: "Excuse Madame Laura because Ridā is" (Rahbani, Z. 1994a: 26). What he is trying to say is that Ridā – the waiter/busboy – has not been able to find it. Ridā's inability to read English is the cause of one of the funniest moments in the play if audience response in the recorded version is taken to be a reliable indicator (Rahbani, Z. 1995b: disc one, 8:45). When Zakariyyā asks Ridā to go and get a bottle of "Dimple" from the storeroom, Ridā is not sure how to identify it. After a few attempts to describe it to him, Zakariyyā tells him that its bottle looks like his sister-in-law. When he comes back with the wrong bottle, Zakariyyā says to him, "Like your sister-in-law, I told you, not like your uncle's wife" (Rahbani, Z. 1994a: 25).

Zakariyyā and others' linguistic limitations are not just the source of comedy, but also of tension. The reason that Thurāyā has to practice prostitution is in order to meet their soaring expenses in the city. One expense is private school tuition for their two children. When Zakariyyā asks why they cannot just send them to the government schools, Thurāyā shames him by responding

> What, do you want your children to grow-up like you, without languages. At the public schools they graduate not knowing languages. You, sir, went to public school for nine years and when you want to ask the customer if he wants ice in his drink you still say to him 'Vous voulez de la neige' [would you like some snow?].
>
> (Rahbani, Z. 1994a: 28)

This last sentence contains the crux of the foreign language issue in the play. You need to speak foreign languages to effectively serve the customers. If you cannot successfully serve the customers, you will never make it in this version of Lebanon. The manager of the bar tries to stress to his staff how important the customers' comfort is. After scolding Zakariyyā, Ridā, and Najīb (the cook) for their service shortcomings, he says

> The operation requires lightness, Ridā. It requires a smile, Najīb. It needs... it needs spirit Zakariyyā. The foreigners must feel that they are surrounded by pleasantness, by sympathy, by "chaleur," by "tendresse," by security. Each one of them must feel that he is in his own house, in his country, among his loved-ones and his friends. The more that they relax, the more they spend. The place is dependent on them. Believe me... believe me, this will benefit us all together, us and you, et c'est tout mes amis.
>
> (Rahbani, Z. 1994a: 48)

Occasionally this "foreign" language is Arabic itself, such as when we see the bar manager apply his own advice when speaking to a wealthy investor from one of the Arabian Gulf countries that the bar's owner is trying to do business with. The manager, Mr Antoine, adopts the wealthy customer's own Gulf dialect when speaking to him (Rahbani, Z. 1994a: 89). As he speaks to the investor, the stage directions say of Antoine: "He speaks in the dialect of the Arabs," meaning the dialect of those from the Arabian Gulf. Not only does Antoine use words typical of those dialects such as "zayn" (good) when speaking to the investor (Rahbani, Z. 1994a: 89), but he also adopts his interlocutor's accent, saying "ānī" for "I" instead of "anā," and pronouncing the letter $qāf$ with the hard "g" sound characteristic of the Gulf dialects (Rahbani, Z. 1995b: disc two, 29:55).

One of the customers is a local poet who spends much of his time in the bar on the phone dictating his nonsensical poetry to editors of the local papers. When he is not on the phone he is often asking some of the bar's workers to listen to his latest poems. Once when the cook Najīb asks the poet to clarify a few things for him, Usāma becomes impatient and tells him: "Sorry Najīb, perhaps this [poetry] isn't for you" (Rahbani, Z. 1994a: 105). After Najīb threatens the poet for this insult, the latter leaves the bar in a huff. There is no question but that the audience is supposed to sympathize with the cook in this instance. Like Ra'ūf in *Hotel, Tomorrow* does not portray the intellectual very sympathetically. Usāma spews such nonsense that the audience laughs at almost every word (Rahbani, Z. 1995b: disc three, 0:15–2:35). At one point, for example, he recites: "The doubts of wool assaulted me, and Haile Selassie was lying prone at the door of the storehouse..." (Rahbani, Z. 1994a: 102).[13] Like the Lebanon of Chiha, the economics of the bar depend on serving the customer well, and serving the customer well means speaking his or her language.

If you cannot speak the foreigner's language, perhaps you can entertain him with your own. Just after the manager's exhortations above, Zakariyyā's cousin enters the stage for the first time. That Rāmiz (played by Joseph Saqr), who has been contracted by the restaurant to supply it with vegetables, is down from the mountain for perhaps the first time in his life is made clear by the difficulty he has had finding the restaurant. Even before we see him we realize that he, like his cousin Zakariyyā, knows no foreign languages. Lost, he has called the restaurant for directions. After Zakariyyā tells him how to get there he asks him if he has memorized the name of the restaurant (which is "Sandy Snack"). Zakariyyā corrects his brother: "not sānghī sanāk, sāndī" (Rahbani, Z. 1994a: 45). Rāmiz may not know English, but he does know how to sing folkloric songs. Later in the play, he and the other workers are sitting around the restaurant eating. The busboy Ridā is told by the cook not to drink too much or it will make it difficult for him to follow his English lesson. Rāmiz asks him if he is studying English, and Ridā says that he does not really study, but rather listens to the English lessons on the radio from London (BBC):

Rāmiz [to Ridā]:   "Why do you study this English?"
Najīb: "Ambition."

| Ridā: | "Brother, Arabic in this place is only worth 300 lira [his very low salary]. Maybe English will raise it a bit." |
| Najīb: | "Ambition." |

(Rahbani, Z. 1994a: 72)

At the end of their meal, Rāmiz asks Najīb to bring some of the lettuce out that he just delivered to the restaurant. Najīb says that he cannot, because this lettuce now belongs to the restaurant. It turns out that the lettuce that Rāmiz just sold the restaurant for half a lira will be sold as four salads for a total of eight lira. Rāmiz goes into a *mawwāl*-type song about the tragedy of this situation. The song addresses Ridā: "Listen Ridā, everything is getting more expensive. Yesterday we were dirt poor, and now we're even poorer." The song goes on to tell Ridā: "Learn a foreign language. This Arabic won't do you any good. Turn on the BBC in the evening; Mary gives spelling and dictation lessons." And then he says in English: "Where is Mary, Ridā?" (Rahbani, Z. 1994a: 77–8). As soon as he finishes this heartfelt song about his real-life problems, one of the bar's foreign customers, a French woman named Christine, asks: "C'est quoi ce que vous chantez?" Communication does not go smoothly between her and Zakariyyā, who is acting as an intermediary for Rāmiz, but when Christine is finally made to understand that Rāmiz is from the mountain, she exclaims: "C'est beau ça. C'est fantastique. C'est bien la montagne" (Rahbani, Z. 1994a: 80). Christine asks if Rāmiz will take her with him to his mountain village. To much snickering and punning by his coworkers, he agrees. Zakariyyā tells Rāmiz that if he plays his cards right, in a few days, he will be able "to take her out." Rāmiz does not understand the urban use of this word, which literally means to "take something or someone out" (*dahhar*): "Where would I take her out?" "Out," replies Zakariyyā, who tells him conspiratorially that soon he will be able to "bring her back inside." When Rāmiz is leaving, Zakariyyā asks him where he is going. "Inside," he confusedly answers him (Rahbani, Z. 1994a: 81–2). The next time we see Rāmiz he is smitten both with Christine and Beirut: suddenly he too is considering moving to the city.

The next time that Rāmiz comes to the restaurant coincides with a meeting between the owner 'Adnān and the business man from the Gulf. Much to Zakariyyā's consternation, 'Adnān asks him to have Thurāyā belly dance for them. Rāmiz inadvertently saves Zakariyyā and Thurāyā from the degradation. Back in the kitchen he has started to sing another *mawwāl*. Zakariyyā yells at him to be quiet, but 'Adnān has another idea. He asks the manager to bring Rāmiz out. The manager replies: "But how can I, he's wearing that cap on his head [obviously referring to his woolen country cap called a *tāsa*]." But 'Adnān's girlfriend Laura has warmed to the idea and says, in English, "Oh, he's funny, bring him." The owner seconds her: "It'll be good. He'll make us laugh for a while and then entertain the customers for a bit" (Rahbani, Z. 1994a: 91–2). Rāmiz comes out and performs an *'atābā*[14] followed by another folkloric song, written by Ziad, called "To the Drone of the Bus" ("'A hadīr al-būsta").

114

If one does not speak foreign languages, then, one has to find some other way to serve the "customers." Personal initiative is, after all, the basis of the service economy. As the bar manager tells Zakariyyā when he threatens to quit if he is not given a raise:

> You should keep in mind that the salary you get is not the main thing.
> It's just a formal thing between you and us. Your main income is from
> tips from… your individual efforts, from your own spirit of initiative….
> You mean to tell me that with your salary and with tips, etc. etc., that you
> are not making thirteen or fourteen hundred lira a month?
>
> (Rahbani, Z. 1994a: 40)

The "etc." is a reference to Thurāyā's prostitution. If Rāmiz has his folklore and Thurāyā her body, what can Zakariyyā offer? If one has nothing to offer the foreigner at home, one may have to travel. It is this line of argumentation that the manager uses to try to get Zakariyyā to go and manage their new luxury restaurant in one of the Arabian Gulf states. When Zakariyyā resists the idea the manager repeats to him: "This is a country without any natural resources or agriculture" (Rahbani, Z. 1994a: 97). Zakariyyā will repeat this phrase over and over after this conversation as something of a mantra. The sentence was also, in fact, something of a mantra for Michel Chiha, which he used as his justification for a lack of industry in Lebanon and of the need for the Lebanese to migrate for work (Traboulsi 1999: 65). Interestingly enough, though a constant foe of the industrialization of Lebanon, Chiha was no friend of local agriculture either. Traboulsi points out that although Chiha originally supported agriculture when calling for the creation of Greater Lebanon (the idea being that the agriculture would help make Lebanon more agriculturally self-sufficient), he went ultimately from calling for the import of industrial products and the export of agricultural products, to supporting the import of agricultural products and the export of services (Traboulsi 1999: 71). In such an environment, it is no wonder that Rāmiz cannot make a living from agriculture and that Zakariyyā would be forced to consider working abroad, no wonder that all of the lower-level employees of the restaurant are suffering from economic and social woes.

It is also no wonder that Zakariyyā would ultimately explode in an act of violence. Though *Tomorrow* does not treat the war directly per se, it does contain much more violence than the Rahbanis' *Petra*. Though the latter is about a war between armies, all of the fighting is offstage. This is nothing new to the theater of the Rahbani Brothers. As early as their 1962 *Moon's Bridge*, violence was usually obviated by the actions, often miraculous or magical, of the character played by Fairouz. Traboulsi sees the absence of violence in *Bridge* as being equivalent to the Rahbani Brothers asking their viewers to forget and put behind them the violence of the short war of 1958 (Traboulsi 2006: 61). And even if there was violence in some of the later plays, such as the death of the Fairouz character

Ghurba in *Granite Mountains*, it takes place, significantly, offstage. Ziad's theater is different in this regard. Even his first two plays, *Celebration* and *Hotel*, contain violent confrontation, though it is almost always framed in a comedic if not outright slapstick way. The violence in *Tomorrow*, however, has a different tone, and I am not referring only to the play's bloody finale, but to smaller incidents throughout. In addition to the confrontation between the cook and the poet that I mentioned above, which results in the cook grabbing the poet's lapels as he yells at him, there is an incident where Zakariyyā is ordered by the manager to make a local drug dealer stop harassing the owner's girlfriend. The confrontation results in a bit of a scuffle between Zakariyyā, the drug dealer, and the cook, who has come out of the kitchen to defend his friend. There is one case of violence, which, though it occurs offstage and is framed comically, is rather chilling: Zakariyyā's son, it seems, maybe expelled from his school for an attack on one of his teachers in the playground. Though the war itself has no presence in this play, the ever-present tension and violence make its message difficult to miss: it is not just that the Chihaistic vision of Lebanon portrayed by the Rahbani Brothers' *Petra* will not save Lebanon from its morass, but that it actually was its cause. *Tomorrow* is a rejection of the idea that the country's troubles come from without. Not only do they come from within, they are the products of the very Chihaism that *Petra* celebrates.

While it would be hard to imagine Ziad going so far as to accuse his parents' project of participating in the precipitation of the war, it does not escape criticism for allowing itself to become a commodity of the project that did. *Tomorrow* is very explicit about the danger of the commodification of culture. The same poet Usāma who writes pretentious and incomprehensible poetry, for example, is trying to sell large numbers of poems and socks to the investor from the gulf. And though both are "counterfeit," he tells his potential patron, no one will ever know the difference between them and the originals. This is how he talks about the poems: "You could never ever distinguish them from the originals, except maybe that they are a bit short. I'm thinking of making 1500 of them Andalusian and the rest [of 4000] split in half between nationalistic and existential [poems]" (Rahbani, Z. 1994a: 115). Even Rāmiz, though not yet as savvy as the urbane Usāma, soon comes to realize that his contribution to the service economy could be through the touristic commodification of culture, in this case folklore. And is this not exactly what the Rahbani Brothers and others did? Did they not appropriate, sanitize, and commodify folklore starting with their very first performances at Baalbeck?

The first song that Rāmiz sings in the play is called "Listen Ridā." This is the title of one of the books written by Anis Frayha in the late 1950s with the goal of appropriating mountain folklore in the name of preserving it. I suggest that Frayha and the Rahbani Brothers were participating in the same project. Ziad himself has admitted that the title of this song is a direct reference to Frayha's book (Harb 1978b). What he intends by this borrowing is left open for interpretation. It might be instructive to look both at the differences between the two Ridās and what they are each supposed to "listen" to. The Ridā of the Frayha book is the son of an urbanized elite who is supposed to listen to the folkloric tales of the recently abandoned countryside and to appreciate them for their childlike simplicity (Frayha 1956: jīm, dāl, and hā'). The Ridā of the Ziad song is a young man struggling to make his way in a brutal urban environment. And the advice given to him is not to cherish his native folklore, but to learn English, or else suffer the fate of the village peasant (Rāmiz) who is just beginning to comprehend the cruel economic lessons of the modern market economy. It has been suggested that the bar in *Tomorrow* is a symbol for Lebanon (Dāwūd 1980, Fāris 1980, al-Mukhkh 1983, and Shāwūl 1989). In such a light, Rāmiz's performance at the bar can be seen as an ironic evocation of the participation of the Rahbani Brothers in the Baalbeck Festival's Lebanese Nights. It is also worth keeping in mind that Rāmiz is played by Joseph Saqr, who acted in a number of Rahbani plays.

Rāmiz, as I mentioned above, may not have to follow his own advice to Ridā to succeed in this environment. His other option is to follow the path of the Rahbani Brothers. This is what he seems to be on the way to discovering. What Ziad himself will soon discover is that parody can be a tricky thing. While he seems to want to have the songs sung by Joseph Saqr and others in this and his previous play to be parodic, he cannot control the reception of them, particularly when they are taken out of the context of the plays themselves. Perhaps it is a realization of this danger that would lead Ziad to reduce the number of songs in each of his subsequent plays. One of the points of resemblance between Ziad's first play *Celebration* and those of the Rahbani Brothers was in its use of plot merely as a string to tie a group of songs loosely together. The play *Celebration* contains twenty-one songs. It was not included in the group of four of his plays published in book form in 1994. This is undoubtedly because of the literal thinness of the script, a characteristic of the Rahbani plays on which Ziad has negatively commented (Fāris 1980: n.p.). *Hotel* had a fair number of songs too: seven. And while *Hotel* is a mere 83-pages long, *Tomorrow*'s script comprises 147 pages, and, also in contrast to the first 2 plays, contains only 3 songs. Less music and more spoken dialogue is the trend for these plays. While the Rahbanis' plays focused on the visual and the musical, for Ziad, the text is the most important element (Baydūn, 'Abbās 1993: 6 and Sa'īd, Kh. 1998b: 657). This growing textual focus comes, perhaps, even at the expense of direction. Ziad likes to say that he does not direct his plays but rather "implements" their texts ('Anīnī 1989–90). He also often stresses that he practices his theater without ever having studied any technical aspect of the medium or even having read much theater itself (Sa'īd, Kh. 1998b: 656). He admits to having read "a book or two on theater by Stanislavski" (al-Ashqar 1994: 6). In terms of theater itself, he says that he has read the "French Classics" in school as well as some plays by Bertolt Brecht later (Bāshā and Dāwūd 1983: 10).

Ziad's focus on the word as opposed to the spectacle may help to explain the great popularity that his works enjoyed both on the radio and on cassette tapes ("13 Nīsān 75" 2000, Matar 1993, Samāha 1976, and Zaytūnī 1994). This was particularly true during certain periods of the war when the staging of theater, not to mention attending it, would have been impossible. There were also certain times when Ziad felt that, even if it had been possible to stage a play, that it would have been dangerous to have a large audience together watching such potentially inflammatory material (Yamīn 1990 and al-Zayn 1980). Ziad's radio presence had such an impact that it has entered the fictional world of the Lebanese novelist Hanan al-Shaykh (Hanān al-Shaykh). Her Zahrā, the narrator of *The Story of Zahra* (*Hikāyat Zahra*, 1980), mentions how Ziad's radio programs kept her and her family laughing during the war (al-Shaykh 1998: 237). Zahra may have been referring to Ziad's plays (none of which, except for *Celebration*, were ever filmed) or to his 1976 radio show on Radio Lebanon called *We're Still Alive, Thank God* (*Ba'dnā tayyibīn, qūl Allāh*), which consisted of a series of skits done with the actor and auteur Jean Chamoun (Jān Sham'ūn). While space and the focus of this book do not allow me to explore this program in any detail, I will say that it has been characterized as one of the civil war's most important works of art (Samāha 1976: 2). It certainly seems to have had a wide following, so much so that cease-fires were called so that the daily nine p.m. episodes would not be missed (Stevens 1981: 275). This is not to say that everyone *liked* the show. In fact, right-wing factions opposed to its content attacked the premises of Radio Lebanon several times (Kāmil, S. 1986: 82). From this, one can surmise that it was this show, more than his *Hotel*, which led to the threats that forced him from East Beirut.[15]

Radio would remain an important medium for Ziad. Many Lebanese became familiar with his plays by listening to them on the radio during the long years of the war (Zaytūnī 1994: 18). Ziad even played a role in the establishment of the leftist station *The Voice of the People* (*Idhā'at sawt al-sha'b*) in 1987 ("Muqābala ma'a Ziad Rahbani" 1993a). In addition to being the subject of many interviews on this station, he also broadcast on it programs similar to *We're Still Alive*, such as the 1986 *Brains Are Just For Decoration* and a music education show *It's Only Music* (*Mannū illā al-mūsīqā*, 1990). As of the summer of 2005, *The Voice of the People* was dedicating one half-hour of every programming day to Ziad's work. In the summer of 2004 his picture was prominently displayed in the station's main studio.

Despite the increasing emphasis on text over music in his plays, *Tomorrow* does contain three songs which, as I mentioned above, would remain popular long after the play itself had ended its run (Bāshā and Dāwūd 1983: 10). This means, of course, that the songs were taken out of their very important folklore-indicting contexts and left to stand on their own.[16] We saw in Ziad's parody of *tarab* in *Hotel* that a number of the songs were written in the Egyptian dialect to signal that they were not to be received "straight." His musical project in general has, in fact, been characterized as "anti-*tarab*" (Murūwa 1998: 347). The anti-*tarab* and anti-folkloric nature of the songs in *Tomorrow*, however, is hard to detect. Part of the problem may have been the increased popularity of Joseph Saqr. It appears that through the popularity of songs like those in *Celebration* and *Hotel*, Saqr himself was coming to be regarded as a major *mutrib* (meaning "singer" or, literally, one who produces *tarab* in others). The problem of this paradox did not escape

Ziad. In 1986 he made a record called *I'm not an Infidel* (*Anā mush kāfir*) without using the voice of Joseph Saqr. Ziad explains the absence of the singer from it by saying that there is no place for *tarab* on it (S. 1986: 24). Elsewhere, Saqr is referred to as "Ziad's *mutrib*" (Wāzin 1995: 22). At the same time, he had a voice that Ziad has described as "baladī" (Wāzin 1995: 22), meaning something like "local," or, in this case, folkloric. This, even though this is the very type of song that Ziad, with the voice of Saqr, was trying to parody (Manganaro 1999a: 6). Ziad would thus often walk a thin line between parody and a kind of homage to *tarab* and folklore.

In *Tomorrow* he deals with this problem by tinkering with the genre's musical and linguistic idioms. A good example of this is the first song performed by Joseph Saqr: "Listen Ridā." That we are in the realm of folklore is made clear by the song's traditional *mawwāl* opening: "*Awf, awf, awf*" (Woe is me). The first two words after this incantation say much about the remainder of the song: "things have changed for us" (Rahbani, Z. 1994a: 77). The word "things" is literally "air" (*hawā*), one of the trademark words in the Rahbani lexicon.[17] The use of this word at the beginning of the song narrows the context from folklore to the folkloric world of the Rahbanis. At the same time, this air has been "changed." How? Does not the narrator then go on to talk about agriculture? Is this not, then, part and parcel of the Rahbani pastoral landscape? Perhaps surprisingly, it is not. Though the setting for many of the Rahbani Brothers' songs and plays is the countryside, what is depicted is almost always the countryside in a state of holiday or celebration ('Āmil 1969: 107). The absence of work in the Rahbani Brothers' plays is not unrelated to their connection to festivals. The content of these works seems to have been permanently impacted by the holiday atmosphere of the festivals at which they were performed. Kirshenblatt-Gimblett has the following to say about such a context for folkloric performance

> To know a society only in its festival mode, filtered through the touristic lens of a spectacle...[raises] another set of problems: the illusion of cultural transparency in the face of undeciphered complexity and the image of a society always on holiday. To festivalize culture is to make every day a holiday.
>
> (Kirshenblatt-Gimblett 1991:419)

Labor of any kind in their works is rare, but especially agricultural work (Abī Samrā 1978: 216). This *mawwāl* of Ziad is different. The "*awf, awf, awf*" of the beginning is not just a caricaturized rural formulaic musical beginning, but rather a true call of despair. Rāmiz, remember, is bemoaning the fact that he cannot afford to buy the very lettuce which he has grown and harvested: "Everything has changed. Everything has changed. The price of everything has gone up. The head of lettuce that I grew is no longer mine" (Rahbani, Z. 1994a: 77). It is after Rāmiz bemoans this economic injustice that he begins to advise Ridā to study English. We are suddenly not only in the context of the city, but in the world of global economics. Ziad marks this shift both linguistically and musically. After imploring Ridā to pursue his English lessons on the BBC, Rāmiz addresses him in English: "Where is Mary, Ridā" (Rahbani, Z. 1994a: 78)? This line is punctuated by a blast of horns and an end to the "eastern" rhythm of the lute (Sahhāb, S. 1986: 12).[18] The song ends on a bleak note: "Yesterday we ate and as far as I know we were full. We laid out everything that we had. We got up early and became hungry again. We must eat all over again. What a tragedy, Ridā" (Rahbani, Z. 1994a: 78–9). In the Rahbani Brothers' oeuvre, even when the topic of poverty – or very rarely hunger – is broached, its causes are not addressed. In this song – as in the play as a whole – Ziad exposes the roots of this poverty and hunger to be caused by the very touristic service economy in which the Rahbanis project so vigorously participated.

The other songs of *Tomorrow*, however, are not so clearly parodic, especially when taken out of the contexts mentioned above: "To the Drone of the Bus" is a pastoral romp, the narrator of which envies his fellow passengers riding between two Mt Lebanon villages – Himlāyā and Tannūrīn – because they have no knowledge of 'Alya's beautiful eyes. "She's Fine Without You" ('Āysha wahdā balāk) is a song urging a spurned lover to stop obsessing about his beloved because she has no interest in him. These two songs, especially when separated from their context, lose any parodic strength that they may have had. One Lebanese informant of mine, who knows the work of Ziad as well as anyone, insisted that the song "To the Drone of the Bus" occurs in the play *A Long American Film* when in fact it appears in *Tomorrow*. This is one example of how over time some of these songs lose their association with the plays for which they were originally written. Ziad seems to try harder to avoid the problem of ambiguity in his next play.

Ziad's 1980 *A Long American Film* follows the daily lives of some of the inmates of a South Beirut mental hospital during the civil war.[19] While its overall structure and theme (the inmates of a mental hospital being in certain senses saner than their doctors and nurses) may have been inspired by the 1975 film version Ken Kesey's novel, *One Flew Over the Cuckoo's Nest* (Zaytūnī 1994: 18), its context is purely Lebanese. The patients have all gone "mad" because they have not been able to cope with the horrors, contradictions, and paradoxes of the war and Lebanon's indefatigable sectarian structures. This work continues the trend of less music and more text in Ziad's plays. Of its three and one half-hour running time, there are only twelve minutes of music (Shāmil 1981: 35). It contains three songs and its text-version is 182 pages long (Rahbani, Z. 1994b), meaning that the song to dialogue ratio is much lower than in any of his previous plays. So text-centric is this work that Ziad said that it could have just as easily been written as an article (Bāshā and Dāwūd 1983). It also continues the trend of simultane-ously critiquing the Rahbanis' project (Fāris 1980: n.p.) as well as the general situation in Lebanon at the time. In addition to reducing the amount of music, Ziad also seems determined to have the songs retain their full parodic or critical strength outside the context of the plays. The beginning of the second act opens, for example, with the music from a song that is a clear parody of the long and repetitive Egyptian *tarab* songs of Oum Kalthoum. The stage directions read: "Eastern music ('This is a Long American Film') 'Oum Kalthoum-like atmosphere' " (Rahbani, Z. 1994b: 116). This musical introduction is replete with the swooning crowd noises in the background like the ones found on many recordings of Oum Kalthoum's live performances (Danielson 1997: 95–6). The soundtrack to the play contains a four-minute version of the song sung by Munā al-Mur'ashlī in clear imitation of Oum Kalthoum. The sole lyrics to the song say, in the Egyptian dialect, "This is a long American film" (Rahbani, Z. 1995d: side two, track one).[20] Another song clear in its message is "In The Time of Sectarianism" ("Fī zamān al-tā'ifiyya"). This song very sharply criticizes the country's sectarian system, which seems to affect all aspects of life except for financial transactions: "In the time of sectarianism.... Keep your hand on your identification card. Hold it as tightly as you can. Look at the lira, oh how beautiful it is, it cuts from here to there" (Rahbani, Z. 1994b: 161). At the same time, poverty cuts across sectarian lines as well. The narrator of the song addresses his fellow Lebanese in East Beirut: "What is your news? How are you doing? I'm thinking of you. We both got the same salary increase, which is sufficient for neither you nor me" (Rahbani, Z. 1994b: 161–2). Ziad then very cleverly appropriates the Phoenician discourse of Lebanon's right-wing factions, parodying their classicization of tradition and their claims to past greatness, while at the same time linking such discourse to sectarianism

> Oh inventor of the alphabet, chemistry, and physics. You who have traveled the seven seas and beat Columbus to America, who extracted the color purple, who made glass and pottery. What do you want with my family name, with letters, with the alphabet? Stay away from my name and its letters....[21]
>
> (Rahbani, Z. 1994b: 162)

The strength of the message of this song can be seen, for example, in a 1996 interview with the singer and actor Sami Hawat (Sāmī Hawwāt) on the occasion of the death of Joseph Saqr. After singing this song on the air, the interviewer says that she just wants to make clear to the listeners outside of Lebanon that this song was written during the civil war, lest they think that this is the current state of things in Lebanon. Before moving on to Ziad's fifth play *A Failure* which, not incidentally, contains no songs, I would like to digress for a few paragraphs and discuss how Ziad approaches this problem of the fine line between parody and tribute on one of his musical records, where, because of the absence of a narrative context, the danger for ambiguity is perhaps even more present than it was in the plays.

Ziad faced this parody/tribute paradox in 1995 when trying to produce a record of songs with Joseph Saqr called *Seeing As That... (Bi-mā innū...)*. He was told that in order to have it distributed, Saqr would have to sing some *'atābā*s on it (Suwayd, M. 2001: n.p.). In *Seeing as that...* the first of four *'atābā*s, " 'Atāba-1," begins conventionally enough, that is with several verses about love and longing: "Distance yourself from me as much as you like. My horses are longing that will reach you. God willing my words will find you and you will respond immediately" (Rahbani, Z. 1995a: track three). The only hint from the beginning that we are not in conventional *'atābā* mode is the sound of drums in between verses. Ziad has said that even the traditional *tabla* drum has no role in the *'atābā*. Despite this, on this record he went so far as to use timpani drums (Shams 1995: n.p.). After a few similar verses, however, we suddenly find ourselves in a very different place: "Is it reasonable, oh people, that you would remain positive when missiles are falling near me? We have asked a lot, but there is no answer except for the missile" (Rahbani, Z. 1995a: track three). Above I mentioned that an important feature of the *'atāba* is its line-ending homonyms. In this verse, the homonyms of the first three lines are "ījābī" (positive), "ijā bī" (came to me), and "ijābī" (answer).[22] The end of " 'Atāba-1" sets the tone for the remaining three *'atābās*. The next one – "files" ("milaffāt") – begins with the clearly political line: "They have seven files on me," obviously referring to some state security apparatus. One of the voices in the background asks: "Only?" The narrator goes on to wonder why they would have all of these files on him when he has not traveled and only associates with other poor people like himself (Rahbani, Z. 1995a: track six). The third *'atābā* – "Olympic" – is similarly unromantic. It is about an athlete being scolded for withdrawing from the Olympic games. Like the *mawwāl* "Listen Ridā," Ziad inserts some English into this *'atābā*. In this case it is one of the three line-ending rhyming words: "qalam bīk" (a Bic pen). The final *'atābā* – "Mai-Juillet" is introduced with the following spoken words: "Here for you is a necessary *'atābā* verse. Perhaps it [the language] is broken. I mean it has some French in it..." (Rahbani, Z. 1995a: track 13). And indeed, the first line ends with "Mai-Juillet." Then we hear a voice say, in French, "This is not how it ['May to July'] is said in French" (Rahbani, Z. 1995a: track 13). The verse is about a man who meets a woman one summer and claims, not only that he generally "behaved honorably with her," but also that there was no sexual contact with her. We can clearly hear her denial of this in the background: "I am pregnant," she says, in French (Rahbani, Z. 1995a: track 13). By the end of this record Ziad has turned the *'atābā* on its head. Not only does he use it to express social concerns and the tragedy of war, but he also scandalously exposes its latent sexual content. This – along with the insertion of English, French and the timpani drums – removes the genre completely from its pastoral folkloric setting. Without the benefit of an outside dramatic framework, we see Ziad on this record dealing with the parody/homage dilemma by clearly manipulating both the form and content of the traditional *'atābā*. For his 1983 play *A Failure*, however, Ziad had to take a completely different approach.

For his fifth play, his 1983 *A Failure*, which I will take up in the next section, Ziad did not leave the danger of musical ambiguity to chance. Though *A Failure* is a play about the making of a musical, it does not include a single complete song. Its lack of music is a reflection of the fact that it embodies Ziad's strongest reaction both to the Rahbani Brothers' project and to the general situation in Lebanon to that date.

A Failure: the power of parody

The headline to a 1983 magazine article about Ziad's new play *A Failure* punned as follows: "*A Failure* succeeds in bringing Fairouz and Asi together" ("fāshil'" 1983: 10). The article is accompanied by photos of the separated couple chatting under the glare of the press' cameras. Though they both congratulated their son at the end of the play, it is hard to imagine that the play did not make them both very uncomfortable. *Failure*, a play about the failure of a folklore-filled Rahbani-esque play to be staged, represents Ziad's clearest critique of that project to that point in time.

Above, I discussed the play *Petra*, which was the last Rahbani Brothers production starring the diva Fairouz. Soon after it ended its run in Beirut, Fairouz and Asi separated (Aliksān, J. 1987: 103). Despite this breakup and Asi's illness, there would be two more musical plays staged under the name of "the Rahbani Brothers:" *The Conspiracy Continues* (*al-Mu'āmara mustamirra*, 1980) and *The Seventh Spring* (*al-Rabī' al-sābi'*, 1981). Neither involved Fairouz. *Conspiracy* marks the first time that the Lebanese civil war was treated directly by a Rahbani Brothers work. While it is replete with soldiers and checkpoints, and contains a commitment-type anthem, the entire production is said to have an artificial and hollow feel to it (Abū Murād 1990: 189–93 and Manganaro 1999a: 5). Ziad himself critiqued the play on many fronts. First of all, he found it typical of the musical decline of the Rahbani Brothers' theater (Shāmil 1981: 34), a downturn manifesting itself in what he calls their "stealing from themselves" after the demise of Asi's health (qtd. in Bāshā 1987b: 42). Ziad admits that his 1979 *A Long American Film* was in part a reaction to their *Conspiracy*:

It is not just a reaction to their play, but to all plays written about the war or about the situation before the war that contain the message that we are all brothers and that the war was just a two-year series of skirmishes.

(Fāris 1980: n.p.)

It is his 1983 effort *A Failure*, however, which contains Ziad's most direct response to both *Conspiracy* and the Rahbani project in general (Bāshā and Dāwūd 1983: 10). This play owes its existence to the 1982 Israeli invasion of Lebanon. Prior to that event, Ziad had been putting the final touches on a play called *He Had* (*Kāna bi-hi*). After the invasion, however, and his disappointment at how little resistance there was to it ("Muqābala ma'a Ziad Rahbani" 1993b), he felt not only that it would have been technically difficult to reschedule the work, but also that the political climate was not right for it (Kāmil, S. 1983b: 68). What the times called for, it seems, was the highly critical and music-less *A Failure*, which he would stage the following year in 1983.

A Failure is about a Lebanese theater group attempting to stage a play in war-ravaged Beirut. It is, in other words, a play within a play. The inner play is a pastoral musical that looks uncannily like the early works of the Rahbani Brothers. Its events take place in a picturesque Lebanese village, complete with a waterfall, a bridge, and a village square – all recognizable elements from the Rahbani theatrical village. The harmonious existence of the village's inhabitants is disrupted when a "stranger" steals the village's shared water jug. Once the jug is restored, the youth of the village resume their joyful dancing and singing in the square. The audience of *Failure*, however, sees only bits and pieces of these events. This is because the rehearsals for the play are full of mishap and tension. Part of the problem is the war itself: supplies cannot easily be procured and various cast members cannot attend the rehearsals regularly. More detrimental to the successful performance (or even rehearsal) of the play, however, are the sectarian clashes between the members of the cast. While the dance troupe is supposed to represent ideal and harmonious village life, the performers come from different social and religious groups and can be seen bickering and backstabbing from the beginning of *Failure* to its end.

Ironically, although the inner play is a musical, *Failure* does not contain a single complete song. Above I have traced the progressive disappearance of music, particularly song, in Ziad's theater. Even *Film*, though containing only three songs, opens with an instrumental introduction. *Failure*, in contrast, opens to the sound of a hammer banging, an indication both of the lack of music and the incessant cacophony to come. The incremental elimination of songs from his plays might have been spurred by the desire to avoid ambiguity, particularly when the songs were removed from the context of the plays. What might be clearly parodic in the context of a play's events, in other words, can take on a life of its own when heard as an isolated song on the radio. Ironically, it has been suggested that the lack of music in *Failure* was the main reason for its relative failure at the box office (Bāshā and Dāwūd 1983: 10 and Kāmil, S. 1983a: 68), and for the fact that many people who did attend it left early (Kāmil, S. 1983b: 68). The play was no better received by many critics. One such critic complained that it was simplistic and full of ideology (Baydūn, 'Abbās 1983: 9). Another bemoaned its excessive cynicism (Shāhīn 1983: 24). A third found it rough, as if the whole thing was the performance of a draft of a play (Shāwūl 1989: 448–54).

What little music one does hear in *Failure* is obviously a parodic reference to the Rahbani school of Lebanese musical theater. It should be remembered that Ziad's first parodic attack on the Rahbani folkloric school came in the comparison of naïve folklore to marijuana in *Hotel*. That was an attack on its content. Then in *Tomorrow* Ziad criticized its commodification. *Failure* criticizes both. The content of Rahbani folklore is scrutinized early in the play when the audience hears part of one of the songs from the internal play – *Mountains of Glory* (*Jibāl al-majd*) – which takes place, true to the Rahbani genre, in the town square.

Accompanied by stage directions from the director Nūr, the actors sing

> We have recovered the water jug. It has been returned to its owners. The village is full of love. We are for you and you are for us. We are with you and you are with us. The village is full of love and we have opened our doors. And he who thought for a moment that he could separate us, he who was drowning us in the sea of foreignness has left for good. The village remains and he's not able to take an inch of our land. We are all brothers and we will remain brothers. We will recapture the beautiful days and our square will be re-illuminated with love and faith and we are going to rebuild Lebanon. It will be rebuilt and we will erect the buildings. We will create a new Lebanon full of songs and vineyards. Oh our country, oh our country.
>
> (Rahbani, Z. 1994d: 27–8)

Many of these words and phrases are frequently recurrent in the songs and plays of the Rahbani Brothers. The village, as I have shown, is the context for most of their works, and frequently, as mentioned above, specifically the village in a state of holiday or celebration. As is the case with this play, these festivals are often occasions to celebrate the resolution of tension and the restoration of love and faith to the village. Many of the lexical items in the above-quoted sample are predominant in the Rahbani Brothers' songs. Above, the word "illuminated" is repeated five times. Of the 353 Rahbani Brothers' songs that I surveyed, the word "light" appears in 39 songs. Building Lebanon is a theme we saw in the early plays such as *Holiday* which came, it should be remembered, on the heels of the civil violence of 1958. Also central to the early plays was the role played by "love and faith" in the resolution of tension.

Later in *Failure*, the cast attempts to rehearse a song and dance number called "The Holiday of Happiness." Again we hear about the village square, the songs and the vineyards. The girls sing of how they are waiting for the boys to appear (Rahbani, Z. 1994d: 60). "Waiting" is a consistent element of the Rahbani song. The word appears – almost always in the colloquial (e.g. *nātir*) – in 52 of the 353 songs that I surveyed. At one point, the female protagonist of *Failure* sings the first few words of a song that begins "good night" (Rahbani, Z. 1994d: 61). "Night" is perhaps the most ubiquitous word in the Rahbani musical-theatrical idiolect. It occurs in no less than 132 songs. Though Fairouz's voice has been described as being "like the morning sun" (Abī Samrā 1999: 8) and is often considered a voice to be listened to in the morning (Currey 2002 and Habib 2005: 130–2), this must be for reasons other than her subject matter. The chorus of the play within the play also sings that the village is "staying up late" (Rahbani, Z. 1994d: 66). Considering how many of the Rahbani Brothers' songs are framed by the night, the high frequency of "staying up late" in their songs should not be surprising: it appears in approximately a fifth of their songs that I surveyed.

If the naïve Rahbani-esque nature of these lines is not enough to convince the viewer/listener of their parodic intent, the hollowness of the words becomes undeniably apparent as soon as the very singers and dancers who utter them begin to bicker along religious and regional lines. Ziad, if fact, reports that he experienced this problem of sectarian tension between actors in real life during rehearsals for his 1979 *Film* (Bāshā and Dāwūd 1983: 10). Just after the troupe finishes rehearsing the above-quoted song about love and unity, a group of Christian dancers approaches the director and asks him why the play is opening in West Beirut as opposed to the mostly Christian eastern part of the city. They assure him that they do not want to be misunderstood, that their complaint has nothing to do with "sectarianism," or "Islam and Christianity" or "East versus West Beirut," but rather that it is a matter of "atmosphere," of "mental state" and of "audience." Nūr scolds them, telling them that there is now no longer such a thing as East and West in Beirut (Rahbani, Z. 1994d: 35–6). Despite such reassurances, tension builds throughout the rehearsals, reaching an apex when the dance coach Muhīb replaces the head dancer – who is Christian – with a Muslim. By this time, opening night is just hours away and the stage is on the verge of turning into a battle-field. The militia that the play's producer has sent for opening-night security has to act as a peacekeeping force between the actors themselves. In light of such turmoil, when the cast rehearses a song at the end of the play with words like "songs of love," "welcome... to our village, to our love" (Rahbani, Z. 1994d: 194), they ring so falsely as to leave Ziad's message starkly clear: the musical mountain and village love of the Rahbani Brothers' theater were not just wishful thinking, not just a "story" or being "on the verge of lying" as the village headman in *The Ring Seller* tells his niece (Rahbani, A. and M. 2003a: 27). Hours before opening night the producer of the play appears for the first time to berate Nūr for, among other things, not staying in touch with him as he had promised. The director swears to him that he has been trying to call him night and day but that he has not been able to get through: "It's unbelievable," he tells him, "it's something like a lie." The producer responds: "It's not like a lie. It's the very definition of a lie" (Rahbani, Z. 1994d: 140). This sentence, coming as it does after eight years of sporadic and brutal civil war, can be read as being directed at the Rahbani Brothers and Fairouz themselves.

While this message comes across without any ambiguity thanks in part to the absence of songs in this play, Ziad is not able to avoid the inherent trap of parody completely in *A Failure*. This can be seen in the periodic unironic applause that follows highly ironic lines in the recording of the play. Joseph Saqr, the voice of Ziad's parodic folklore in the previous plays, acts in *Failure* as an arrogant singer and actor playing the role of the village headman (*mukhtār*) in *Mountains of Glory*, the play within a play, a role that is reminiscent of that ubiquitous character in the Rahbani Brothers' musical-theatrical oeuvre. Unlike the *mukhtār* of the musical-theatrical world of the Rahbani Brothers, though, in this play Saqr does not have any songs to sing. Furthermore, unlike his characters in Ziad's earlier plays, he also has very few spoken lines. This is perhaps because Ziad feared the unironic authority that his voice had come to carry for Lebanese audiences. Such fears are perhaps confirmed when his character, rehearsing some of his lines as the village headman, delivers the following sentence after the village water-jug has been stolen: "If we unite, there is no power that can defeat us" (Rahbani, Z. 1994d: 82). This sentence, delivered in a melodramatic way that makes its irony hard to miss, is received with apparently unironic applause in the recorded version of the play (Rahbani, Z. 1993c: disc one, 41:55). Moreover, the context of the headman's speech should have helped the audience to appreciate its sarcasm. The rehearsal of this scene is being conducted in conditions of total chaos that resemble anything but "unity:" the mother of one of the actresses keeps calling the theater every time she hears an explosion or a piece of potentially dangerous news; the actor playing the village policeman, another common element in the Rahbani oeuvre, is spreading rumors that the rehearsal has been cancelled; while rehearsing a song that has been prerecorded certain actors' voices are heard but they are not present on the stage; and the dancers are stepping on each other and subsequently arguing, partly because the sound man has set up his equipment where they are meant to dance. This sound equipment, which has been temperamental throughout the rehearsals, finally gives out after making a series of loud and irritating buzzing noises. Chaos is increased by the creative liberties taken by the lighting technician. The prima donna female protagonist, who is often accompanied onstage by her hairdresser, complains about the low height of the arch that she is supposed to walk through because it does not allow her and her lofty hair to easily pass under it. Meanwhile, the actor playing the village headman is suffocating in the little room in which he is supposed to hide before delivering his line about unity. Furthermore, none of the bit characters are able to get their simple lines or movements right, one of the director's technicians is absent because he is engaged in battle in the mountains, and the female star's hairdresser contradicts the director until the former is chased offstage by the latter. All of this is the context of the line about unity. The line about unity itself is punctuated by the character playing the policeman blowing loudly into his microphone to test it. Despite these clues, part of the audience still responds to these lines with enthusiastic applause.

The source of this ambiguity can be attributed to the fact that parody is always a matter of quoting (Bakhtin 1981a). Parody involves, in other words, a dialogue between the language of the text being parodied and the language of the parody. Baydūn, then, is right to characterize *Failure* as a "war of texts" (Baydūn, 'Abbās 1983: 9). In his "From the Prehistory of Novelistic Discourse" Bakhtin writes about the prevalence of parody in the classical Greek and Roman traditions. So common was it in the Roman tradition that "the Romans could not imagine a serious form without its comic equivalent" (Bakhtin 1981b: 58). The practice was well known in Medieval Europe as well, where the parody of sacred texts was common. The problem for today's reader of these classical and medieval texts is that even when one can identify the text being quoted, one cannot always determine to what extent "the author is quoting with reverence or, on the contrary, with irony or with a smirk" (Bakhtin 1981b: 68). Ziad's work demonstrates the possibility of such ambiguity with a contemporary audience as well, as it too points to the persevering power of the original Rahbani texts.

Despite the inability to avoid ambiguity and to escape from his own ambivalence completely, the fact that Ziad is attacking his parents' school of work if not their work directly is repeatedly made clear elsewhere in the play. The very name of the play within the play – *Mountains of Glory* – can be read as a pastiche of the titles of *Granite Mountains* and *Holiday of Glory* ("Glory" in that title is given as *'izz* instead of *majd*). We also know that Ziad was upset by a post-1975 practice that the Rahbani Brothers were not above indulging in. Not only would they stage some of their plays in both East and West Beirut, but they would also make textual changes depending on which side of the capital the play was being performed. According to Ziad, the Rahbani Brothers were planning on adding scenes praising the occupied (and pre-dominantly Muslim) South of Lebanon when they moved their *Conspiracy* from East to West Beirut (Fāris 1980: n.p.). In *Failure*, when Nūr admits to the producer Nazīh that he forgot to insert a few sentences about the South, he is told: "Here in this region the audience likes that sort of thing. Put a small sentence in and later when we stage it in East Beirut you can put something else" (Rahbani, Z. 1994d: 147).

The brief appearance of the play's producer contains within it several other critiques of the Rahbani Brothers' project. His main complaint about the play within the play is that the director Nūr has gone way over budget

Nūr: "It's a simple folkloric work."

Nazīh: "Ok, folkloric. Didn't you tell me from the beginning that it was just a small play?"

Nūr: "Yeah. I mean... that is to say, it is, it would be considered small...."

Nazīh: "May God curse the father of folklore and the hour of its birth. What do you have in the play? How many people? What, do you have a thousand Roman soldiers? Is there a battle on horseback or what?"

Nūr: "It's not about horses Mr Nazīh, but these expenses, man. What quality! What do you think? Of course quality costs you a lot.... Here, I have the original receipts."

Nazīh: "But I don't understand anything from these receipts. They're folkloric receipts. What? What is this: 'the villagers got angry' 10,000 lira? What is this 'the villagers got angry'? Is it in the play?"

Nūr: "Yes. It's a scene. It's when the villagers get angry."

Nazīh: "What happens?"

Nūr: "It's a scene, Mr Nazīh. We see the villagers being happy, and then some-thing specific happens, and they get mad."

Nazīh: "And what do they do with ten thousand lira?"

Nūr: "They don't do anything. No, these 10,000 lira are for the pants when the villagers get angry."

Nazīh: "Hmm, is it necessary for the villagers to change their pants when they get angry?"

Nūr: "Of course. The pants of anger are different than the pants of happiness, Mr Nazīh."

(Rahbani, Z. 1994d: 141–4)

This is an obvious reference to the ever-escalating extravagance of the Rahbani Brothers' folkloric plays.

This scene humorously critiques another aspect of the Rahbani theater, namely the dehumanizing (in this case de-sexualizing) of the characters. The producer asks Nūr if the play has "sex" [in English] in it

Nūr: "What do you mean by sex?"
Nazīh: "You work it out. Put some sex in it. Sex is good."
Nūr: "I know Mr Nazīh but, you know, this is the story of a village."
Nazīh: "So?"
Nūr: "How can I explain this? You have a village headman, a policeman, a girl; this kind of thing. A village headman having sex?! Are you kidding?"
Nazīh: "I don't know Mr Nūr. How about sex between the village headman and the girl, for example."
Nūr: "Nope."
Nazīh: "It wouldn't work?"
Nūr: "The girl is supposed to be pure. She's devoted to her country, to freedom. You can't have her all of a sudden having sex. Do you know what I mean?"
Nazīh: "Ok, what about the villagers?"
Nūr: "No."
Nazīh: "Can't the villagers, after getting angry for 10,000 lira, for example, talk a bit about sex. I'm not saying that they should be nude or anything."
Nūr: "No, Mr Nazīh. How would it fit in? It's a popular Lebanese story. It has things like nationalism in it, there's no way . . . [Nazīh interrupts him]."
Nazīh: "That's great that it has nationalism. Nationalism also brings people [to the theater]."

(Rahbani, Z. 1994d: 146–7)

Here Ziad is commenting on the fact that the Rahbani Brothers have taken popular rituals like the *dabka*, that are originally not without some relationship to sexuality (al-Rīhānī 1970 and Traboulsi 1996), and completely neutered them. Anyone familiar with the Rahbani Brothers' works, as most in attendance would have been, would have found it almost impossible to imagine those folkloric singing characters in their elaborate costumes as being capable of expressing any measure of sexuality. Hence, the source of comedy of this scene and the reason behind the audience's enthusiastic laughter (Rahbani, Z. 1993c: disc two, 17:16–18:02).

In the scene of his conversation with Mr Nazīh, Ziad achieves one of the goals of parody. According to Bakhtin, texts are parodied in order to eradicate the distance that they create between themselves and their recipient. The Rahbani theatrical oeuvre achieved almost sacred status through its classicization of tradition and appropriation of the popular in the context of the post–1958 nation-building project of Fouad Chehab. The 1975 civil war itself raised questions not just about the sacredness of those icons, but also about their ideological intent. This play can be seen as an artistic articulation of those questions. The dialogue between Nūr and Nazīh is an example of how parody results in a new kind of proximity between an audience and the object being parodied. As Bakhtin puts is

> Laughter has the remarkable power of making an object come up close, of drawing it into a zone of crude contact where one can finger it familiarly on all sides, turn it upside down, inside out, peer at it from above and below, break open its external shell, look into its center, doubt it, take it apart, dismember it, lay it bare and expose it, examine it freely and experiment with it. Laughter demolishes fear and piety before an object, before a world, making of it an object of familiar contact and thus clearing the ground for an absolutely free investigation of it. Laughter is a vital factor in laying down that prerequisite for fearlessness without which it would be impossible to approach the world realistically.
>
> (Bakhtin 1981a: 23)

The conversation between director and producer attacks this very distance: by exposing the sartorial extravagance of their works and the inhuman sexlessness of their characters, Ziad exposes this epic distance of the Rahbanis' theater from the majority of the Lebanese while at the same time reducing it.

With this distance eradicated, Ziad can safely move in for the metaphorical kill. He saves his most frontal attack on the Rahbani Brothers' project for the very end of *Failure*. Just as rehearsal for the play is about to be disrupted terminally by the internecine squabbling of the cast, the director Nūr somehow gets them to carry on. The chorus starts to dance and sing: "Oh Mījānā oh Mījānā oh Mījānā. Abū al-Zuluf and al-Mījānā. These are the songs of our country" (Rahbani, Z. 1994d: 194). Ziad takes the names of these traditional folk songs, which were prevalent particularly in the early plays and records of the Rahbani Brothers and Fairouz, and literally personifies them.[23] While the chorus is singing these words, the lights start flickering and strange loud noises are heard. Suddenly a spotlight is fixed on a large figure on the bridge who says, "*Hi*. I'm Abū al-Zuluf. How is everyone?" (Rahbani, Z. 1994d: 195).[24] After telling everyone to take off their folkloric pants and go home because the play is called off, he seats Nūr in the middle of the stage and tells him: "I have come from heritage especially to see you, in the name of my colleagues Abū al-Mīj, Dal'ūna, Rūzānā, Mījānā, Abū al-Hayba, *and everybody*."[25] The final eighteen minutes of the play are taken up by Abū al-Zuluf's interrogation of Nūr.

Through the personification of Abū al-Zuluf, Ziad critiques the opportunistic commodification of folklore. While the Rahbani Brothers certainly did not have a monopoly on such practices, they were in many respects leaders of the folklore industry that arose in the late 1950s and early 1960s (Abī Samrā 1999: 8). This corresponds roughly to the time frame to which Abū al-Zuluf refers when he says to Nūr, "By whose authority have you been coming down on me for the past twenty years?" (Rahbani, Z. 1994d: 196). He announces that he does not appreciate being left back in the middle ages, but wants to participate in urban modernity just like everyone else: he does not ride a donkey as the songs that invoke his name report, but rather a late-model Kawasaki motorcycle. Nor does he wear the baggy folkloric *shirwāl* trousers, but rather the latest designer jeans. In fact, he is the agent for many of the Western clothing brands and counts Fakhr al-Din among his customers. He also does not spend much time in the countryside these days. In fact, the last time he tried to visit the ubiquitous valley of the Abū al-Zuluf songs he was almost killed by a militia group training there. He complains to Nūr: "Stop regressing and leave us alone. We are progressing and you are regressing" (Rahbani, Z. 1994d: 197). This protest extends to anachronistic song lyrics. He asks Nūr

> Why is it that every time you use the word *'īd* [holiday] straightaway you put either *'anāqīd* [bunches of grapes] or *mawā 'īd* ["assignations" in this context]. And for the past three years or so you've added to these, *Lubnān jadīd* [a new Lebanon]...?[26]
>
> (Rahbani, Z. 1994d: 198)

Abū al-Zuluf goes on to suggest another word that rhymes with holiday, assignations, and bunches of grapes that might be more in line with the current environment: *labīd* (the sound of explosions). Such a sound might come, he suggests, from a cluster bomb. Here Ziad is playing on the relationship between the word for "a bunch of grapes" ('unqūd) and the second word in the term cluster bomb (*qunbula 'unqūdiyya*) which share the same root. If you were to hear such a bomb explode, he goes on to suggest, you might find yourself *rakkīd* (running), another word that rhymes with the above. He then says that despite the fact that the year is 1983, after one hears the word *layālī* (nights) in a song, he is likely to hear *li-ḥālī* (by myself), *'alālī* (heights), *'a bālī* (on my mind), or *dawālī* (grape vineyards) right after it. Why don't you put instead, he asks, *millālī* (troop carriers), as he saw nothing but armored vehicles on his way to the theater. Nūr asks: "Are you kidding, can we really put 'troop carriers' in a song!?" Abū al-Zuluf responds that the better question is "Can we put songs in troop carriers?" (Rahbani, Z. 1994d: 199).

In this play Ziad is also commenting on the opportunistic use of the "Other" by the Rahbanis and others. Above I cited an example of unironic applause to an ironic line. The audience of *Failure* similarly applauds when one of the Christian actresses, responding to a question from a reporter, says, "The play [*Mountains of Glory*] talks about a nationalistic village, because we see it standing against this foreign enemy, and against the people who are pretending to be Lebanese but are working with them [the enemy]" (Rahbani, Z. 1994d: 110 and 1993c: disc one, 64:39). Despite this applause, this line represents the very opposite of Ziad's message in this play. At one point during Abū al-Zuluf's tirade, he asks Nūr why he must always repeat the phrase "We are all brothers" in his works: "If we are all brothers why do we need to keep saying it?" (Rahbani, Z. 1994d: 200). Nūr responds that this is because of "the stranger." Exactly which "stranger" are you talking about, Abū al-Zuluf asks him. He is referring here to two interviews that Nūr gave during the course of the play. The first interview was with a journalist from the leftist daily newspaper *al-Safīr*. When the journalist suggests that the "stranger" in Nūr's play represents Israel, Nūr readily agrees (Rahbani, Z. 1994d: 101). Subsequently when a journalist from the French-language and East-Beirut-based newspaper *L'Express* asks him the same question, he replies: "The Palestinians" (Rahbani, Z. 1994d: 165).

In plays such as *Petra*, the Rahbani Brothers were suggesting that the causes of the civil war lay outside of Lebanon. Ziad turns this view on its head in his play by saying that if the "stranger" is the cause of the war it is because this stranger and strangeness is none other than Lebanon and the Lebanese themselves (Traboulsi "Mā huwa 'al-shay' al-fāshil," n.d.). Ziad is not only criticizing the discourse of his parents here, but rather one that was widespread throughout Lebanon during the war.[27] Abū al-Zuluf, for example, further presses Nūr to tell him exactly which "stranger" he is talking about: if it is the Palestinians, for example, then why would you accept ration stamps from one of their militias? If it is the non-Lebanese in general, then how could you have written a national anthem for Iraq? Who is the stranger? Abū al-Zuluf asks him

> What do you want with this stranger? The stranger. The stranger. The stranger. What stranger? Is not your situation strange? Is not the situation of the country strange? The international forces were thwarted.... Anyone who thinks about coming to Lebanon in the future will be thwarted. Is this not strange? No? There is no longer a Lebanon except in your stories. The village no longer exists except in your stories.
> (Rahbani, Z. 1994d: 202)

What, Abū al-Zuluf goes on to ask him, has happened to your *kibba* mortar and pestle? Abū al-Zuluf reminds him that it, along with other traditional appliances and goods such as the grill, heater, griddle, and even *'araq* now come from abroad? (Rahbani, Z. 1994d: 203). Additionally, who is the stranger, he asks, when you can get a PhD in the *dabka* in America, when the Europeans are playing backgammon, and when women all over the world are belly dancing? The rest of the world has taken everything Lebanese, developed it, then turned around and sold it back to you (Rahbani, Z. 1994d: 204).[28]

The play ends with Abū al-Zuluf forcing Nūr to dress in the very folkloric garb of his play in preparation for taking him to a real village to see if his clichés of "we are all brothers," "love" and "faith" can save him. Nūr is terrified, saying that he is a stranger in that village, that they might think that he has come to do them harm. Distribute "assignations" and "bunches of grapes" to them, Abū al-Zuluf suggests (Rahbani, Z. 1994d: 207). The play ends with Nūr, now dressed in his folkloric clothes, being sent off to the countryside to test the Rahbanis' version of Lebanon against Ziad's own.

Ziad and the novelization of the Rahbanis' Lebanon

Ziad's musical-theatrical work clearly can be categorized as a parody of his parents' project. To what extent, however, does it represent a rejection of it? Bakhtin has pointed out that classical parody was in no way nihilistic: a parody of Homer, even by Homer himself, did not scandalize the ancient Greeks. This is because it was not the events and characters of his tales that were being parodied, only the "epic heroization" of them (Bakhtin 1981b: 55–6). Perhaps it is in this spirit that Ziad's project has been characterized as a continuation of that of the Rahbanis (Bāshā 1987b; "Ilā Asi" 1995; Manganaro 1999a; Shams 2000a; and Traboulsi "Mā huwa 'al-shay' al-fāshil," n.d.). Manganaro, for example, concludes that despite its parodicizing, Ziad's project confirms the nationalism of the work of the Rahbani Brothers because "... he revels in one of the most unique aspects of the nation – language itself. Ziad's insistence on utilizing to the fullest his own national dialect, reinforces his loyalty to his nation" (Manganaro 1999a: 4). While this may be true, it is important to recognize that the nation to which he is being loyal is not necessarily the Rahbani nation. One place to test this hypothesis is to see whether, in fact, his "national dialect" is their "national dialect." This brings us back to parody, for if we agree that his works are parodies of theirs, then we must also agree that his language is not their language.

Though there are many different forms of parody, all of them, according to Bakhtin, share a main subject: language itself (Bakhtin 1981b: 55). For Bakhtin, there exists an inextricable link between parody and linguistic change. Parody flourishes in conditions when monolingualism has been freed from the "tyranny of its own language and its own myth of language" (Bakhtin 1981b: 61). This libera- tion comes at the hands of polyglossia and heteroglossia (Bakhtin 1981b: 61). Parody, in fact, can be seen as part of the shift from monoglossia to polyglossia. Bakhtin is careful to point out – and this is a very important observation for our case – that there is never really such a thing as true monoglossia (Bakhtin 1981b: 66). I hope to have shown, however, that the theatrical project of the Rahbanis represents a *fantasy* of monolingualism and its cousin, monoculturalism, which Bakhtin associates with real political tyranny (Hirschkop 1986: 75). Their attempt to render the regionally diverse *dabka* into a single "Dabka of Lebanon" based on the Mt Lebanon version of the dance is one such example. Their attempts to order and nationalize popular culture extended to language itself. In Ziad's 1993 play *Regarding Honor and the Stubborn People*, one of the characters accosts people in a mask at gunpoint as if to rob them. Instead, he asks them linguistic questions. During one such incident this character asks another how she says the word for "distances:" *masāfaet* or *masāfāt*. In a televised press conference after the opening of this play, Ziad is asked about the function of these linguistic interrogations. He says that in this case he is commenting on the way that the Rahbani Brothers had Fairouz pronounce this word in one of their songs. Whereas most Lebanese would pronounce the word *masāfaet*, Fairouz, despite the fact that the remainder of the song is in colloquial Arabic, pronounces the word as it would be said in classical

Arabic, for example, *masāfāt*. Coincidentally, Ziad's uncle Mansour is at the press conference. Ziad asks him: "Isn't that right uncle?" Mansour agrees that it was not done randomly, but that they wrote their songs by a "selective process." We wanted, he goes on to explain, to select what was beautiful from all regions of Lebanon. We wanted, he continues, a language that would be understood everywhere ("Mu'tamar sahafī li-Ziad" 1993). In their zeal to present a unified Lebanese front and in their inevitable move away from Mt Lebanon specific folklore, the Rahbani Brothers attempted to standardize a Lebanese Arabic which had actually become infinitely more diverse with the creation of Greater Lebanon in 1920. When they were not attempting to standardize the dialect, they were showcasing a version of mountain Lebanese Arabic (Abū Murād 1990: 37 and 77). While their plays contain a variety of voices, the accent and register is relatively uniform. There are exceptions to this rule, especially in their later plays. For example in their 1974 play *Loulou*, language is used as an indicator of social position (Shāwūl 1988: 258). Even as late as the 1977 *Petra*, however, the Rahbani Brothers, according to Asi, were attempting to present what he called "the white dialect" that could be widely understood (Harb 1978a: n.p.). These efforts to promote a standardized Lebanese Arabic based on a Christian or mountain dialect were not carried out, of course, alone. One way to look at Said Akl's project to come up with a system of transliteration of Lebanese Arabic is as such a project of systematization. Since short vowels are rarely included in written Arabic texts, be they standard or colloquial, there is room for flexibility in the pronunciation of words. In Beirut alone, there are at least four different pronunciations for the word "here," all of which could be represented by the Arabic letters *hā'*, *waw*, *nūn* plus a variety of long and short vowels (Cadora 1979: 86). When such a word is written out in Latin script, as Akl did for a series of books, such flexibility is lost. Akl renders the word "*hawn*" (Akl 1978: 128), which is the way that Cadora records the word being pronounced in Ashrafiyya, the predominantly Christian section of East Beirut (Cadora 1979: 86). It is also no coincidence that Akl played a role in convincing the Rahbani Brothers to "purify" their language by writing solely in "Lebanese" Arabic (Abī Samrā 1992b: 14). This is further proof of the Rahbanis' ever-increasing distance from the "folk" of folklore. For Bakhtin, it is the folk and their lore that are the very source of both parody and heteroglossia (Bakhtin 1981a). The metaphorical public square is their stage (Hirschkop 1990: 71). The Rahbanis too have theatricized – more literally – that space. For them, however, this process involves the very opposite processes, that is, sanitizing and standardizing.

Part of Ziad's project is to recapture the polyphony that is the reality of Greater Lebanon. We can see such a project beginning to take shape in *Hotel*. In that play we are introduced to Ziad's first Armenian character. This figure is the butt of a series of linguistic jokes. Bakhtin reminds his reader that comedy at the expense of difference of dialect is nothing new. In the context of national language formation, however, it takes on added significance (Bakhtin 1981b: 82). This is certainly the case in the instance of *Hotel*. Above I discussed the intellectual revolutionary's wedding speech and his citing of Gibran. It is significant that it is not the intellectual himself who owns up to his literary borrowing, but rather the Armenian that points out his sentence's source (Rahbani, Z. 1994c: 75). The Armenian may have trouble speaking "Lebanese" Arabic, but there is no mistaking his Lebanese-ness.

Compared to the modest but significant start in theatrical heteroglossia that is *Hotel, Tomorrow* is a virtual tower of Babel, as I have shown above. In addition to the cacophony of foreign languages and accents, this play foregrounds generational and class differences glossed over in the Rahbani Brothers' plays. There is, first of all, the pompous use of classical Arabic by the poet Usāma. Ziad's parody of this language is highlighted by the failure of the cook and vegetable deliverer to make any sense of his poetic spewings. There is also the idiolect of the Westernized Lebanese teenagers characterized by their use of Western names and nicknames; their mixture of Arabic, English, and French; and their adjective-starved language. One of them, Sāmī, calls Zakariyyā either "Zāk" or "Champ" and asks after friends such as Mike, Mark, Gabbie, and Steve (Rahbani, Z. 1994a). He and his girlfriend pepper their speech with words like "gentleman" and "maximum" (Rahbani, Z. 1994a: 109). At one point, they are talking about popular Western music, comparing the merits of bands like Pink Floyd and Led Zeppelin. In this conversation they repeat, to a degree that the audience finds amusing (Rahbani, Z. 1995b: disc three, 10:50) variations of the word "fahl" ("fahil" in the local pronunciation). In classical Arabic, this word literally means "stallion." Here, in its various adjectival (*fahl, fahhīl, fahliyya,* and *afhal*), verbal (*fahhal* and *yatafahhal*) and nominal (*tafhīl* and *fuhhūla*) forms (Rahbani, Z. 1994a: 112), the word means something like "cool."

Though itself a piece of fiction, the play is also an important reminder that heteroglossia does not occur unattached from specific socioeconomic circumstances. In talking about the formation of the novel, the ultimate artistic representation of heteroglossia, Bakhtin writes that

> All of these processes of shift and renewal of the national language that
> are reflected *by* the novel do not bear an abstract linguistic character *in*
> the novel: they are inseparable from social and ideological struggle,
> from processes of evolution and of renewal of society and the folk
> [italics in the original].
>
> (Bakhtin 1981b: 67–8)

Elsewhere he writes that the

> catastrophic nature of Russian capitalism was a condition of the emer-
> gence of polyphony: such a coexistence of discrete voices, he argued,
> could only arise when communities which had existed in a condition of
> isolation were thrown together by a moment of sudden modernization.
>
> (Hirschkop 1990: 72)

This is nothing less than the very process that the viewer or reader of *Tomorrow* witnesses. The irony, then, is that the very social and economic system supported and informed by the theater of the Rahbani Brothers not only led to the civil war, but was also a prerequisite for the heteroglossia that would enrich the literary work of Ziad and others.

This heteroglossia reaches a peak in *A Failure*. It is the paramount example of 'Anīnī's observation about the peculiarity of language in Ziad's theater:

> This characteristic shows itself first in his use of lexical items from the depths of popular language, second in the composition of his sentences and dialogues and lastly in the variety of dialects and playing with foreign accents: the mountain dialect, the southern dialect, the village dialect, the Armenian and Italian accents, the defective pronunciation of French and American accents, etc.
>
> ('Anīnī 1989–90: 148–9)

We have already seen the comic effect of Ziad's character attempting to speak French in *Tomorrow*. In *Failure*, the director Nūr has a similarly difficult time when speaking to the Francophone journalist from East Beirut. When she asks him to describe the play *Mountains of Glory* to her, he obviously does not understand the questions, and responds as if she had just complimented him: "Merci. Merci. May God preserve you" (Rahbani, Z. 1994d: 164). And when he does finally understand the question, he speaks in an almost incomprehensible melange of Arabic, French and English (I will only translate the Arabic, but will put it in italics to distinguish it from the English in the text): "C'est la folklore libanaise qui parle au nom du Liban *in the* oui et la pays...*not* pays, la village libanaise.... Oui. *In* tu...we are...there is...Abū al-Zuluf. Abū al-Zuluf. Dal'ūna. Mījānā et encore Rosana" (Rahbani, Z. 1994d: 164). These scenes are more than simply funny, for as Bakhtin observes, when "sacred languages" [and French and English are certainly seen as being almost "sacred" by some in Lebanon] are spoken "by the accents of vulgar folk languages," they are seen in a new light, their artificiality highlighted (Bakhtin 1981b: 77).

The same holds for the pompous use of classical Arabic. In *Hotel*, Ziad parodied a certain kind of armchair revolutionary intellectual. In *Tomorrow* his target was pretentious poetry. In *Failure*, it is the discourse of a certain kind of showy journalism that comes under fire. The Arabic speaking journalist establishes the absurdity of his own language by very formally and dryly telling Nūr that he does not want the interview to be formal and dry, but rather like a normal "chat" (Rahbani, Z. 1994d: 97). Similar to his interview with the Francophone journalist later in the play, Nūr does not always understand what is being asked of him. When the writer employs a kind of formal journalistic language to ask Nūr to specify what he means when he says that his play is new, Nūr, as the stage directions tell us, does not really understand what he is being asked. At one point he comically responds to a question he does not understand: "Welcome,

welcome" (Rahbani, Z. 1994d: 99). And finally, as with his mangling of French, when Nūr himself attempts to respond to a question in formal Arabic, he makes a common grammatical mistake, saying for "one day" "*ihdā hādhihi al-ayyām*" (Rahbani, Z. 1994d: 100) instead of "ahad hādhihi al-ayyām."

Various regional Lebanese dialects are represented in *Failure* as well: from the broken and poorly pronounced Arabic of the journalist from East Beirut, to the Armenian assistant director (whose language is much less caricature-like than that of the Armenian in *Hotel*, but still distinctive enough for one of the characters to ask him if he is Armenian) (Rahbani, Z. 1994d: 180). The assistant director, for example, often does not match the gender of nouns and adjectives correctly. Just before being asked about his identity, for example, he says for "Lebanese village" "dayʻa Lubnānī" (Rahbani, Z. 1994d: 180), instead of "dayʻa Lubnāniyya." The dialect of the Druze is represented in the character of the technician Fu'ād. The Druze in Lebanon and elsewhere are known for their tendency to pronounce the letter *qāf* as a hard consonant, whereas most other Lebanese almost always pronounce it as a glottal stop. The contrast can be seen where the Druze character Fu'ād asks "shū qarrartum?" (what did you decide?), and the director responds with a question: "'arrarnā?" (what did we decide?) (Rahbani, Z. 1994d: 40). We also know that Fu'ād is a Druze because at one point he is late for rehearsal because he is in the mountains fighting with the "socialists" (Rahbani, Z. 1994d: 76). It is well known that Druze of this time tended to fall in line politically with their leader Kamal Jumblat (Kamāl Junbalāt), the head of the Lebanese Socialist party. The play also contains the dialect of a resident of the northern city of Tripoli. Again, Ziad has two characters say the same word in close proximity to one another to emphasize the contrast. At one point Nūr asks his technical crew "What do we want to do (*na 'mil*)?" Sāmir from Tripoli repeats the question, asking Nūr, "So, what do you want me to do (*a 'mul*)?" (Rahbani, Z. 1994d: 43 and 1993: disc one, 12:03). And while Ziad may often be making fun of these linguistic and dialectic differences, it is important to note that he is also, by the very act of including them in his plays, celebrating them.[29]

Both the dialogism with his parents' discourse and the heteroglossia outlined above are indicative of what Bakhtin refers to as the "novelization" of all genres of literature in times when the novel is ascendant. The novel, he claims, is not a fixed genre but an ever morphing vessel for discourse to fill in periods of hetero- and polyglossia. This because the novel is nothing less than the parody of other genres (Bakhtin 1981a: 5). He describes the features of novelized genres as follows:

> They become more free and flexible, their language renews itself by incorporating extraliterary heteroglossia and the 'novelistic' layers of literary language, they become dialogized, permeated with laughter, irony, humor, elements of self-parody and finally – this is the most important thing – the novel inserts into these other genres an indeterminacy,

a certain semantic open endedness, a living contact with unfinished, still-evolving contemporary reality (the open ended present).

(Bakhtin 1981b: 6–7)

This contact with the present is an important distinction between the two projects. If theater in the hands of Ziad has been novelized, then the Rahbani Brothers' work can be characterized as its opposite: epicized. What characterizes the epic, according to Bakhtin and others like Lukács (Lukács 1971), is its remoteness, its sealed off-ness from any present. Whereas the epic is backward looking, the novel and the novelized genres are rooted in the present and even forward looking. The novel, according to A.S. Byatt, is the most "imperfect" of all art forms (qtd. in Updike 2001: 106). Imperfect, however, does not just mean flawed, but also unfinished and incomplete. The imperfect, in the grammatical sense, is contingent on a future. Unlike the Rahbani plays that end with the closure of marriage or military victory, Ziad's endings are more problematic, more, in the grammatical as well as plot-resolution sense, imperfect: the incomplete revolution in *Hotel*, the uncertain fate of Thurāyā and Zakariyyā at the end of *Tomorrow*, the suspect "cure" of the patients at the end of *Film*, the never performed play of *Failure*. It is no wonder that Ziad's plays are often seen as the predictors of future events (Amīn 1997; Baydūn, 'Abbās 1996; al-Mukhkh 1983; and Zaytūnī 1994) whereas the Rahbani theater has been characterized, as I've shown, as a consistent expression of nostalgia for some utopian past.

The "imperfection" of Ziad's individual works is paralleled in his ever-evolving and self-contradicting career, which would come to include a series of records and concerts with his mother Fairouz in the 1980s and 1990s. I will examine their collaboration in Chapter 4. Before doing that, however, I will first return to her long career with the Rahbani Brothers to focus more closely on her role and signification in that project. Until now I have only cursorily examined Fairouz's crucial place in this musical and musical-theatrical project. The beginning of Chapter 4 will trace the transformation of this young woman into a symbol for a certain vision of the Lebanese nation. Above I have discussed some of the wider implications of this project as an identity-forming agent. In Chapter 4, I will discuss its effect on Fairouz herself, not without an attempt to address the question of her own agency in that project, an attempt that will be made all the more difficult in light of her paradoxical silence. I will then ask to what extent Ziad's collaboration with Fairouz freed both Lebanon and Fairouz herself from her own earlier iconization as the main symbol of the Rahbanis' Lebanon.

4

FAIROUZ AND/AS THE NATION

> If Fairouz were not a singer, what would she be?
>
> a. a housewife
> b. an ambassador
> c. a nun
>
> Fairouz is?
>
> a. our mother
> b. our sister
> c. our neighbor
>
> Which image of Fairouz is the quickest to come to mind?
>
> a. the wife of Asi
> b. the mother of Ziad
> c. the daughter of Mudallaj [the character played by Fairouz in *Granite Mountains*]
>
> questions from a survey as part of a special tribute to Fairouz in a 1992 edition of the weekly cultural supplement of the Beirut newspaper *al-Nahār* ("al-Istiftā' " 1992: n.p.)

The Egyptian President Gamal Abdel Nasser is rumored to have expressed regret that Fairouz was not born Egyptian. Apocryphal or not, it is a pregnant sentiment. Was not Nasser the father of revolutionary postcolonial Arab nationalism? Did not his pan-Arab radio station Voice of the Arabs invite the Rahbanis to compose songs for Palestine in the 1950s? Theoretically, it should not have mattered to Nasser whether Fairouz was Egyptian, Lebanese, or Iraqi. On the one hand, Nasser's wish points to the tension between individual state and pan-Arab nationalisms in the region. More important for the purposes of this book is the anecdote's indication not just of the importance of cultural production to postcolonial nation building, but also of the role of gender in that process. The phenomenon of the star in this region was not only a twentieth-century mass-media creation, but also a hand-maiden of postcolonial nationalism. For the purposes of this chapter, the gendered nature of that metaphor is apropos. Not only were many of these stars women, but it has also become abundantly clear that nationalism is a gendered phenomenon.

In Ziad Rahbani's 1972 musical play *Celebration*, there is a singing competition at the village café to see who is going to sing in place of the aging owner. One of the participants is a married woman escorted to the competition and spoken for there by her husband. After just a few bars of singing, someone in the audience exclaims " 'āh," a typical response of a *tarab*-filled listener. The husband becomes enraged, wanting to know who would say such a thing to his wife. He repeats again and again, more insistently each time: "Who said 'Ah Madam'?" (Rahbani, Z. 1997b: side two, track three). The melee that follows threatens to break up the competition. These two anecdotes raise a number of questions relevant not only to the long career of Fairouz, but also to the role of women – and women performers in particular – in modern nation-building projects.

As the first anecdote demonstrates, women performers were called upon to participate actively in projects of nation building. The second anecdote, on the other hand, reveals that these performers had to contend with problematic social status. Chatterjee demonstrates that this was the case in nineteenth-century India as well. He categorizes this paradox of nation building as "betrayal." While performers were an integral part of national subject formation, they themselves were often cast as "Others" by their audience (Chatterjee 1993: 154). This phenomenon is related to the problematic status held by performers, particularly but not exclusively female, in different parts of the world (van Nieuwkerk 1995). Chatterjee's discussion of the actress Binodini points to the possibility that the very artistic participants in certain nationalist projects can themselves, on certain levels, embody the Otherness upon which unity is predicated.

The Rahbani family has not been immune to this phenomenon. When still serving as a policeman, for example, Mansour was once rebuked by a superior for moonlighting as an artist: "Shame on you, son of my friend and brother Hannā, for singing on a stage" (Zoghaib 1993: part three, 71). Another story has Mansour, early in his career, trying to publish poetry in the magazine *al-Sayyād*, edited by Suhayl Idrīs, future editor of *al-Ādāb*, the leading "commitment literature" organ in the region. His poems kept getting rejected until he sent them in under a pseudonym ("Sab' wa-Makhūl" 1969: 4). In the next generation, Ziad Rahbani apparently found his future wife's father unenthusiastic about the match (Fadl Allāh 1995). The song "A Spoiled Upbringing" ("Marbā al-dalāl"[1]) on his 1995 record *Seeing as That* is about a man going to request Dalāl's hand in marriage from her father. The father says to him: "You know, a lawyer has requested my daughter's hand; those who come to us are from the best families. It is not every day that a lawyer comes, but there are plenty of your ilk" (Rahbani, Z. 1995a: track 11). If we assume that on one level this song is autobiographical, its message is worth pondering. That the son of not only the most famous artistic couple in Lebanon, but also the authors of such highly influential Self-Other boundary demarcating narratives could be thus "betrayed" speaks volumes about the power of such borders to subsume those who participate in their very demarcation.

Such examples are not limited to Lebanon. One well-known Arab-World example of similar artist-society tension is that of the Egyptian author of one of the first novels in the region. Muhammad Husayn Haykal signed that 1913 work with a pseudonym out of fear of societal disapproval (Kilpatrick 1992: 227). For similar reasons, the Egyptian novelist and playwright Tawfīq al-Hakīm did not sign his surname to his first two plays. Drama was even less respected than narrative writing: "Dramatic art was looked down upon as being the occupation of, at best, bizarre people; at worst, of people of doubtful morals, who lived a life of license, very low on the social scale" (al-Rā'ī 1992: 368). The pioneer of Egyptian musical theater Sayyid Darwish faced similar problems. Early in his career his brother-in-law told him that if he did not stop singing he would force him to divorce his wife (Zakī 1988: 116). There is no question, however, that it is female performers who have borne the brunt of this tension (Armbrust 2000a: 201).

In previous chapters I have been in dialogue with the work of Partha Chatterjee on Indian nationalism in nineteenth-century India. Here I will note some of the differences between the Indian and Lebanese contexts to show that despite divergent contexts, women in a variety of places and times have played similar roles in modern nation building. While in both locales the phenomena of the classicization of tradition and the appropriation of the popular were instrumental in the formation of identities, the main thesis of Chatterjee's work is that elite Indian nationalists initially began pressing for independence from the British not on the political plane, but rather on the cultural one. Using Gramsci's theory of incremental revolution, he describes how Indian nationalists assimilated in the public sphere, all the while carving out a private – and in their minds superior – cultural space (Chatterjee 1993). This had important implications for the role of women in society.

The context of this national struggle led, because of this separation between the external and internal worlds, to the reification of false dichotomies such as "spiritual/material, home/world, and feminine/masculine" (Chatterjee 1993: 126). Women became the main vessels to symbolize all that this culturally superior internal world came to mean. Women were, in other words, supposed to be authentic and pure, to "have the qualities of self-sacrifice, benevolence, devotion, religiosity, and so on" (Chatterjee 1993: 131). Ironically, perhaps, this new status had the effect of allowing women more and more to exit the home. Thus desexualized and stripped of any ambiguity as far as their social role was concerned, women could more readily enter the public sphere, with the caveat, of course, that they remain good ambassadors and representatives of that space. This is because "the 'spiritual' signs of her femininity... [were] now clearly marked – in her dress, her eating habits, her social demeanor, her religiosity" (Chatterjee 1993: 130). This meant that women in public who did not conform to these ideal notions of Indian womanhood would almost automatically be "Othered" and set up as foils. This category of foils included performers (Chatterjee 1993: 151).

In what ways does this account of nineteenth-century Bengali nationalism help us to think about the case of Fairouz and Lebanon? In Lebanon, the national identity formation projects in which the Rahbanis, Fairouz, and others participated were, in fact, an extension of a discourse encouraged by Lebanon's French colonizers (Kaufman 2004). Fairouz was, in other words, part of a national project that significantly *was not* predicated on difference with Europe. And although there was pressure for the French to quit the country ultimately, the national Maronite elite, as represented in the Baalbeck Festival committee members, continued to look to Europe – and to France in particular – as a cultural and civilizational model (Sa'īd, Kh. 1998b). Such leanings were not limited to the cultural activity of the Baalbeck Festival. In his study of Lebanese theater in general, Abū Murād notes that during the mandate period only one play was written on the subject of independence from France (Abū Murād 1997: 2).

Differences notwithstanding, I hope to show below that Fairouz's public and theatrical persona seem to fit the nineteenth-century Indian model for the role of women in postcolonial nationalist projects. This is the case both in terms of her centrality to the specific national project discussed at length above and in the focus on her qualities of Virgin Mary–like chastity onstage and domestic maternity offstage. At the same time, her position in these projects also resembles the role of Muslim women in nationalist movements in countries of the region with Islamic majorities, who until now have been the focus of most of the writing on the relationship between women and nationalism in the Arab World.[2]

A common complaint of feminist academics about studies of nationalism focusing both on the Middle East (Moghadam 1994) and other parts of the world (Mayer 2000, McClintock 1997, Meyer 2000, Ranchod-Nilsson 2000, and Yuval-Davis 1997) has been that despite the fact that gender inarguably plays a large role in the formation of national and other subjectivities, studies of identity formation until very recently have largely ignored this fact. Another almost equally common observation is that even when nationalism began to be studied with gender in mind, too often the focus has been on the direct political role played – or not played depending on the specific case – by women in various nationalist projects, as opposed "to broader exploration[s] of the ways in which conceptual categories like 'the state' and 'citizen' are based upon particular gender identities" (Ranchod-Nilsson 2000: 164). This, according to Abu-Lughod, was the state of the field until very recently in writing on women and nationalism in the Middle East (Abu-Lughod 1998a). The collection of essays in the book she edits proposes to rectify this problem by treating nationalism "as a cultural or discursive project in which ideals of womanhood and notions of the modern were key elements" (Abu-Lughod 1998a: 17). Another trend in writing about women in the region that the volume sets out to remedy is not to pose the question of the status and role of women in the context of a monolithic "Islam," but rather to look at speci-ficities of time and place. While the essays in her volume succeed to a great extent in accomplishing this, they fall somewhat short in contrast to similar recent studies on India – according to the final essay in the work by Deniz Kandiyoti – in that they contain "little critical reflection on how the everyday landscape of modernity in the Middle East (including tastes, styles, mores, and consumption patterns) was shaped through relations among different classes and communal groups (Muslims, Levantines, Armenians, Jews, and Copts, to name but a few)" (Kandiyoti 1998: 276).

Recent scholarly work on female performers in the region takes up this challenge by examining, among other things, the status and popularity of these figures in the context of factors like class and confessional background.[3] In her work on female performers in Egypt, van Nieuwkerk describes how, by examining issues of class among other factors, the status of dancers has declined over time to the point that audiences now equate almost all such women with prostitutes (van Nieuwkerk 1998: 21). Such associations are not restricted to dancers. She also discovered that singers, in her estimation due to the fact that their performances also center on their bodies, have only slightly higher status than dancers (van Nieuwkerk 1998: 27).[4] Rare are the performers that are able to avoid such classification (Abu-Lughod 1997: 505). One such exception is Oum Kalthoum.

While stardom and professionalization could help the performer gain social acceptance (Armbrust 2000a), this was not always the case. Danielson concludes that it was not the nature of Oum Kalthoum's voice but rather her "character" that allowed her to escape the usual social disapproval of female performers (Danielson 1997: 5). Oum Kalthoum succeeded in projecting the image of "bint al-balad" (van Nieuwkerk 1998: 30) or "bint al-rīf" (daughter of the country) (Danielson 1997: 4). She jealously guarded her image as a simple and religious woman organically connected to her modest rural background. An example of a star not as successful in this regard is Asmahan, a rival of Oum Kalthoum and the sister of singer/actor Farid El Atrache. Not only did her career as a singer and actress problematize her relationship to her own Syrian-Druze family and clan, but

> Asmahan's story [also] confirms the theses of scholars who observed
> that in many different cultures performers were given special status but
> not necessarily high status.... Entertainers' special status evolved in the
> Middle East from the necessity of patronage for musical creation and
> thus the linkage of the performer to the courts and to concubinage.
> Although all recognize the twentieth century as a new era, old attitudes
> die hard and slowly....
>
> (Zuhur 2000: 215)

Not unrelated to her "bint-al-balad-ness," Oum Kalthoum may have avoided the fate of other performers like Asmahan by eventually framing herself as a nationalist performer. Oum Kalthoum's songs and performances, like Fairouz's, resonated both within her own country and across the Arab World. The two singers are similar in that Fairouz was also able to avoid social disapprobation. This did not come, however, without certain costs. In other words, while in the previous chapters I examined some of the consequences and effects of the Rahbani project on subject formation in Lebanon, this chapter will comment on the effects that embodying that project had on, if not Fairouz "herself," then on her public persona. This will come through an examination of Fairouz's musical-theatrical characters and the way that her offstage persona has been represented.

Many aspects of Fairouz's artistic and personal life – at least what we can gauge from her public persona – were profoundly influenced by her central role in the Rahbani Brothers' project. I contend that the very combination of the processes by which tradition is classicized and the popular appropriated that had such a powerful subject forming effect on its audience at Baalbeck and elsewhere worked its magic equally powerfully, if not somewhat paradoxically, on Fairouz herself. I will discuss, in other words, how the public Fairouz was in certain ways imprisoned by the weight of the project that she was embodying. Why am I examining the career of Fairouz in this manner and not those of Asi, Mansour, and Ziad Rahbani? I will actually do this to a limited extent in the remainder of this chapter and in the Conclusion. Here, however, I focus on the role of Fairouz in these projects and the effect this role had on her because one of the things I hope to confirm is that, despite the important differences between various postcolonial nation-building projects, women in a variety of places and times – like other "Others" – were fated to bear the brunt of these nation-building projects' inconsistencies.

Fairouz as metaphor for the nation

It has been noted that whereas men are often seen as metonyms of the nation, women are cast as its metaphors. Men, in other words, are contiguous to one another and the nation whereas women are heavily laden symbols for all sorts of ideal notions of nationhood, and their bodies repositories for collective national honor (McClintock 1997). It can be argued that Fairouz's musical theatrical characters were metaphoric in that they embodied many of the ideals of nationhood, but metonymic in their nation or community-building activities within the individual works. At the same time, these characters came to stand as both metaphors and metonyms for "herself," or at least for the "public" persona that she presented – and that was presented for her – offstage.

On the closeness of these two personas, Fairouz has commented that what she did onstage was not really acting, as the characters she played were always so close to her life (Bāsīlā 1973: part one, 57). We have also seen above how her husband Asi thought that the story of their marriage resembled the stories in their theatrical works (Aliksān, J. 1987: 168). My conflation of Fairouz's characters and Fairouz "herself" below should not be understood as taking such statements at face value, but rather as an assumption that Fairouz and the Rahbani Brothers were always performing. I use the word performance in the way meant by Greg Dening (Dening 1996), that is as the constant narrating of the past (including the most recent past), and Judith Butler. Performance, for Butler, is neither "a singular 'act'," nor necessarily "theatrical" (Butler 1993: 12). And though for Butler, who builds on Lacan, performance – because of its present-ness – always

144

"conceals or dissimulates" the conventions it is citing (Butler 1993: 12), the word does not imply disingenuousness.

I discussed above how for nineteenth-century Indian national elites, the core of their imagined nation lay in their internal family lives. In that regard, I showed how it was women who bore the brunt of representing the values of the authenticity of the Indian nation. In other contexts as well, despite different types of colonization and various kinds of postcolonial national projects, women were often imbued with this symbolic role of "guard[ing] the home and creat[ing] domesticity against which men construct their fictive manliness" (Einstein 2000: 42). This was not only the case for the nationalisms of formerly colonized countries, as demonstrated by Kirsten Belgum for nineteenth-century Germany (Belgum 1998), Nancy Armstrong for eighteenth- and nineteenth-century England (Armstrong 1987), and Logan Sparks for the contemporary US (Sparks 2000). Whether via representations in essays, popular journals, or novels – or in the lack of combat participation by women in even a highly militarized society like Israel (Levy 2000) – women have been cast as the producers of citizens and not as citizens themselves (Heng 1992, Levy 2000, Ranchod-Nilsson 2000, and Yuval-Davis 1997). They have been represented, in other words, as symbolic mothers of the national family (Belgum 1998 and Einstein 2000). While having its own particularities and paradoxes, the case of Fairouz mostly corroborates such observations on the role of women in national projects.

The folkloric acts staged by the Rahbani Brothers at Baalbeck were not only a huge success with audiences, but also ultimately pleased the Festival committee members as well as other members of the ruling elite. This was due in part to the powerful combination of the classicization of tradition and the appropriation of the popular that those acts represented. They confirmed, in other words, that in Lebanon's folk traditions were echoes of the great Phoenician civilization that had been the very inventor of culture. These works must have also pleased their audience and patrons at Baalbeck due to their more direct nationalist messages. Above I have shown how the Rahbani Brothers' 1960 *Holiday of Glory* ends with a marriage uniting two villages. The young bride is told that she is to devote herself to her husband and to her children, whom she is to teach to worship both God and Lebanon (Rahbani, A. and M. 1960: 55). The role of women in this imagined nation, then, is a domestic one, central to the functions of procreation and social reproduction: the woman is to take care of her citizen husband and to produce and raise her Lebanon-worshipping citizen children.[5] The role of the mother in *Holiday of Glory* was played, not by Fairouz, but by the singer Sabah. It was the first and one of only two times that the Rahbanis would stage a work at Baalbeck or elsewhere without Fairouz in the lead role. It is important to note that these absences were caused by pregnancy.

In many of the Rahbani Brothers' plays in which Fairouz did play the lead role, it is striking – if we are assuming that she was a symbol for the nation in the maternal model explicated above – how few of her characters *literally* fit this mold. For her characters, love and its socially acceptable manifestation marriage are often delayed for the sake of the community. In *Night and the Lantern*, for example, Mantūra is not only the main breadwinner and treasurer of the village-family, but also the producer of the huge lantern that is going to light up the erstwhile dark corners of the play's imaginative geography and make them safe for travel and for commerce. In the 1967 *Hala and the King*, Hala refuses to become the king's bride despite her abject poverty. In the 1964 *The Ring Seller*, Rīma happily agrees to become engaged to a complete stranger in a year's time so that all of the other girls of the village can get engaged immediately. In the 1966 *Days of Fakhr al-Din*, 'Atr al-Layl's role as singer laureate of the nation forces her to advise her fiancé to look for another bride. And even in the 1978 *Petra*, where Fairouz plays a wife and a mother, she is willing to sacrifice her daughter's life for the health of the nation as a whole. While there is no doubt as to the dedication of these characters to the health and unity of the communities to which they belong, such roles cannot easily be interpreted to fit into the mold of women as the producers and care givers of the nation's male citizens and defenders.

It is perhaps for this very reason that in Fairouz's "private" life, so much stress has been placed upon her being a devoted mother and wife. I would like to suggest that this is not only because her characters often represent such daring divergence from the role usually allotted to women in the nation-building process, but also because she herself, when she is in the process of presenting such roles, is obviously not at that very moment being a devoted mother and wife. In contrast to the numerous pictures of her in the press with her children (e.g. Jarkas n.d.: 46–50 and Nāsir 1986: part three, 47 and part four, 45) or in the hospital after having given birth to one of them (e.g. "Hakadhā kānū" 19: 51), Ziad has commented on the fact that he saw very little of his parents growing up due to their busy schedules. He says that the person he is closest to in his family is the nanny who raised him (al-'Abd Allāh n.d.: 18). And not only is Fairouz not being a devoted mother and wife when onstage, she is also *performing*, an act which is problematic both in and outside of the region, especially for women. It is perhaps for all of these reasons, then, that she and others place so much emphasis on her offstage role as model mother and wife.

If the characters she plays in these works tend to take on male-oriented metonymic characteristics of the nation or community, the offstage Fairouz comes to be a metaphor for the nation. It is not surprising that this would be stated in terms of sanctioned domesticity. At one of her concerts a fan commented that she "is the only mother who speaks to all of us" (Aylett 1994: 52). The reaction to another one of her performances is described as follows:

> They showered her with flowers on stage because she is the bride of the nation which every countryman feels as if he is her groom, but she remains a bride without a groom, because she is engaged to the nation, which is incapable of inviting its citizens to its wedding.
>
> (Mahfūz, 'I. 1986: 41)

146

In writing on women performers in the region, Zuhur notes that so-called good women are usually portrayed in connection with a man (Zuhur 2000: 188). And if this man cannot always be depicted as the nation itself, second best is an actual man who is seen as devoting his artistic life to the service of the nation. Thus is it any surprise that the first choice readers are given in the survey at the beginning of the chapter as to how they think of Fairouz is as "Asi's wife"? Fairouz reports that after her separation from him in the late 1970s, the church refused to give them a divorce. The Patriarch of the Greek Orthodox Church is reported to have said to her: "Divorce, no way. You are not a woman. You are a model for the woman and a symbol for her" (al-Zībāwī 1992: 9). When asked in an interview if she thought that she had succeeded as a woman, Fairouz queried back: "You mean as a wife?" (Nasrī 1983: 10).

Being a model wife in the Lebanese and other contexts does not mesh so well with being a performer, even if what Fairouz was performing was the very nation itself. It is perhaps for this reason that interviews with her and articles and texts about her stress the fact that Fairouz remains a housewife at heart despite her fame and success. This was a strategy used by and about "ordinary" female performers in Egypt: "Female performers divert attention from the fact that they are working women in public to the private facets of their lives: they speak of being mothers and housewives…" (van Nieuwkerk 1998: 30). The Egyptian singer and composer Mohamed Abdel Wahhab is said to have remarked on Fairouz's skill as a housewife, opining that she did not let her servants do enough (Nāsir 1986: part seven, 47). When once asked whether she cooked, Fairouz said that she often does, adding that at the very least she always oversees the cooking in her house. In the same interview she was asked how she spends her days. She responded: "like any other housewife" (qtd. in Aliksān, J. 1987: 154–5). While Fairouz herself may have been emphasizing this aspect of her home life out of concern for her social status, she was at the same time reconfirming herself as a suitably domestic symbol for the nation. It is clear that all of this talk about her housewifery had some impact, as "housewife" is one of three possible responses to the 1992 survey question at the beginning of this chapter which asks what would Fairouz be were she not a singer. One of the other three responses is "nun." Are not the roles of housewife and nun contradictory? In some contexts, perhaps. In the case of Fairouz, however, both signify an appropriation of sexuality: a housewife's sexuality has been harnessed by her functions of social and biological reproduction and a nun's sexuality has been sacrificed to her devotion to God. It is the representation of Fairouz's relationship to sexuality that I take up next.

Above I discussed the scene in Ziad Rahbani's 1983 play *A Failure* in which the producer asks the director if he can put some "sex" into the play within the play in order to attract a larger audience. The director is appalled that the producer is suggesting that the village headman have sex with the "girl" of the village. The director tries to assuage the producer by assuring him that the play contains "nationalism," and that this is also a draw for audiences (Rahbani, Z. 1994d: 148). While nationalism and sex may have been equally appealing to theatrical audiences in that context, the two are, in another sense, mutually exclusive phenomena.[6] As Einstein writes

> As mother of the nation, woman is invisibly visible as a symbolic fantasy.... [The] fantasmatic woman becomes the body of the nation. In the process she is desexualized and "regulated" as the mother of us all. Her maternal body fictionalizes motherhood and the nation simultaneously. She represents safety through the boundaries of her body. She is embraced by the glorification of womanhood. She represents morality itself.
>
> (Einstein 2000: 43)

The point that the scene from *Failure* comically makes is that it is not the idea of sexual relations between two villagers that was *a priori* objectionable. Rather, it is the fact that the village "girl" had come to stand for the nation in the Rahbani musical theatrical project and elsewhere that required her to remain desexualized.

Fairouz and her characters, as the leading "village girls" of her time, were completely stripped of even the slightest hint of sexuality. How can this be when so many of these works have love as their theme, when Fairouz's characters were said to be "engaged to love" ("Asi Rahbani muwassi' hudūd al-hubb" 1986: 11)? It is, in fact, precisely because she is "engaged to love" and not to an actual human being that this love is represented as spiritual, not bodily. As "the girl" in *The Moon's Bridge* says, "Love is absolute, not the love of the lover or the love of the world" (qtd. in "Asi Rahbani muwassi' hudūd al-hubb" 1986: 11). Romantic love for her characters, as mentioned above, is always put off. As Abī Samrā writes, "Waiting is the fate of Rahbani love, though the waiting does not lead to anything" (Abī Samrā 1999: 9). It is also important to keep in mind that not only was Fairouz playing nation-symbolizing female *characters*, but that she was at the same time a female *performer*. Thus the need to keep any hint of sexual love away from her characters was, in a sense, doubled.

van Nieuwkerk concludes that this similarly problematic status of female singers and dancers is because both acts involve the use of the body. One of the reasons she gives for both Oum Kalthoum and Farida Fahmi pursuing the "girl of the country" image was that it was "a way of deconstructing notions about the sexual body" (van Nieuwkerk 1998: 30). She goes on to explain that "female entertainers are ambivalent in their attitude to their bodies.... Female performers accordingly try to neutralize and even deny the femininity of their bodies in order to counter balance the image of looseness or immorality" (van Nieuwkerk 1998: 34). This would be doubly true if the body in question were not only performing onstage, but performing nothing less than the nation itself. It is perhaps for this reason that Fairouz almost always appeared to be virtually motionless during her concerts.

Fairouz is known for her striking stillness during her performances (Asmar 1999: 14; Aylett 1994: 51; Jarkas n.d.: 92; Sam'ān 2002: n.p.; and Singh-Bartlett 2000d: n.p.). It was a notable event, for example, when she was going to play a small drum (*darabukka* in classical Arabic and *dirbakki* in the Lebanese dialect) for the first time onstage ("Fairouz tazhar 'alā masrah Qasr al-Bīkādīlī" 1967: 12). This is not, I would argue, only because it would entail playing a simple musical instrument, but also because it would involve movement. And just as her love is described as spiritual, so is her stillness. The Lebanese poet Unsī al-Hājj somewhat cryptically explains it as follows:

> Fairouz sings with her whole body, and her still position on the stage without restlessness, swaying... gestures or waving is not from coldness but, quite the opposite; it is a total separation from the outside world for the sake of the complete concentration on the role which she is living the moment she is singing it.
>
> (al-Hājj, U. 1987: vol. one, 274)

I would like to suggest that this utter stillness comes from much more mundane concerns. While it could very generally be described as stage fright, I wonder if part of that fear was not rooted in this quandary of female performers and their bodies. The following statement by Fairouz makes it clear that there are many factors contributing to this fear

> I look forward to my return [to the stage] and I fear it. There is the fear of life and there is the fear of the stage. I fear both. Fear in one's life is exhausting. In life I'm afraid of loneliness... hatred, malice and envy. As for my fear on the stage, it is an ever-present fear. As an artist succeeds, new fears take residence inside him. His name becomes fear. I fear for my art. He who has a sense of responsibility fears everything that calls for fear. Fear is the head of responsibility. As soon as someone loves me my responsibility increases and with it my fear. Stage fright can perhaps be summarized in the moment in which the artist gives everything he has when he meets people. Each of my appearances on stage was a risk of my whole being.
>
> (qtd. in al-Zībāwī 1992: 8)

It is perhaps out of this fear of risking her "whole being" that Fairouz remained so still, that she never joined in the folkloric *dabka*, a dance that is not unconnected to sexuality. Perhaps this is what Bāshā had in mind when he commented that Fairouz had become "frozen" with the Rahbani Brothers (Bāshā 1995: 151). This stillness, this sexlessness, this chasteness is not unrelated to a certain literal loftiness in the representations of Fairouz and her musical theatrical characters, for, as with women in nineteenth-century Bengal, "the image of woman as goddess or mother served to erase her sexuality in the world outside the home" (Chatterjee 1993: 130). In this light, it is not surprising that the poet Jūrj Ibrāhīm al-Khūrī would write: "She is a spirit more than she is a body" (qtd. in Tirād and Khalīfa 2001: 48). It is this etherealness that I take up presently.

The official history of the Baalbeck Festival describes Fairouz's 1957 debut there as follows: "She appeared like the Virgin Mary on a cloud and she let loose with her strong voice: 'Lubnān yā akhdar halū' [Lebanon oh green and sweet]..." (Munassā 1994: 14). It is important to note that this description was written more than thirty-five years after the event itself. How did Fairouz become so closely associated with things celestial? In a 1992 tribute to Fairouz in the *al-Nahār* newspaper,[7] a handful of prominent Arab literati offer testimonials as to her significance. As if they were following the same guidelines, all of their statements mention Fairouz's connection to the sky or to heaven. The Palestinian poet Mahmoud Darwish writes that Fairouz's songs are like our letters to the angels (Darwish 1992: 19). The Egyptian novelist Yūsuf al-Qa'īd quips that "her voice reminds us of heaven's water" (al-Qa'īd 1992: 19). The Lebanese poet Unsī al-Hājj says,

> Her voice adds to life from above and from inside.... It is the purest voice I have ever heard in my life. And in its extreme pureness it is like a ghost coming to you, like an idea, and it seems to you to be abstract, without form, and thus their saying that it is angelic
>
> (al-Hājj, U. 1992: 18)

And the Lebanese writer Jūrj Shahhāda recommends that you

> Close your eyes and listen to Fairouz. Her voice is the voice of angels. We cannot see the angels, but sometimes we hear them sing. It seems as if the sky has forgotten Lebanon but perhaps Fairouz's voice can remind us of this beloved nation.
>
> (Shahhāda 1992: 19)

It is said that Said Akl first called Fairouz Lebanon's Ambassador to the stars. There is no shortage of other references to her proximity to the celestial bodies. Her voice, for example, is that of "the moon shining" (Nāsir 1986: part one, 36), and Fairouz herself "will forever remain the moon of the contemporary Lebanese and the Arab song..." (Wāzin 1996: 20). al-Hājj requests that she "shine always, oh star, shine above the night" (al-Hājj, U. 1987: vol. three, 932). It is no wonder that when asked if she dreams of going to the moon, she responds: why do I have to dream when "we and the moon are neighbors (qtd. in N. 1970: 11)," which is simultaneously a pun on the name of one of her songs written by the Rahbani Brothers and a reference to the general association of herself with the heavens. Whence all of these celestial and heavenly similes and metaphors? Fairouz's pun offers some clue for at least one place to look: the songs. Of the approximately 350 songs that I surveyed, it is worth noting that the word "moon" is found in seventy-one of them. It should be mentioned that there is an arguable connection between all of these references to the moon and stars in her songs, and the fact that the stated or implied context of many of the plays and songs is the

150

Lebanese mountain village. As the song "We and the Moon are Neighbors" ("*Nahnā wa-al-qamar jīrān*") goes: "We and the moon are neighbors. Its house is behind our hills and it rises in front of us to hear our tunes. It knows the time of our assignation and bathes our [roof] tiles in a beautiful light...." This song appears on at least five Fairouz records.

More pertinent to the focus of this book is the content of the plays. How did the plays feed this association of Fairouz with the heavens? I will begin by looking at the plots of the works and then return to the significance of Baalbeck as the context of their production. I have already shown how from her very first second on the stage at Baalbeck, it appeared as if Fairouz was some sort of celestial being hovering up above the audience. Many of her subsequent roles would strengthen this impression. The premise of the 1961 play staged at Baalbeck – *The Woman from Baalbeck* – is that before the gods abandoned that site thousands of years ago, they wanted to take one of the town's inhabitants (the character played by Fairouz) with them so that she could sing for them up in their high places. The other townspeople convince the gods to let her stay and sing for them, as if sealing for Fairouz's characters the role of mediation between the earth and the heavens. In plays such as the 1962 *The Moon's Bridge* and the 1966 *Days of Fakhr al-Din*, the characters played by Fairouz appear and disappear as if they are not of this earth (Abū Murād 1990: 117 and Traboulsi 2006: 47–8). And of her character Ghurba in the 1969 play *Granite Mountains*, 'Āmil writes that she always appears on the stage as if she is descending from the sky to the people ('Āmil 1969: 2–3).

This etherealness is at least in part the result of starring in these nationalistic plays at such a symbolically infused site. It should be remembered that much of the early writing on the Festival in its annual brochures makes the connection between these performances and the worship of the gods in ancient times, making the claim that the singing and dancing that went on at that site thousands of years ago and which is now being revitalized, is "nothing but a prayer to the gods in thanks and supplication" ("Mahrajān al-fann al-sha'bī al-Lubnānī" 1961: 166). There is also a whole book written on the relationship between Fairouz's songs and prayer (e.g. 'Ubayd 1974). Said Akl, who penned the introduction to that book, wrote elsewhere that Asi and Mansour Rahbani were careful in writing and choosing material for her only to give her that which would "make people lift their eyes up to the sky" (qtd. in Zoghaib 1993: part seven, 117). When they did so, if they happened to be attending a performance at Baalbeck, there was some chance that they might actually see Fairouz.

It is thus no surprise that Fairouz is described alternately as "angelic," as I demonstrated above, and "virginal." One of her characters is even called "Halo" (Hala in the 1967 *Hala and the King*). This is only one instance of a general pattern of the concept of the halo being used in conjunction with her life and work. As Abū Murād writes: "Her characters are surrounded by a magical halo, which imposes on the plays a magical atmosphere" (Abū Murād 1990: 234). And when making the connection between the Rahbani-conceived performances at Baalbeck and the ancient rites performed there, he reiterates the image of the halo: "For on these steps her voice rang out for the first time 'Lebanon, oh green and sweet' and this voice embraced the voice of the distant past which erects a halo of piety and dignity on top of those edifices..." (Abū Murād 1990: 58–9). It was Fairouz, according to Khālida Saʿīd, who bestowed on her listeners "the daily halo of sacredness" through her songs (Saʿīd, Kh. 1992: 12). Unsī al-Hājj wrote that without Fairouz, the Rahbani Brothers would not have been nearly as successful as they were. She was, he says, "the halo and the crown" of their project (al-Hājj, U. 1987: vol. three, 848). Even more common than depictions of Fairouz as haloed angel, are the comparisons between her and the Virgin Mary.[8]

Above, I showed how this comparison is made starting with her very first appearance at Baalbeck in 1957. Her character in the 1962 *The Moon's Bridge* is also meant to evoke images of the Christian version of that religious figure. At the end of the 1960s her characters were still inspiring comparisons to the Virgin Mary. This, at least, is how ʿĀmil reads the signification of Ghurba's white dress in the 1969 *Granite Mountains*, as well as that character's role as a mediator between God and the people (1969). And when Fairouz returned to Baalbeck after a quarter-century hiatus in 1998, these associations were once again brought to the fore. One account describes her in her white dress as being "like a statue of the Pure Virgin" (Wāzin 1998: 18). This haloed and ethereal virginity is not only appropriate for the symbol of the historic sanctity of Baalbeck, but also for the mother of all the Lebanese, and the wife of Lebanon itself. Fairouz was not just an ambassador between Lebanon and the heavens, but a haloed and chaste ambassador.

"Fairouz Was and Remains a Villager:" the appropriation of the popular, part three

When Fairouz's characters were not appearing to descend from the sky virgin–like and haloed, they were very much tied to the earth. It should be remembered that with her debut at Baalbeck, Fairouz was suddenly transformed from a young urban radio performer into "Lebanon's leading folklore singer" ("Mahrajān al-fann al-shaʿbī al-Lubnānī" 1959: n.p.). It should also be remembered that what was being enacted in the folkloric "Lebanese Nights" at Baalbeck was portrayed not as a mere *imitation* of the ancient celebratory religious rights that went on there, but rather an actual *reenactment* of these rites by representatives of the descendants of those first supplicants. These descendants are none other than the northern mountain villagers, the progeny of the very Phoenicians who had been driven into the hills by wave after wave of invaders over the centuries (Kaufman 2001: 174). How did this transformation from the urban to the rural take place?

As with her association with the stars and the heavens, the cultivation of the image of Fairouz as a legitimate vessel for folk culture was achieved through the repetition of a certain type of theatrical role, as well as the presence of a consistent discourse about her mountain village roots in a variety of media texts. This was not merely to legitimize her credentials to represent the folk but also – as we have seen in the case of Oum Kalthoum and Farida Fahmi – to preserve her respectability and social status. In terms of her musical theatrical roles, it was not until the beginning of the 1970s that Fairouz ceased to play the innocent childlike mountain village girl. The Rahbanis, particularly in their early works at Baalbeck, were keen on the appropriation of the popular. It is perhaps no coincidence that the centerpiece of this project was a female character. As Chatterjee reminds us

> The popular enters hegemonic national discourse as a gendered category. In its immediate being, it is made to carry the negative marks of concrete sexualized femininity.... But with the mediation of enlightened leadership, its true essence is made to shine forth in its natural strength and beauty: its capacity for resolute endurance and its ability to protect and nourish.
>
> (Chatterjee 1993: 73)

The fact that the Janus-faced discourse of national projects looks back to a legitimizing past and forward to a modernizing present and future has been much commented on. Only recently has this aspect of nationalism begun to be analyzed as gendered. It has become a well-observed fact that it is very often women who represent the past and men who stand for the progress of the future (McClintock 1997: 91–2). Who better to play this past-looking role than a lower middle class woman with strong rural ties and a beautiful voice whose raw talents could be "polished" (Abū Murād 1990: 40) by her mentors?

It has been written that when you hear Fairouz's voice "in the urban prison that is your room," that "space opens and you discover the sky ... and you feel that the sky has returned to the city, or that you have returned to the village" (Kishlī 1992: n.p.). This effect comes not just from Fairouz's link to the sky, as we saw above, or because the songs she sang were about the village, but rather because she herself, as the texts on her repeat, "was and remains a villager" (Nāsir 1986: part one: 36). Fairouz, though brought up in Beirut, would often talk about the childhood summers spent in her village, describing activities very similar to those she would undertake in her theatrical roles, such as carrying a water jug on her head (Nāsir 1986: part one, 37) or singing on her way to fetch water from the spring (Aliksān, J. 1987: 170), while collecting firewood (Haddad 1981: 24), or while sitting on a boulder on the side of the road (Jarkas n.d.: 22). It is worth noting that in the same context as relating these anecdotes, Fairouz would cheerfully mention her childhood poverty in a way reminiscent of her character Hala in *Hala and the King* (Bāsīlā 1973: part one, 56), describing, for example, how she only had one pair of shoes for each year, and just one coat for her whole childhood (Aliksān, J. 1987: 170). The privations of village life are given a romantic glow: there was no electricity in the village and if they heard any kind of motorized sound it might be the once-daily arrival of the rickety local bus (Jarkas n.d.: 22). It was for all of this that she would "count the days until the end of the school year" (Aliksān 1987: 170). And like for Asi and Mansour Rahbani, it was a grandmother who was the center of her world in the village (Bāsīlā 1973: part one). It was she, for example, who would come to Beirut to accompany the young Fairouz back to the village, arriving in the city with a bit of the countryside with her in the form of "hand-picked and roasted almonds" (Aliksān, J. 1987: 170). It was also she who taught Fairouz that village soil was as good as gold (Aliksān, J. 1987: 172).

Though Fairouz would continue to visit either her or Asi's village throughout her life, it was almost always these childhood memories that she would recollect. This is not just a matter of nostalgia, but also perhaps an issue of the child and the childlike being prioritized as the ideal vessels of folklore. Maybe it is for this reason, among others, that the adult Fairouz is so frequently described as a child. Fairouz's voice has been said to be that of an "eternal gentle child" (al-Naqqāsh 1992: 19) as having "the nightingale warbling [quality] of a child" (Aliksān, J. 1987: 147) and of having the voice of a frightened child needing protection (Unsī al-Hajj qtd. in 'Azzām 2002: n.p.). Mahmoud Darwish has described her songs as those which "always forget to grow up" (Darwish 1992: 19). And Fairouz herself has been described as "the child, the mother who forgot to grow up" (Bāsīlā 1973: part one, 56). This striking image brings us back to one of the unifying themes of this chapter: the importance of "desexualizing" the female national symbol, particularly when that symbol is also a performer. The most famous child-mother is, of course, the Virgin Mary. What better analogy could be found for a female performer who represents not just any nation, but a nation the creation and survival of which is so often described as a miracle (e.g. Akl 1964). Both Fairouz's musical theatrical characters and Fairouz herself have often been imbued with the power to perform miracles. We have already seen how her very first night at Baalbeck has been described as a miracle (Munassā 1994: 14), just as we have seen her characters in plays such as *The Moon's Bridge*, *Fakhr al-Din*, *The Station*, and *Granite Mountains* perform or predict miracles. Like her initial appearance at Baalbeck, her very arrival onto the music scene in Lebanon is similarly described as a miracle (Tirād and Khalīfa, R. 2001: 49). Fairouz herself has been attributed with ending a drought in Brazil by singing the song "Rain, Oh World" ("Shattī yā Dinī," 1960) at a concert there (Bāsīlā 1973: part one, 56). al-Hajj has written, "Her voice is responsible for many miracles" (al-Hajj, U. 1987: vol. three, 848). Traboulsi has remarked that *The Moon's Bridge*, the Lebanese "miracle play par excellence" (Traboulsi 2006: 48), was written in reaction to the civil violence of 1958. He has theorized that the role of Fairouz in that play is in part a theatrification of the frequent reported sightings of the Virgin Mary during those events (Traboulsi 2006: 48). From very early in her career, then, Fairouz became associated with miracles and the Virgin Mary. Below I will show that while these symbolic associations were considered by Fairouz to be a great honor, they also put her in something of a bind.

Fairouz: "Prisoner of the Mold"

A woman on the street once called out to Fairouz: "Oh queen, oh great one, oh Mary, oh Pure One." She describes this incident as having "really shaken" her (qtd. in Nasrī 1983: 10). This occurrence is not dissimilar to the fate faced by her character Hala in *Hala and the King*. Hala, a poor mask seller from the countryside is mistaken for the king's bride to be. It is on this basis that the town's authorities detain her. When she declines to be taken to the king's palace, saying that she prefers to wait in the town square, the police chief tells the people that she is to be welcomed and treated with respect. They should fulfill any of her wishes except her desire to leave (Rahbani, A. and M. 1967: 38). To hear Fairouz and some others describe it, the predicament of Hala is not so different from her own.

In some respects, her "imprisonment" is no different from that of any celebrity. This is the sense one gets from the following lament:

> Who would believe that on my trips I don't see anything of the countries I visit? I get off of the plane and go directly to my hotel room where I imprison myself out of fear of illness.... Members of the group have a good time and that is their right. They see the sights of the country, while I am left to my own devices until it's time to appear before the fans. This despite the fact that I am among those who love looking at faces and moving among them. But this pleasure is denied me even in Beirut.
>
> (qtd. in Aliksān, J. 1987: 180)

In the same interview she expresses the usual celebrity ambivalence about fame

> Fame is a golden cage. The artist's freedom is locked away and he lives as a prisoner among his iron bars.... What can I say about fame.... Its bitterness is stronger than its sweetness, except that there are moments I find it impossible to describe.
>
> (qtd. in Aliksān, J. 1987: 180)

More than just a prisoner of fame in general, however, Fairouz seems to have become a captive of the symbol that she came to represent. Elsewhere she says,

> The mold into which I find myself having been poured frightens me.... In art and in normal life I feel that I'm the prisoner of this mold.... My life has become like that of the trapeze artist in the circus of whom it is required that he walk along the wire without falling.
>
> (qtd. in al-Zībāwī 1992: 9)

It is notable that the majority of these prison descriptions are phrased in the passive voice, as if she herself had no control over her fate. Compounding this sense of passivity is Fairouz's paradoxical silence. Despite being the veritable "voice" of this musical theatrical project Fairouz's voice, outside of the context of her onstage performances, was and remains seldom heard. In some of her early statements to the press, Fairouz presents herself as a vessel for the voice of the

Rahbani Brothers. When asked whether she would sing on a desert island that was free of song-writers, Fairouz answers that she would sing only if she had been put in that situation after having met Asi ("Fairouz wa-al-Rahbāniyyān bi-al-fushā" 1964: 2). It is as if without the Rahbani Brothers she would never have sung, despite the fact that she already had a burgeoning career when she started to work with them. The Rahbani Brothers are not just credited with the *fact* of her voice, but with its *content* as well. Later, for example, she would say, "their language became my language..." (qtd. in al-Zībāwī 1992: 7).

This belief may help to explain why she spoke so little in public. When asked once about her famous silence, Fairouz quipped: "I don't know how to talk and don't like to talk. Mansour knows how to talk but doesn't like to talk. Asi knows how to and likes to talk, so we made him 'the talker' " (qtd. in " 'Alā masrah al-haram fī al-Qāhira" 1966: 15). Silence would become one of her trademarks. With regard to all of the controversy surrounding her separation from Asi, it was her silence that was perhaps most frequently remarked upon

> If the Rahbanis have occasionally spoken about the problems, Fairouz has remained silent.... The prophesizing, the whispers, the statements are very many, but despite that, Fairouz has remained silent.... She does not respond, comment or clarify even in cases of injustice and accusations against her.
>
> ('Abdullāh n.d.: 10)

In another interview that remarks on her silence throughout the controversy, she says

> The day that they chose war I chose silence. From the beginning I've been one of the friends of silence. In Egypt they asked me how I felt to be singing in front of the Sphinx.[9] I said that the Sphinx has been my friend for a long time. I love him because he's silent. I want to emphasize that I am from the family of silence. True language is that which passes from heart to heart. Speech does not decide the truth.... Words are impotent....
>
> (qtd. in al-Zībāwī 1992: 8)

One multi-part interview with Fairouz makes her silence one of its main themes, perhaps in order to explain her sometimes short and cryptic answers during the interview itself. The reader is told things like "Of the secrets of speech, she knows only silence" (Nāsir 1986: part one, 35), "You look at her today and find in her strange features of silence, as if she and silence were inseparable twins" (Nāsir 1986: part two, 45), "Fairouz only likes silence" (Nāsir 1986: part two, 45), and "Fairouz preferred silence, leaving the talking to Asi" (Nāsir 1986: part five, 46). This final observation can be confirmed from that fact that in some interviews with Fairouz, Asi interrupts her and ultimately does much of the talking himself (e.g. Bāsīlā 1973). As Nāsir puts it: "Asi used to think and speak for Fairouz" (Nāsir 1986: part eight, 42).

At a 1972 press conference on their upcoming participation in that year's Baalbeck Festival, Fairouz is present but silent. At one point someone asks whether Fairouz will be singing live or if her voice will be prerecorded. The article reports that in response to this question "Fairouz the silent whispers something to Salwā al-Sa'īd [the chairperson of the Baalbeck Festival Committee]." Someone in the audience asks: "Doesn't Fairouz speak? Doesn't she say anything?" The article reports that everyone present responded to this question as if they were a chorus: "She sings" (Ghurayyib 1972: 7). In another interview she quips: "Is not my singing speaking?" (qtd. in Aliksān, J. 1987: 150).

Is it? If Fairouz is more or less silent offstage, and singing other people's words on it, to what extent can she be said to have "a voice" in this project? In the collection of essays on women and modernity in the Middle East mentioned above, Lila Abu Lughod is keen to avoid the trap that some have accused the subaltern studies group of having fallen into, that is of leaving female voices unheard in their study of the underrepresented in Indian historiography (Abu-Lughod 1998a: 23–4).[10] The essays, then, focus on texts produced by women when possible, not without acknowledging the difficulty of recouping voices other than the upper and upper middle class (Abu-Lughod 1998a: 24). The collection of essays in her book is also careful to show that despite the fact that projects of modernity such as nationalism bound women, as Chatterjee puts it, "to a new … subordination" (Chatterjee 1993: 130), that "one need to be attuned to the way that these projects might have been simultaneously regulatory and emancipatory" (Abu-Lughod 1998a: 12). As an example, Abu-Lughod points out that some of the discourses on domestic discipline became the source for movements to provide education to women (Abu-Lughod 1998a: 12). The essays also show some awareness that what was emancipatory for some was regulatory for others (Abu-Lughod 1998a: 24–5). This introduction and the essays included in the volume are part of a positive trend in writing on women in the region, a trend where specific contexts are central and broad generalizations are rare. Even so, if the methodology of such work is based largely on extant texts produced by women, how can they help us to locate the voice of someone as silent as Fairouz?

The concept of agency is a complex one. De Certeau and Appadurai have found there to be a certain amount of agency in consumption (of texts, images, products, etc.) (Appadurai 1996 and de Certeau 1984). De Certeau considers his work on agency and resistance to power to be a foil to Foucault's work on the uses and manifestations of power. It is similar to Foucault's work, however, in that he too is interested in micro mechanisms, that is the small things that "consumers" of power can do to resist power. While de Certeau himself seems to be aware of the danger of setting up power and resistance as a binary, Butler is more explicit about stating that resistance cannot be seen as being separate from power (Butler 1993). In other words, there is no one without certain amounts of both agency and power. Thus, when McClintock writes that "Women are typically constructed as the symbolic bearers of the nation but are denied any direct relation to national agency" (McClintock 1997: 90), one has to approach her use of the word agency with some caution.

In the spirit of the realization that resistance is not simply the antipode of power, it has been argued that silence itself can be a powerful form of agency. In an essay on the effect of the partition of India and Pakistan very literally on the bodies of women, Veena Das talks about the large-scale abduction and rape of women that was carried out by men on both sides. When she tried to interview the victims about these acts, she found a "... zone of silence around the event" (Das 1997: 84). For Das, this silence becomes a form of resistance because these acts were obviously carried out with the knowledge that women's bodies are powerful symbols of the nation. The women, she found, turned this passivity into agency by hiding their pain and by talking about their ordeals by employing the metaphor of pregnancy. But unlike a true pregnancy, the pain would be kept inside never to be born (Das 1997: 85).

In a footnote above I cited the writing of Das and Yang on India/Pakistan and Korea respectively to demonstrate how the sexualization of women's bodies can be central to national discourses. In terms of the issue of silence, however, Yang's findings contradict those of Das and are more in line with my own conclusions about Fairouz's silence. Yang found that the Korean women who had been conscripted as "comfort women" by the Japanese during World War Two were keen to discuss what had happened to them when the issue began to be aired publicly in the early 1990s, but found themselves shamed into silence (Yang 1998). It is possible, in other words, that the women interviewed by Das were not *able*, not only out of shame but also for the sake of their nations, to speak about their traumatic experiences.

In an article about women's literary autobiographies in Arabic, Magda al-Nowaihi took a different tack in arguing that silence can be a powerful form of resistance. Her article compellingly argues that the production of texts after long periods of silence as well as women characters' silences within those texts can be seen as effective forms of resistance in a patriarchal society (al-Nowaihi 2001). Since she is discussing both periods of literary activity preceded by periods of silence and silences within literary texts, however, her study is a powerful reminder that silence is an effective form of resistance when it can be contrasted to periods of non-silence. Though we will see below a case of Fairouz using her silence in this strategic way, by and large it is a challenge to find a voice to contrast to her otherwise striking silence.

This is not to say, of course, that Fairouz was agency-less in this project. There is no question that on the level of day-to-day practice that Fairouz did participate in the choice of material that she would sing and on the manner in which she would perform it (Kāmil, S. 1983b; Nāsir 1986 and al-Wanīn 1991). There is also no question that Fairouz's performance of the songs and roles written for her distinctly added something to them (Murūwa 1998 and Sa'īd, Kh. 1992). But the way that this kind of agency is depicted is telling: "If the Rahbani Brothers are the architects of this image and sound, then Fairouz is that which *embodies* [italics mine] it" (Sa'īd, Kh. 1992: 12). Thus we are back to the image of women "embodying" the nation while men "enact" it. Unsī al-Hājj once wrote, "They do not write the songs 'for her,' but they write them 'by her' " (al-Hājj, U. 1987: vol. one, 337). This sentence can also be read as saying, "They do not write the songs 'for her,' but they write her 'with them'." In Arabic, the sentence reads: "wa-humā lā yaktubāni 'la-hā' al-ughniyya bal yaktubānihā 'bi-hā'." At the end of the sentence the pronoun that can mean "her" or "it" (hā) occurs twice. It is relatively clear from the statement's context that the first hā is referring to "the song" (al-ughniyya) and the second hā to Fairouz. Because of the ambiguity intrinsic in the pronominal suffix hā, however, the second reading remains a possibility. The letter "bi" above is called "bā' al-isti'āna" (Na'ma 1973: 152), that is, the bā' of "instrumentality." If he had wanted to say that she participates in the writing of these songs, he would have used the preposition "ma'a," which, the grammarian Wright explains, "indicates association in time or place" (Wright 1981: vol. two, 264). In his next sentence, in fact, al-Hājj says that when Fairouz performs their songs, she is not singing them "for them [the Rahbani Brothers]," but rather "with them" (ma'ahumā) (al-Hājj, U. 1987: vol. one, 337). While they get to participate in her performance of their songs, she is at best a passive tool in the writing of these songs, if not actually created by them. Whether an instrument or a product, it is clear that al-Hajj's impression is that Fairouz is certainly not an active partner in the production of these texts.

This is not to say that such was the fate of every nation-symbolizing female performer in the region. Oum Kalthoum stands as a case in point. While, like Fairouz, Oum Kalthoum did not write or compose her songs, she did, from a very early stage, take firm artistic and financial control of her career

> She was an entertainer who convinced her conservative family that she could direct her career independently. She eventually bought out her relatives, a prudent and independent move, and ceased performing with them. She made exceedingly canny business decisions on her own, and adopted the fashionable and more revealing garments of the 1930s and 1940s.
>
> (Zuhur 2000: 8–9)

We know too from her English-language biographer Virginia Danielson that despite the fact that Oum Kalthoum had some of the most famous poets of the twentieth century pen the lyrics to her songs and some of the best known composers write her music, that she maintained artistic control over their production (Danielson 1997: 117).[11] One such composer described working with her as being like "building the High Dam [of Aswan]" (Danielson 1997: 129). Oum Kalthoum was also a strong presence on the Egyptian music scene in general. For a period of time she headed the committee that chose what music would be broadcast on Egyptian radio, and in 1945 she nominated herself – and was subsequently elected – to the presidency of the musicians' union. Oum Kalthoum was also more than a passive symbol representing the nation. After the defeat of the Egyptians in the 1967 war with Israel, she staged a famous series of concerts throughout the Arab World and Europe, the proceeds of which she donated to the Egyptian treasury (Danielson 1998: 117).[12]

To question Fairouz's agency in the nation-building project in which she participated is not to say that other Lebanese women of the same time period had no agency in this and other projects. We have already seen, for example, how the "ladies of the [Baalbeck Festival] committee" and the wife of President Chamoun played an active role in shaping this festival and its related folklore movement. The contrast between these elite women and Fairouz raises an important issue. As Sita Ranchod-Nilsson and Mary Ann Tetreault remind us, we must

> acknowledge the diversity of nationalistic projects, which range from organized national liberation movements to multiple and competing discourses about national identity, and to recognize that women, like men, can be found on all sides of these projects.
>
> (Ranchod-Nilsson and Tetreault 2000: 6)

And even when these women are technically on the same side of a certain project, they have greatly varying degrees of power. The comparison between the Baalbeck Festival committee members and Fairouz serves as a reminder of another important fact: that the practice of such agency sometimes results in ambiguous consequences. McClintock cautions

> There is not only one feminism, nor is there one patriarchy. Feminism is imperialist when it puts the interests and needs of privileged women in imperialist countries above the local needs of disempowered women and men, borrowing from patriarchal privilege.
>
> (McClintock 1997: 91–2)

I think that we can for the sake of argument include in this "privileged" category the female national elite of Lebanon at the time of its independence from France.

While it would be difficult to categorize Fairouz as among the "disempowered," it arguable that Fairouz the public persona was a "prisoner" of sorts: once to the nationalist project(s) for which she became an important symbol and once to a cultural environment – not necessarily unique to the Arab or Muslim World – in which the price for being a national symbol was perhaps matched by the price a female performer paid for cultural respectability. Below I will ask to what extent she remained a "prisoner" in her artistic collaboration with her son Ziad, whose goals included freeing Lebanon itself from the constraints of the Rahbani nation.

Fairouz and Ziad: from sky to earth, from mother to daughter

One repeated theme of the writing about the collaboration between Ziad and his mother is that Ziad took Fairouz the icon and "brought her down to earth"

("Hiwār al-'umr" 1997). For some this is a positive development ('Abd al-Amīr 2001 and Khūrī 2000), while for others, it is tantamount to a crime (Baydūn, 'Abbās 2000 and Talīs 1979). What does it mean for Fairouz to be brought down to earth? It means, among other things, the partial transformation of Fairouz from the realm of the allegorical to that of the private. Fairouz, the impression was, gave up her celestial ambassadorship when she began working with Ziad. She went, in other words, from representing a collective to being an individual.

These impressions, while containing a great deal of truth, need to be nuanced. Before looking at Ziad and Fairouz's collaboration, it should be stated that there had already been some variation of the characters "embodied" by Fairouz in her singing and theatrical roles with the Rahbanis over the years, that "her voice had always been changing" (al-'Awīt 1987: 20). Mansour is quoted as saying that though he and Asi never gave up their belief in the love song, their work was always evolving, and along with it so was Fairouz. She went from singing about flowers and birds to singing "I loved You in the Summer" ("Habbaytak bi-al-sayf"). She became, according to Mansour, a mature woman (Aliksān, J. 1987: 87).

Regardless of whether her collaboration with Ziad constitutes a break with the past for Fairouz, this is how many *perceived* it (Aliksān, 'A. 1995 Aliksān, J. 1987, Kabbāra 1991, "Song of Lebanon" 1986, and Suwayd 2000 and 2001). This impression is no doubt bolstered by the cotermination of this collaboration with her separation from Asi. Ziad's writing for Fairouz began, of course, well before the split up, with songs like "The People Asked Me" ("Sa'alūnī al-nās") for the 1973 Rahbani Brothers' production *The Station*. It was after the 1979 separation of Fairouz and Asi, however, that the two began collaborating more extensively and no longer under the aegis of the Rahbani Brothers. Ziad and Fairouz's collaboration differed from that of Fairouz and the Rahbani Brothers in that it was purely musical. Ziad has admitted that he has not thought about writing theatrical roles for Fairouz because he finds the writing of musical dialogues, like those found in the Rahbani Brothers' works, too difficult. While Ziad has continued to pursue a variety of musical and theatrical projects outside of the context of his work with Fairouz, Fairouz herself has come to work more and more exclusively with Ziad. One writer has described this process as the transformation of Fairouz from Ziad's "mother" on that first song to his "daughter" by some of the later projects (Talīs 1991: 41).

Talīs sees this process as nearing completion with Ziad's 1991 effort with Fairouz entitled *How are You?* He comments

> He who did not believe that the Fairouz of Asi and Mansour had become
> the Fairouz of Ziad, now must believe and must be convinced by *How*
> *are You? . . . How are You?* does not ask about the condition of Fairouz,
> but it does offer a response to the question, and it is Ziad who responds.
> (Rahbani, Z. 1991: 40)

'Ammār Aliksān says that Ziad's goal from this record was "to break the myth and challenge accepted truths, to light a fire under the memory of the Rahbanis, under everything that he thought was a counterfeit of reality" (Aliksān, 'A. 1995: 28). Kabbāra writes that the songs on the record speak "the language of all of the people and their daily concerns with bitter and true sarcasm. They leave the traditional behind... and diverge from the Rahbani experiment" (Kabbāra 1991: 16).

For this record, Ziad wrote the music and the lyrics to almost all of the songs. This in contrast to his first two records with his mother, *Alone Together* (*Wahdon*, 1970) and *My Knowledge of You* (*Ma'riftī fīk*, 1987). On both of these earlier records Ziad wrote the lyrics for less than half of the songs. The title track of *How Are You?* in particular was seen as marking a transition. It is not that, as we have seen above, Fairouz did not sing love songs for the Rahbani Brothers or for Ziad in their earlier work together, but on this record, and perhaps on the title track in particular, Fairouz is singing in a new language, both in terms of form and content. At one point the narrator of the song says to her interlocutor: "How are you, what a guy you are" (Rahbani, Z. 1995c: track seven). This phrase "what a guy" is repeated several times and are some of the last words uttered by Fairouz in the song. This phrase, for its colloquial quality[13] and its sarcastic use, became emblematic of the new Fairouz, by both supporters and detractors of this phase. The Iraqi writer Dayzī al-Amīr complains about the "everydayness" of the language on this record, explaining that "we are a people who are imbued with *tarab* by the word" (al-Amīr 1992: n.p.). It is perhaps not just the level of the language, but a combination of its form and content that made this song, and thus the whole record, emblematic of the "new Fairouz." I have commented several times in this book on a speech made in the early Rahbani Brothers' play *Holiday of Glory* in which a wise old man tells a young bride that after her marriage she is to dedicate herself wholly to her husband and children, even if this devotion comes at the expense of her other family members. I have previously mentioned Ziad's reworking of this advice in his play *Happiness Hotel*. Here we have yet another (sub)version of that original speech, this time uttered by Fairouz herself. In the song, she is meeting a past lover after many years of having not seen him. She says that she heard that he now has children, "may God keep them." In the very next line, with the knowledge that this man has a family, she admits to him: "I think about us getting back together." She has this thought, she confesses later in the song, "despite your dependents and the people." She ends the song telling him that she loves him. While the Rahbani project may have stood for a certain kind of sanctioned love, it never came at the expense of the family, and often seemed to be in the service of, if not the nation itself, at least the community. Here we have Fairouz expressing a new kind of love in a new kind of language. On this record, in other words, the personal and private is placed above the collective.

Another version of this song on the same record offers the listener a glimpse not only of the "new" Fairouz, but also of the artistic control that Ziad seemed to be gaining over his mother. The song just prior to the title track consists of a three and a half-minute exchange between himself and his mother as they rehearse the title track. I think that at least part of what Ziad wants to convey via this banter is that Fairouz is not to be confused with the personas she adopts onstage and in songs. She is merely a performer of these roles. At the same time the segment, intentionally or not, gives the impression that Ziad has complete artistic control over the project. At one point during this banter, in order to give Fairouz a sense of how he wants the song to sound, he offers his mother a sample in *his* voice. "Fairouz and I are normal people, a mother and son, working together artistically," seems to be the overt message. What is also made clear is that it is Ziad who is in charge. He is the author, not only of content, but of form as well. Once again the impression given is that Fairouz is more of an instrument than a partner, that like the Rahbani Brothers, Ziad has written these songs "through" (*bi*) Fairouz, not "with" (*ma'a*) her.

Above I discussed aspects of Fairouz's silence, concluding that in her case it was not an apparently effective form of resistance to her iconization. This was not always the case. Fairouz chose not to sing in Lebanon during the long years of the civil war, for example, for fear that her appearance and voice would be exploited by various sides in the conflict (Baydūn, 'Abbās 1994). While she could not control her recorded voice from being co-opted, the goal of her silence was to prevent her live voice from being exploited. It is certainly natural, however, that as soon as the war ended, Fairouz would want to perform in Lebanon after a nearly twenty-year artistic absence. Thus in 1994 she accepted an invitation to sing at the Beirut Festival to be held in what was left of war-devastated downtown Beirut.

The announcement that Fairouz would participate in this Festival led to an uproar. This because the highly controversial consortium of companies called Solidere that had been formed after the war to rebuild downtown Beirut was sponsoring the concert.[14] The fear, it seemed, was that Fairouz's singing at this concert would appear to be an endorsement of the politics of this consortium. The announcement led not only to a slew of articles about the controversy (e.g. Abī Sa'b 1994, 'Assāf 1994, Baydūn 'Abbās 1994, H., J. 1994, al-Hājj, B. 1994, Himsī 1994, "Kull ahad wa-intū bi-khayr" 1994, Qasīr 1994, "Sawt Fairouz yatla' min qalb Beirut" 1994, and al-Sha'shā' 1994), but also to the distribution of pamphlets calling on Fairouz to withdraw from the Festival as well as the circulation of a petition with the same goal.[15] Around this time, Ziad held a public meeting with university students to discuss his new play *If Not for the Possibility of Hope*. The meeting ended up focusing almost solely on the upcoming Fairouz concert, for which Ziad was to be responsible for the music. Ziad explained to his audience that though he agreed with them in principle and had himself signed the petition asking Fairouz not to sing, that he would still arrange the music for the concert and Fairouz would still sing because they were contractually obligated to do so (al-Sha'shā' 1994: 19).

This reaction to her announced plans to participate in this 1994 event shows, despite Ziad's attempts to "bring her down to earth," that Fairouz remained a powerful symbolic figure in Lebanon. The writer 'Abbās Baydūn, while having reservations about the concert, pointed out that perhaps it was not appropriate to protest the Solidere project by trying to embarrass Fairouz. No one, he says "thought much about Fairouz the woman and Fairouz the singer, and no one understood how much a singer would hurt after a silence of fifteen years" (Baydūn, 'Abbās 1994: 52). In the end, both the organizers of the Festival and its opponents partook in the symbolization of the concert and of Fairouz. Baydūn wanted to remind his readers that Fairouz is not only a symbol, but a woman as well.

The concert was, at least in terms of numbers, a huge success, with some 40,000 fans watching the show, many of them having been bussed in from various parts of the country. The fact that Fairouz did participate in the Festival explodes the notion of her as a completely pliant figure. Though she is often portrayed as being a tool of one Rahbani project or another, her appearance at this event – regardless of what one thinks of its prudence – was, among other things, a clear indication of a certain measure of independence, an independence that had already manifested itself in other, if more subtle ways, as well.

Fairouz's first album with Ziad – *Alone Together* – contains a rendition of the song "To the Drone of the Bus" that was originally sung by Joseph Saqr in Ziad's 1988 play *What About Tomorrow*. This song was originally meant as a kind of faux-pastoral. I also mentioned in that chapter the trouble Ziad had had in walking the fine line between parody and homage and how such balance became particularly challenging as Joseph Saqr's voice became more and more popular and as the songs were heard more and more outside of the context of the plays. Thus "To the Drone of the Bus" had become extremely popular not *because* of its parodic nature but rather *despite* it. Not all observers, however, missed the sarcastic nature of that and the less popular song from that play, "I sent you." Some were surprised that both of these songs were included on Ziad's first record with Fairouz. When the music critic Nizār Murūwa asked Ziad how he could have had his mother sing these songs, Ziad seems to be at a rare loss for words, finally saying that the song is transformed when Fairouz sings it. In another interview, Ziad has said that when Fairouz sings the song, the rickety old-fashioned bus (*būsta*) turns into a more modern bus (*awtūbūs*) (al-Zayn 1980: n.p.). When Murūwa presses him on the issue, however, Ziad admits that maybe if he had thought more about it, or maybe if he had had this interview earlier, he would never have let her sing those songs (Murūwa 1998: 334–5).

More confrontationally and punningly, Talīs asks: "Does Fairouz develop or decline to the drone of the bus?" (Talīs 1979: 6). In the article of that title he concludes that the song is not suitable for her, that her voice is such that she cannot convince us that she is singing on a run-down old bus (Talīs 1979: 6). Rūmiyyū Lahhūd's criticism is more pointed. He says that this work is not a song but rather "an adolescent tale." Fairouz's talents and energies, he goes on to say, need great poetry. It is fine for her to collaborate with her son on a song or two, but it is unreasonable to think that she would continue her work with him (qtd. in Aliksān, J. 1987: 285–6). Fairouz herself was asked if it was not demeaning for a performer of her stature to sing songs that were originally written for someone else? She responded that it did not matter for whom the song had been written, but rather who had written the song ('Abdullāh n.d.: 12).

Perhaps these critics were missing the point. First of all, this song seemed to establish the start of a new stage for Fairouz in people's minds. Jān Aliksān says that this song met with immediate success and that it allowed her to enter "a vast world" which she had not been able to enter previously because of "the 'siege' that had been imposed on her" (Aliksān, J. 1987: 103). What he seems to be implying is that with this song the siege was lifted. While Fairouz had always been associated with both the heavens and the countryside, her association with the latter was always in the context of the sanitized representation of the folk in "The Lebanese Nights" of the Rahbani Brothers. It was as if Fairouz the angel had descended from the heavens and taken up residence in a village on Mt Lebanon. In her rendition of this song, in contrast, the words are those of the poor village farmer whom Joseph Saqr played in the original theatrical context of this song, not of the angel or savior Fairouz had come to embody. The only change made to the song for Fairouz was the addition of a two-line *mawwāl* at the beginning in which she poetically expresses the effect that the eyes of her beloved have had on her. She then proceeds to sing the song almost exactly as Joseph Saqr had. Not only is the narrator of this song riding in an old broken-down bus, he seems to be doing so without paying the fare, all the while remarking on the ugliness of a fellow passenger's ill wife, the oppressively hot weather and, perhaps most shockingly, asking God to "destroy the house" of the eyes of the beloved. The narrator of the song says, "Oh Alyā, may [God] destroy the house of your eyes" (Rahbani, Z. 2000: track five). While the expression "May God destroy your house" (*Allāh yikhrib baytak*) is often used in jest, it is not the kind of expression that the followers of Fairouz were used to hearing from her. It is easy to see how the use of such language and imagery by Fairouz would be disconcerting to some. It is equally easy to see how the use of just such imagery and language could have been, in a sense, liberating to her.

While the singing of "To the Drone of the Bus" can be interpreted as an emancipating act for Fairouz, it can also be seen as a marker of the ambivalence both she and Ziad had toward the Rahbani Brothers' project. While the song may have originally been written as a parody, one of the effects of Fairouz's performance of it was to neutralize its critical dimension, to complete its transformation into a kind of homage. The musical collaboration of Fairouz and Ziad would continue to vacillate between the two poles represented in the history of this song. In the same year that they released this first collaborative record together, Fairouz performed a concert in Paris. The concert was dominated by songs either by the Rahbani Brothers or songs that *sounded* like songs by the Rahbani Brothers (Talīs 1979: 6), a testament to the slow and never complete transition to a new repertoire.[16] A few years later – in 1981 – Fairouz made her second trip to the US for a series of concerts where she sang a similar repertoire, even though these concerts were directed by Ziad. Eleven out of the fourteen songs that Fairouz sang on that tour were by the Rahbani Brothers. The show also included a series of folkloric dances of a type that Ziad had previously and would subsequently parody in his own work. The producer of that tour was none other than Ziad himself. The tour's brochure informs us that he "prepared the entire program," including the choreography for the folkloric dance scenes (Boullata 1981: 68).

In his 1986 radio show *Brains are Just for Decoration*, Ziad talks about the expectations of the Lebanese who have been living outside of the country and getting their information on Lebanon solely from the Rahbani Brothers' musicals. He says that if such a person decides to go back to Lebanon, he will expect to see so much greenery upon his arrival that he will need an eye doctor. He corrects this person's expectations, telling him that he will not see Fakhr al-Din (from the play *The Days of Fakhr al-Din*) in the airport, and that the "mountains of which there are none higher" have all been bombed. What do you expect, he asks, that Fātik (from the play *Granite Mountains*) will carry your suitcases and that Hala and the king (from the play *Hala and the King*) will help you fill out your papers? Hala and the king have gone to Brazil like everyone else (Rahbani, Z. 1987: disc one, track two, 13:10). What about Fairouz and Ziad's concerts abroad? Would they have done anything to change the expectations of the migrant Lebanese who imagines his country to be like the Lebanon of the Rahbani Brothers' plays?

I bring up these apparent contradictions as a way of demonstrating the significant pull that the Rahbani project continued to have, not only on its audience, but on both Fairouz, who had been its main voice, and Ziad, who in other contexts had reacted so strongly against it. In 1986, for example, just around the time that the radio show *Brains are Just for Decoration* would begin to be broadcast, the mother-son duo teamed up for a concert in London. By all accounts the show – featuring Ziad on the piano – was a great success. One article reports that the audience was most responsive to two songs: the Lebanese national anthem and "I Love you Lebanon" (Mahfūz, H. 1986: 42). It should be remembered that the release of the latter song by the Rahbanis and Fairouz ten years earlier had marked a dramatic ideological and even physical rift between Ziad and his family. What is Ziad doing ten years later – Lebanon still in the grip of civil war – accompanying Fairouz through this song on the piano in London, even though his 1986 radio show targets, if not that very song, at least the use of the word "stubborn" in it?[17] The fact that the other song to receive the greatest response was the national anthem provides perhaps our best clue to the puzzle this question represents. In London, Fairouz was not singing primarily for a European audience, but rather for a diasporic Lebanese one, for whom such songs would have been particularly appealing. If the intersection of mass media, migration, the appropriation of the popular and the classicization of tradition in the form of the Rahbani Brothers project had had tremendous subject forming powers, these powers were not limited to the subjectivities of its audience. As I demonstrated above, Fairouz was, in a sense, imprisoned by the Lebanon that she enacted and embodied. She was not the only one. The fact of the inclusion of these works in his repertoire with her make it clear that Ziad himself was not exactly "free" to do with Fairouz as he wished. I do not suggest a rigid dichotomy between producers and consumers, but wish to point to the participation of all subjects in the discursive conditions of their existence. Therefore, those most active in the discursive production of the nation could not go untouched by the transformative capacity of discourses of the nation. In fact, as we have seen, they sometimes come to embody it in a most profoundly personal way.

Michel De Certeau argues against a passive notion of structured subjectivity that a Foucauldian framework might seem to imply. For him, objects of discourse are transformed by consumers, and in this sense subjectivity is formed through a productive process, which he refers to in terms of "tactics" (De Certeau 1984: xx). Lila Abu-Lughod has shown how this works with popular culture in her study on the reception of soap operas on Egyptian television, where she shows that the poor rural women whom she studied often found lessons in this programming that its producers did not intend (Abu-Lughod 1995). But what can be said about the producers themselves? If consumption can be seen as an act that disrupts the binary relationship between an active producer and a passive consumer, then might not production be invaded by a certain measure of consumption as well? Fairouz, Ziad, and the Rahbani Brothers are not only consumers of their own products, but also consumers of the *reception* of their products. It is almost as if Ziad had no choice but to lead Fairouz through the national anthem and the song that he claims drove him from his family home and from East Beirut.

After the death of Asi in 1986 there were a number of events held to honor his memory. Controversially, neither Ziad nor Fairouz participated in any of them. Despite his well-known ambivalence towards his father, Ziad's absence from these commemorative occasions was explained as being not out of respect for Asi, but rather because he felt that such events had ideological agendas behind them (Hamāda, M. 1992: 53). Ziad and Fairouz would wait almost ten years before marking the death of Asi publicly. In 1995 they released a record called *To Asi* which consists of seventeen of Asi and Mansour's songs, rearranged by Ziad and sung anew by Fairouz.

Most of the reactions in the press to this musical tribute were positive. Writers like Bāshā and Wāzin found that the rearrangement of the songs was done tastefully without doing violence to the memory of Asi (Bāshā 1995 and Wāzin 1996). Ziad himself has said that he had wanted to remain true to the atmosphere of the original versions and to that end he tried to use as many of the original instruments in his rearrangements as possible, taking great care over five years of work and tinkering to get everything right (Fadl Allāh 1995). There were, however, some dissenters (e.g. Aliksān, 'A. 1995 and Baydūn 'Abbās 2000). 'Ammār Aliksān contends that instead of adding to the Rahbani collage, Ziad in this record has "painted over it" (Aliksān, 'A. 1995: 28). He implies that Ziad has done some violence to the songs that he rearranged, in light of the fact that the songs he chose to be reworked were still very much in circulation. By choosing these popular songs to redo Ziad had, in his opinion, museumified the originals. He says that the black and white photo of Asi on the album cover is emblematic of what Ziad has done to the memory of the man's work: he has taken a project full of color and made it seem archaic and monochromic (Aliksān, 'A. 1995: 28–31).

167

In light of the sum of Ziad's musical theatrical parodies of his parents' work and his more direct statements to the press about his family's project, it is easy to see why there would be some suspicion as to the intentions behind this project. In a variety of interviews, for example, Ziad has indicated that though he had a large measure of appreciation for the Rahbani Brothers' – and particularly Asi's – music, he did not think much of the lyrics (al-Ashqar 1981 and Bāshā 1987b). Well before Ziad and Fairouz released this record, Nizār Murūwa said he understood that one important aspect of Ziad's collaboration with Fairouz was the continuation of the Rahbani artistic mission by writing new songs for her and by rearranging the old Rahbani songs without words (Murūwa 1998: 317). Perhaps he was think-ing of a song like "'Ayntūrā" (name of a Lebanese mountain town thirty-eight kilometers northeast of Beirut) on the record *My Knowledge of You*, which is a lyric-less rearrangement of a song originally composed by Asi.[18] On *To Asi* however, Ziad does the exact opposite, rearranging the music for seventeen classic Rahbani Brothers' songs without changing a single word. He has, in other words, altered the musical compositions, which he has said he respected, and kept the lyrics, which he spent much of his artistic career countering and parodying. This is not to say, of course, that the mood of the songs is not altered by some of the brooding and jazzy arrangements, but the fact remains that he has made no significant alterations to the lyrics of these songs.

Did he, one might wonder, choose songs with lyrics that were not representative of the Rahbani Brothers' general oeuvre? Actually, in terms of their vocabulary and general themes, the songs on the record are quite representational of the Rahbani folkloric lexicon that Ziad had previously parodied. For example, in the play *A Failure* Ziad mocks the frequent use of words like "'īd" (holiday), "mawā'īd" (dates or appointments), and "'anāqīd" (clusters of grapes), particu-larly the repeated juxtaposition of these items for purposes of rhyming. In *To Asi*, these words appear with an even greater frequency – separately and as rhyming units – than they do in the greater Rahbani's oeuvre itself. Whereas some version of the word "appointment" appears in 11 percent of the 353 Rahbani songs which I surveyed, it appears in a full 35 percent of the 17 songs on *To Asi*. And while the word "clusters of grapes" appears with an equal relative frequency in both sets of songs, the word "holiday" occurs 3 times more frequently in the songs that Ziad chose for *To Asi* than it does in the 353 Rahbani Brothers songs that I examined. And some combination of these words is used for rhyming purposes on at least two songs on Ziad's record as well. In Ziad's second play *Happiness Hotel* he mocked his parents' frequent use of certain lexical items having to do with birds and flight, flowers, and the village spring. Without exception, these words occur much more frequently in the songs that Ziad chose for *To Asi* than they do in the Rahbani song collection as a whole. For example, the generic word for flower (*zahr*) appears in 24 percent of the Rahbani songs that I surveyed, but is in almost half of the songs chosen by Ziad for this record. Other ubiquitous words in the Rahbani lexicon that appear with high frequency in the songs on this record are: "moon," "high," "heart," "air," "light," and words related to "waiting," "night," and "nighttime parties," "mountains," and "memory" or "remembrances." In other words, Ziad chose some of the most rural-mountain centric songs in the Rahbani oeuvre for this record. This might prove not only the record title's claim that this project was a tribute to Asi, but also that the very material that he had reacted against so strongly earlier and even while working on this record, had taken hold of him and Fairouz at least as much as it had the rest of Lebanon and the Arab World.

Perhaps the imperative question to ask here is not whether Ziad released Fairouz from some sort of prison, or even how much agency Fairouz had in the formation of either project, but rather whether or not Fairouz, Ziad, and even the Rahbani Brothers themselves were all prisoners of the Lebanon that they created in conjunction with the Baalbeck Festival starting in 1957? Whatever conclusion one reaches, however, I hope to have shown that of all of the participants in these two projects, it was Fairouz whose public persona was the most affected. While Asi, Mansour, and Ziad themselves were all arguably "prisoners" of the Rahbani nation, Fairouz can be seen as a "captive" of the Rahbanis *and* their nation.

CONCLUSION
Beiteddine 2000 and beyond

I began this book with a description of Fairouz's controversial concert at the 1998 Baalbeck Festival. I shall end by focusing on her contrasting appearance at the 2000 Beiteddine Festival and then by commenting on some of her more recent activities. Whereas Ziad had withdrawn from the 1998 Baalbeck Concerts at the last minute in protest, he was not only present in 2000 at Beiteddine, he was also in complete charge. Also in contrast to 1998, most accounts describe the 2000 show as a great success, particularly in terms of the rabidly enthusiastic reception Fairouz received from her fans, "who had not had their thirst quenched when she sang at Baalbeck in 1998, because her voice had not been live and because it had had the taste of the old Rahbani Brothers' material" (Wāzin 2000b: 13). This is how one commentator describes the audience's response on the first night of the three-concert series: when Fairouz finally took the stage "... any lingering doubts were washed away by a standing ovation and by the time the first notes left her mouth, she had already won the hearts and souls of the audience. The applause only got louder, the cheering only became warmer..." (Singh-Bartlett 2000c: n.p.). Elsewhere, the same writer describes the concert's end similarly

> The three-song encore... drove the audience into a frenzy, [and] seemed in retrospect, part of an almost 30-minute ovation. While certain songs drew the hard core to their feet throughout the performance of over 2 hours, the applause barely stopped at all for the last four songs, morphing during the songs into rhythmic clapping in time to the music. By the encore, people were on their feet in the aisles, if not dancing, then shouting their approval. It was a perfect end with Fairouz giving the crowd exactly what they wanted, the chance to tell her that, in the words of one of her songs, they love her and only her.
>
> (Singh-Bartlett 2000b: n.p.)

This in contrast to the 1998 concert at Baalbeck, which had been described as having had the atmosphere of a funeral (Abī Samrā 1999: 9).

The commentaries on the 2000 Beiteddine concert focus centrally on what they describe as a "new" and a "newly born" Fairouz. Ilyās Khūrī, comparing the event

170

to the 1998 concert, comments that her very appearance provided a stark contrast to the event of 1998, where, in her white dress, she had looked like the Virgin Mary (Khūrī 2000: n.p.). He is not alone in focusing on the striking contrast of her red and black dresses at Beiteddine to her appearance at Baalbeck two years earlier ('Ināya 2000, Shams 2000a, and Wāzin 2000b). It is at Beiteddine, he conjectures, that she was finally brought down to earth, that she was reborn and, perhaps most important of all, released from the prison of her past (Khūrī 2000: n.p.).

The concert itself included many of the old but rearranged Rahbani songs that Fairouz had sung on *To Asi*. The best received songs, however, were those written by Ziad (Shams 2000a). Several writers, including Ilyās Khūrī, comment on her rendition of a song originally sung by Joseph Saqr on his and Ziad's 1995 record *Seeing as That...* (Khūrī 2000: n.p.). In Chapter 3, I focused on the parodic *'atābās* of that record. It also contains a number of other sarcastic pieces. Fairouz seemed to catch the audience off guard when she sang, for the first time, one of these latter songs – "'Ayyāsh phoned" ("Talfan 'Ayyāsh") – which is about an unreliable handyman. For 'Abd al-Amīr, it is at this moment that she conclusively enters Ziad's world of irony and sarcasm ('Abd al-Amīr 2001: n.p.). For Shams it was at this juncture that she became a citizen of, as she puts it, "the second Rahbani Republic" (Shams 2000a: n.p.). Behind these comments is perhaps an observation about Fairouz's physical bearing while singing this song. While Fairouz had been her usual stiff self on the stage at the beginning of the concert, several writers comment on her surprising and playful interaction with the chorus during this song on subsequent nights. In general, she seemed more relaxed and at ease physically than ever before (Shams 2000a and Wāzin 2000b).

Another defining moment comes when during the multiple-song encore of each of the three concerts she sang a new song written by Ziad "Morning and Evening" ("Sabāh wa-masā"). As opposed to the other songs of the show, this one was performed without the chorus and without the orchestra. Her only accompaniment came from Ziad on the piano. One writer describes the crowd reacting, not only in "a storm of applause," but also in a euphoric attempt to rush the stage (Shams 2000a: n.p.). Another reviewer described the crowd's response as "an emotional revolution among the fans [who] knew that the song was extremely new and belonged to Ziad Rahbani's school" (Wāzin 2000b: 13). Perhaps it was this song that Ilyās Khūrī was referring to when he said Fairouz's rebirth meant that her words were no longer spoken through a mythic filter (Khūrī 2000: n.p.).

The concert was thought not only to be a great success, but also as being representative of the completion of Fairouz's entry into Ziad's world. Aside from one writer who suggests that it was Fairouz who chose which songs to sing (Singh-Bartlett 2000a), others go out of their way to stress Ziad's complete artistic control over every aspect of the event, including "the administration, the supervision of the orchestra, the chorus, the stage directions; and the choice and arrangement of the songs and the musical introductions" ('Ināya 2000: n.p.). Wāzin adds that this total artistic control was evident from the very start of the show, testifying to Ziad's "dominating the atmosphere of the concert" in his capacity as Fairouz's "current monopolizer." It is at this concert, he adds, that Fairouz "surrenders to him" (Wāzin 2000b: n.p.).

While there seems to have been little debate over whether or not this concert represented a new phase for Fairouz, the question of agency remains unresolved. One writer describes the transition that this concert represents as happening when Fairouz finally gave Ziad a free hand and entrusted him with overseeing all artistic aspects of the concerts ("Saharāt Fairouz al-thalāth fī Beiteddine" 2000: n.p.). Another puts it that for these concerts Ziad received complete control of the project's reins. The same article goes one to talk about Fairouz of 2000 as being "drawn by Ziad," but then says that it is Fairouz who has chosen "to wash with the youth of her son" (al-Abtah 2000: n.p.).

It has been said that Ziad had rescued the late singer Joseph Saqr from one bottle only to imprison him in another ("Jūzīf Saqr" 1996: n.p.).[1] Can this concert be seen to confirm that Fairouz too had escaped from one prison find herself, to a certain extent, in another? Through her work with Ziad, Fairouz seems, on the one hand, to have been released, to a great extent, from the prison of allegory. A septuagenarian, she no longer sings as a child, as a savior, or as the Virgin Mary, but rather – as we started to see glimpses of on the 1991 album *How Are You?* – as a mature lover suffering the vicissitudes of romantic love. On the other hand, there is some sense that in releasing her from the allegorical, he had imprisoned her in his own project of subversion.

I have shown that though Fairouz achieved great success and fame during her thirty-year collaboration with the Rahbani Brothers, she also ended up a prisoner of a very particular sort. This is not just a case of the normal paradox of fame and freedom, for Fairouz had come to represent nothing less than the nation itself, a position which required that she be an incarnation of romantic ideals about the female Lebanese mountain peasant while at the same time being virtually a bodiless, sexless, motionless, mute, and haloed angel. This result was very much connected to the context of her and the Rahbani Brothers' participation in Lebanon' nation-building process, to their shaping of "The Lebanese Nights" section of the Baalbeck Festival. Their project, in the context of the Festival, was the musical-theatrical enactment of an idea of Lebanon's past and the connection of that past to the present day peasant, which demanded that Fairouz be both daughter of the earth and queen of the sky simultaneously. I have also explored how Fairouz's post–Rahbani Brothers' collaboration with her son Ziad did not succeed in completely freeing her from her symbolic status. I hope to have shown, in fact, that Ziad himself, despite musical-theatrical and musical projects that often parodied his parents' work directly, could himself never completely break free from the strong aesthetic and ideological pull of the Rahbani Brothers' representations of the nation.

I have shown how these representations, reiterated at the Baalbeck Festival and elsewhere in Lebanon and abroad, largely served, not "the nation" as a whole, but rather a particular and elite vision that considered the representational epicenter

172

of the nation to be the rural northern Christian Mt Lebanon. This comprised the land roughly contiguous with the Mt Lebanon area of self-rule under French protection from 1860 until the Ottomans reclaimed it during World War One. The Rahbanis' performances at Baalbeck, then, were one manifestation of a project that meant to give cultural assistance to the imposition of the rule of the mainly Christian mountain on the conglomeration of former Ottoman districts that came to be called Greater Lebanon, and then just Lebanon. I also argued that these representations gained much of their force not just from the fact of being performed at Baalbeck under the aegis of the International Baalbeck Festival, but also because their staging coincided with the rapid development of mass media and the increase of internal and external migration in Lebanon. The combination of these factors made their musical-theatrical representations extremely powerful, but problematically so. While the power – and eventual adaptability – of this project is reflected in its influence beyond the borders of Lebanon, its darker side can be seen in the suggestion that it played some role first in the reification and then the heating up of sectarian differences that in turn played some part in the start of the civil war in 1975. One of the many paradoxes of this outcome is that the Rahbanis' project gained important impetus from the unifying efforts of the Chehab regime whose policies, cultural and otherwise, were shaped by the short-lived civil violence of 1958. It was a project, in other words, both predicated on the importance of national unity and state building but participating in the preclusion of those goals.

If the Rahbani Brothers' project had an indirect impact on the production of sectarian and political instabilities in Lebanon, it had an even much more traceable role in the formation of the musical and musical-theatrical project of Ziad Rahbani – Fairouz and Asi's son. After it appeared initially as if their project would be continued through him, Ziad turned against his parents politically and artistically. Even before the start of the civil war, Ziad began to parody his parents' simplistic and opportunistic use of Lebanese folklore with his *Happiness Hotel*. His assault on their representations of Lebanon became more direct with the start of the civil war and can be said to have reached a crescendo with his 1983 *A Failure*. It was not only his most directly critical work, but also his most polyglossic. In sum, the Lebanon of his plays – not to mention his radio programs and songs – is not the Lebanon of his parents' works. It is a Lebanon that reflects to a great extent what Greater Lebanon had become through decades of rural urban migration and the continued marginalization of various groups, a marginalization that is reflected in the attempted monoglossia of his parents' work, that is, their fantasy version of a pre–Greater-Lebanon Lebanon.

Even in his most critical phases, however, Ziad was never able to break free from his parents' project completely. This ambivalence showed itself, for example, in the fineness of the line between homage and parody in some of his theatrical songs. This is easiest to see, perhaps, in his ongoing collaboration with his mother Fairouz. Though this project has done much to free Fairouz from a certain kind of symbolic role in the Rahbani nation, it also reflects, particularly in their ex-Lebanon concerts and in their tribute record *To Asi*, that neither Fairouz nor Ziad are completely free from the Rahbani nation itself.

This is clear even from the 2000 Beiteddine concert, over which Ziad appears to have had so much control, and where Fairouz was said to have succumbed to his artistic wishes. Although each of the three nights of the concert ended with a different song, when Ziad released a recording of the concerts a few months later, he chose to end the record with the climactic song from the third night, the old Rahbani standard "The Breeze Gently Blew On Us" ("Nassam 'alaynā al-hawā") from the 1968 film *Daughter of the Guard* (*Bint al-hāris*). With this choice, old Rahbani songs frame the record. The first song on the record, after a musical intro-duction, is "You Are not my Lover" ("Lā inta habībī"), which Ziad had previously rearranged for *To Asi*. Though this series of concerts may have witnessed the "rebirth" of Fairouz and though Ziad may have played "midwife," the framing of the record by these two songs makes it clear that neither they nor Lebanon, after more than fifteen years of civil war – are totally free of the "Rahbani nation."

Nostalgia is a powerful force. If the first Rahbani project had centered on nostalgia for the pre–World War One period of self-rule on Mt Lebanon, perhaps the second project expresses nostalgia, not for the Lebanon envisioned by the Rahbanis in their folkloric musical-theatrical performances, but for the Lebanon which was the *context* for those performances, that is the pre-*naksa* and pre–civil war Lebanon. What better voice than Fairouz to express this new nostalgia and who better to orchestrate it, literally and figuratively, than Ziad? This is what Jonathan Bach calls "modernist nostalgia," which "is less a longing for an unredeemable past as such than a longing for the fantasies and desires that were once possible in that past" (Bach 2002: 547).

In the Introduction I asked why the fact that Fairouz's voice was not live at her 1998 Baalbeck Festival appearance was so controversial when this technique had apparently been used widely by the Rahbani Brothers in their prewar productions. Here I would like to suggest a partial answer. Even though Fairouz's voice had been recorded in the days leading up to that concert, there was a widespread rumor that what was played at the concert were actually the original prewar recordings of those songs (al-Zībāwī 1998). This impression added to the sense that these songs were out of date and full of empty slogans (Wāzin 1998). At the Beiteddine Festival in the year 2000, many of the songs, such as the songs that had been rearranged for Fairouz by Ziad for their 1995 tribute album *To Asi*, were Rahbani Brothers' songs from the same prewar era. Why was the same type of songs better received in 2000 than in 1998? One reason is the location.

Though Beiteddine is an important historical site in Lebanon and though Fairouz had sung there previously, it was not associated with the elite nationalist project that the Rahbanis and Fairouz had contributed so centrally to at Baalbeck. The Beiteddine Festival was founded in 1985 by the leader of the Progressive Socialist Party (PSP), Walid Jumblat (Walīd Junbalāt). It ran for three successive summers (1985–7) and then continuously every summer since 1994 ("History of the Festival" 2002). The PSP was founded in 1949 by Walid's father Kamal. It was a relatively left-wing Arabist party concerned about the poor that sought and succeeded in extending its base beyond its roots in the Druze community (Petran 1987: 47–8). The Beiteddine Palace lies in the southern part of Mt Lebanon known as the Chouf. Though the palace was built in the early nineteenth century by the Maronite Prince Bashīr Shihāb II, and though it was the seat of government during the period of self-rule on the mountain, this part of the mountain had always been a stronghold of the Druze, despite the steady growth of the Maronite population southward in the mountain until they constituted a majority there by the mid-nineteenth century (el Khazen 2000: 34). During the civil war, the Druze, under the leadership of Walid Jumblat, were able to gain control of much of the Chouf in what has come to be known as "The Mountain War" (Petran 1987: 318–22). It is at this time and in this context that the Festival was launched. Since 1987, the Festival has been run by Walid Jumblat's wife Nūra ("History of the Festival" 2002). And although the palace has long reverted to government control, in addition to the Annual Festival, it houses a permanent museum dedicated to the memory of Kamal Jumblat. The year 2000 was not the first time that Fairouz had sung at the site. In the summer of 1965 she and the Rahbani Brothers staged a concert there (Bāshā 1995: 153).

Important too is the fact that the songs at Beiteddine – unlike Baalbeck in 1998 – were not presented in the context of the original Rahbani Brothers' plays. As we saw above, some of Ziad's songs for Joseph Saqr had previously suffered when they were taken out of their parodic musical-theatrical context. Ziad seems to have learned a lesson from this experience. In this case, removing the songs from the context of their original plays served Ziad's goals quite well. Fairouz no longer symbolized the Christian village mountain nation. If she remained a symbol for anything through these old rearranged songs, it was a symbol of the nostalgia for the hope of the days when she first sang them. This is why the fans reacted so differently to these songs being sung live. This is not Fairouz in her nation-symbolizing prison cell as her 1998 performance was interpreted as being, but rather the new fully humanized and sexualized postwar Fairouz singing, in her new songs written for her by Ziad, of adult love and, in her old rearranged songs, of a nostalgia for the hope of those prewar days.

The fact of this nostalgia for the pre–civil war period is not to say that no lessons were learned from the mistakes of the original Rahbani project or from the long war that followed it. Fairouz may be Ziad's prisoner to a certain extent, but she is no longer just an allegory for the nation. Even the Baalbeck Festival seems to have learned some lessons. With the diva's switch to Beiteddine, the Summer Arts Festival scene in Lebanon has become so competitive as to be described as a war (Talīs 2000). Because of the great success of the two scheduled appearances by Fairouz at Beiteddine that summer, a third night was added. This night was scheduled, perhaps provocatively, to coincide with the opening night of the Baalbeck Festival's "Lebanese Nights," which, like in prewar times, was to showcase Lebanese folklore. But unlike the folklore of the Rahbanis – which had begun as being representative of the folklore of Mt Lebanon and which had developed into a synthetic amalgamation of all Lebanese folklore based on mountain folklore – the "Lebanese Nights" of the 2000 Baalbeck Festival was to include – for the first time since the late 1950s – folkloric performances said to represent *each* of Lebanon's five provinces. I would like to argue that this apparently small gesture toward the recognition of the diversity of the *dabka* in Lebanon at the 2000 Baalbeck Festival is an important sign of a realization that, for there to be one Lebanon, there has to be recognition that there are many Lebanons. This realization may have been catalyzed not only by the civil war itself but also by the critical, polyphonic, and parodic musical theater and music of Ziad Rahbani.

Events since that summer only further demonstrate the ambivalence that both Ziad and Fairouz seem to have toward the original Rahbani project. In the summer of 2001 Fairouz and Ziad returned to Beiteddine and performed a series of concerts quite similar to the ones they staged in 2000. In describing this concert 'Ināya echoes Ilyās Khūrī from the previous year when she says that Ziad has brought Fairouz down from the heavens ('Ināya 2001). The comments of others echo much of what was written about the 2000 concerts, that is that this concert was further proof of Fairouz's submission to Ziad's artistic vision (see, for example, al-Abtah 2001: n.p.).

Both Ziad's apparent control of this collaboration and Fairouz's new nonallegorical status were again confirmed by her most recent release with Ziad, *Or What* (*Walā Kīf*, 2002), which came out at few months after their second collaboration at Beiteddine. On this record, Ziad marries his love of jazz with his proclivity toward having Fairouz sing nonallegorical love songs. Except for the fact that the songs are in Arabic, Fairouz is no longer an "Arab singer," but rather "a singer." On this album, Ziad seems to approach his goal of de-allegorizing Fairouz. One might argue that this is not true of the whole album. Does she not sing an old religious song – "Oh Mary" ("*Yā Maryamu*") – about the Virgin Mary that she had first sung on a record of religious songs in the early 1960s? Is not the song full of the very adjectives that used to describe Fairouz's theatrical characters and Fairouz's public persona: virgin like and flying up above the moon, sun and stars? Yes, but of all of the religious songs that she sang it is interesting to note that this is one of the few that is sung in the second person. Fairouz and Ziad are once and for all announcing her separation from the Virgin Mary by having Fairouz sing a song *to* her. And in case the second-person voice of the song is not enough to remind the listener that the singer is not to be identified with what is being sung about, the song is sung, not to sonorous church music as it was in the original, but rather to the jazzy Latin sound with which Ziad has become associated (Rahbani, Z. 2002: track 5). Furthermore, the song is placed literally in the middle of eight love longs full of sarcasm, pain, and longing and a protest song originally written by Ziad at the beginning of the civil war for the leftist singer Khālid al-Hibr about a street sweeper killed in the early days of the civil war. For example, the song "He Reminds Me of the Autumn" ("Biyadhakkir bi-al-kharīf"), an adaptation of Jaque Prevert's "Autumn Leaves" goes: "I remember you every

176

time autumn comes around. Your face reminds me of autumn. You come back to me every time the weather gets dark, just like a breeze that starts out lightly. This is not about the weather, my love. This is about the past, which was violent" (Rahbani, Z. 2002: track seven).

While it is certainly arguable that this album and the first two appearances at the Beiteddine Festival combine to represent a kind of submission to Ziad's project, the events surrounding her appearance at the 2002 version of the same Festival are perhaps a good example of the trickiness of the issue of agency. It appears that shortly before the scheduled late-summer dates of the show, Ziad decided not to accompany his mother on stage as he had done for the previous two Beiteddine concerts. Accounts of the concert comment on the fact that the 2002 event also featured many fewer of Ziad's songs than did the 2000 and 2001 concerts and was advertised by the Festival organizers as a "retrospective." One observer noted that there were just a few cries for the absent Ziad at the concert, but just a few (Bashar 2002: n.p.). By the next summer Ziad was back with Fairouz at Beiteddine, and that concert is described by some in similar terms to 2000 and 2001. Abi Saab writes, for example, that "many came to meet Fairouz only to find themselves spending a special evening with Ziad Rahbani" (Abi Saab 2003: n.p.). Hazīn, on the other hand, sees more similarities between Beiteddine 2003 and the "retrospective" of 2002 than the Ziad dominated concerts of 2000 and 2001 (Hazīn 2003: n.p.).

If one were looking for a decline in Ziad's influence on Fairouz since 2000, one might point to the fact that since then Fairouz has performed more concerts without Ziad than she has with him, and that the majority of these Ziad-less concerts are dominated by her pre-Ziad work. For example, in February of 2005 Fairouz performed two concerts in Montreal Canada. Of the 20 songs she sang on the first night, only 3 were written or rearranged by Ziad: all the others were older Rahbani classics. One could argue, of course, that over the past few decades Fairouz has often sung outside of Lebanon without her son and without presenting a majority of her songs with him. On the other hand, one might also point to the fact that Ziad and Fairouz are said to be working on a new album together, their first since the 2002 *Or What?*

Many observers of the artistic scene in Lebanon were shocked when in May of 2006 it was announced that Fairouz would return to the Baalbeck Festival to kick off its fiftieth anniversary season. More surprising was the news that she would be performing the Rahbanis' 1970 Work *Wake Up (Sahh al-nawm)*, a play about a king who would rather sleep than stamp his subjects' petitions and the girl, played by Fairouz, who steals his seal from him while sleeping and thus gets the kingdom up and running again. More surprising still was the announcement that Ziad would be overseeing the event. Ziad at Baalbeck? Ziad directing the very kind of Rahbani play he so often parodied? Because of the Israeli invasion of Lebanon in the summer of 2006, the work was postponed and then moved to Beirut in December of 2006 where it played to mostly positive reviews, though there was speculation that the songs were lip-synched, the very technique that prevented Ziad from participating in Fairouz's 1998 return to Baalbeck.

177

What is clear is that the story of their collaboration or lack of collaboration since 2000 certainly complicates the issue of agency. In other words, the trend traced by many through the second Beiteddine Festival concerts of Fairouz slowly but inextricably entering Ziad's orbit has to be nuanced. At the same time, it also bears out what was said earlier in the work about ambivalence. Neither Ziad nor Fairouz can completely let go of the Rahbani brother heritage.

Nor can Lebanon, it seems, completely resolve the sectarian issues that have plagued it since its formation. Recent events – that is the string of assassinations beginning with that of former Lebanese Prime Minister Rafik al-Hariri – have made this clear. Fairouz and Ziad chose silence for approximately a year after the assassination, perhaps knowing fully well the potential potency of their words and works. This has not prevented multiple sides from conscripting their works to their cause. Just as all factions during the fifteen-year conflict used Fairouz as an artistic mascot, it has been reported that both the anti-Syrian demonstrators in Beirut and the demonstrators in Damascus in support of the Syrian presence in Lebanon were blasting songs by Fairouz. This makes the question of to whom Fairouz belongs most. What it confirms, on the other hand, is the astonishing power of popular culture in some contexts, and certainly in the context of contemporary Lebanon.

APPENDIX

The musical theater of the Rahbanis

Fairouz and the Rahbani Brother's musical plays

*Traditions and Customs**	*Taqālīd wa-'ādāt*	1957	Baalbeck
*Wedding in the Village**	*'Urs fī al-day'a*	1959	Baalbeck – Damascus
*The Holiday of Glory***	*Mawsim al-'izz*	1960	Baalbeck
The Woman from Baalbeck	*al-Ba'labakkiyya*	1961	Baalbeck – Damascus
The Moon's Bridge	*Jisr al-qamar*	1962	Baalbeck – Damascus
The Army's Return	*'Awdat al-'askar*	1962	Beirut
The Night and the Lantern	*al-Layl wa-al-qindīl*	1963	Beirut – Damascus
The Ring Seller	*Bayyā' al-khawātim*	1964	The Cedars – Damascus
The Ring Seller (film)	*Bayyā' al-khawātim*	1965	dir. Youssef Chahine
*Windmills***	*Dawālīb al-hawā*	1965	Baalbeck
The Days of Fakhr al-Din	*Ayyām Fakhr al-Dīn*	1966	Baalbeck
Exile (film)	*Safar barlak*	1966	dir. Henri Barakat
Hala and the King	*Hāla wa-al-malik*	1967	The Cedars – Beirut – Damascus
Daughter of the Guard (film)	*Bint al-hāris*	1968	dir. Henri Barakat
The Person	*al-Shakhs*	1968	Baalbeck – Damascus
		1969	Beirut
Granite Mountains	*Jibāl al-sawwān*	1969	Baalbeck – Damascus
Live Live	*Ya 'īsh ya 'īsh*	1970	Beirut

179

Wake Up	*Sahh al-nawm*	1971	Beirut – Damascus
The Guardian of the Keys	*Nātūrat al-mafātih*	1972	Baalbeck
Paper People	*Nās min waraq*	1972	Beirut – Damascus
Love Poem	*Qasīdat hubb*	1973	Baalbeck
The Station	*al-Mahatta*	1973	Beirut – Damascus
Loulou	*Lūlū*	1974	Beirut – Damascus
Mays al-Rim	*Mays al-rīm*	1975	Beirut – Damascus
Petra	*Batrā*	1977	Amman – Damascus
		1978	Beirut

* In participation with other artists
** Featured Sabah instead of Fairouz

Ziad Rahbani's musical plays

An Evening's Celebration	*Sahriyya*	1973	Beirut
Happiness Hotel	*Nazl al-surūr*	1974	Beirut
What Do We Need to Do Tomorrow	*Bi-nisba li-bukrā shū?*	1977	Beirut
A Long American Film	*Fīlm Amīrkī tawīl*	1979	Beirut
A Failure	*Shī fāshil*	1983	Beirut
Regarding Honor and the Stubborn People	*Bi-khusūs al-karāma wa-al-sha'b al-'andīd*	1993	Beirut
If Not for the Possibility of Hope	*Law lā fushat al-amal*	1994	Beirut

NOTES

INTRODUCTION

1 For a complete listing of their musical-theatrical works and films, please see the appendix. The 1998 Festival program calls these musical-theatrical works *masrahiyyāt* (plays) ("Fairouz fī al-layālī al-Lubnāniyya" 1998: 1), just one of the many names that had been applied to them over the years. Part of this variation is due, no doubt, to the differences between the individual works. The lack of generic stability is perhaps best summed up in the Lebanese poet Unsī al-Hājj's characterization of the 1966 work *The Days of Fakhr al-Din (Ayyām Fakhr al-Dīn)*: "It is not an operetta, nor a spectacle, play or opera. It is a mix of all of these things" (al-Hājj 1987: vol. one, 273). The following are some of the names that have been used to describe these works: "ūbarīt sha'biyya" (a popular operetta) ("Mawsim al-'izz" 1960: 85 and "al-Layālī al-Lubnāniyya" 1962: 183), "ūbarīt" (operetta) (al-Rahbani, A. and M. 1960: 1), "hikāyat al-mahrajān" (the Festival's story) ("Bayyā' al-khawātim" 1964: 14), "masrah ghinā'ī" (singing theater) ("Fairouz bi-alhān Najīb Hankash" 1964: 6), "mashhad al-fūlklūr al-Lubnānī" (scenes from Lebanese folklore) ("al-Fasl al-thānī min: 'Dawālīb al-hawā'" 1965: 14), "'amal masrahī fannānī isti'rādī dakhm" (a huge spectacular artistic theatrical work) ("10 Layālin fī Baalbeck" 1966: 9), "masrahiyya ghinā'iyya sha'biyya" (a popular singing play) ("al-Fann al-sha'bī al-Lubnānī" 1966: n.p. and "al-Layālī al-Lubnāniyya: 'Jibāl al-sawwān'" 1969: n.p.), "munawwa'āt ghinā'iyya rāqisa" (dancing and singing medleys) (*"Qasīdat hubb*: munawwa'āt ghinā'iyya rāqisa li-al-Akhawayn Rahbani" 1973: 153), "'amal ghinā'ī isti'rādī" (a spectacular singing work) ("Mādhā 'an al-layālī al-Lubnāniyya fī Baalbeck?" 1973: 63), "mughannāt" (songs) (Abī Samrā 1992b: 14 and M. 1972: 7), "masrahiyyat mughannāt" (a play of songs) (al-Hājj 1987: vol. one, 24) "tāblūhāt isti'rādiyya wa-fūlklūriyya" (spectacular and folkloric tableaux) (Abī Samrā 1992b: 14), and "tarājīdiyyā ghinā'iyya" (a singing tragedy) (Munassā 1994: 24). When asked about the issue of nomenclature in a 1977 interview, Mansour Rahbani says that he prefers that their works be called "masrah shāmil" (complete theater) (qtd. in Aliksān, J. 1987: 108). Nomenclature in Western musical theater has been similarly unstable. On nomenclature issues in Western musical theater see Bordman 1981.

2 See Knapp 2005 for ideas about the marginalization of musical theater in US academic circles. His work also treats the impact of plays like *Oklahoma!* (1943), *Guys and Dolls* (1950), and *The Music Man* (1957) on the formation of identity in the US. Andrea Most 2004 focuses less on the audience than on those making and performing in these works, arguing that US musical theater in roughly the second quarter of the twentieth century was an important space for Jews to assimilate themselves into US culture: "The Broadway stage was a space where Jews envisioned an ideal America and subtly wrote themselves into that scenario as accepted members of the mainstream American

community" (Most 2004: 1–2). For other works onstage and film musicals in the US and Europe see Lamb 2000, Marshall and Stilwell 2000, and Everett and Laird 2002. On US musicals specifically, see Feuer 1982, Smith 2005, and Walsh and Platt 2003.

3 For further reading on the use of spoken Arabic in written literature, see 'Awad 1986 and Sa'īd, N. 1964.

4 In addition to the exceptions that will be mentioned below, for writing on Arab theater that treats musical theater centrally, see 'Ismat 1995, Kāmil, M. 1977, and Zakī 1988.

5 There are exceptions to this trend. See, for example, Paul Shāwūl's book on contemporary Arab theater, which contains sections on both the Rahbani Brothers and Ziad (Shāwūl 1989: 440–54 and 466–511).

6 See, for example Abū Murād 1990; Aliksān, J. 1987; Murūwa 1998; and Traboulsi 2006, all of which I draw on in the chapters to come.

7 For a complete list of Ziad's musical-theatrical works see appendix.

8 For an impressively detailed site on Fairouz and the Rahbani Brothers, see "www.fairouz.com." Most of the sites dedicated to Ziad have been taken down apparently due to legal action by Ziad. One remaining site of interest is "ziad-rahbani.tripod.com."

9 For such works see Habib 2005 and Weinrich 2006.

10 There has been a proliferation of writing on popular culture in the Arab World in the past decade or so. See, for example, Abu-Lughod 1995, Armbrust 1996, 2000c, Danielson 1997, Gordon 2002, Shafik 1998, Shannon 2006, Stauth and Zubaida 1987, Stein and Swedenburg 2005, van Nieuwkerk 1995, Zuhur 1998, 2000, and 2001a. See also the October 1996 issue of *Popular Music* 15(3), which is devoted to articles on the Middle East. Also see the 1998 triple issue of *Visual Anthropology* 10(2–4) dedicated to popular culture in the region.

11 See, for example, Khalidi 1995, Lustick 2000, Tessler 1999, and issue 205 of *Middle East Report* October–December 1997, 27 (4).

12 For a discussion of the problem of "exceptionalism" in Middle Eastern Studies, see the essays in the spring 1998 issue of *Arab Studies Journal* 6(1).

13 While all of Foucault's corpus concerns itself with the various sites at which the matrix of power/knowledge operates to generate truth about the self, see particularly Foucault 1980 and 1972 for a theory of the relationship between language, truth, and the production of subjectivity.

1 BAALBECK AND THE RAHBANIS: FOLKLORE, ANCIENT HISTORY, AND NATIONALISM

1 While I use this term throughout the book, I realize fully that Chatterjee is not the author of the idea that history is often employed for ideological purposes in the present. This concept is perhaps most famously formulated by Hobsbawm 1983 as "The Invention of Tradition." See also the essays in Boswell and Evans 1999.

2 For an account of the discovery of this tomb, see Winstone 1991. Reid 1997 offers an account of the impact of this and other European-led Egyptology breakthroughs on the Pharaonic movement in Egypt at the beginning of the twentieth century. For a history of the translation of the Hieroglyphs by European scholars, see Adkins 2000.

3 For a discussion of the place of *Zaynab* in the history of the Arab novel, see Allen 1998.

4 Almost all present-day researchers disagree with Allūf's conclusions. While they do not deny that the city owed its name to the deity Baal, there is neither textual nor archeological evidence that it was a major religious center in pre-Hellenistic times (Sader 1998). Some nationalist historians, however, continue to argue for the site's Phoenician provenance. See, for example, Nehme 1997.

5 For more information on Lebanese migration to Egypt in the nineteenth and early twentieth centuries, see Dāhir 1986 and Hourani and Shehadi 1992.

6 By "official history" and "official narrative" I mean *Baalbeck, Festival Days* (*Baalbeck, ayyām al-mahrajān*, 1994) which was commissioned by the Baalbeck Festival committee.

7 For more information on this period of Lebanese history see Chevallier 1996, Harris 1997, Laurens 1990, and Salibi 1988.

8 It should be said that though Chiha's affiliation with this organization is mentioned by both the French and Arabic sections of the official history of the Baalbeck Festival (Munassā 1994: 8; Tueni 1994: 34), in his recent authoritative book on Chiha, Fawwaz Traboulsi does not mention any such connection (Traboulsi 1999).

9 For more on Chiha see Hartman and Olsaretti 2003.

10 The *mawwāl* is a folksong with versions in most Arab countries. It often consists of one verse inserted into a song of a different style. The song that Farid El Atrache's *mawwāl* is inserted into is "I've been missing you" ("Ishtaqtilak"). For more on the *mawwāl*, see Būdhayna 1999 and Salīm 1999. On the *mawwāl* in Egypt, see Cachia 1977.

11 For a definition of Folklore, as well as a history of the academic field of Folklore Studies, see Kirshenblatt-Gimblett 1998.

12 I will talk more about the *dabka* in the next two chapters. For more information on this form of folkdance, see Traboulsi 1996 and 2006.

13 For an interesting study of a nationalistic project with intriguing similarities and differences to the case of Lebanon, see Baram 1991 on the official uses of archeology and folklore in Ba'thist Iraq.

14 For a thought provoking study of the drawing of such boundaries, see Thongchai 1994.

15 Other examples of folklore playing key roles in nation building are the cases of Greece (Herzfeld 1986) and Finland (Wilson 1976). Folklore as an object of study and nationalism has also been linked in Germany, Great Britain, China, and Japan (Tamanoi 1998).

16 In other accounts by Mansour, Habib Abou Chahla or "the government" is credited with authoring the idea of their inclusion into the Festival (Abī Samrā 1993: 63 and Aliksān, J. 1987: 109).

17 *Tatrīb* is a transitive verbal noun meaning to cause *tarab*. *Tarab* most often refers to a state of music-induced ecstasy. The terms are usually used either neutrally or positively. As can be seen here, however, they can also have negative connotations. For more on *tarab* see Racy (2003) and Shannon (2003 and 2006).

18 This may be a reference to the Egyptian diva Oum Kalthoum (Umm Kulthūm), famous for singing long *tarab*-inducing songs whilst clinging to a handkerchief. It is no small irony that Oum Kalthoum herself, who was very popular in Lebanon, would appear at the Baalbeck Festival in 1966, 1968, and 1970. For book-length studies of the singer, see Danielson 1997, Fu'ād 2000, and al-Najmī 1993. I would also recommend *Umm Kulthum: a Voice Like Egypt* (1996). This documentary film is particularly useful in demonstrating the meaning of *tarab*.

19 The exception to this rule was – starting in 1970 – the first day to each year's version of The Lebanese Nights. For this performance only, tickets were theoretically free for residents of Baalbeck (Abī Samrā 1993). In reality, however, many of these tickets were sold on the black market. At least once the police had to break up a demonstration by locals unable to procure tickets because of this practice ("Fairouz fī Baalbeck" 1998). One writer has even read the chaos that reigned on the evening that tickets were free for locals in the summer of 1973 – the Rahbanis' final prewar appearance at Baalbeck – as a precursor to the civil war itself (Abī Samrā 1992a: 10).

20 This figure is based on World Bank statistics from the year 2005 ("Lebanon at a Glance" 2006).

21 The Festival committee was divided into subcommittees. The folklore committee was formed in 1957, and for a time included under its umbrella the nonfolkloric Lebanese

theater that was staged at the Festival beginning in 1964. In 1962 a separate "Arab theater committee" was formed (Saʿīd, Kh. 1998b: 58).

22 Beiteddine palace lies in the Chouf mountains of Lebanon and was built in the early nineteenth century for the local Emir, Bashīr Shihāb the Second. Beginning in 1943 the palace became a summer residence of the Lebanese President. It also houses a number of museums. It is now the site of a Summer Arts Festival – founded in 1985 – which has become a competitor of the Baalbeck Festival and about which I will have more to say in the book's conclusion.

23 According to Racy, a similar phenomenon was occurring all over the Arab World due to rural to urban migration. This phenomenon allowed for the appearance of new musical movements "whose context was unmistakably urban but whose inspiration was folk and rural" (Racy 1981: 37). Danielson, commenting specifically on the Egyptian form of the folkloric *mawwāl* writes that it is "Egypt's 'country' music, widely known in cities and towns as well, which tended to evoke nostalgia for the village and its ostensible purer lifestyle" (Danielson 1997: 26, footnote 28). Another example of this trend can be seen in the Syrian/Egyptian performer Farid El Atrache whom we saw above, singing folklorically at the ruins of Baalbeck in the 1962 Egyptian Film *Letter From an Unknown Woman*: "Farid El Atrache exhibited a special flair for composing, or incorporating and elaborating on, folk melodies in his work. This became a characteristic of composers of the twentieth century whether in Egypt or in the Levant, as compared to the previous inspirations included in the Ottoman repertoire" (Zuhur 2000: 175).

24 The 1994 official history of the Festival reproduces the language ratio of the annual programs. Two hundred and forty of its pages are in French or English, whereas the Arabic section is just sixty-three pages long. While the work as a whole is elaborately produced to the point that some of the photographs are originals hand-pasted onto the pages, the production quality is noticeably higher for the French and English portions of the book. See Tueni 1994.

2 THE MUSICAL THEATER OF THE RAHBANI BROTHERS: REPRESENTATION AND THE FORMATION OF SUBJECTIVITIES

1 For more information on this war, which resulted in approximately 2,500 deaths, see Abū Sālih 1998, Agwani 1965, and Alin 1994.

2 In Egypt, a similar phenomenon can be found in the folk dancer Farida Fahmi (Farīda Fahmī), daughter of the famous Egyptian engineer Hassan Fahmi (Hasan Fahmī). Marjorie Franken writes that Farida, "... daughter of a university professor, graduate of the elite English School and Cairo University, whose mother was English and paternal grandfather an estate manager for King Farouq, married to a film director – Farida Fahmi danced in the dress of a Delta peasant girl, covered her head with traditional veils, [and] wore her hair in long pleats that whirled as she danced like any village girl. This was spectacle indeed..." (Franken 1998: 278).

3 While he does not clarify what type of dance music he is referring to, others are more specific, and thus we learn that the Rahbani Brothers were Arabicizing Latin dance music (Abū Murād 1990: 41 and Racy 2002: n.p.) such as tangos (Aliksān, J. 1987: 88) rumbas (al-Zībāwī 1994: 55), and sambas (al-ʿAwīt 1987: 22), as well as classical dance music such as Mozart's waltzes ("Mansour Rahbani baʿda khrūjihi min al-mustashfā" 1995: 18). The production of this type of music was not limited to the days before they started working with Fairouz, for apparently they also wrote many tangos (Aliksān, J. 1987: 89) and "light, dance tunes" for her as well (Boulus 1981: 22). In fact, the first song they ever wrote for her – "Mārūshkā" (woman's name) – was just such a song

(Nāsir 1986: part four, 45). A 1951 study of the radio audience in Lebanon confirms the popularity of "dance music" at that time ("The Radio Audience of Lebanon" 1951: 21), as does a comment by the director of Radio Damascus in (Aliksān, J. 1987: 88). The liberal use of Latin dance rhythms had become widespread in Egyptian film music in the 1940s. Notable efforts to combine Eastern scales with Latin dance rhythms were composed by Mohamed Abdel Wahhab (Muhammad 'Abd al-Wahhāb) (e.g. the use of the rhythm of swing in the song "A-B-C" ("Abjad Hawaz") sung by Leila Mourad (Laylā Murād) in the film *The Flirtation of Girls* (*Ghazal al-banāt*, 1949)), Riyad al-Sunbati (Riyād al-Sunbātī) (e.g. the waltz in "The Two of Us" ("Ihnā al-ithnayn") sung by Leila Mourad in the film *Poor Layla* (*Laylā bint al-fuqarā'*, 1944), and Mohammed al-Qasabji (Muhammad al-Qasabjī) (e.g. the tango "When Will You Know" ("Imtā hā ta'rif")) sung by Asmahan (Asmahān) in the film *Love and Revenge* (*Gharām wa-intiqām*, 1944) (Sahhāb, F. 1987: 12). Also, the Rahbanis were not the only producers of such music in Lebanon, where Western dance tunes reached their peak of popularity in the 1950s. Khaled Abou Nasr (Khālid Abū Nasr) has been cited as very successfully combining Latin rhythms with Eastern scales (Sahhāb, S. 1986: 12). For more information on the composer and singer Mohamed Abdel Wahhab, see Armbrust 1996, Murūwa 1998, al-Najmī 1993, and Sahhāb, F. 1987. For information on al-Qasabji, see Sahhāb, F. 1987. For further reading on Leila Mourad, see Armbrust 2000b. I will discuss Asmahan at greater length below.

4 Commercial broadcasts began in Europe and the US in the early 1920s ("Broadcasting" 2007). Radio sets were first available in Lebanon in 1932 (al-Zughbī 1969). For a survey of the history of electronic media in the Middle East, see Boyd 1999.

5 In 1942 "Radio of the East" had become more Lebanon-centered as the result of the founding of a separate station in Syria that same year. The departure of the French, however, did not mean the end of foreign Language programming. In 1946, for example, the daily breakdown of programming by language at "Radio of the East" was as follows: 335 minutes in Arabic, 235 in French and 145 in English (al-Hasan 1965: 94–5).

6 For more information on Tawfiq al-Basha see Bāshā 1995 and Ghazāla 1998. All of these figures, along with Asi and Mansour, made up the remainder of the "gang of five," a group of artists that worked together in various configurations at Near East Radio (Bāshā 1995: 145). Sabri Sharif would go on to direct most of their musical-theatrical performances at Baalbeck and elsewhere.

7 Abū Murād, for example, cites the following for their pioneering work in this regard: 'Umar al-Za'nī, Naqūla al-Mannī, Yahyā al-Labābīdī, Sāmī al-Saydāwī, Matrī al-Murr, the Fulayfil Brothers, Wadī' Sabrā, Iskandar Shalfūn, and 'Abd al-Qādir al-Tannīr (Abū Murād 1990: 34).

8 The top four were Farid El Atrache, Mohamed Abdel Wahhab, Oum Kalthoum, and Asmahan. Though El Atrash and Asmahan were brother and sister born in the Levant, they moved to Egypt early in their lives. The majority of their songs are in the Egyptian style and they are more often than not treated as Egyptian singers. For an example of such treatment and for more information on all four of the above, see Sahhāb, F. 1987. For a book length study of Asmahan, which includes a great deal of information on her brother Farid El Atrache as well, see Zuhur 2000.

9 In a survey of the lyrics of 353 songs sung by Fairouz I came across the words "wild" and "boulder" only once. I did not come across the word "thorn." I found the words "wild" and "boulder" not only in the same song – "The Mij dance" ("Dabkat al-Mīj") – but also in the same line of that song. Incidentally, that very line contains two words that are similar to the very "perfumed and sappy words" mentioned disparagingly above, for example, "flowers" and "roses."

10 Some of the songs written in this new style before they began to collaborate with Fairouz were "The Ship of Love is Ours" ("Markab al-hubb la-nā"), "We are the Hens

of Love, We are the Cocks of Dreams" ("Nahnu dajājāt al-hubb, Nahnu duyūk al-ahlām") and, "Rain, Lightening and Thunder" ("Shitī wa-barq wa-ra'd") (Aliksān, J. 1987: 69).

11 Nasser used mass media shrewdly and aggressively both in and outside of Egypt (Franken 1998: 272). To learn more about his "Voice of the Arabs" radio network specifically, see Boyd 1977. In it, Boyd informs us that "Egypt has probably committed more resources to the establishment and programming of its radio and television systems than any other developing country" (Boyd 1977: 1).

12 One source claims that after the closure of the Near East Radio station the Rahbani Brothers broadcast their work on the Voice of America ("Sab' wa-Makhūl" 1969: 4). If true, this only strengthens the argument about the challenges and opportunities offered by the proliferation of radio at this time.

13 At the same time it should be kept in mind that the Rahbani Brothers did not have a monopoly on the shortened song. In talking about the shortening of songs for Oum Kalthoum's film appearances, Danielson writes: "The short song itself was nothing new to the singer or to the audience, as both were already accustomed to commercial recordings and broadcast performances constrained by time limitations" (Danielson 1997: 88).

14 For works on musical theater in the Arab World, see Kāmil, M. 1977 and Zakī 1988.

15 This genealogy demonstrates the inextricable nature of the relationship between theater and music in the Arab World. Abū Murād calls theater the "offspring of song" (Abū Murād 1997: 410) and Shāwūl comments that "Theater began with song" (Shāwūl 1988: 253).

16 For reading on Levantine migrants in Egypt in general, see Dāhir 1986, Hourani 1992 and Philipp 1985. For reading about the contribution of Levantines to theater in Egypt, see Badawi, M.M. 1992a and Landau 1958.

17 For more information on the life and works of Sayyid Darwish, see, in addition to the works on musical theater listed above, Darwish, H. 2000, Dawwāra 1996, Murūwa 1999, Sahhāb, F. 1987, and Zakī 1991. For further reading on El-Rihani, see Abū Sayf 1972, al-'Antablī 1999, Armbrust 2000c, Farīd 2000, and al-Rā'ī 1993. For more information on al-Kassar, see Kassār 1991 and 1993.

18 For more information on the traditional distinctions between Arab and Western music, see Touma 1996.

19 For a more detailed study of the relationship between the Rahbanis and the Palestinian resistance song, see Stone 2007. For a detailed survey of the Palestinian resistance song in general, see Massad 2003.

20 For example, though clearly a proponent of liberalism a la Chiha, Chamoun's government did not allow the establishment of private radio stations during his tenure, though there was considerable interest in such a development in the business community (al-Hasan 1965: 128).

21 For an account of a similar transformation of violent historical event into melodrama in American Musical theater, see Beidler 1993. The article describes the transformation of James Michener's World War Two novel *South Pacific* into Broadway melodrama as one example of "something called American remembering" (Beidler 1993: 222). The musical theater of the Rahbani Brothers show that similar rewritings and re-rememberings were also occurring elsewhere.

22 al-'Īd is ironically quoting Pierre (Biyār) Jumayyil's (the founder of the strong-arm youth movement Phalange (al-Katā'ib) party), who famously referred to the real and perceived enemies of the Maronites as "the other Lebanons:" "al-Lubnānāt al-ukhrā."

23 This does not mean that others did not participate in future versions of the folkloric Lebanese Nights, but that they did so only in years when the Rahbani Brothers and Fairouz did not perform at the Festival. After sharing the Lebanese Nights stage in

1957 and 1959, between 1960 and 1966 the Rahbani Brothers and Fairouz were absent from the Festival just two out of seven summers, and in those five summers in which they performed, they were the sole presenters of The Lebanese Nights.

24 For more information on this last type of song in both the Arab east and west, see Touma 1996: 83–6. For further reading on the significance of this musical genre specifically in the Levant, see Shannon 2006 and Currey 2002.

25 This is equal to approximately 16,000 US dollars in 1966, or around 85,000 US dollars in 2002.

26 This subtitle was removed when the play was printed in book-form in 2003. See Rahbani, A. and M. 2003c.

27 For more on this figure, about whom I will have more to say in the next chapter, see Hawi 1982, Naima 1951, and Waterfield 1998.

28 "Sayyida Harīsā," (the Lady of Harissa) is a reference to a statue of the Virgin Mary at a Maronite convent in the village of Harissa, which overlooks Jounieh (Jūnīh), a coastal village that is now considered to be a suburb of East Beirut.

29 These sentences are reproduced verbatim in Traboulsi 2006: 48 except that he removed the words "Christian" in the later version.

30 Other references to them as a trinity can be found in Abī Samrā 1999: 8 and Nāsir 1986, part 1: 35.

31 Said Akl made a similar claim just before the outbreak of the civil war in the mid-1970s: "Lebanon has become, thanks to my writings and to what I spread in the consciousness of the Lebanese luminaries, a nation that is difficult to kill" (qtd. in "Said Akl" 1996: vol. two: 956).

32 Unlike most of the scripts of the Rahbani Brothers' plays in my possession, this one does not contain the lyrics to the songs, thus the reference to the recording of the play.

33 It should be noted that Chiha himself had no roots in Mt Lebanon, and that for him the mountain and its villages were not central to his writing about Lebanese nationalism. Though he referred to the mountain as the "spine of the Lebanese state," many of his best known works did not contain any references to the mountain (Kaufman 2004: 166).

34 Of course, Fairouz and the Rahbani Brothers were not the only Arab artists to combine a blend of local and regional messages in their works. Farid El Atrache, for example, also attempted "...to play both sides of the fence – projecting both an Arab and an Egyptian image" (Zuhur 2001c: 291). Zuhur gives as an example his song "Mail by Wind" ("Būstat al-rīh") of the early 1970s which was a city by city tour of the Arab World. El Atrache himself or other singers performing this song would often improvise lyrics related to the city or country in which the song was being sung (Zuhur 2001c: 292).

3 ZIAD RAHBANI'S THEATRICAL "NOVELIZATION" OF THE RAHBANIS' LEBANON

1 For further reading on the Lebanese theatrical responses to the *naksa* and about the figures and works mentioned above, see Sa'īd, Kh. 1998b.

2 Paul Fussel's *The Great War and Modern Memory* masterfully outlines the dramatic effects that that war had on the language, lives and literatures of those affected by it in Europe.

3 For more on this prize and for a view of Akl that approaches hagiography, see Salameh 2004.

4 For information on the strikes and demonstrations taking place in Beirut in the early 1970s, see Petran 1987.

5 In a 1997 speech marking the thirtieth anniversary of the death of Che Guevera in Beirut, Ziad saluted Jihād Sa'd, the man who carried out this action, reminding his listeners that Jihād threw money from the windows of the bank onto to the street to

show that the action was not motivated by money. He also mentions that Jihād's brother Mīshāl plays the trombone in his band (Rahbani, Z. 1997a: 10).

6　The "Abū al-Zuluf" is a type of folkloric song about which I will have more to say below.

7　I will talk more about this type of folk-song below.

8　While the vast majority of them were sung by Fairouz, and written and composed by the Rahbani Brothers, some were written by others (e.g. Said Akl and Philemon Wehbe), composed by others (e.g. Mohamed Abdel Wahhab and Sayyid Darwish), or sung by others (e.g. Wadī' al-Sāfī and Nasrī Shams al-Dīn). Some of the songs surveyed also include Christian hymns, children's songs, and songs adapted from classical Arabic poetry. This survey in no way attempts to be exhaustive. It has been estimated that Fairouz has sung more than 1,500 different songs ('Ubayd 1974: 13). Boulus puts the number at "over 800" (Boulus 1981: 28). This survey does not include the unsung lyrics of the plays. For a complete discography of Fairouz's singing, see Habib 2005.

9　Touma defines this type of song as follows: "The *layālī* is a solo vocal form whose text consists of the words *yā laylī yā 'aynī* (Oh my night! Oh my eye!), referring in poetic metaphor to a beloved woman. Usually the *layālī* is performed by a singer who also accompanies him or herself on the *'ūd...*" (Touma 1996: 96).

10　By "stubborn," the Rahbanis clearly meant defiant, for example, *sāmid*, but this word does not rhyme with words like "'īd" (holiday) and "jadīd" (new), which end the surrounding lines. In his 1993 play Ziad means us to understand the word "karāma" (honor) sarcastically, as actual "honor" in the play is in very short supply. As for "stubbornness," Ziad uses it in its negative sense, as in unwilling to change or unwilling to change one's mind ("Hadīth ma'a Ziad Rahbani" 1993: 22 and "Muqābala ma'a Ziad Rahbani" 1993b). In his 1986 radio show *Brains are Just for Decoration (al-'Aql zīna)* Ziad, talking about this Lebanese stubbornness, says, "you will find him [the Lebanese] stubborn, but not stubborn for nothing... stubborn about something stupid.... He has gone mad, grasping onto his sectarianism stubbornly" (Rahbani, Z. 1987: disc one, track two, 14:05–24).

11　The words used for "our income" and "our expenses" – *madkhūlnā* and *masrūfnā* – are of the same "weight," in Arabic, meaning more or less that they rhyme, thus adding to the humorous effect of the line.

12　The play does not specify whether the music is coming from the radio or a tape player. In any case, it is worth noting that commercial FM radio underwent a boom in Lebanon in the 1970s (Boyd 1991: 281). A recent dissertation on identity among Lebanese youth counts more than 100 FM radio stations operating in Lebanon by the late 1990s. It claims that English and French are the predominant languages of these stations (Kraidy 1996: 10–11). My own experience with FM stations in Beirut or with searching for Lebanese radio stations on the Internet confirms these findings. And even on some of stations for which Arabic is the language of broadcast, the music played is predominantly in European languages. There are exceptions to this trend, one of which will be discussed below.

13　Ziad may even have had a particular poet in mind for Usāma, or at least a particular type. When asked in an interview when the events of this play take place, he says that they can be seen as happening either before or after the war. He continues to say, "Look at a poet like Adonis for example, he and those who publish him... were around both before and after the war" (Harb 1978b: 11). Adonis (Adūnīs, i.e. 'Alī Ahmad Sa'īd) is a Syrian poet and critic well known for his interest in modernizing Arabic poetry in a way that is not completely disconnected from its own past modernizing traditions (Jayyusi 1992: 172). On his use of classical poetry, see Marāshda 1995. To read about Adonis's own views on Arabic poetry, see Adonis 1990.

14 The '*atābā* is a "non-metric strophic folksong" (Asmar 2000) that is characterized by its romantic themes and its series of line-ending homonyms. I will have more to say about this type of song below.

15 For more information on the program and for summaries of some of the episodes, see Stevens 1981.

16 In addition to releasing complete recordings of all seven of his plays, Ziad also put out separate sound tracks for three of them: *Tomorrow, A Long American Film*, and *If Not for the Possibility of Hope*. It is understandable that *Celebration* would not have a separate soundtrack, as there is much more music than dialogue in the work. Similarly understandable is the lack of soundtracks for *A Failure* and *Regarding Honor and the Stubborn People*, as neither play contains any complete songs. It is perhaps surprising, however, that there is no soundtrack to the play *Hotel* with its seven songs.

17 The classical Arabic word "*hawā'*," becomes "*hawā*" in the Lebanese dialect (Abū Saʿd 1987: 343), as it often does in the Egyptian dialect as well (Badawi, E. and Hinds, M. 1986: 918). This word appears in almost one-third of the Rahbani Brothers' songs that I have surveyed. In its colloquial form it becomes identical to one of the classical Arabic words for "love" (*hawā*), and thus is sometimes used punningly.

18 Salīm Sahhāb notes that Ziad is not the first Arab to use horns in his music. Mohamed Abdel Wahhab used them in a somewhat tentative way in "I Love You When You Remember Me" ("Uhibbuka wa-anta fākirnī"). A jazzier use of horns can be noted in the songs that ʿAlī Ismāʿīl composed for Abdel Halim Hafez (ʿAbd al-Halīm Hāfiz), such as in the two Mambos "Lovers" ("Mughrimīn") and "Sing, Sing" ("Ghannī ghannī") (Sahhāb, S. 1986: 12).

19 I am focusing here only on the question of parody in *Film* for reasons of space. As Ziad's most direct theatrical response to the Lebanese Civil War, it is certainly deserving of a more detailed study. For more information on the play, see ʿAnīnī 1989–90, Amīn 1997, and Shāwūl 1989.

20 Ziad has said that he considers Oum Kalthoum to be "a disease" (qtd. in Baydūn, ʿAbbās 1996: 53). His main complaint about her style seems to be the length of her songs. In one interview he commented that in the duration of one of her pieces a hundred different things could be invented or discovered (Kāmil, S. 1983b: 68).

21 This section of the song is not included on the recorded version of the play that I have (Rahbani, Z. 1993a). It is, however, in the text version of the play (Rahbani, Z. 1994b) and on the play's soundtrack (Rahbani, Z. 1995d: side two, track two).

22 Please note that in Lebanese Arabic the letter "tā marbūta" is usually pronounced like a *kasra* ("i") or long *yā'* ("ī"), as opposed to as a *fatha* ("a") as in classical Arabic.

23 A section of the entry on rural Lebanese folklore in the Grove's online dictionary reads: "During the wedding party…song genres typically performed include the *Abū al-Zuluf* and the '*atābā*. The *Abū al-Zuluf* is a strophic love song performed by an individual man or woman, usually with a short chorus refrain after each verse; the melody displays a degree of improvisatory flexibility. The '*atābā* consists of verses sung by a man or woman alone, usually with an added refrain (*mījānā*) and typically opening with the expression *yā mījānā*. Sometimes these songs are accompanied by a *mijwiz* [a reed instrument of two parallel pipes] or an urban instrument such as the '*ūd* [lute]" (Racy 2002).

24 When quoting Abū al-Zuluf, I will place the words that he says in English in italics.

25 These are names of other types of folkloric songs.

26 The Rahbani Brothers used the word "holiday" in a tenth of the songs that I surveyed. The word "bunches of grapes" appears in 23 of the 353 songs that I surveyed. And some form of the word "assignation" appears in 42 of the songs. At least two of these words appear together in eight of the surveyed songs, including "Summer Oh Summer" ("Sayf yā sayf") and "The Holiday's Sound" ("Sawt al-ʿīd"). A combination

of all three occurs in two songs, "Rain oh World" ("Shattī yā dinī") and "Night Holiday" ("ʿĪd al-layl"). In terms of the amendment of "a new Lebanon" to their post-1975 songs, we find such a case in the song that Ziad disparaged above: "I love you Lebanon," which indeed rhymes ʿīd (holiday) with jadīd (new), in the context of the creation of Lebanon anew.

27 For more on the idea of "the stranger" or "the Other" during this period in Lebanon, see Nasr, M. 1996.

28 In other contexts, Ziad has complained about the West's appropriation of Eastern music (Bāshā 1987a: 37) in its constant search for new sounds (al-Ashqar 1981: part one, 70).

29 For an interesting article on the language of Ziad's 1995 album *Seeing as That...* see al-Jawharī 1996. She says, for example, that Ziad "Unearths all that the upper classes find to be dirty or base..." (al-Jawharī 1996: n.p.).

4 FAIROUZ AND/AS THE NATION

1 The title is a pun on his ex-wife's name. By simply dropping the definite article "al" from "al-dalāl," the title would mean "the rearing of Dalāl." Because of phonetic rules of Arabic, the "l" of the definite article is elided with the following consonants, which makes it difficult to hear whether the title of the song is "a spoiled upbringing" or "the rearing of Dalāl." In fact, some Lebanese with whom I discussed this song assumed, understandably, that the title was the latter.

2 Examples of such important and groundbreaking works are Ahmed 1992, Badran 1995, and Kandiyoti 1991. It is perhaps because such studies are often framed around the theme of Islam that many of them do not treat the case of Lebanon, which has a large Christian population. Examples of other important works on gender and nationalism in the Middle East that do not include Lebanon are Abu-Lughod 1998b and Moghadam 1994. It is also quite likely that the Civil War in Lebanon has contributed to this lack, as writing about the connection between gender and nationalism in the region began to appear in significant numbers only after the start of the war. Perhaps bolstering the argument of the importance of the war as a factor in this silence is the fact that some of the works on women in the Middle East that both pre and postdate the war do include the case of Lebanon (e.g. Beck 1978, Hamāda *et al.* 2000, and Joseph 2000). Also adding to the viability of this argument is the fact that a number of critical texts that deal centrally with the question of the relationship of women to the civil war in Lebanon have recently appeared, including Accad 1990, Cooke 1993 and 1988, *al-Marʾa al-Lubnāniyya* 1987, and Shehadeh 1999.

3 See, for example, Danielson 1997, Franken 1998, van Nieuwkerk 1998, and Zuhur 2000. Studies that takes such factors into consideration are not restricted to those on female performers. See, for example, Armbrust 2000a, 2000b, and 1996.

4 The problematic social status of women performers is not limited, of course, to the Middle East. Kano's study of the historical link between the theater and prostitution in Japanese theater provides an important reminder of this fact (Kano 2001: 5).

5 As Heng and Devan point out, however, not all women of the nation are equally encouraged to reproduce. They cite the example of Singapore where, since 1983, economic incentives have been used to encourage so-called graduate women to have more children, and less educated women to have fewer. It turns out that the majority of these "graduate women" are from the ruling ethnically Chinese classes, whereas the majority of the less educated women are from the poor and rapidly growing portion of the population with Malay or Indian roots (Heng and Devan 1992).

6 Veena Das writes of a context – the partition of Pakistan and India – where female sexuality became tragically central to national causes. See Das 1997 for a study of the use of rape as a way to make territorial claims. Yang demonstrates how female

sexuality became linked to national honor during the recent revelations of the use of Korean women as sexual "comfort women" for the Japanese during World War Two (Yang 1998). Such examples are potent reminders of the fact that one of the ways that nationalism is gendered is in its rendering of female sexuality subservient to the nation.

7 It should be noted that the "official history" of the Festival was published by the same company that puts out the Christian center-right *al-Nahār* newspaper, Lebanon's most circulated daily newspaper.

8 For a study of the role of the Virgin Mary in Irish Nationalism, see Martin 2001.

9 Fairouz performed concerts in Cairo in 1976 and 1989.

10 This criticism has come, most notably, from "within" the group. See Spivak 1988 for a critique of the group's approach to questions of gender.

11 In addition to Danielson, for further reading on the relationship between Oum Kalthoum and her composers, see Sahhāb, I. 2001.

12 Though she is known to have had close ties to Nasser personally, Danielson has noted that despite their relationship, to cast her as his weapon "is to simplify in the extreme" (Danielson 1998: 114).

13 The phrase, as pronounced by Fairouz, is "mallā inta." In his dictionary of Lebanese Arabic, Frayha has this phrase as "millā," and says that it is an "exclamatory participle" short for "min man la mathīl lahu" (Frayha 1995: 174) that is, "from whom there is no equal."

14 This project was and remains controversial for myriad reasons: because it was seen to benefit Rafik Hariri, the late Lebanese businessman and Prime Minister, personally; because it is said have been an attempt to architecturally erase the memory of the war; because it involved the forced buying-out of the area's property owners; because it required that even some structurally sound buildings be torn down so that the rebuilding could be done in a uniform manner; and so on. For further reading about this massive project as well as the general reconstruction of Beirut after the war, see: Kabbani 1992, Khalaf and Khoury 1993, Makdisi, S. 1997, Thabet 1999, and Volk 1994.

15 Some of these pamphlets contained slogans taken from Fairouz's songs: "Stay at home" ("Khallīkī bi-al-bayt") from the song of that name from her 1987 record with Ziad *My Knowledge of You* and "Fairouz killed us twice" (Fairouz qatalatnā marratayn) from the song "Oh Knitter of the Brows" ("yā 'āqid al-hājibayn") from the 1968 film *Daughter of the Guard* (the lyric reads: "If you meant to kill me, you killed me twice") (Baydūn, 'Abbās 1994: 52, al-Sha'shā' 1994: 18).

16 Of the 31 songs on the recorded version of the concert, only 7 were not written by the Rahbani brothers. And even some of these songs, according to Talīs, *sounded* as if they had been written by the Rahbanis. Such songs included "Oh Bird of Summer" ("Yā tayr al-sayf") by Elias Rahbani, Mansour and Asi's younger brother (Talīs 1979: 6).

17 See note 10 in Chapter 3.

18 This song originally appears as part of a medley of songs in musical play *Love Poem*, first performed in Baalbeck in 1973. On the recorded version of the play the song can be found under the track "Reconciliation" ("Musālaha"). It can also be found on the live recording of her 1986 London concert *Fairouz at the Royal Festival Hall London* (Rahbani, Z. 1989). All of the songs on this latter album, except for two tracks, were arranged by Ziad.

CONCLUSION: BEITEDDINE 2000 AND BEYOND

1 Though the writer is not explicit, I am assuming that he or she means that Ziad had saved Joseph Saqr from the folkloric world of the Rahbani Brothers only to place him in the prison of his own project. It is a fact that Joseph Saqr, once he started to work

for Ziad, did very little work on his own or for anyone else, including long periods of time when Ziad was either himself dormant artistically or working with others. We have already seen that Saqr had only a very small part in the 1983 play *A Failure*. After this play, the next time that Saqr would work extensively with Ziad would not be until Ziad's 1993 play *Regarding Honor and the Stubborn People*. As both of those plays were virtually song-less, however, the period of time that Saqr produced no music with Ziad was even longer: between the 1979 *A Long American Film* and Ziad's 1994 play *If Not for the Possibility of Hope*. Saqr did indicate, however, that he sang abroad a lot during this period (Fadl Allāh 1995: 53). Saqr died in 1997 at the age of fifty-five, shortly after the release of his and Ziad's highly successful 1995 record *Seeing as That*.... It is also possible that the bottle metaphor refers to rumors that a possible cause of Saqr's demise was an addiction to alcohol. It is also thought that after the death of Saqr Ziad himself received treatment for alcoholism.

BIBLIOGRAPHY

"10 Layālin fī Baalbeck li-al-Akhawayn Rahbani" (1966) *Mulhaq jarīdat al-nahār*, June 19, pp. 8–10.

"13 Nīsān 75: kay lā nansā – 13 Nīsān 2000: hattā lā tatakarrar: yawm min hayātī fī al-harb" (2000) *Jarīdat al-safīr*, April 14, n.p.

VIIème festival international de Baalbeck (1962) Beirut: Association du festival international.

'Abd al-Amīr, 'A. (2001) " 'Fairouz fī Beiteddine' istawāna bayna al-qadīm wa-al-'hadīth'," *Jarīdat al-hayāt*, March 26, n.p.

al-'Abd Allāh, 'I. (n.d.) "Ziad Rahbani: 'Ba'dnā tayyibīn 'ūl Allāh'," *Majallat alhān, n.d.*, pp. 16–19.

'Abd Allāh, M. (1977) "Fī awwal hadīth lahu ba'da al-harb: Ziad Rahbani: lan utājir bi-al-khurāb irdā'an li-al-jumhūr," *Majallat al-hasnā'*, n.d., pp. 51–2.

—— (n.d.) "Fairouz: asbahnā mahkūmīn bi-hādhā al-fann wa-'azamatihi wa-lā majāl li-itlāq sarāh ayy minnā," *Majallat alwān*, n.d., pp. 10–13.

Abi Saab, P. (1994) "al-Ghinā' 'alā anqād Beirut!" *Majallat al-wasat*, September 19, p. 51.

—— (2003) "Fairouz at the 2003 Beit Eddine Festival: The Return of Fairouz by way of Ziad," *aljadid*, 9(Summer), n.p.

Abī Samrā, M. (1978) "Tajribat al-Rahābina wa-Fairouz: muhāwala fī tarh al-su'āl wa-ru'yat al-ufuq," *al-Tarīq*, 37(4–5): 211–19.

—— (1992a) "Fairouz: mahattāt min sīra," *Mulhaq jarīdat al-nahār*, November 7, pp. 9–10.

—— (1992b) "Fairouz wa-al-akhawān Rahbani," *Mulhaq jarīdat al-nahār*, May 9, p. 14.

—— (1993) "Ma'a Mansour Rahbani bahthan 'an al-zaman al-dā'i': mā alladhī yabqā min al-ustūra al-Rahbāniyya?," *Majallat al-wasat*, February 8, pp. 60–5.

—— (1998) " 'Majd Lubnān' u'tā lahā," *Mulhaq jarīdat al-nahār*, August 22, p. 9.

—— (1999) "Asi Rahbani fī sawt Fairouz: hanīn al-jabal ilā nafsihi," *Mulhaq jarīdat al-nahār*, May 22, pp. 6–9.

al-Abtah, S. (2000) "Fairouz tatull jarī'a mughāmira fī 'Mahrajānāt Beiteddine'," *Jarīdat al-sharq al-awsat*, August 23, n.p.

—— (2001) "Shaghaf Lubnānī ismuhu Fairouz: li-al-'ām al-thānī fī mahrajānāt Beiteddine," *Jarīdat al-sharq al-awsat*, July 29, n.p.

Abū al-Asbar, M. (1998) " 'Awdat Fairouz ilā Baalbeck," *Jarīdat al-anwār*, August 15, pp. 1, 24.

Abu-Lughod, L. (1995) "The Objects of Soap Opera: Egyptian Television and the Cultural Politics of Modernity," in Miller, D. (ed.) *Worlds Apart: Modernity Through the Prism of the Local*, London: Routledge, pp. 190–210.

193

Abu-Lughod, L. (1997) "Movie Stars and Islamic Moralism in Egypt," in Lancaster, R.N. and Leonardo, M.D. (eds) *The Gender/Sexuality Reader: Culture, History, Political Economy*, London: Routledge, pp. 502–12.

—— (1998a) "Introduction: Feminist Longings and Postcolonial Conditions," in Lughod, L.A. (ed.) *Remaking Women: Feminism and Modernity in the Middle East*, Princeton: Princeton University Press, pp. 3–31.

—— (ed.) (1998b) *Remaking Women: Feminism and Modernity in the Middle East*, Princeton: Princeton University Press.

Abū Murād, N. (1990) *al-Akhawān Rahbani: hayāt wa-masrah*, Beirut: Dār Amjad li-al-nashr wa-al-tawzī'.

—— (1997) "al-Masrah fī Lubnān: marāhiluhu, anwā'uhu, qadāyāhu (1900–75)," unpublished thesis, al-Jāmi'a al-Lubnāniyya.

—— (2000) "Lebanon," in Rubin, D. (ed.) *The World Encyclopedia of Contemporary Theatre: The Arab World*, London: Routledge.

Abū Sa'd, A. (1987) *Qāmūs al-mustalahāt wa-al-ta'ābīr al-sha'biyya*, Beirut: Maktabat Lubnān.

Abū Sālih, A. (1998) *al-Azma al-Lubnāniyya 'ām 1958: fī daw' wathā'iq yukshaf 'anhā li-awwal marra*, Beirut: al-Manshūrāt al-'Arabiyya.

Abū Sayf, L. (1972) *Najīb al-Rīhānī wa-tatawwur al-kūmūdiyya fī Misr*, Cairo: Dār al-ma'ārif.

Accad, E. (1990) *Sexuality and War: Literary Masks of the Middle East*, New York: New York University Press.

Adkins, L. and R. (2000) *The Keys of Egypt: the Race to Read the Hieroglyphs*, London: Harper Collins Publishers.

Adonis (1990) *An Introduction to Arab Poetics* (trans.) C. Cobham, London: Saqi.

Aghacy, S. (2001) "Lebanese Women's Fiction: Urban Identity and the Tyranny of the Past," *International Journal of Middle East Studies*, 33: 503–23.

Agwani, M.S. (ed.) (1965) *The Lebanese Crisis, 1958: A Documentary Study*, New York: Asia Publishing House.

Ahmed, L. (1992) *Women and Gender in Islam*, New Haven: Yale University Press.

Akl, S. (1944) *Qadmūs*, Beirut: Manshūrāt dār al-fikr.

—— (1960) "Tamhīd," in Rahbani, A. and M. *Mawsim al-'izz: ūbarīt bi-faslayn*, Beirut: Manshūrāt Raymūn Haddād, pp. 3–4.

—— (1964) *Falsafat al-Shihābiyya*, Beirut: Manshūrāt "al-Akl."

—— (1974) "Introduction" in 'Ubayd, J. *al-Sālāt fī-aghānī Fairouz*, Jounieh, Lubnān: al-Matba'a al-būlusiyya.

—— (1978) *Kumasiyyaat*, Beirut: Mancuraat Cadmuus.

" 'Alā masrah al-haram fī al-Qāhira sanat 1968: Fairouz wa-'Abd al-Wahhāb wa-300 Misrī wa-Lubnānī yashtarikūn fī taqdīm masrahiyya ghinā'iyya kabīra" (1966) *Mulhaq jarīdat al-nahār*, November 6, p. 15.

Aliksān, 'A. (1995) "Sharīt Fairouz wa-Ziad (Ilā Asi): fikra ūdībiyya muhaddāt ilā sūrat al-ab," *Majallat marāyā al-madīna*, July, pp. 28–31.

Aliksān, J. (1987) *al-Rahbāniyyūn wa-Fairouz*, Damascus: Dār talās.

Alin, E. (1994) *The United States and the 1958 Lebanon Crisis: American Intervention in the Middle East*, New York: University Press of America.

Allen, R. (1998) *The Arabic Literary Heritage*, Cambridge: Cambridge University Press.

Allūf, M.M. (1914) *History of Baalbek by One of Its Inhabitants*, 12th edn, Beirut: Catholic Printing Press.

—— (1922) *History of Baalbek by One of Its Inhabitants*, 30th edn, Beirut: Catholic Printing Press.

—— (1926) *Tārīkh Baalbeck*, 4th edn, Beirut: al-Matba'a al-adabiyya.

'Āmil, M. (1969) "Hawla masrahiyyat al-Rahābina al-akhīra 'Jibāl al-sawwān'," *al-Tarīq*, 28: 97–112.

Amīn, A. (1997) "'Bi-khusūs' masrah Ziad al-Rahbani 1970–90," *al-Hadātha*: 71–89.

al-Amīr, D. (1992) "Tabqā ma'ānī al-kalimāt nāqisa hattā tughanniyyhā Fairouz," *Mulhaq jarīdat al-nahār*, November 7, n.p.

Anderson, B. (1991) *Imagined Communities: Reflections on the Origin and Spread of Nationalism*, New York: Verso.

—— (1994) "Exodus," *Critical Inquiry*, 20: 314–27.

—— (1998) "Nationalism, Identity, and the World-in-Motion: On the Logics of Seriality," in Chea, P. and Robbins, B. (eds) *Cosmopolitics: Thinking and Feeling beyond the Nation*, Minneapolis: University of Minnesota Press, pp. 117–33.

'Anīnī, Rafīq (1989–90) "Ru'yat al-hayāt wa-al-fann fī masrah Ziad Rahbani," *al-Tarīq*, 48(6) and 49(1): 147–62 and 175–96.

al-'Antablī, 'U. (1999) *Najīb al-Rīhānī*, Cairo: al-Hay'a al-'āmma li-qusūr al-thaqāfa.

Appadurai, A. (1966) *Modernity at Large: Cultural Dimensions of Globalization*, Minneapolis: University of Minnesota Press.

Arab Studies Journal (1998). 6(1).

Armbrust, W. (1996) *Mass Culture and Modernism in Egypt*, Cambridge: Cambridge University Press.

—— (2000a) "Farid Shauqi: Tough Guy, Family Man, Cinema Star," in Ghoussoub, M. and Sinclair-Webb, E. (eds) *Imagined Masculinities: Male Identity and Culture in the Modern Middle East*, London: Saqi, pp. 199–226.

—— (2000b) "The Golden Age before the Golden Age: Commercial Egyptian Cinema before the 1960s," in Armbrust, W. (ed.) *Mass Mediations: New Approaches to Popular Culture in the Middle East and Beyond*, Berkeley: University of California Press, pp. 292–327.

—— (2000c) "Introduction: Anxieties of Scale," in Armbrust, W. (ed.) *Mass Mediations: New Approaches to Popular Culture in the Middle East and Beyond*, Berkeley: University of California Press, pp. 1–31.

Armstrong, N. (1987) *Desire and Domestic Fiction: A Political History of the Novel*, Oxford: Oxford University Press.

al-Ashqar, B. (1981) "Ziad al-rajul al-'āmm," *Jarīdat al-nahār al-'Arabiyya al-dawliyya*, January 19 and 26 and February 2, pp. 68–70, 56–8, and 60–1.

—— (1994) "Safar fī a'māq al-nafs al-Lubnāniyya," *Mulhaq jarīdat al-nahār*, May 14, p. 6.

"Asi Rahbani muwassi' hudūd al-hubb" (1986) *Jarīdat al-nahār*, June 25, p. 11.

Asmar, S. (1999) "Fairouz: a Voice, a Star, a Mystery," *aljadid*, 14(27): 14–16.

—— (2000) "The Two Tenors of Arab Music," *Turath. org*. Online. Available HTTP: http://www.turath.org/Articles/TwoTenors.htm (accessed January 2, 2007).

'Assāf, R. (1994) "al-Samt wa-mukabbirāt al-sawt," *Mulhaq jarīdat al-nahār*, September 17, p. 18.

'Awad, L. (1986) *Tārīkh al-fikr al-Misrī al-hadīth: min 'asr Ismā'īl ilā thawrat 1919*, Cairo: Maktabat madbūlī.

al-'Awīt, 'A. (1987) "Hādhā mā fa'alahu Ziad wa-hādhā mā ghannathu Fairouz," *Majallat al-hasnā'*, July 24, pp. 20–2.

Aylett, H. (1994) "Fairuz," *New Statesman and Society*, 7(294): 51–2.

'Azzām, F. (2002) "Fairouz: sawtī risālatī," *Majallat al-mar'a al-yawm*, May 14, n.p.

"Baalbeck bi-khayr raghm al-zilzāl" (1964) *Mulhaq jarīdat al-nahār*, June 21, p. 6.

Bach, J. (2002) " 'The Taste Remains': Consumption, (N)ostalgia, and the Production of East Germany," *Public Culture*, 3(14): 545–56.

Badawi, E. and Hinds, M. (1986) *A Dictionary of Egyptian Arabic: Arabic-English*, Beirut: Librairie du Liban.

Badawī, F. (1966) *Jārat al-qamar*, Cairo: al-Dār al-qawmiyya li-al-tibā'a wa-al-nashr.

Badawi, M.M. (1992a) "Arabic Drama: Early Developments," in Badawi, M.M. (ed.) *Modern Arabic Literature*, Cambridge: Cambridge University Press, pp. 329–57.

—— (1992b) "Introduction: I. The Background," in Badawi, M.M. (ed.) *Modern Arabic Literature*, Cambridge: Cambridge University Press, pp. 1–23.

Badran, M. (1995) *Feminists, Islam, and Nation*, Princeton: Princeton University Press.

Bakhtin, M.M. (1981a) "Epic and Novel: Toward a Methodology for the Study of the Novel," in Bakhtin, M.M. and Holquist, M. (ed.) Emerson, C. and Holquist, M. (trans.) *The Dialogic Imagination*, Austin: University of Texas Press, pp. 3–40.

—— (1981b) "From the Prehistory of Novelistic Discourse," in Bakhtin, M.M. and Holquist M. (ed.) Emerson, C. and Holquist, M. (trans.) *The Dialogic Imagination*, Austin: University of Texas Press, pp. 41–83.

Barakāt, Kh. (1996) "Mulāhaza hawla al-tajriba al-Rahbāniyya: al-khalfiyya al-tārīkhiyya, wa-al-ibdā' alladhī lā yamūt," *aljadid*, March, pp. 28–9.

Baram, A. (1991) *Culture, History and Ideology in the Formation of Ba'thist Iraq, 1968–89*, New York: St. Martin's Press.

Baron, B. (2005) *Egypt as a Woman: Nationalism, Gender, and Politics*, Cairo: The American University in Cairo Press.

Bāshā, 'Abīdū (1987a) "Hiwār shāmil ma'a ākhir al-kibār fī sulālat al-Rahābina 1: Ziad Rahbani: min man takhāf Fairouz? li-mādhā takhāf Fairouz?" *Majallat al-usbū' al-'Arabī*, August 2, pp. 36–8.

—— (1987b) "Hiwār shāmil ma'a ākhir al-kibār fī sulālat al-Rahābina 2: hattā al-Rahābina saraqū min al-Rahābina," *Majallat al-usbū' al-'Arabī*, August 17, pp. 42–3.

—— (1995) *Kitāb al-rāwī (siyar)*, Beirut: Dār al-tanwīr.

—— (1998) "Fairouz al-Ba'labakkiyya īqūna tatajaddad," *Jarīdat al-safīr*, August 15, p. 1.

—— and Dāwūd, H. (1983) "Hiwār ma'a Ziad Rahbani: a'īsh min al-masrah wa-ufakkir bi-al-hijra kay atafarragh li-al-mūsīqā," *Jarīdat al-safīr*, August 20, p. 10.

Bashar (2002) "Live from Beiteddine 2002," Fairouzonline.com. Online Posting. Available HTTP: http://www.fairuzonline.com/wwwboard/messages/115.shtml (accessed August 9, 2002).

Bāsīlā, N. (1973) "Dhikriyyāt Fairouz," *Majallat al-usbū' al-'Arabī*, July 9, 23 and 30, pp. 56–9, 68–71, 54–8.

Bayat, A. (2001) "Studying Middle Eastern Societies: Imperatives and Modalities of Thinking Comparatively," *Middle East Studies Association Bulletin*, 35(2): 151–8.

Baydūn, 'A. (1983) "Hawla masrahiyyat Ziad Rahbani 'Shī fāshil': tafāhat al-īdiyyūlūjiyyā wa-tafāhat al-wāqi'," *Jarīdat al-safīr*, May 21, p. 9.

—— (1993) " 'An masrah Ziad Rahbani aydan: kūmīdiyyā al-qaswa: al-aghānī ru'ūs sarākhāt wa-al-fukāha tajāwazat khatt al-mut'a," *Mulhaq jarīdat al-nahār*, July 10, pp. 6–7.

—— (1994) "al-Wuqūf 'alā atlāl al-dhākira bayna istifrāgh al-mādī wa-istinfādihi: thalāth lahazāt fī rihlat al-bahth 'an 'huwiyya Lubnāniyya': lā tufarritū bi-Fairouz... laysa dhahabunā kathīran!" *Majallat al-wasat*, May 12, pp. 50–3.

—— (1996) "Muqābala ma'a Ziad," *Majallat al-wasat*, July 22 and 29 and August 5, pp. 50–3, 52–4, and 52–5.

196

—— (2000) "'Awdat al-Rahbani al-dāll wa-hafl al-taslīm al-'ā'ilī," *Jarīdat al-safīr*, August 8, n.p.

Baydūn, A. (1979) "Muqaddima," in 'A. al-Zayn *Fusūl min tārīkh al-Shī'a fī Lubnān*, Beirut: Dār al-kalima, pp. 9–29.

"Bayyā' al-khawātim" (1964) *Mulhaq jarīdat al-nahār*, August 9, p. 14.

Bayyā' al-khawātim (1965) direction: Youssef Chahine, production and screenplay Asi and Mansour Rahbani, with Fairouz, Salwā Haddād, Mansour Rahbani, Nasrī Shams al-Dīn and Fīlmūn Wahbī, Phenicia Films.

Beck, L. and Keddie, N. (eds) (1978) *Women in the Muslim World*, Cambridge, MA: Harvard University Press.

Beidler, P. (1993) "South Pacific and American Remembering; or, 'Josh, We're Going to Buy This Son of a Bitch!'," *Journal of American Studies*, 27(2): 207–22.

"Beiteddine Festival History" (n.d.). Online. Available HTTP: http://www.beiteddine.org/main.html (accessed January 2, 2007).

Belgum, K. (1998) *Popularizing the Nation: Audience, Representation, and the Production of Identity in Die Gartenlaube, 1853–1900*, Lincoln: University of Nebraska Press.

Berman, M. (1982) *All That Is Solid Melts Into Air: The Experience of Modernity*, New York: Simon and Schuster.

"Bi-mā innū" (1993) "Interview with Ziad Rahbani and Joseph Saqr," produced by M. Suwayd, Lebanese Television, n.d.

Biani, N. (1972) *A Trip to Lebanon*, n.p.: n.p.

Bītār, M. (1978) "Muqāranat al-muthannā: Fairouz wa-Ziad Rahbani," *Jarīdat al-safīr*, July 26, n.p.

Bordman, G.M. (1981) *American Operetta: From H.M.S. Pinafore to Sweeney Todd*, Oxford: Oxford University Press.

Boswell, D. and Evans, J. (eds) (1999) *Representing the Nation: A Reader: Histories, Heritage and Museums*, London: Routledge.

Boullata, K. (ed.) (1981) *Fayruz, Legend and Legacy*, Washington, DC: Forum for International Art and Culture.

Boulus, S. (1981) "Origins of a Legend," in Boullata, K. (ed.) *Fayruz, Legend and Legacy*, Washington, DC: Forum for International Art and Culture, pp. 17–35.

Boyd, D.A. (1977) *Egyptian Radio: Tool of Political and National Development*, Lexington: Association for Education in Journalism.

—— (1991) "Lebanese Broadcasting: Unofficial Electronic Media During a Prolonged Civil War," *Journal of Broadcasting and Electronic Media*, 35(3): 269–87.

—— (1999) *Broadcasting in the Arab World: A Survey of the Electronic Media in the Middle East*, Ames: Iowa State University Press.

"Broadcasting" (2007) *Encyclopedia Britannica* in *Encyclopedia Britannica Online*. Online. Available HTTP: http://search.eb.com/eb/article-9106100 (accessed January 4, 2007).

Brosman, C. (1999) *Visions of War in France: Fiction, Art, Ideology*, Baton Rouge: Louisiana State University Press.

Būdhayna, M. (1999) *al-Mawwāl fī al-ghinā'al-'Arabī, al-Hammāmāt*, Tūnis: Manshūrāt M. Būdhayna.

Būlus, M. (2001) *Allāh, al-ard wa-al-habīb fī "al-Layl wa-al-qindīl" wa "Jibāl al-sawwān,"* Beirut: Dār 'Isām Haddād.

Butler, J. (1993) *Bodies That Matter: On the Discursive Limits of "Sex,"* London: Routledge.

Cachia, P. (1977) "The Egyptian Mawwāl – Its Ancestry, its Development, and its Present Forms," *Journal of Arabic Literature*, 8: 77–103.

Cadora, F.J. (1979) *Interdialectal Lexical Compatibility in Arabic: An Analytical Study of the Lexical Relationships among the Major Syro-Lebanese Varieties*, Leiden: E.J. Brill.

Celik, Z. (1992) *Displaying the Orient: Architecture of Islam at Nineteenth-Century World's Fairs*, Berkeley: University of California Press.

de Certeau, M. (1984) *The Practice of Everyday Life* (trans.) Rendall, S.F., Berkeley: University of California Press.

"Chat Iskandaria." (n.d.) *Fairouz.com*. Online. Available HTTP: http://www.fairouz.com/fairouz/articles/arsi.html (accessed June 19, 2002).

Chatterjee, P. (1993) *The Nation and Its Fragments: Colonial and Postcolonial Histories*, Princeton: Princeton University Press.

Chevallier, D. (1996) "Reflections on France, Lebanon and the Syria Area," in Brown, L.C. and Gordon, M. (eds) *Franco-Arab Encounters: Studies in Memory of David C. Gordon*, Beirut: American University of Beirut, pp. 179–200.

Cooke, M. (1988) *War's Other Voices: Women Writers on the Lebanese Civil War*, Cambridge: Cambridge University Press.

Cooke, M. and Rustomji-Kerns, R. (eds) (1994) *Blood into Ink: South Asian and Middle Eastern Women Write War*, Boulder: Westview Press.

Cooke, M. and Woollacott, W. (eds) (1993) *Gendering War Talk*, Princeton: Princeton University Press.

Currey, N.E. (2002) "History in Contemporary Practice: Syria's Music Canon," *Middle East Studies Association Bulletin*, 36(1): 9–19.

al-Dāhir, H. (1995) "Yukmil al-masīra al-Rahbāniyya al-ibdāʿiyya baʿda ghiyāb Mansour," *Jarīdat al-anwār*, March 26, p. 1.

Dāhir, M. (1986) *al-Hijra al-Lubnāniyya ilā Misr: "hijrat al-Shuwām*," Beirut: al-Jāmiʿa al-Lubnāniyya qism al-dirāsāt al-tārīkhiyya: tawzīʿ al-maktaba al-sharqiyya.

Danielson, V. (1997) *The Voice of Egypt: Oum Kalthoum, Arabic Song, and Egyptian Society in the Twentieth Century*, Chicago: University of Chicago Press.

—— (1998) "Performance, Political Identity, and Memory: Umm Kulthum and Gamal ʿAbd al-Nasir," in Zuhur, S. (ed.) *Images of Enchantment: Visual and Performing Arts of the Middle East*, Cairo: The American University in Cairo Press, pp. 109–22.

Darkūb, M. (1998) "Nizār Murūwa/nāqidan mūsīqiyyan: al-ruʾya al-talīʿiyya, wa-al-wudūh al-ʿamīq," in Darkūb, M. (ed.) *Fī al-mūsīqā al-Lubnāniyya al-ʿArabiyya wa-al-masrah al-ghināʾī al-Rahbani*, Beirut: Dār al-Farābī.

Darwish, H. (2000) *Sayyid Darwish bayna al-ʿabqariyya wa-al-muʾāmarāt al-fanniyya*, Cairo: Dār al-ahmadī li-al-nashr.

Darwish, M. (1992) "Ughniyyat hayātinā," *Mulhaq jarīdat al-nahār*, November 7, p. 19.

Das, V. (1997) "Language and Body: Transactions in the Construction of Pain," in Das, V., Kleinman, A. and Lock, M. (eds) *Social Suffering*, Berkeley: University of California Press, pp. 67–91.

Dāwūd, H. (1980) "Ziad Rahbani fī masrahiyyatihi al-jadīda: kathīr min al-mawhiba, kathīr min al-iddiʿāʾ," *Jarīdat al-safir*, October 5, p. 11.

Dawwāra, M.M. (1996) *Sayyid Darwish: al-fannān wa-al-insān*, Cairo: al-Hayʾa al-ʿāmma li-qusūr al-thaqāfa.

Deeb, Lara (2006) *An Enchanted Modern: Gender and Public Piety in Shiʿi Lebanon*, Princeton: Princeton University Press.

Dening, G. (1996) *Performances*, Chicago: The University of Chicago Press.

Einstein, Z. (2000) "Writing Bodies on the Nation for the Globe," in Ranchod-Nilsson, S. and Tetreault, M. (eds) *Women, States, and Nationalisms: At Home in the Nation?*, London: Routledge, pp. 35–53.

Everett, W.A. and Laird, P.R. (2002) *The Cambridge Companion to the Musical*, Cambridge: Cambridge University Press.

Fadl Allāh, H. (1995) "Ziad Rahbani: Kullunā taghayyarnā, lākin bi-al-mabda' 'anā mā taghayyarnā'! Joseph Saqr: 'kunnā muballishīn dahk, wa-ba'dnā," *Majallat al-hasnā'*, November 24, pp. 50–3.

"Fairouz bi-alhān Najīb Hankash" (1964) *Mulhaq jarīdat al-nahār*, June 21, p. 6.

"Fairouz fī Baalbeck…min dūn ahlihā" (1998) *Jarīdat al-safīr*, August 14, p. 1.

"Fairouz fī al-layālī al-Lubnāniyya: mukhtārāt min masrahiyyāt al-Akhawayn Rahbani: Jisr al-qamar – Jibāl al-sawwān – Nātūrat al-mafātīh" (1998) *Festival international de Baalbeck*, Beirut: Association du festival international de Baalbeck pour 1998, pp. 119–29.

"Fairouz tazhar 'alā masrah Qasr al-Bīkādīlī bi-qinā' 'alā al-wajh wa-darabukka fī al-yadayn" (1967) *Mulhaq jarīdat al-nahār*, January 1, pp. 12–15.

"Fairouz wa-al-Rahbāniyyān bi-al-fushā" (1964) *Mulhaq jarīdat al-nahār*, May 24, pp. 2–3.

"al-Fann al-sha'bī al-Lubnānī min ayyām Fakhr al-Dīn" (1966) in *XIème festival international de Baalbeck*. Beirut: Association du festival international de Baalbeck pour 1966, n.p.

Farīd, S. (2000) "Najīb al-Rīhānī bayna al-masrah wa-al-sīnamā," *al-Kutub wijhāt nazar*, June, pp. 60–7.

Fāris, Sh. (1980) "'Fīlm Amīrkī tawīl' radd 'alā tajribat al-Rahābina wa-'alā tajārib masrahiyya ukhrā," *Jarīdat al-nidā'*, November 16, n.p.

"al-Fasl al-thānī min: 'Dawālīb al-hawā'" (1965) *Mulhaq jarīdat al-nahār*, August 1, pp. 14–16.

Feuer, J. (1982) *The Hollywood Musical*, Bloomington: Indiana University Press.

Fisk, R. (1992) *Pity the Nation*, Oxford: Oxford University Press.

Foucault, M. (1972) *The Archeology of Knowledge* (trans.) Sheridan Smith, A.M. New York: Pantheon Books.

—— (1980) *Power/Knowledge: Selected Interviews and Other Writings, 1972–7*, Gordon, C. (ed. and trans.), Brighton: Harvester.

"Foul and Fair: Ziad al-Rahbani and the Nightmare of Postwar Culture" (1993) *The Lebanon Report*, 4(4): 6–7.

Franken, M. (1998) "Farida Fahmy and the Dancer's Image in Egyptian Film," in Zuhur, S. (ed.) *Images of Enchantment: Visual and Performing Arts of the Middle East*, Cairo: The American University in Cairo Press, pp. 265–82.

Frayha, A. (1956) *Isma'yā Ridā!*, Beirut: Maktabat Khayyāt.

—— (1957) *al-Qarya al-Lubnāniyya: hadāra fī tarīq al-zawāl*, Tripoli, Lebanon: Jarrūs bris.

—— (1995) *A Dictionary of Non-Classical Vocables in the Spoken Arabic of Lebanon*, Beirut: Librairie Du Liban.

Fu'ād, N.A. (2000) *Oum Kalthoum: 'asr min al-fann*, Cairo: Dār al-hilāl.

Fussell, P. (1975) *The Great War and Modern Memory*, Oxford: Oxford University Press.

Gershoni, I. and Jankowski, J. (1986) *Egypt, Islam, and the Arabs: The Search for Egyptian Nationhood, 1900–30*, Oxford: Oxford University Press.

Ghazāla, M. (1998) *Tawfīq al-Basha: Yaqazat al-mūsīqā*, Beirut: M. Ghazāla.

Ghurayyib, L. (1972) "al-Layālī al-Lubnāniyya 'alā sharāshif zarqā' Fairouz: man yughannī fī al-sabāh," *Jarīdat al-nahār*, July 11, p. 7.

Gibran, K. (1923) *The Prophet*, New York: Knopf.

—— (1956) *al-Nabī*, (trans.) Naima, M., Beirut: Admūn Dahba.

Good Friday Eastern Sacred Songs ((1962, 1964, 1965)/1990) performed by Fairouz. Arranged by Asi and Mansour Rahbani. A. Chahine and Fils. (produced by). Beirut: Voix De l'Orient, VDLCD 516.

Gopnik, A. (2001) "That Sunday," *The New Yorker*, August 13, pp. 30–3.

Gordon, J. (2002) *Revolutionary Melodrama: Popular Film and Civic Identity in Nasser's Egypt*, Chicago: Middle East Documentation Center on behalf of the Center for Middle Eastern Studies at the University of Chicago.

H., J. (1994) "Fairouz hiya al-hadath," *Majallat al-dalīl*, August 19, p. 3.

Habib, K. (2005) "The Superstar Singer Fairouz and the Ingenious Rahbani Composers: Lebanon Sounding," unpublished thesis, University of California, Santa Barbara.

Haddad, J.W. (1981) "My Sister and I," in Boullata, K. (ed.) *Fayruz, Legend and Legacy*, Washington, DC: Forum for International Art and Culture, pp. 24–5.

"Hādhā huwa al-fūlklūr fī al-mūsīqā wa-al-ghinā' " (1964) *Mulhaq jarīdat al-nahār*, September 13, p. 15.

"Hadīth ma'a Ziad Rahbani" (1993) *Majallat nagham*, April 6, pp. 22–6.

al-Hājj, B. (1994) "Min qalb Beirut salām li-Fairouz," *Jarīdat al-nahār*, September 14, p. 6.

al-Hajj, U. (1987) *Kalimāt Kalimāt Kalimāt*, 3 vols, Beirut: Dār al-nahār li-al-nashr.

—— (1992) "Shā'irat al-sawt: mukhtārāt min kitābātihi fīhā," *Mulhaq jarīdat al-nahār*, November 7, pp. 18–19.

"Hakadhā kānū" (1991) *Majallat al-shabaka*, August 9–16, 1: 51.

Hamāda, M. (1992) "Fī muqābala khāssa sarīha wa-shāmila 'an al-Rahābina wa-fannihā," *Majallat al-wasat*, November 30, pp. 48–53.

Hamāda, M., Joseph, S., and Makdisi, J. (eds) (2000) *al-Muwātaniyyafī Lubnān bayna al-rajul wa-al-mar'a*, Beirut: Dār al-jadīd.

Harb, N. (1978a) "al-I'lām al-rasmī yudhī' a'mālanā al-fanniyya mabtūratan," *Jarīdat al-safīr*, n.d., n.p.

—— (1978b) "Ziad Rahbani 'ashiyyat taqdīm 'Bi-al-nisba li-bukra shū:' masrahī lā yatrah ayy badīl" *Jarīdat al-safīr*, February 12, p. 11.

Harding, G. (1963) *Baalbek: a new guide*, Beirut: Khayats.

Harris, W. (1997) *Faces of Lebanon: Sects, Wars and Global Extensions*, Princeton: Markus Wiener Publishers.

Hartman, M. and Olsaretti, A. (2003) '"The First Boat and the First Oar': Inventions of Lebanon in the Writings of Michel Chiha," *Radical History Review*, 86: 37–65.

Harvey, A. (1998) *A Muse of Fire: Literature, Art and War*, Rio Grande, Ohio: Hambledon Press.

al-Hasan, H. (1965) *al-I'lām wa-al-dawla*, Beirut: Sādir.

Hawi, K.S. (1982) *Kahlil Gibran: His Background, Character, and Works*, London: Third World Centre for Research and Publishing.

Hazīn, Gh. (2003) "Fairouz tughannī fī Bayt-Dīn li-al-sha'b al-maskīn wa-Ziad yuqaddim mufāji'āt min qadīmihi wa-jadīdihi," *Jarīdat al-rā'y*, n.d., n.p.

Heng, G. and Devan, J. (1992) "State Fatherhood: The Politics of Nationalism, Sexuality, and Race in Singapore," in Parker, A., Russo, M., Sommer, D., and Yaeger, P. (eds) *Nationalisms and Sexualities*, London: Routledge, pp. 343–64.

Herzfeld, M. (1986) *Ours Once More: Folklore, Ideology, and the Making of Modern Greece*, New York: Pella Publishing Company, Inc.

Himsī, H. (1994) "Hiwār tullāb al-jāmiʿāt maʿa Ziad Rahbani: mādhā ʿan al-shuyūʿiyya wa-al-tāʾifiyya wa-Fairouz wa-al-Sūlīdayr," *Jarīdat al-safīr*, September 1, p. 10.

Hirschkop, K. (1986) "A Response to the Forum on Mikhail Bakhtin," in Morson, G.S. (ed.) *Bakhtin: Essays and Dialogues on His Work*, Chicago: The University of Chicago Press, pp. 73–88.

—— (1990) "Heteroglossia and Civil Society: Bakhtin's Public Square and the Politics of Modernity," *Studies in the Literary Imagination*, 23(1): 65–98.

Hiwār al-ʿumr (1997) narr. J. Khūrī, dir. ʿI. ʿAbbūd, with Z. Rahbani and K. Hamdān, Lebanese Broadcasting Company, Broadcast in two episodes, December.

Hobsbawm, E. and Ranger, T. (eds) (1983) *The Invention of Tradition*, Cambridge: Cambridge University Press.

Hourani, A. (1992) "Lebanese and Syrians in Egypt," in Hourani, A. and Shehadi, N. (eds) *The Lebanese in the World: A Century of Emigration*, London: Centre for Lebanese Studies in association with I.B. Tauris, pp. 497–507.

Hourani, A. and Shehadi, N. (eds) (1992) *The Lebanese in the World: A Century of Emigration*, London: Centre for Lebanese Studies in association with I.B. Tauris.

al-ʿĪd, Y. (1978) "Qirāʾāt shiʿriyya – Said Akl bayna al-ramz wa-al-mutlaq," *al-Tarīq*, 37(2): 165–82.

"Ilā Asi" (1995) *Khallīk fial-bayt*, prepared by S. Tāhā and N. ʿArnūq, presented by Z. Wahbī, dir. M. al-Maghribī, with N. Abū Murād, N. Hasan, R. Khūrī and S. al-Sāyigh, Future Television, Beirut, Lebanon, July 2.

ʿInāya, J. (2000) "Haflat Fairouz fī Beiteddine khayr min alf hafl," *Jarīdat al-safir*, August 5, p. 1.

—— (2001) "al-ʿAsr al-jadīd fī ughniyat Fairouz wa-Ziad," *Jarīdat al-nidāʾ*, August 2, n.p.

Inchbold, A.C. (1906) *Under the Syrian Sun: The Lebanon, Baalbek, Galilee and Judea*, 2 vols, London: Hutchinson and Co.

ʿIsmat, R. (1995) *al-Masrah al-ʿArabī: suqūt al-aqniʿa al-ijtimāʿiyya*, Damascus: Muʾassasat al-shabība li-al-iʿlām wa-al-tibāʿa wa-al-nashr.

"al-Istiftāʾ " (1992) *Mulhaq jarīdat al-nahār*, November 7, n.p.

Izzard, R. and M. (1959) *Smelling the Breezes: A Journey through the High Lebanon*, London: Hodder and Stoughton.

Jarkas, R. (n.d.) *Fairouz: al-Mutriba wa-al-mishwār*, Beirut: Sharikat ʿashtarūt li-al-tibāʿa wa-al-Nashr.

al-Jawharī, A. (1996) "Lughat Ziad Rahbani," *Jarīdat al-nahār*, August 22, n.p.

Jayyusi, S.K. (1992) "Modernist poetry in Arabic," in Badawi, M.M. (ed.) *Modern Arabic Literature*, Cambridge: Cambridge University Press, pp. 132–79.

Joseph, S. (1999) *Intimate Selving in Arab Families: Gender, Self, and Identity*, Syracuse: Syracuse University Press.

—— (2000) *Gender and Citizenship in the Middle East*, Syracuse: Syracuse University Press.

—— (2005) "Learning Desire: Relational Pedagogies and the Desiring Female Subject in Lebanon," *Journal of Middle East Women's Studies*, 1(1): 79–109.

"Jūzīf Saqr: laysh ʿamilt hayk?!" (1996) *Majallat alwān*, January 11, n.p.

Kabbani, O. (1992) *The Reconstruction of Beirut*, Oxford: Centre for Lebanese Studies.

Kabbāra, R. (1991) "Ziad Rahbani: lastu maʿa sawt ʿAmr Diyāb... bal maʿa mā yuhāwil an yubarhinahu," *Jarīdat al-anwār*, September 12, p. 16.

Kāmil, M. (1977) *al-Masrah al-ghināʾī al-ʿArabī*, Cairo: Dār al-Maʿārif.

Kāmil, S. (1983a) "ʿShī Fāshilʾ: lā taqraʾū al-masrahiyya min al-ʿunwān!" *Majallat al-shirāʿ*, March 7, pp. 68–9.

Kāmil, S. (1983b) "Ziad Rahbani fī hiwār hawla 'Shī fāshil': al-Rahābina lā yasma'ūn mūsīqā," *Majallat al-shirā'*, March 7, p. 68.

—— (1986) "Ziad Rahbani, mustaqbalunā al-fannī," *Jarīdat al-shirā'*, December 29, p. 82.

Kandiyoti, D. (ed.) (1991) *Women, Islam, and the State*, Philadelphia: Temple University Press.

—— (1998) "Afterword: Some Awkward Questions on Women and Modernity in Turkey," in Lughod, L.A. (ed.) *Remaking Women: Feminism and Modernity in the Middle East*, Princeton: Princeton University Press, pp. 270–88.

Kano, A. (2001) *Acting like a Woman in Modern Japan: Theater, Gender and Nationalism*, New York: Palgrave.

Kassār, M. (1991) *'Alī al-Kassār: barbarī Misr al-wahīd*, Cairo: Dār akhbār al-yawm.

—— (1993) *'Alī al-Kassār wa-thawrat al-kūmīdiyya*, Cairo: Dār al-Ma'ārif.

Kaufman, A. (2000) "Reviving Phoenicia: The Search for an Identity in Lebanon," unpublished thesis, Brandies University.

—— (2001) "Phoenicianism: The Formation of an Identity in Lebanon in 1920," *Middle Eastern Studies*, 37(1): 173–94.

—— (2004) *Reviving Phoenicia: In Search of an Identity in Lebanon*, London: I.B. Tauris.

Khalaf, S. and Khoury, P. (eds) (1993) *Recovering Beirut: Urban Design and Post-War Reconstruction*, Leiden: Brill.

Khalidi, R. (1995) "Is There a Future for Middle East Studies," *Middle East Studies Association Bulletin*, 29(1): 1–7.

Khalīfa, Marālīn (1998) "Ilyās Rahbani: 'dhahabnā ilā Baalbeck wa-intazarnā Ziad fa-lam ya'ti': fī radd 'alā al-ittihāmāt al-sahāfiyya wa-al-ma'ākhidh," *Jarīdat al-hayāt* August 25, p. 18.

Khalīfa, Marsīl (1985) "Ziad Rahbani wa-jāz 'al-ūryāntāl'," *Jarīdat al-nidā'*, January 31, p. 7.

el Khazen, F. (2000) *The Breakdown of the State in Lebanon: 1967–76*, London: I.B. Tauris.

al-Khāzin, W. and Ilyān, N. (1970) *Kutub wa-udabā': tarājum wa-muqaddimāt wa-ahādīth li-al-udabā' min Lubnān wa-al-'ālam al-'Arabī*, Beirut: al-Maktaba al-'asriyya.

Khūrī, I. (2000) "Fairouz al-thāniyya," *Mulhaq jarīdat al-nahār*, August 12, n.p.

Kilpatrick, H. (1992) "The Egyptian Novel from *Zaynab* to 1980," in Badawi, M.M. (ed.) *Modern Arabic Literature*, Cambridge: Cambridge University Press, pp. 223–69.

Kirshenblatt-Gimblett, B. (1991) "Objects of Ethnography," in Karp, J. and Lavine, S. (eds) *Exhibiting Cultures: The Poetics and Politics of Museum Display*, Washington, DC: Smithsonian Institution Press, pp. 387–443.

—— (1998) "Folklore's Crisis," *Journal of American Folklore*, 111(440): 281–327.

Kishlī, M. (1992) "Shatahāt Fairouziyya," *Mulhaq jarīdat al-nahār*, November 7, n.p.

Knapp, R. (2005) *The American Musical and the Formation of National Identity*, Princeton: Princeton University Press.

Kraidy, M.M. (1996) "Towards a Semiosphere of Hybrid Identities: A Native Ethnography of Glocalization," unpublished thesis, Ohio University.

"Kull ahad wa-intū bi-khayr: Warda wa-Ziad Rahbani: mamnū' istikhdām Fairouz li-al-di'āyā al-siyāsiyya" (1994) *Majallat fann*, September 5, p. 8.

Kuntz, B. (2000) *Lebanon: An Insiders Guide*, Beirut: Prana Publishers.

Kurayyim, M. (2000) *al-Masrah al-Lubnānī fī nisf qarn: 1900–50*, Beirut: Dār al-maqāsid.

Lamb, A. (2000) *150 Years of Popular Musical Theatre*, New Haven: Yale University Press.

Landau, J.M. (1958) *Studies in the Arab Theater and Cinema*, Philadelphia: University of Pennsylvania Press.

Laurens, H. (1990) *Le royaume impossible: la France et la genèse du monde arabe*, Paris: Armand Colin.

"al-Layālī al-Lubnāniyya: alhān wa-raqasāt shaʻbiyya" (1962) *VIIème festival international de Baalbeck*, Beirut: Association du festival international, pp. 180–3.

"al-Layālī al-Lubnāniyya: 'Jibāl al-sawwān:' masrahiyya ghinā'iyya shaʻbiyya: ghinā' wa-tamthīl Fairouz" (1969) *XIème festival international de Baalbeck*, Beirut: Association du festival international de Baalbeck pour 1969, n.p.

"Lebanon at a Glance" (2006) Washington, DC: The World Bank Group. Online. Available HTTP: http://devdata.worldbank.org/AAG/lbn_aag.pdf (accessed January 2, 2007).

Levy, E. (2000) "Women Warriors: the Paradox and Politics of Israeli Women in Uniform," in Ranchod-Nilsson, S. and Tetreault, M. (eds) *Women, States, and Nationalisms: At Home in the Nation?*, London: Routledge: pp. 196–214.

Lukács, G. (1971) *The Theory of the Novel; a Historico-Philosophical Essay on the Forms of Great Epic Literature*, Cambridge, MA: M.I.T. Press.

Lustick, I.S. (2000) "The Quality of Theory and the Comparative Disadvantage of Area Studies," *Middle East Studies Association Bulletin*, 34(2): 189–92.

M., ʻ. (1972) "Baalbeck 1972," *Jarīdat al-nahār*, May 26, p. 7.

McClintock, A. (1997) "'No Longer in a Future Heaven': Gender, Race and Nationalism," in Mufti, A., Shohat, E. and McClintock, A. (eds) *Dangerous Liaisons: Gender, Nation, and Postcolonial Perspectives*, Minneapolis: University of Minnesota Press, pp. 89–112.

"Mādhā ʻan al-layālī al-Lubnāniyya fī Baalbeck?" (1973) *Majallat al-usbūʻ al-ʻArabi*, July 30, p. 63.

Mahfūz, H. (1986) "Fairouz: anā ramz Lubnān al-muwahhad," *Majallat al-sayyād*, June 27–July 3, pp. 40–3.

Mahfūz, ʻI. (1986) "Rūh al-shaʻb," *Majallat al-kifāh al-ʻArabī*, June 30, p. 66.

"Mahrajān al-fann al-shaʻbī al-Lubnānī: 28, 29, 30, 31 Āb 1959" (1959) in *IIIème festival international de Baalbeck*, Beirut: Association du festival international de Baalbeck, n.p.

"Mahrajān al-fann al-shaʻbī al-Lubnānī" (1961) in *Vème festival international de Baalbeck*, Beirut: Association du festival international de Baalbeck, pp. 145–66.

"Mahrajānāt Baalbeck fī kitāb" (1994) *Mulhaq jarīdat al-nahār*, December 3, p. 3.

Makdisi, S. (1997) "Laying Claim to Beirut: Urban Narrative and Spatial Identity in the Age of Solidere," *Critical Inquiry*, 23: 661–705.

Makdisi, U. (1998) "The 'Rediscovery' of Baalbek: A Metaphor for Empire in the Nineteenth-Century," in Scheffler, T., Sader, H., and Neuwirth, A. (eds) *Baalbek: Image and Monument: 1898–1998*, Beirut: In Kommission Bei Franz Steiner Verlag Stuttgart, pp. 137–56.

Manganaro, E.S. (1999a) "Imagining Lebanon Through Rahbani Musicals," *aljadid*, 29: 4–6. (same as Salem, E.)

——— (1999b) "Lebanon Mythologized or Lebanon Deconstructed: Two Narratives of National Consciousness," in Shehadeh, L.R. (ed.) *Women and War in Lebanon*, Gainesville: University Press of Florida.

"Mansour Rahbani baʻda khrūjihi min al-mustashfā bi-al-Qāhira" (1995) *Jarīdat al-safīr*, September 29, p. 18.

Marāshda, ʻA. (1995) *Adūnīs wa-al-turāth al-naqdī*, Irbid, Jordan: Dār al-Kindī.

Marshall, B. and Stilwell, R.J. (2000) *Musicals: Hollywood and Beyond*, Exeter, England: Intellect.

Martin, A. (2001) "Death of a Nation: Transnationalism, Bodies and Abortion in Late Twentieth-Century Ireland," in Mayer, T. (ed.) *Gender Ironies of Nationalism: Sexing the Nation*, London: Routledge, pp. 65–88.

Massad, J. (2003) "Liberating Songs: Palestine Put to Music," *Journal of Palestine Studies*, 32: 21–38.

Matar, 'A. (1993) "'Awdat Ziad," *Majallat marāyā al-madīna*, January 15, n.p.

"Mawsim al-'izz: awparīt sha'biyya: ta'līf al-Akhawayn Rahbani" (1960) in *IVème festival international de Baalbeck*. Beirut: Association du festival international de Baalbeck, pp. 86–96.

Mayer, T. (ed.) (2001) *Gender Ironies of Nationalism: Sexing the Nation.* London: Routledge.

Meyer, M.K. (2000) "Ulster's Red Hand: Gender, Identity, and Sectarian Conflict in Northern Ireland," in Ranchod-Nilsson, S. and Tetreault, M. (eds) *Women, States, and Nationalisms: At Home in the Nation?*, London: Routledge, pp. 119–42.

Middle East Report (1997) 4 (27).

Mīna, H. and al-'Attār, N. (1976) *Adab al-harb*, Damascus: Manshūrāt wizārat al-thaqāfa.

Mitchell, T. (1988) *Colonising Egypt*, Berkeley: University of California Press.

—— (1999) "The Stage of Modernity," in Mitchell, T. (ed.) *Questions of Modernity*, Minneapolis: University of Minnesota Press.

Moghadam, V. (ed.) (1994) *Gender and National Identity: Women and Politics in Muslim Societies*, London and Oxford: Zed Books, Ltd. and Oxford University Press.

Moran, J. (2002) *Interdisciplinarity*, London: Routledge.

Most, A. (2004) *Making Americans: Jews and the Broadway Musical*, Cambridge, MA: Harvard University Press.

"Mu'assasat Rahbani" (2000) *Lubnān al-dhākira wa-al-ams*. Prepared and presented by S. Bayrūtī, direction A. Hilmāwī, with N. Abū Murād, Lebanese Television, April 4.

Mufarrij, T.B. (1969) *al-Mawsū'a al-Lubnāniyya al-musawwara*, 3 vols, Beirut: Maktabat al-bustān.

al-Mukhkh, M. (1983) "Masīrat Ziad Rahbani al-fanniyya: 'Shī Fāshil' wa-al-bahth 'an al-hall," *Jarīdat al-safīr*, May 8, p. 11.

Munassā, M. (1991) "Mansour Rahbani yukmil al-risāla," *Jarīdat al-nahār*, June 4, p. 7.

—— (1994) "Baalbeck...Mahrajān al-ard wa-al-insān," in Tueni, Gh. (ed.) *Baalbeck: les riches heures du festival*, Beirut: Editions Dar an-Nahar, pp. 6–63.

"Muqābala ma'a Ziad Rahbani" (1993a) *Idhā'at sawt al-sha'b*, n.d.

—— (1993b) with F. Abū 'Absī, K. Libbus, Z. Rahbani, J. Saqr and 'A. Shāhīn, Lebanese Television, May 11.

Murūwa, N. (1998) *Fī al-mūsīqā al-Lubnāniyya al-'Arabiyya wa-al-masrah al-ghinā'ī al-Rahbanī*, Beirut: Dār al-Farābī.

—— (1999) "Sayyid Darwish, Major Arab Music Pioneer" (trans.) S. Asmar, *aljadid*, 5(29): 11, 32–4.

Musawwih, M. (2006) *Jamāliyyāt al-ibdā' al-Rahbanī: dirāsa tahlīliyya li-al-a'māl al-masrahiyya li-al-Akhawayn Asi wa-Mansour al-Rahbani*, Beirut: Bīsān li-al-nashr wa-al-tawzī' wa-al-i'lām.

"Mu'tamar sahafī li-Ziad Rahbani bi-khusūs 'amalihī al-jadīd: 'Bi-khusūs al-karāma wa-al-sha'b al-'anīd" (1993) with M. Rahbani, Z. Rahbani, K. Libbus, J. Saqr, Lebanese Broadcasting Company, April 5.

N., S. (1970) "Sālat al-Kūmūdūr tughayyir huwiyya wa-tuhzinunā," *Jarīdat al-nahār*, June 12, p. 11.

Naima, M. (1974) *Jubrān Khalīl Jubrān: hayātuhu, mawtuhu, adabuhu, fannuhu*, Beirut: Mu'assasat naufal.

al-Najmī, K. (1993) *Turāth al-ghinā' al-'Arabī bayna al-Mawsilī wa-Ziryāb.wa-Oum Kalthoum wa-'Abd al-Wahhāb*, Cairo: Dār al-Shurūq.

Na'ma, F. (1973) *Mulakhkhas qawā'id al-lugha al-'Arabiyya*, Cairo: Nahdat Misr li-al-tibā'a wa-al-nashr wa-al-tawzī'.

al-Naqqāsh, R. (1972) "Nās min waraq: bayna alhān al-Rahbāniyyayn wa-sawt Fairouz tajriba fanniyya jarī'a: Sayyid Darwish yahlum bi-talhīn al-jarā'id . . . wa-al-akhawān Rahbani yulahhinān al-nathr!," *Majallat al-musawwar*, May 5, pp. 36–7.

—— (1992) "al-Zahra," *Mulhaq jarīdat al-nahār*, November 7, p. 19.

Nāsir, M. (1986) "Fairouz wa-al-Rahābina . . . hikāyat nagham." *Majallat alwān*, August 16, 23, and 30; September 6, 13, 20, and 27; and October 4 and 11, pp. 35–7, 44–7, 46–9, 42–5, and 40–2.

Nasr, M. (1996) *"al-Ghurabā' " fī khitāb Lubnāniyyīn 'an al-harb al-ahliyya*, London: Dar Al Saqi.

Nasr Allāh, H. (1984) *Tārīkh Baalbeck*, 2 vols, Beirut: Mu'assasat al-wafā'.

Nasr Allāh, R. (1986) "al-Ard, al-insān, al-watan: thulāthiyyat al-intimā' 'inda al-Rahābina," *Majallat al-kifāh al-'Arabī*, June 30, pp. 64–6.

Nasrī, S. (1983) "Fairouz munshidat mahrajānāt Jarash," *Jarīdat al-nahār*, August 19, p. 10.

Nehme, L.M. (1997) *Baalbek: monument phénicien*, Beirut: Aleph et Taw.

Nimr, N. (1981) "al-Nazariyya wa-al-barhana wa-Asi Rahbani (2)," *Jarīdat al-anwār*, n.d., p. 7.

al-Nowaihi, M. (2001) "Resisting Silence in Arab Women's Autobiographies," *International Journal of Middle East Studies*, 33(4): 477–502.

Petran, T. (1987) *The Struggle over Lebanon*, New York: Monthly Review Press.

Phares, W. (1995) *Lebanese Christian Nationalism: The Rise and Fall of an Ethnic Resistance*, Boulder: Lynne Rienner Publishers.

Philipp, T. (1985) *The Syrians in Egypt: 1725–1975*, Stuttgart: Franz Steiner Verlag.

Piterberg, G. (1997) "The Tropes of Stagnation and Awakening in Nationalist Historical Consciousness," in Jankowski, J. and Gershoni, I. (eds) *Rethinking Nationalism in the Arab Middle East*, New York: Columbia University Press, pp. 42–62.

Popular Music (1996) 13.3.

al-Qa'īd, Y. (1992) "Sawtuhā yudhakkir bi-mā' al-janna," *Mulhaq jarīdat al-nahār*, November 7, n.p.

"Qasīdat hubb: munawwa'āt ghinā'iyya rāqisa li-al-akhawayn Rahbani" (1973) in *XVIIème festival international de Baalbeck*, Beirut: Association du festival international: pp. 148–53.

Qasīr, S. (1994) "Na'mat al-ikhtiyār," *Mulhaq jarīdat al-nahār*, September 17, p. 18.

Racy, A.J. (1977) "Musical Change and Commercial Recording in Egypt, 1904–32," unpublished thesis, University of Illinois at Urbana-Champaign.

—— (1981) "Legacy of a Star," in Boullata, K. (ed.) *Fayruz, Legend and Legacy*, Washington, DC: Forum for International Art and Culture, pp. 36–8.

—— (2001) "Musical Attitudes and Spoken Language in Pre-Civil War Beirut," in Zuhur, S. (ed.) *Colors of Enchantment: Theater, Dance, and the Visual Arts of the Middle East*, Cairo: The American University in Cairo Press pp. 336–51.

—— (2002) "Urban-Based Folklore" in "Modern Developments" in "Lebanon." Online. Available HTTP:http://www.grovemusic.com/shared/views/article.html?section= music.16186.4.3.4#music.16186.4.3.4 (accessed January 2, 2007).

—— (2003) *Making Music in the Arab World: The Culture and Artistry of Tarab*, Cambridge: Cambridge University Press.

"The Radio Audience of Lebanon" (1951) New York: Columbia University, Bureau of Applied Social Research.

Ragette, F. (1980) *Baalbek*, Park Ridge, NJ: Noyes Press.

Rahbani, A. and M. (1960) *Mawsim al-'izz: ūbarīt bi-faslayn*, Beirut: Manshūrāt Raymūn Haddād.

—— (1966) *Ayyām Fakhr al-Dīn: masrahiyya ghinā'iyya sha'biyya*, n.p.: privately printed.

—— (1967) *Hāla wa-al-malik*, Beirut: al-Mu'assasa al-sahafiyya.

—— (1975) *Nās min waraq*, n.p.: privately printed.

—— (1977) *Batrā*, Damascus: n.p.

—— (1988) *Fairuz*, performed by Fairouz, produced by A. Chahine and Fils, Beirut: Voix de l'Orient Series, VDLCD 502.

—— (1991) *Fairuz: The Days of Fakhr Eddeen: Complete Original Cast Recording*, 2 records, directed by S. al-Sharif, produced by A. Chahine and Fils, With Fairouz, N. Shams al-Dīn, F. Wahbī, R. 'Assāf, Beirut: Voix de l'Orient Series, VDLCD 525/526.

—— (1992a) *Fairuz: Lebanon Forever*, performed by Fairouz, produced by A. Chahine and Fils, Beirut: Voix de l'Orient Series, VDLCD 544.

—— (1957/1992b) *Fairouz, Rāji'ūn*, performed by Fairouz, Beirut: A. Chahine and Fils, VDLCD 546.

—— (1972, 1974, 1993) *Fairuz: Return of the Soldiers, AlBaalbakiya*, performed by Fairouz et. al., produced by A. Chahine and Fils, Beirut: Voix de l'Orient Series, VDLCD 569.

—— (2003a) *Bayyā' al-khawātim: masrahiyya ghinā'iyya min faslayn. al-a'māl al-masrahiyya al-kāmila*, Zoghaib, H. (ed.), Jounieh, Lebanon: Dīnāmīk gharāfīk li-al-tibā'a wa-al-nashr.

—— (2003b) *Jibāl al-sawwān: masrahiyya ghinā'iyya min faslayn. al-a'māl al-masrahiyy*a al-*kāmila*, Zoghaib, H. (ed.), Jounieh, Lebanon: Dīnāmīk gharāfīk li-al-tibā'a wa-al-nashr.

—— (2003c) *Jisr al-qamar: masrahiyya ghinā'iyya min faslayn. al-a'māl al-masrahiyy*a al-*kāmila*, Zoghaib, H. (ed.), Jounieh, Lebanon: Dīnāmīk gharāfīk li-al-tibā'a wa-al-nashr.

—— (2003d) *al-Layl wa-al-qindīl: masrahiyya ghinā'iyya min fasl wāhid. al-a'māl al-masrahiyy*a al-*kāmila*, Zoghaib, H. (ed.), Jounieh, Lebanon: Dīnāmīk gharāfīk li-al-tibā'a wa-al-nashr.

—— (2003e) *al-Mahatta: masrahiyya ghinā'iyya min faslayn. al-a'māl al-masrahiyya al-kāmila*, Zoghaib, H. (ed.), Jounieh, Lebanon: Dīnāmīk gharāfīk li-al-tibā'a wa-al-nashr.

—— (2003f) *Ya'īsh ya'īsh: masrahiyya ghinā'iyya min faslayn. al-a'māl al-masrahiyy*a al-*kāmila*, Zoghaib, H. (ed.), Jounieh, Lebanon: Dīnāmīk gharāfīk li-al-tibā'a wa-al-nashr.

Rahbani, Z. (1987) *al-'Aql zīna*. 2 records, produced by al-Sharaka al-'ālamiyya li-al-bathth, narration Ziad Rahbani, Beirut: Sharakat lūrd sāwand, TMP 991–2.

—— (1989) *Fairouz at the Royal Festival Hall London*, performed by Fairouz, produced by A. Chahine and Fils, Beirut, VDL CD 509.

—— (1985/1991) *Anā mush kāfir*, performed by Z. Rahbani and S. Hawwāt, produced by M. and A. Moussa, Beirut: Relax In, REL.

—— (1993a) *The American Motion Picture by Ziad Rahbani: Complete Original Cast Recording of the Popular Musical Play*. 3 records, performed by Z. Rahbani, J. Saqr, S. Hawwāt, Z. Abū 'Absī, et al., produced by A.J. Samaha, Beirut: Voice of Beirut, VOBCD 523–5.

—— (1993b) *L'auberge du bonheur by Ziad Rahbani: Complete Original Cast Recording of the Popular Musical Play*, 2 records, performed by Z. Rahbani, J. Saqr, *et al.*, produced by A. Chahine and Fils, Beirut: Voix de l'Orient Series, VDLCD 558–9.

—— (1993c) *Failure... Complete Original Cast Recording by Ziad Rahbani.* 2 records, performed by Z. Rahbani, J. Saqr, Z. Abū 'Absī, M. Sa'īdūn, *et al.*, produced by A. Samaha, Beirut: Voice of Beirut, VOBCD 526–7.

—— (1994a) *Bi-al-nisba li-bukrā shū*, Beirut: Mukhtārāt.

—— (1994b) *Fīlm Amīrkī tawīl*, Beirut: Mukhtārāt.

—— (1994c) *Nazl al-surūr*, Beirut: Mukhtārāt.

—— (1994d) *Shī fāshil*, Beirut: Mukhtārāt.

—— (1995a) *Bi-mā innū...*, performed by Z. Rahbani and J. Saqr, produced by A. Chahine and Fils, Beirut: Voix de l'Orient Series, VDL 607.

—— (1995b) *Bennesbeh Labokra... Chou*, 3 records, performed by Z. Rahbani, J. Saqr, S. Hawwāt, *et al.*, produced by Relax-In International, Beirut: A. Moussa and Co., RELCD 625–7.

—— (1991/1995c) *Fairuz: Kifak inta*, performed by Fairouz, produced by A. Moussa and Co., Lyrics to track 2 J. Harb. Beirut: Relax-In International, RELCD 528.

—— (1995d) *Fīlm Amīrkī tawīl: mūsīqā wa-aghānī al-masrahiyya*, performed by Z. Rahbani, J. Saqr, S. Hawwāt, *et al.*, produced by A.J. Samaha. Beirut: Voice of Beirut, TC VOB.

—— (1995e) *Ilā Asi*, performed by Fairouz and Z. Rahbani, produced by A. Chahine and Fils, lyrics by A. and M. Rahbani except lyrics to tracks 4 and 5 (S. Aql), composed by A. and M. Rahbani, re-orchestration by Z. Rahbani, Beirut: Voix de l'Orient Series, VDLCD 600.

—— (1997a) "Ghīfārā 'ād 'alā nashīd Ziad Rahbani," *Jarīdat al-diyār*, October 11, p. 10.

—— (1973/1997b) *Sahriyya: a Popular Musical Play by Ziad Rahbani*, performed by Z. Rahbani, J. Saqr, M. Mahfūz, produced by A. Chahine and Fils., Beirut: Voix de l'Orient Series, TC LVDL 78–9.

—— (1979/2000) *Fairuz: Wahdon*, performed by Fairouz, produced by Relax-In International. Vocals Fairouz, lyrics to track 1 J. Harb, to track 3 A. and M. Rahbani, and to track 5 T. Haydar, Beirut: EMI Music Arabia, REL 586.

—— (2001) *Fairuz live at Beiteddine: 2000*, performed by Fairouz, produced and arranged by Ziad Rahbani, lyrics to tracks 2, 9, 13, and 17 – A. and M. Rahbani; to track 14 – J. Harb; and to track 12 – S. Darwish, Beirut: Relax-In and EMI Music Arabia, EMI 531599.

—— (2002) *Fayruz... wa-la kif*, performed by Fairouz, produced by Relax-in Music, composition for track 2 – L. Bonfa and A. De Maria and for track 7 – J. Cosma and J. Prevert, Beirut: Relax-In and EMI Music Arabia, EMI 53806.

"Rahbani yarudd 'alā lajnat mahrajānāt Baalbeck" (1997) *Jarīdat al-safīr*, July 2, p. 9.

al-Rā'ī, 'A. (1980) *al-Masrah fī al-watan al-'Arabī*, Madīnat al-Kuwayt, al-Kuwayt: Manshūrāt al-majlis al-watanī li-al-thaqāfa wa-al-funūn wa-al-ādāb.

—— (1992) "Arabic Drama Since the Thirties," in Badawi, M.M. (ed.) *The Cambridge History of Arabic Literature: Modern Arabic Literature*, Cambridge: Cambridge University Press, pp. 358–403.

—— (1993) *Masrah al-sha'b*, Cairo: Dār sharqiyyāt.

Ranchod-Nilsson, S. and Tetreault, M.A., (2000) "Gender and Nationalism: Moving Beyond Fragmented Conversations," in Ranchod-Nilsson, S. and Ann Tetreault, M. (eds) *Women, States, and Nationalism: At Home in the Nation?*, London: Routledge, pp. 1–17.

Reid, D.M. (1997) "Nationalizing the Pharaonic Past: Egyptology, Imperialism, and Egyptian Nationalism, 1922–52," in Jankowski, J. and Gershoni, I. (eds) *Rethinking Nationalism in the Arab Middle East*, New York: Columbia University Press, pp. 127–49.

Republic of Lebanon at the New York World's Fair (1939) New York: n.p.

al-Rīhānī, A. (1970) *Qalb Lubnān*, Beirut: Mu'assasat al-Rīhānī.

S., A.M. (1986) "Ziad Rahbani: ilā Urūbbā al-Gharbiyya ma'a atyab al-tamanniyyāt wa-al-simfūniyyāt," *Majallat al-shabaka*, January 28, pp. 22–4.

"Sab' wa-Makhūl wa-Abū Fāris wa-Umm Fāris wa-Nasrī wa-al-Sitt Zumurrud kulluhā shakhsiyyāt fūlklūriyya min atraf mā ibtada'ahu al-Rahbāniyyān" (1969) *Jarīdat al-nahār*, June 8, p. 4.

Sader, H. and Van Ess, M. (1998) "Looking For Pre-Hellenistic Baalbek," in Sader, H., Scheffler, T. and Neuwirth, A. (eds) *Baalbek: Image and Monument: 1898–1998*, Beirut: In Kommission Bei Franz Steiner Verlag Stuttgart, pp. 247–68.

"Saharāt Fairouz al-thalāth fī Beiteddine: shā'irat al-sawt 'laysat gharīmat al-zaman'" (2000) *Jarīdat al-nahār*, August 12, n.p.

Sahhāb, F. (1987) *al-Sab'a al-kibār fī al-mūsīqā al-'Arabiyya al-mu'āsira*, Beirut: Dār al-'ilm li-al-milāyīn.

Sahhāb, I. (2001) "Min Abū al-Muhammad Ilā Sayyid Makkāwī ... Umm Kulthūm uu-mulahhinūhā," *al-Kutub wijhat nazar*, March, pp. 52–8.

Sahhāb, S. (1986) "Ziad Rahbani fī 'Anā mush kāfir' al-tadarruj al-kūmīdī tudākhil al-kalām ma'a al-mūsīqā" *Jarīdat al-safīr*, March 1, p. 12.

"Said Akl" (1996) in R. Campbell (ed.) *A'lām al-adab al-'Arabī al-mu'āsir: siyar wa-siyar dhātiyya*, 2 vols, Beirut: In Kommission Bei Franz Steiner Verlag Stuttgart, 1: 955–7.

Said, E. (1979) *Orientalism*, New York: Vintage Books.

—— (1999) *Out of Place: A Memoir*, New York: Vintage Books.

Sa'īd, Kh. (1992) "Sāhat al-ustūra," *Mulhaq jarīdat al-nahār*, November 7, p. 12.

—— (1998a) "Fairouz, risālat amal," in *Fairouz fī al-layālī al-Lubnāniyya: mukhtārāt min masrahiyyāt al-Akhawayn Rahbani*, Beirut: Lajnat mahrajānāt Baalbeck al-dawliyya, p. 125.

—— (1998b) *al-Haraka al-masrahiyya fī Lubnān, 1960–75: tajārib wa-ab'ād*, Beirut: Lajnat mahrajānāt Baalbeck al-dawliyya.

Sa'īd, N.Z. (1964) *Tārīkh al-da'wa ilā al-'āmmiyya wa-āthāruhā fī Misr*, Alexandria: Dār nashr al-thaqāfa bi'l-Alexandria.

Salām, 'A. (1986) "al-Ughniya al-musawwara, al-ūbrā al-idhā'iyya wa-al-masrah al-ghinā'ī: thulāthiyyat al-ibdā' fī masīrat al-Rahābina," *Majallat al-kifāh al-'Arabī*, pp. 62–3.

Salameh, F. (2004) "Inventing Lebanon: Lebanonism in the Poetry and Thought of Said Akl," unpublished thesis, Brandeis University.

Salem, E. (2003) *Constructing Lebanon: A Century of Literary Narratives*, Gainesville: University Press of Florida (same as Manganaro, E.S.).

Salibi, K. (1988) *A House of Many Mansions: The History of Lebanon Reconsidered*, London: I.B. Tauris.

Salīm, 'A. (1999) *Funūn al-wāw: al-mawwāl, al-muwashshāh: dirāsa naqdiyya*, Cairo: Ittihād kuttāb Misr: Dār zawīl li-al-nashr.

Samāha, J. (1976) "'Ba'dnā tayyibīn ... 'ul Allāh:' Ziad Rahbani: 'al-wataniyya al-Lubnāniyya' ... wa-al-taqaddumiyya 'al-fawdawiyya'," *Jarīdat al-safīr*, November 15, p. 4.

Sam'ān, Mādūnā (2002) "'Fairouz' Ziad tath'ar min 'Fairouz' Asi," Riyad: al-Riyād al-alaktarūnī, January 21. Online. Available HTTP: http://www.geocities.com/darina_station/articles/05_wala_keef2.htm#1 (accessed January 2, 2007).

"Sawt Fairouz yatla' min qalb Beirut 'al-mustaqbal'" (1994) Majallat al-wasat, August 29, p. 48.

al-Sāyigh, S. (1986) "al-Intisār al-mahzūm," Majallat al-kifāh al-'Arabī, June 30, pp. 60–1.

Seligman, G. (1997) Jacket notes in The Legendary Fairuz, Hemisphere 8235722.

Selim, S. (2004) The Novel and the Rural Imaginary in Egypt, 1880–1985, London: RoutledgeCurzon.

Sh., A. (1966) "al-Qāhira: Fairouz tudhhil al-atfāl," Mulhaq jarīdat al-nahār, October 30, p. 15.

Shafik, V. (1998) Arab Cinema: History and Cultural Identity, Cairo, Egypt: The American University in Cairo Press.

Shahhāda, J., Rahbani A. and M. (1964) "Nadwat al-Tarīq hawla qadāyā al-masrah al-Lubnānī," al-Tarīq, 23(2): 4–15.

—— (1992) "Sawt al-malā'ika," Mulhaq jarīdat al-nahār, November 7, p. 19.

Shāhīn, J. (1983) "'Shī fāshil' li-Ziad Rahbani: matā tanqadī 'mawāsim' al-tahakkum wa-al-'abathiyya?," Majallat al-shabaka, March 7, pp. 24–6.

al-Shamālī, J. (1978) "al-Wahda al-dākhiliyya manzūran ilayhā min wijhatayn mutanāqidatayn: min 'Batrā' Fairouz wa-al-Rahābina ilā 'Sanāk bār' Ziad," Jarīdat al-safīr, March 26, p. 10.

Shāmil, Y. (1981) "Ziad Rahbani: yastahwīnī al-bahth 'an hanjara nisā'iyya qādira 'alā al-'itā'!," Majallat alhān, July 4, pp. 32–5.

Shams, D. (1995) "Ziad Rahbani 'an jadīdihi ma'a Joseph Saqr 'Bi-mā innū:' ta'aththartu bi-al-mūsīqā al-Kurdiyya wa-lastu min ansār 'al-fīdiyyū kalīb'," Jarīdat al-safīr, October 27, n.p.

—— (2000a) "Iqtala'ū siyāj al-zuhūr wa-natharūhu 'ala 'al-Sitt': majānīn Fairouz wa-dawlat al-Rahābina al-thāniyya," Jarīdat al-safīr, August 8, n.p.

—— (2000b) "Ziad Rahbani 'ashiyyat Beiteddine: kunnā nufakkir afdal ayyām al-harb," Jarīdat al-safīr, July 28, n.p.

Shannon, J. (2003) "Emotion, Performance, and Temporality in Arab Music: Reflections on Tarab," Cultural Anthropology, 18(1): 72–98.

—— (2006) Among the Jasmine Trees: Music and Modernity in Contemporary Syria, Middletown: Wesleyan University Press.

al-Sha'shā', S. and Hadshītī, L. (1994) "Hamla sha'biyya li-inqādh Fairouz," Majallat al-fann, September 12, pp. 18–23.

Shāwūl, B. (1988) "Tajribat al-Rahābina," al-Hayāt al-masrahiyya, 34–5: 253–64.

—— (1989) al-Masrah al-'Arabī al-hadīth: 1976–89, London: Riad al-Rayyes Books.

al-Shaykh, H. (1998) Hikāyat Zahra: riwāya, Beirut: Dār al-ādāb.

Shehadeh, L. (ed.) (1999) Women and War in Lebanon, Gainesville: University Press of Florida.

'"Shī fāshil' tanjah fī jam' Fairouz wa-Asi!," (1983) Majallat alhān, March 15, p. 10.

Shukr Allāh, A. (1978) '"Bi-al-nisba li-bukrā shū?' masrahiyya ahsanat al-tasdīd," al-Tarīq, 37(4–5): 259–67.

Singh-Bartlett, W. (2000a) "Fairouz and Ziad Rahbani Renew a National Legend," The Daily Star, August 8, n.p.

Singh-Bartlett, W. (2000b) "Fairouz Concert Could Be Best Ever: Ziad Rahbani's Direction Has Breathed New Life into Her Career," *The Daily Star*, August 8, n.p.

—— (2000c) "A Long Time Coming but Fairouz is Still Magic," *The Daily Star*, August 5, n.p.

—— (2000d) "National Legend: Beiteddine," *The Daily Star*, August 7, n.p.

al-Sir'alī, Y. (1966) *Sa'ih fī Lubnān*, Beirut: al-Maktab al-tijārī li-al-tibā'a wa-al-tawzī' wa-al-nashr.

Smith, S. (2005) *The Musical: Race, Gender and Performance*, London: Wallflower.

"Song of Lebanon" (1986) *The Economist*, July 5, p. 82.

Sparks, C.L. (2000) "Citizen-Soldiers or Republican Mothers?," in Ranchod-Nilsson, S. and Tetreault, M. (eds) *Women, States, and Nationalisms: At Home in the Nation?*, London: Routledge, pp. 181–95.

Spivak, G. (1988) *In Other Worlds: Essays in Cultural Politics*, London: Routledge.

Stauth, G. and Zubaida, S. (eds) (1987) *Mass Culture, Popular Culture, and Social Life in the Middle East*, Boulder, Colorado: Westview Press.

Stein, R. and Swedenburg, T. (eds) (2005) *Palestine, Israel and the Politics of Popular Culture*, Durham: Duke University Press.

Stevens, J. (1981) "'We're Still O.K.' – The Lebanese Tapes," *Arab Studies Quarterly*, 3(3): 275–84.

Stone, C. (2007) "Fairouz, the Rahbani Brothers, Jerusalem and the Leba-stinian Song," in Mayer, T. and Mourad, S. (eds) *Jerusalem: Idea and Reality*, London: Routledge.

Suwayd, H. (1997) "Yastakthirūn 'alā Fairouz wa-al-Rahābina mā yadfa'ūnahu li-al-ajānib," *Majallat al-wasat*, June 14, pp. 58–60.

Suwayd, M. (2000) "Ziad Rahbani: Fairouz atlaqat yadī wa-sa-tuqaddim jadīdan wa-aghānī lam takhtārhā min qabl," *Mulhaq jarīdat al-nahār*, July 31, p. 5.

—— (2001) "'Mūnūdūz' ma'a Salmā wa-mūsīqā yuzayyinuhā al-shaghaf sihran wa-jamālan," *Mulhaq jarīdat al-nahār*, April 9, n.p.

T., J. (1987) "Mansour Rahbani: masrahunā lā yuqaddim al-hulūl li-annanā lā nurīd li-al-nās an tatanaffas!: fī hiwār hawla 'Sayf 84' wa-al-masrah al-Rahbani," *Majallat al-sayyād*, June 12, pp. 44–6.

Talīs, 'A. (1979) "Fairouz tatatawwar am tatadahwar 'a hadīr al-būsta?," *Majallat al-shabaka*, September 3, pp. 6–7.

—— (1981) "Mādhā yaf'al Ziad Rahbani?," *Jarīdat al-anwār*, August 11, p. 7.

—— (1991) "Fairouz wa-Ziad Rahbani fī 'Kayfak inta'! huwa ibnuhā am-hiya ibnatuhu?!," *Majallat al-shabaka*, July 8, pp. 40–1.

—— (1993) "Diddahu wa-lākin ma'ahu!," *Majallat sahar*, April 23, 3.

—— (2000) "Wadī' al-Sāfī wa-Fairouz...ma'rakat Āb al-luhāb: bayna mahrajānāt Baalbeck wa-Beiteddine: ayy niyyāt?," *Jarīdat al-hayāt*, July 30, p. 13.

Tamanoi, M.A. (1998) *Under the Shadow of Nationalism: Politics and Poetics of Rural Japanese Women*, Honolulu: University of Hawaii Press.

Tessler, M., Nachtwey, J., and Banda, A. (eds) (1999) *Area Studies and Social Science: Strategies for Understanding Middle East Politics*, Bloomington: Indiana University Press.

Thabet, J. (1999) The Tragedy of Heritage in the Age of Lebanon's Reconstruction, *aljadid*, 5: 8–10.

Thongchai, W. (1994) *Siam Mapped: A History of the Geo-Body of a Nation*, Honolulu: University of Hawaii Press.

Tirād, M. and Khalīfa, R. (2001) *Fairouz: hayātuhā wa-aghānīhā*, Tripoli, Lebanon: al-Mu'assasa al-hadītha li-al-kuttāb.

Touma, H. (1996) *The Music of the Arabs*, Portland: Amadeus Press.

Tourist and Hotel Guide for Lebanon (1962) Beirut: The Catholic Press.

Traboulsi, F. (1996) "La dabké: sexe, folklore et fantaisie," *l'Orient-Express*, September, pp. 44–9.

—— (1997) "Khaybāt wa-āmāl: masrah al-Rahābina 'ashiyyat al-harb al-ahliyya," *al-Hadātha*, 21/22: 45–9.

—— (1998) "Filastīn fī fann Fairouz wa-al-Rahābina: 'Jibāl al-sawwān' aw mu'jizat al-sha'b al-muqāwim," *al-Karmal*, 57: 203–12.

—— (1999) *Silāt bi-lā wasl: Michel Chiha wa-al-īdiyulūjiyyā al-Lubnāniyya*, Beirut: Riad El-Rayyes Books.

—— (2000) *Reflections on Culture and Folklore in Lebanon*, manuscript of paper presented at Center for Behavioral Research, The American University in Beirut.

—— (2006) *Fairouz wa-al-Rahābina: masrah al-gharīb wa-al-kanz wa-al-a'jūba*, Beirut: Riyād al-Rayyis li-al-kutub wa-al-nashr.

—— (n.d.) "Fann al-Rahābina fī harb 1958: 'Jisr al-qamar' aw-al-mu'jiza 'alā al-masrah," *Zawāyā*, pp. 73–9.

—— (n.d.) "Mā huwa 'al-shay' al-fāshil' fī masrahiyyat Ziad Rahbani?," manuscript of unpublished article.

Tueni, Gh. (ed.) (1994) *Baalbeck, ayyām al-mahrajān*, Beirut: Dār al-nahār li-al-nashr.

'Ubayd, J. (1974) *al-Sālāt fī-aghānī Fairouz*, Jounieh, Lebanon: al-Matba'a al-būlusiyya.

Umm Kulthum: A Voice Like Egypt (1996) directed by Michal Goldman, narrated by Omar Sharif, Arab Film Distribution.

Updike, J. (2001) "Young Iris: A New Biography Focuses on the Novelist's Early Questings," *The New Yorker*, October 1, pp. 106–10.

van Nieuwkerk, K. (1995) *"A Trade Like Any Other:" Female Singers and Dancers in Egypt*, Austin: University of Texas Press.

—— (1998) "Changing Images and Shifting Identities: Female Performers in Egypt," in Zuhur, S. (ed.) *Images of Enchantment: Visual and Performing Arts of the Middle East*, Cairo: The American University in Cairo Press, pp. 21–35.

—— (1998) *Visual Anthropology* 10 (2–4).

Volk, L. (1994) "Reconstruction through Deconstruction: A Critical Reading of the Discourse on Lebanon since the Civil war," *Arab Studies Journal*, 2: 17–23.

al-Walī, T. (1992) "Fairouz li-al-fatayāt wa-li-Lubnān al-jabal" *Mulhaq jarīdat al-nahār*, November 7, p. 18.

Walsh, D. and Platt, L. (2003) *Musical Theater and American Culture*, Westport: Praeger.

al-Wanīn, R. (1991) "Mu'dilat Fairouz wa-Ziad: 'Kīfak inta'," *Majallat al-hasnā'*, October 4, pp. 66–7.

Waterfield, R. (1998) *Prophet: The Life and Times of Kahlil Gibran*, New York: St. Martin's Press.

Wāzin, 'A. (1992) "Fairouz wa-al-akhawān Rahbani yaltazimūn 'al-qadiyya:' mughannat 'Rāji'ūn' ba'da khamsa wa-thalāthīn 'āman," *Jarīdat al-hayāt*, October 21, p. 21.

—— (1995) "'Bi-mā innū...' istawāna jadīda li-Ziad Rahbani tasdur khilāl ayyām," *Jarīdat al-hayāt*, October 14, p. 22.

—— (1996) "Fairouz al-mutajaddida dawman fī jaww Rahbani badī': istawānatān dammatā ajmal ughniyāt al-khamsīnāt wa-al-sittīnāt," *Jarīdat al-hayāt*, June 16, p. 20.

211

Wāzin, 'A. (1998) "al-Layālī al-Rahbāniyya fī Baalbeck tasta'īd al-mādī wa-sawt Fairouz huwa al-ustūra al-sāmida: Ziad Rahbani insahab ihtijājan 'alā khid'at 'al-balay-bāk'," *Jarīdat al-hayāt*, August 18, p. 18.

—— (1999) "Fushat al-liqā' bayna Fairouz wa-al-Masīh," *Mulhaq jarīdat al-nahār*, April 3, n.p.

—— (2000a) "Fairouz al-sabiyya al-Mutamarrida taqūl li-al-hākim 'Sahh al-Nawm': hiwārāt ghinā'iyya majhūla sudirat fī al-istiwāna al-kāmila," *Jarīdat al-hayāt*, January 24, n.p.

—— (2000b) "Sawt Fairouz yunāfis mūsīqā Ziad Rahbani siban wa-wāqi'iyyatan… wa-'awdatan ilā al-mādī," *Jarīdat al-hayāt*, August 6, p. 13.

Weber, J. (2002). "Long Playing Records and Tape Recording" in "History of Recording" in "Recorded Sound." Online. Available HTTP: http://www.grovemusic.com/shared/views/article.html?section=music.26294.1.4#music.2694.1.4 (accessed January 2, 2007).

Weinrich, I. (2006) *Fayrūz und die Brüder Rahbānī. Musik, Moderne und Nation im Libanon*, Wuerzburg: Ergon Verlag.

Williams, R. (1968) *Drama from Ibsen to Brecht*, London: Chatto and Windus.

Wilson, W. (1976) *Folklore and Nationalism in Modern Finland*, Bloomington: Indiana University Press.

Winstone, H.V.F. (1991) *Howard Carter and the Discovery of the Tomb of Tutankhamun*, London: Constable.

Wright, W. (1981) *A Grammar of the Arabic Language*, 2 vols, Beirut: Librairie du Liban.

Yabroudi, P., Karam, E.G., Chami, A., Karam, A., Majdalani, M., Zebouni, V., Melhem, N., Mansour, C. and Saliba, S. (1999) "Substance and Abuse: The Lebanese Female and the Lebanon Wars," in L.R. Shehadeh (ed.) *Women and War in Lebanon*, Gainesville: University of Florida Press, pp. 282–320.

Yamīn, Jūrj (1985) "Mansour Rahbani, barnāmij li-al-talafizyūn al-Sūrī wa-afkār 'al-intāj al-ghinā'ī al-rasūlī fī ghaybūba'," *Jarīdat al-nahār*, February 14, p. 11.

—— (1990) "Ziad Rahbani, a'tinā khubzanā jumalan mūsīqiyyan," *Jarīdat al-nahār*, October 12, n.p.

Yang, H. (1998) "Re-membering the Korean Military Comfort Women: Nationalism, Sexuality, and Silencing," in Kim, E.H. and Choi, C. (eds) *Dangerous Women: Gender and Korean Nationalism*, London: Routledge, pp. 123–41.

Yuval-Davis, N. (1997) *Gender and Nation*, London: Sage Publications.

Zaatari, Z. (2006) "The Culture of Motherhood: An Avenue of Women's Civil Participation in South Lebanon," *Journal of Middle East Women's Studies* 2(1): 33–64.

Zakī, 'A.T. (1988) *al-Masrah al-ghinā'ī fī sab'at ālāf sana*, Cairo: al-Hay'a al-Misriyya al-'āmma li-al-kitāb.

—— (1991) *al-Sayyid Darwish fī 'īd mīlādihi al-mi'awī*, Cairo: Dār al-Ma'ārif.

al-Zayn, D. (1980) "Ziad Rahbani ya'zif 'alā al-waj'," *Majallat al-hawādith*, October 24, n.p.

Zaytūnī, B. (1994) "Ziad Rahbani fī 'Law lā fushat al-amal'," *Mulhaq jarīdat al-nahār*, May 28, p. 18.

al-Zībāwī, M. (1994) "al-Hulm al-Rahbani jassadatahu Fairouz thumma tamazzaq: zā'ira gharība fatahat al-hayāt 'alā al-mudhish wa-al-mustahīl," *Majallat al-wasat*, February 28, pp. 54–6.

—— (1998) "'a 'add al-mahabba al-'atab kabīr," *Mulhaq jarīdat al-nahār*, August, 22, p. 10.

al-Zībāwī, M. and Marshalīn, I. (1992) "Fairouz: laytanī baqīt kamā kunt: ba'īda 'an al-wāqi'," *Mulhaq jarīdat al-nahār*, November 7, pp. 7–9.

Zoghaib, H. (1993–94) "Hikāyat al-Akhawayn Rahbānī 'alā lisān Mansour Rahbani," *Majallat al-wasat*, November 15, 22, and 29, 1993, pp. 68–72, 68–71; December 6, 13, 20, and 27, 1993, pp. 70–3, 72–5, 73–5, 116–19; and January 3, 1994, pp. 68–71.

—— (1998) "al-Zaman al-Rahbānī," *Fairouz fī al-layālī al-Lubnāniyya: mukhtārāt min masrahiyyāt al-Akhawayn Rahbani*, Beirut: Lajnat mahrajānāt Baalbeck al-dawliyya, p. 127.

—— (2001) *al-Akhawayn Rahbani: Tarīq al-nahl*, Beirut: al-Awdīsiyya li'l-nashr wa-al-i'lām.

al-Zughbī, I. (1969) "Rādiyū al-sharq," *Mulhaq jarīdat al-nahār*, October 12, pp. 6–12.

Zuhur, Sh. (ed.) (1998) *Images of Enchantment: Visual and Performing Arts of the Middle East*, Cairo: The American University in Cairo Press.

—— (2000) *Asmahan's Secrets: Woman, War, and Song*, Austin: The Center for Middle Eastern Studies, The University of Texas at Austin.

—— (ed.) (2001a) *Colors of Enchantment: Theater, Dance, Music, and the Visual Arts of the Middle East*, Cairo: The American University in Cairo Press.

—— (2001b) "Introduction," in Zuhur, S. (ed.) *Colors of Enchantment: Theater, Dance, and the Visual Arts of the Middle East*, Cairo: The American University in Cairo Press, pp. 1–17.

—— (2001c) "Musical Stardom and Male Romance: Farid al-Atrash," in Zuhur, S. (ed.) *Colors of Enchantment: Theater, Dance, and the Visual Arts of the Middle East*, Cairo: The American University in Cairo Press, pp. 270–97.

INDEX

Note: Names of plays, songs, publications and the like are in italics, as are words transliterated from Arabic (but not the names of persons). References such as "178–9" indicate (not necessarily continuous) discussion of a topic across a range of pages, whilst "192n22" indicates a reference to note 22 on page 192. A reference in the form "192nn" indicates that the topic is referred to in multiple notes on page 142. Wherever possible in the case of topics with many references, these have either been divided into sub-topics or the most significant discussions of the topic are indicated by page numbers in bold.

INDEX

Bāsīlā, N. 144, 153, 154, 157
Bayat, A. 9
Baydūn, 'Abbās 84–5, 127, 163–4
Beck, L. 190n2
Beidler, P. 186n21
Beirut: as capital 10, 23, 54, 74, 86;
east v. west 93, 110, 118, 121, 126, 128,
132, 167; and Fairouz 153–5; language
differences 134, 136–7; location of
performances 2, 42, 53, 67–8, 82, 95, 99,
110, 123, 163, 177; migration to 26, 79;
rebuilding 163, 191n14; setting for plays
104, 111, 114, 120, 124; as subject of
A Failure (Shī fāshil) 123–32;
and Ziad 93
Beirut Festival, and Fairouz 163–4
Beiteddine 34, 174–5, 184n22
Beiteddine Festival 170–2, 174–8
Bekaa 17–18, 21, 23, 54, 75, 80, 86
Belgum, Kirsten 145
Berman, Marshall 78
Biani, N. 18
Binodini 62, 140
Bītār, M. 107, 111
Bordman, G.M. 181n1
Boswell, D. 182n1
Boullata, K. 166
Boulus, S. 41, 184n3, 188n8
Boustani, Fouad 22
Boyd, D.A. 45, 185n4, 186n11, 188n12
Brains are Just for Decoration (al-'Aql zīna)
118, 166, 188n10
Brazil 95, 154, 166
Brecht, Bertolt 117
Būdhayna, M. 183n11
Būlus, M. 80
Butler, Judith 144–5, 157
Byatt, A.S. 138

Cachia, P. 183n10
Cadora, F.J. 134
Canada 177
capitalism 44, 90, 109, 135
Casino du Liban 61, 67
Cedars Festival 67–8, 73–5, 78, 95
Chahine, Youssef 75–6, 80
Chamoun, Camille 3, 53; and Baalbeck
Festival 19–20, 24, 31, 40–1, 54–5, 160;
and Chiha, Michel 54
Chamoun, Jean 118
Chamoun, Zalfa 28, 41, 160
Chatterjee, Partha: appropriation of
the popular 10, 25–6, 29; classicization of
tradition 10, 14, 182n1; and colonialism
14; on exclusion of Islam 38; on female

characters 153, 157; Indian nationalism
62, 141; nation building as "betrayal 140;
presentation of the folk in childlike
terms 27
Chehab, Fouad: aims 54–5, 173; ascent
to power 10, 42, 53–4; and Baalbeck
Festival 42, 51, 54–5; and Chiha, Michel
108; and commitment 53; and *The
Moon's Bridge (Jisr al-qamar)* 58; and
radio 54; and Rahbani Brothers 58, 75,
88–9, 129, 173; and Syrians 53; and
village, mountain Lebanon 85;
see also Chehabism
Chehabism 54, 56, 58, 86, 88, 104, 108;
see also Chehab, Fouad
Chevallier, D. 183n7
Chiha, Michel 20, 22–4, 34, 113, 183nn,
186n19, 187n33; and Chihaism 108–11;
and *Petra (Batrā)* 109–10; and Rahbani
Brothers 57, 108–9; and Ziad 115–16
China 183n15
Chouf, the 21, 23, 86, 175, 184n22
Christian elite, attitudes 37
"Christian" Lebanon *see* Maronites;
"village" Lebanon
Christian villagers *see* "village" Lebanon
Christopher, Warren 106
cinema: Egyptian 17–18, 25, 38, 75–6,
185n3; and musical theater 50;
parodied by Ziad 11, 93, 120–4;
and Rahbani Brothers 8, 42, 75–7, 79,
174, 181n1
civil war 1, 2, 12; and Fairouz 163; and
gender 190n2; and *Happiness Hotel
(Nazl al-surūr)* 101–2; and Rahbani
Brothers 91, 107–10, 123; and Ziad
115–16, 118, 132, 173
classicization of tradition: Baalbeck 15–25,
31, 38, 145; Egypt 14–15, 31; Greece 14,
21; India 14, 26, 141; Rahbani brothers
38, 41, 129, 145, 166; Ziad 121, 129
Clinton, Bill 106
colonialism: and ethnography 73; fight
against 43, 45, 47, 52; justification 14;
and popular culture 25; post-colonial
nation building 21, 26, 48, 53, 139,
142, 144–5
commitment 49, 52–3, 94, 123, 140
*Conspiracy Continues, The (al-mu'āmara
mustamirra)* 123, 128
Cook, Mrs 49
Cooke, M. 190n2
Cooper, James Fenimore 80
Corm, Charles 23, 37
Currey, N.E. 125, 187n24

217

Harding, Gerald 18–19
Hariri, Rafik 1, 178, 191n14
Harris, W. 54, 183n7
Hartman, M. 183n9
al-Hasan, H. 54, 185n5, 186n20
Hawi, K.S. 187n27
Hawat, Sami 121
Hayek, Joseph 37
Haykal, Muhammad Husayn 15, 141
Hazīn, Gh. 177
He Had (*Kāna bi-hi*) 123–4
Helou, Charles 23, 88
Heng, G. 145, 190n5
Herzfeld, M. 183n15
heteroglossia 12, 93, 133–7
al-Hibr, Khālid 176
Himsī, H. 163
Hinds, M. 189n17
Hirschkop, K. 133, 134, 135
Hobsbawm, E. 182n1
Holiday of Glory, The (*Mawsim al-'izz*) 10,
   58–61, 64–5, 67, 84, 101, 104, 106, 128,
   145, 162, 179
Hourani, A. 74, 182n5, 186n16
How Are You? (*Kīfak inta*) 12, 161–2, 172
Hrawi, Elias 3

I'm not an Infidel (*Anā mush kāfir*) 119
al-'Īd, Y. 62, 186n22
identity: and Chiha, Michel 110; cultural
   62; and duality 70–1, 73; European 14;
   formation 73, 83, 85, 138, 142, 160,
   181n2; and integration 80; Lebanese 1,
   11, 36, 71, 188n12; sectarian 29
ideoscapes 89
Idrīs, Suhayl 140
If Not for the Possibility of Hope
   (*Law lā fushat al-amal*) 93, 163, 180,
   189n16, 192n1
'Ināya, J. 176
Inchbold, A.C. 19
incremental revolution 26
India: classicization of tradition 14, 26, 141;
   nationalism 10, 38, 62, 140–1, 145;
   women in postcolonial projects 12, 142,
   157–8, 190nn
Iraq 90, 132, 139, 162, 183n13
Ireland: and The Virgin Mary 191n8
Islam: classicization of tradition 15;
   exclusion by Christian elite 37;
   and Fairouz 81; and women 142;
   and Ziad 126
Ismā'īl, Alī 189n18
'Ismat, R. 182n4
al-'Itānī, Khālid 99

It's Only Music (*Mannū illā* al-m
   ūsīqā) 118
Izzard, R. 19

Jabbāra, Raymūn 94
Jankowski, J. 15, 31
Japan 158, 183, 190n4, 191n6
Jarkas, R. 146, 148, 153
Jarrār, Wadī'a and Marwān 29, 65
al-Jawharī, A. 190n29
Jayyusi, S.K. 188n13
jazz 77, 189n18
Jerusalem 95
Jordan 90, 107–8; Ajloun 110;
   Amman 90, 110
Joseph, S. 190n2
Jounieh 187n28
journalistic sources 7–8
Jumayyil, Pierre 186n22
Jumblat, Kamal 137, 174–5; and
   civil war 175
Jumblat, Nūra 175
Jumblat, Walid 174–5

Kabbani, O. 191n14
Kabbāra, R. 162
Kāmil, M. 182n4, 186n14
Kāmil, S. 107, 111, 118, 123, 124, 158,
   189n20
Kandiyoti, D. 142–3, 190n2
Kano, A. 190n4
al-Kassar, Ali 50, 186n17
Kassār, M. 186n17
Kaufman, Asher 20, 35
Kesey, Ken 120
Kettaneh, Aimée 17–20
Khalaf, S. 191n14
Khalidi, R. 182n11
Khalīfa, Marālīn 5, 6, 149, 154
Khalīfa, R. 149, 154
el Khazen, F. 55, 175
al-Khāzin, W. 57
Khoury, Bishara 22–3
Khoury, P. 191n14
Khūrī, Ilyās 170–1, 176
Khūrī, Jalāl 94
al-Khūrī, Jūrj Ibrāhīm 149
Kilpatrick, H. 141
Kirshenblatt-Gimblett, B. 28, 31, 32, 33,
   69, 85, 119, 183n11
Kishlī, M. 153
Klat, Hektor 20, 34–5
Knapp, R. 181n2
Korea 158, 191n6
Kraidy, M.M. 188n12

INDEX

Kuntz, B. 19
Kurayyim, M. 50

al-Labābīdī, Yahyā 185n7
Lacan, Jacques 144
Lahhūd, Rūmiyyū 164
Laird, P.R. 182n2
Lamb, A. 182n2
Landau, J.M. 186n16
Laurens, H. 183n7
al-layālī 105, 188n9
Le Bon, Gustave 14
Lebanese National Committee for
   UNESCO 28–9
Lebanese Nights 175; Baalbeck Festival 30,
   32; beginnings 29, 40; and Beiteddine
   175; and Chehabism 42, 54; and civil
   war 183n19; and diversity 176; and
   Fairouz 2, 43, 63, 152, 165; in Festival
   program 34; later works 70; and Rahbani
   Brothers 30–2, 43, 63, 67, 69–70, 117,
   172, 186–7n23; revenue 33, 183n19;
   and social realism 96; and "village"
   Lebanon 35; and Ziad 117
"Lebanese Song" 46–8, 185–6n10
Lebanese-ness 70–4, 135; see also
   "village" Lebanon
Lebanon and miracles 2, 35, 41, 56, 58,
   98, 154
Letter from an Unknown Woman (Risāla min
   imra'a majhūla) 17, 18, 25, 38, 184n23
Levy, E. 145
Litani River plan 56–7
Live Live (Ya'īsh ya'īsh) 95, 97, 100,
   108, 179
Long American Film, A (Fīlm Amīrkī tawīl)
   11, 93, 120–1, 123, 124, 138, 180,
   189nn, 192n1
Loulou (Lūlū) 95–7, 99–100 134, 180
Love and Revenge (Gharām wa-intiqām)
   185n3
Love Poem (Qasīdat hubb) 95–6, 180,
   191n18
Lukács, G. 138
Lustick, I.S. 182n11

McClintock, A. 142, 144, 153, 157–8, 160
Mahfūz, H. 74, 84, 166
Mahfūz, 'I. 7, 46, 94
Mais al-Rim (Mays al-Rīm) 97,
   99–100, 180
Makdisi, S. 191n14
Makdisi, Ussama 9, 15–17
Manganaro, Elise Salem 76, 80, 90,
   111, 119, 123, 133

al-Mannī, Naqūla 185n7
Marāshda, 'A. 188n13
Maronites: and Baalbeck Festival 22, 24, 32,
   142; and Chehabism 54; and east Beirut
   110, 187n28; and Fakhr al-Din 88; and
   the French 16, 21–2, 24, 26, 77, 142; on
   history of Lebanon 20; image of Lebanon
   32; migration 26; mountain-dwelling 16,
   26, 79, 175; and "other Lebanons" 24,
   186n22; and the Phalange Party 186n22;
   and the Virgin Mary 187n28
Marshall, B. 182n2
Martin, A. 191n8
mass media: and Abdel Nasser, Gamal
   186n11; and capitalism 44, 90; and
   migration 10–11, 38, 43–4, 73, 85, 89–9,
   166, 173; and producing "localities" 44;
   technology 11
Massad, J. 186n19
Matar, 'A. 117
mawwāl 25, 114, 119, 122, 165,
   183n10, 184n23
Mayer, T. 142
mediascapes 89
methodology 8
metonymy 13, 31, 41, 144, 146
Meyer, M.K. 142
Michener, James 186n21
migration: external 10–11, 62, 74, 79,
   90, 166, 173, 182n5; internal 10–11,
   26, 62, 74, 79–80, 173, 184n23;
   and mass media 11, 38, 43–4, 73, 85,
   89–91, 166, 173
mījānā 66, 130, 136
mijwiz 189n23
mimesis 31, 85
Mīna, Hannā 94
Mitchell, Timothy 11, 14, 70–1
Moghadam, V. 142, 190n2
Moiseyev, Igor 28–9
Moon's Bridge, The (Jisr al-qamar) 4,
   10, 56–8, 67, 77, 103, 148, 151, 152, 154,
   179, 187n26
Moran, J. 9
Most, A. 181n2
"mountain" Lebanon see "village" Lebanon
Mt Lebanon 82, 107; and Beiteddine 175;
   and Chiha, Michel 187n33; as core of
   Greater Lebanon 10, 16, 20–1, 54, 86,
   89–90, 172–3; and dabka 133; imagery
   47, 55, 107; and migration 74, 111;
   al-Mutasarrifiyya 77–9, 172, 174–5;
   and Phoenicians 35, 88, 152; and
   "village" Lebanon 10, 47, 134, 165,
   172, 175; and Ziad 114, 120

221